Common SAP R/3 Functions Manual

Springer
London
Berlin
Heidelberg
New York
Hong Kong
Milan
Paris
Tokyo

William Lawlor

Common SAP R/3
Functions Manual

 Springer

William Lawlor, MSc

British Library Cataloguing in Publication Data
Lawlor, William
    Common SAP R/3 functions manual. – (Springer professional computing)
    1. R/3 (Computer file) 2. ABAP/4 (Computer program language)
    I. Title
    650′.028553769
    ISBN 1852337753

Library of Congress Cataloging-in-Publication Data
Lawlor, William, 1972-
    Common SAP R/3 functions manual / William Lawlor.
      p. cm. -- (Springer professional computing)
    Includes index.
    ISBN 1-85233-775-3 (alk. paper)
      1. Integrated software. 2. SAP R/3. 3. Client/server computing. I. Title. II. Series.

QA76.76.I57L38 2003
005.75′85--dc22   2003060693

ISBN 1-85233-775-3 Springer-Verlag London Berlin Heidelberg
A member of BertelsmannSpringer Science + Business Media GmbH
springeronline.com

Typeset by Gray Publishing, Tunbridge Wells, UK
Printed and bound by The Cromwell Press, Trowbridge, UK
34/3830-543210 Printed on acid-free paper SPIN 10954911

Foreword

It is well recognised that programs written to the standard and in the style of the host system are inherently easier to maintain and upgrade. SAP is no different. Those programs that are written with as much standard SAP code as possible are better equipped to cope with changes in the system that could otherwise cause a custom program to malfunction.

Customised code can be notoriously difficult to decipher and change during upgrade projects. It is much better to utilise existing SAP code, which offers a degree of standardisation in programs. Reducing the amount of re-coding for problems, for which SAP has already written, tested, and provided solutions, in turn eliminates further sources of program errors and cuts the all-important program development time, and hence costs.

The growing complexity of SAP has resulted in over 105,000 individual function modules in the 4.6B system, and this number will continue to increase as new features are added to the system. With no existing or consistent documentation for most of these modules, the author has undertaken the task of producing the first concise reference of a broad range of modules designed to solve common problems encountered in most ABAP-programming projects.

The modules chosen were based on analysis of thousands of custom developments and the author's own many years of ABAP development. The modules described herein offer application developers the most complete and consistent documentation available and should be a welcome addition to any ABAP developer's library.

David Quirke
Project Manager, SAP

About the Author

William Lawlor has been involved in the IT industry, since the late 1980s. He has been programming and involved in application development for over 10 years in several languages, such as C and C++, Visual Basic, and COBOL. As a consultant, he has spent the last 6 years working almost exclusively in ABAP. During this time he worked on three full SAP implementations and numerous version upgrades. He has also developed several ABAP utilities, such as an authorisation-reporting tool for IMG transactions and a utility program to secure transportable objects between systems.

He has attended numerous courses provided by SAP in ABAP, BASIS, Finance and Costing, Sales and Distribution, Material Management, and Production Planning. He currently works as an ABAP Consultant and Author.

Contents

Contents   ix

Introduction   xix

Layout of Reference Entries   xxi

An Introduction to SAP xxiii

Using Function Modules xxvii

1. System   1
    ABAP4_CALL_TRANSACTION – Initiates a transaction in a separate window   1
    ARFC_GET_TID – Returns IP address of the server (in hexadecimal)   2
    AUTHORITY_CHECK_DATASET – Checks file access authorization   3
    BP_ EVENT_RAISE – Triggers background event   5
    CAT_CHECK_RFC_DESTINATION – Checks the RFC destinations and connections   6
    CAT_PING – Checks RFC system and configuration   7
    DEQUEUE_ES_PROG – Releases program locks   8
    ENQUEUE_ES_PROG – Prevents parallel execution of program   8
    FTP_COMMAND – Executes a command on the FTP server   9
    FTP_CONNECT – Opens connection to the FTP server   10
    FTP_DISCONNECT – Closes connection to the FTP server   12
    GET_JOB_RUNTIME_INFO – Retrieves detailed job information   13
    GUI_EXEC – Starts an external program asynchronously   13
    GUI_GET_DESKTOP_INFO – Returns information about the end-users desktop   14
    GUI_RUN – Starts program with ShellExecute   16
    GWY_READ_CONNECTIONS – Checks gateway connection   17
    HLP_MODE_CREATE – Creates another session in system   18
    IW_C_GET_FRONTEND_VERSION – Version of SAP front-end installed on a PC   19
    RFC_MAIL – Sends e-mail to another SAP system   20
    RSPO_FIND_SPOOL_REQUESTS – Finds a spool number   20
    RSPO_OUTPUT_SPOOL_REQUEST – Outputs same request on a different printer   22
    RSPO_RPRINT_SPOOLREQ – Triggers spool to print automatically   23
    SAPWL_GET_SUMMARY_STATISTIC – Summary of object usage statistics   23
    SAPWL_WORKLOAD_GET_DIRECTORY – Timeframe of statistics on SAP database   25
    SAPWL_WORKLOAD_GET_STATISTIC – Object usage statistics   26
    SHOW_JOBSTATE – Checks the status of a job   27
    SO_SPOOL_READ – Returns printer spool information   29

SO_WIND_SPOOL_LIST – Dialogue to browse printer spool numbers 30
SXPG_CALL_SYSTEM – Calls command external to the SAP system 31
SXPG_COMMAND_CHECK – Checks authorization to execute a command 33
SXPG_COMMAND_EXECUTE – Executes a command on remote system 34
SXPG_COMMAND_LIST_GET – Reads a list of external OS commands 35
TERMINAL_ID_GET – Returns IP address and the terminal ID 35
TH_DELETE_USER – Logs off a user 36
TH_ENVIRONMENT – Gets values in SAP environment variables 37
TH_REMOTE_TRANSACTION – Runs a transaction on a remote server 38
TH_SERVER_LIST – List of RFC servers 39
TH_USER_INFO – Returns information about user 39
TH_USER_LIST – Displays users logged onto server 41
TRANSACTION_CALL – Initiates a transaction in a separate window 42
USER_EXISTS – Checks whether user ID is valid 42
WS_EXECUTE – Calls another program from ABAP 43
WS_QUERY – Executes query function on front-end 44

2. Conversions 47

BAPI_CURRENCY_CONV_TO_EXTERNAL – Converts currency format to external format 47
BAPI_CURRENCY_CONV_TO_INTERNAL – Converts currency format to internal format 48
CF_UT_UNIT_CONVERSION – Converts material unit quantities 49
CONVERSION_EXIT_ALPHA_INPUT – Converts number to a string filled with zeroes 50
CONVERSION_EXIT_ALPHA_OUTPUT – Converts number with zeroes into an integer 51
CONVERSION_EXIT_AUART_INPUT – Converts sales document type to SAP format 51
CONVERSION_EXIT_AUART_OUTPUT – Converts sales document type to display format ... 52
CONVERSION_EXIT_CUNIT_INPUT – Converts external unit to SAP's internal unit 53
CONVERSION_EXIT_CUNIT_OUTPUT – Converts internal unit to commercial unit 54
CONVERSION_EXIT_LUNIT_INPUT – Converts technical unit for internal unit 55
CONVERSION_EXIT_LUNIT_OUTPUT – Converts internal unit to technical unit 56
CONVERSION_FACTOR_GET – Returns conversion factors for a unit 57
CONVERT_ABAPSPOOLJOB_2_PDF – Converts ABAP spool output to PDF 59
CONVERT_OTFSPOOLJOB_2_PDF – Converts an OTF (SAPscript) spool to PDF 61
CONVERT_TO_FOREIGN_CURRENCY – Converts local currency to foreign currency 63
CONVERT_TO_LOCAL_CURRENCY – Converts foreign currency to local currency 64
CURRENCY_AMOUNT_SAP_TO_IDOC – Converts currency to IDOC format 66
CURRENCY_CODE_ISO_TO_SAP – ISO currency code to SAP's currency code 67
CURRENCY_CODE_SAP_TO_ISO – SAP currency code to ISO currency code 68
DATE_STRING_CONVERT – Converts string date into DATE type 68
DIMENSION_CHECK – Checks internal unit of dimension 69
DIMENSION_GET – Retrieves internal ID of specified dimension 71
DIMENSION_GET_FOR_UNIT – Textual description of dimension 71
HR_ROUND_NUMBER – Rounds a number according to rules 72
HRCM_AMOUNT_TO_STRING_CONVERT – Converts an amount to a character string 73
HRCM_STRING_TO_AMOUNT_CONVERT – Converts a character string to an amount 74
MATERIAL_UNIT_CONVERSION – Converts base unit to alternative unit 75
MD_CONVERT_MATERIAL_UNIT – Conversion of material units 76
ROUND – Rounds value to a number of decimal places 77

ROUND_AMOUNT – Rounding based on company and currency 79

SI_UNIT_GET – Retrieves international unit of measure 80

SX_OBJECT_CONVERT_OTF_PDF – Conversion from OTF (SAPscript) to PDF 81

SX_OBJECT_CONVERT_OTF_PRT – Conversion from OTF to printer format 84

SX_OBJECT_CONVERT_OTF_RAW – Conversion from OTF (SAPscript) to ASCII 84

UNIT_CONVERSION_SIMPLE – Converts measurement unit values and rounds 85

UNIT_CONVERSION_WITH_FACTOR – Converts value according to the factor passed 86

UNIT_CORRESPONDENCE_CHECK – Checks if units belong to same dimension 87

UNIT_GET – Returns unit for dimension and factor 88

UNIT_OF_MEASURE_ISO_TO_SAP – Converts ISO unit to SAP unit of measure 90

UNIT_OF_MEASURE_SAP_TO_ISO – Converts SAP unit to ISO unit of measure 91

UNIT_OF_MEASUREMENT_HELP – Displays all units of a specified dimension 92

3. Dates and Times 93

ADD_TIME_TO_DATE – Adds months/days/years to a date 93

C14B_ADD_TIME – Adds a time value to a date and time 95

COMPUTE_YEARS_BETWEEN_DATES – Number of years between two dates 95

CONVERSION_EXIT_LDATE_OUTPUT – Converts date format 96

CONVERT_DATE_INPUT – Conversion exit routine for inverted date 97

CONVERT_DATE_TO_EXTERNAL – Formats date from internal to display format 98

CONVERT_DATE_TO_INTERNAL – Formats date from display to internal format 99

COPF_DETERMINE_DURATION – Calculates difference between date and time 100

DATE_CHECK_PLAUSIBILITY – Checks if the value of a field is a date format 101

DATE_CHECK_WORKINGDAY – Determines if a single date is a working day 102

DATE_CHECK_WORKINGDAY_MULIPLE – Checks date across multiple factory calendars .. 103

DATE_COMPUTE_DAY – Determines the day of the week for a date 105

DATE_CONV_EXT_TO_INT – Conversion of dates to SAP's internal format 106

DATE_CONVERT_TO_FACTORYDATE – Converts calendar date into factory day 107

DATE_CONVERT_TO_WORKINGDAY – Converts a calendar date into working day 109

DATE_CREATE – Calculates a date from the input parameters 110

DATE_GET_WEEK – Determines the week in a year for a date 110

DATE_IN_FUTURE – Calculates a future or past date 112

DATE_TO_PERIOD_CONVERT – Returns the period of a date 113

DATUMSAUFBEREITUNG – Formats date as per the user settings 115

DAY_ATTRIBUTES_GET – Returns information about a day 116

DAY_IN_WEEK – Returns the day of the week for a date 117

DAYS_BETWEEN_TWO_DATES – Calculates number of days between two dates 118

EASTER_GET_DATE – The date of Easter Sunday 118

FACTORYDATE_CONVERT_TO_DATE – Converts factory day into calendar date 119

FIMA_DAYS_AND_MONTHS_AND_YEARS – Calculates the difference between two dates . 120

FIRST_AND_LAST_DAY_IN_YEAR_GET – First and last days of a period 121

FIRST_DAY_IN_PERIOD_GET – Gets first day of a period 122

GET_CURRENT_YEAR – Gets the current fiscal year for a company 122

HOLIDAY_CHECK_AND_GET_INFO – Determines if a date is a holiday 123

HOLIDAY_GET – All holidays in a factory calendar 124

HR_BEN_GET_DATE_INTERSECTION – Checks if dates overlap another date range 126

HR_GET_LEAVE_DATA – Gets all leave information 128

HR_HK_DIFF_BT_2_DATES – Days, months and years between two dates 130
HR_IE_NUM_PRSI_WEEKS – Number of weeks between two dates 131
HR_PAYROLL_PERIODS_GET – Gets the payroll period for a particular date 132
HR_TIME_RESULTS_GET – Gets the time results for a payroll period 134
LAST_DAY_IN_PERIOD_GET – Gets last day of a period 135
MONTH_NAMES_GET – Names of all the months 135
MONTH_PLUS_DETERMINE – Adds or subtracts months to/from a date 137
PERIOD_DAY_DETERMINE – Starts and finishes date for period-fiscal year 137
RE_ADD_MONTH_TO_DATE – Adds or subtracts months to/from a date 138
RH_GET_DATE_DAYNAME – Returns the day based on the date provided 139
RKE_ADD_TO_PERIOD – Calculates period from any period 139
RKE_TIMESTAMP_CONVERT_INPUT – Converts display to TIMESTAMP fields 140
RKE_TIMESTAMP_CONVERT_OUTPUT – Converts TIMESTAMP fields for display 141
RP_CALC_DATE_IN_INTERVAL – Adds/subtracts years, months, days to/from date 142
RP_CHECK_DATE – Checks if value is in date format 142
RP_LAST_DAY_OF_MONTHS – Gets the last day of the month 143
SD_DATETIME_DIFFERENCE – Difference in days and time for two dates 144
SUBTRACT_TIME_FROM_DATE – Subtracts months, days, and years from a given date .. 145
SWI_DURATION_DETERMINE – The time between two events in seconds 146
WDKAL_DATE_ADD_FKDAYS – Number of working days in a date range 147
WEEK_GET_FIRST_DAY – Returns the date of the Monday of a week 148
WEEK_GET_NR_OF_WORKDAYS – The number of workable days in a week 149
WEEKDAY_GET – Names of all the days of the week 150

4. Files 151
C13Z_FILE_DOWNLOAD_ASCII – Downloads a file in ASCII format 151
C13Z_FILE_DOWNLOAD_BINARY – Downloads a file in binary format 155
C13Z_FILE_UPLOAD_ASCII – Uploads a file in ASCII format 156
C13Z_FILE_UPLOAD_BINARY – Uploads a file in binary format 157
DOWNLOAD – Downloads a file to the PC 157
EPS_GET_DIRECTORY_LISTING – Lists filenames from the application server 160
EPS_GET_FILE_ATTRIBUTES – Returns attributes for a file 161
GUI_CREATE_DIRECTORY – Creates a directory on the presentation server 162
GUI_DELETE_FILE – Deletes a file on the presentation server 164
GUI_DOWNLOAD – Downloads a file to the presentation server 165
GUI_REMOVE_DIRECTORY – Deletes a directory in the presentation server 166
GUI_UPLOAD – Uploads a file from the presentation server 166
LIST_DOWNLOAD – Downloads report to local file 167
PROFILE_GET – Reads an entry in an INI file on the frontend 168
PROFILE_SET – Writes an entry to an INI file on the frontend 169
RS_DELETE_PROGRAM – Deletes an ABAP program 170
RSPO_DOWNLOAD_SPOOLJOB – Downloads program spool to a file 171
RZL_READ_DIR – Reads a directory 172
RZL_READ_FILE – Reads a file 173
RZL_WRITE_FILE_LOCAL – Saves internal table to the presentation server 174
SO_SPLIT_FILE_AND_PATH – Splits a path into a filename and a path 175

STRR_GET_REPORT – Downloads ABAP source code 175
STRUCTURE_EXPORT_TO_MSACCESS – Downloads data into MS Access 176
TABLE_EXPORT_TO_MSACCESS – Downloads data into MS Access 178
TMP_GUI_DIRECTORY_LIST_FILES – Lists files and subdirectories 179
TMP_GUI_READ_DIRECTORY – Lists files in a directory 180
UPLOAD – Uploads a file into SAP 181
UPLOAD_FILES – Uploads multiple files into SAP 182
WS_DOWNLOAD – File transfer from internal table 183
WS_FILE_DELETE – Deletes file in the presentation server 184
WS_FILENAME_GET – Calls file selector popup 184
WS_UPLOAD – File transfer to internal table 185

5. **Lists** 189
DYNP_VALUES_READ – Reads screen values before PAI transport 189
DYNP_VALUES_UPDATE – Changes screen field contents without PBO 193
F4IF_INT_TABLE_VALUE_REQUEST – Standard help at process on value-request 193
HR_DISPLAY_BASIC_LIST – Provides a table control for data 194
K_ABC_DOKU_SHOW – Reads documentation from local program 195
LIST_FROM_MEMORY – Retrieves the output of report from memory 196
LIST_TO_ASCI – Converts an ABAP report to ASCII 197
RPY_DYNPRO_READ – Reads screen objects, including screen flow 198
RS_COVERPAGE_SELECTIONS – Returns the selection parameters for a report 199
RS_CREATE_VARIANT – For creating dynamic variants 200
RS_REFRESH_FROM_SELECTOPTIONS – Returns the selection parameters for a report 202
RS_SET_SELSCREEN_STATUS – Deactivates function codes on screen 203
RS_TOOL_ACCESS – Reads documentation from another program 204
RS_VARIANT_CONTENTS – Values of a variant returned in a table 206
RS_VARIANT_DELETE – Deletes a variant from a program 206
RS_VARIANT_EXISTS – Checks whether a variant exists for a report 207
RS_VARIANT_TEXT – Returns short description of variant 207
RS_VARIANT_VALUES_TECH_DATA – Reads variant parameters of a report 208
RZL_SUBMIT – Submits a remote report for execution 209
SAPGUI_PROGRESS_INDICATOR – Displays a progress bar on the SAP GUI 209
SAVE_LIST – Saves report as list container 210
VRM_SET_VALUES – Customises values on a drop-down field 211
WRITE_LIST – Contents from LIST_FROM_MEMORY 212
WWW_ITAB_TO_HTML – Converts internal table to HTML format 213
WWW_LIST_TO_HTML – Converts report list to HTML format 214

6. **Long Texts** 217
COMMIT_TEXT – Moves long texts from memory into log file 217
CREATE_TEXT – Creates header long text 218
DELETE_TEXT – Deletes long text(s) from SAP 220
EDIT_TEXT – Edits long text in fullscreen text editor 221
INIT_TEXT – Initialises long text header and line table 222
PRINT_TEXT – Formats text for printing 222
PRINT_TEXT_ITF – Formats text into ITF for printing 223

READ_TEXT – Reads text module into SAP 224
SAVE_TEXT – Saves long text in SAP 224

7. Number Ranges 227

NUMBER_GET_NEXT – Obtains next number from number object 227
NUMBER_RANGE_DEQUEUE – Unlocks the number range object 227
NUMBER_RANGE_ENQUEUE – Locks the number range object 228
NUMBER_RANGE_INTERVAL_LIST – Gets existing intervals of a number object 228
NUMBER_RANGE_OBJECT_CLOSE – Writes all changes to the database 229
NUMBER_RANGE_OBJECT_DELETE – Deletes the definition of a number object 229
NUMBER_RANGE_OBJECT_GET_INFO – Gets information for a number range object 230
NUMBER_RANGE_OBJECT_INIT – Initialises local memory for a number object 230
NUMBER_RANGE_OBJECT_LIST – Lists all number objects with their attributes 231
NUMBER_RANGE_OBJECT_MAINTAIN – Provides screens to maintain number object 233
NUMBER_RANGE_OBJECT_READ – Gets texts and attributes of number object 235
NUMBER_RANGE_OBJECT_UPDATE – Copies and changes number range objects 236

8. Office Integration 237

ALSM_EXCEL_TO_INTERNAL_TABLE – Uploads Excel spreadsheet to internal table 237
EXCEL_OLE_STANDARD_DAT – Starts Excel and transfers internal table data 238
EXECUTE_WINWORD – Opens MS Word on the PC 240
KCD_EXCEL_OLE_TO_INT_CONVERT – Uploads data directly from Excel sheet 241
MS_EXCEL_OLE_STANDARD_DAT – Builds a file and automatically starts Excel 242
RH_START_EXCEL_WITH_DATA – Starts Excel with contents of an internal table 244
RS_SEND_MAIL_FOR_SPOOLLIST – Sends message from program to SAPoffice 245
SAP_CONVERT_TO_XLS_FORMAT – Downloads internal table to Excel 246
SO_NEW_DOCUMENT_ATT_SEND_API1 – Attaches a document to an e-mail 247
SO_NEW_DOCUMENT_SEND_API1 – Sends an express mail (SAPoffice) 249
WS_EXCEL – Starts MS Excel on the PC 250

9. Popup Dialogues 253

Confirmation Prompt Dialogues 253
C14A_POPUP_ASK_FILE_OVERWRITE – Asks if file can be overwritten 253
CJDB_POPUP_TO_HANDLE_TIME_OUT – Asks for next step if timeout occurs 254
POPUP_TO_CONFIRM – Confirms an action before carrying out 256
POPUP_TO_CONFIRM_DATA_LOSS – Confirms an action before carrying out 257
POPUP_TO_CONFIRM_LOSS_OF_DATA – Confirms an action before carrying out 258
POPUP_TO_CONFIRM_STEP – Asks whether to perform processing step 259
POPUP_TO_CONFIRM_WITH_MESSAGE – Informs about a specific point during action ... 260
POPUP_TO_CONFIRM_WITH_VALUE – Displays a numeric value with a message 261

Display Input Check Dialogues 262
POPUP_GET_VALUES – Creates a dialogue box for display and input 262
POPUP_GET_VALUES_DB_CHECKED – Inputs data to be checked against database 264
POPUP_GET_VALUES_SET_MAX_FIELD – Specifies number of fields to display in dialogue ... 265

POPUP_GET_VALUES_USER_BUTTONS – Requests values and displays pushbuttons 267
POPUP_GET_VALUES_USER_CHECKED – Input data to be checked in a user exit 268
POPUP_GET_VALUES_USER_HELP – Branching in a user F1 or F4 help 270

Popup Screens 272
COPO_POPUP_TO_DISPLAY_TEXTLIST – Dialogue box displaying help when F1 is pressed . . . 272
CORRESPONDENCE_POPUP_EMAIL – Dialogue box for requesting e-mail address 273
EPS_PROGRESS_POPUP – Creates a number of graphical popups 274
ERGO_TEXT_SHOW – Shows text in a documentation window 276
F4_CLOCK – Displays a clock in a popup window 277
F4_DATE – Displays a calendar in a popup window 278
F4_FILENAME – Displays selection of files on local PC 279
F4_FILENAME_SERVER – Displays selection of files on server 281
F4_USER – Pops up logon IDs 282
FITRV_CALCULATOR – A working popup calculator 283
HELP_START – Help values on database fields 284
HELP_VALUES_GET_NO_DD_NAME – Help values for any field 286
HELP_VALUES_GET_WITH_DD_NAME – Help values on database fields 288
HELP_VALUES_GET_WITH_DD_TABLE – Help values on database tables 290
HELP_VALUES_GET_WITH_TABLE – Lists help values on selection screen 291
KD_GET_FILENAME_ON_F4 – Selects files on the local PC 293
MD_POPUP_SHOW_INTERNAL_TABLE – Pops up contents of internal table 294
POPUP_CONTINUE_YES_NO – Popup with the responses "Yes" and "No" 296
POPUP_DISPLAY_TEXT – Displays help documentation 297
POPUP_DISPLAY_TEXT_WITH_PARAMS – Displays help documentation with parameters . 298
POPUP_FOR_INTERACTION – General purpose popup box 300
POPUP_NO_LIST – Displays standard dialogue box if no data 302
POPUP_TO_DECIDE – Provides user with several push buttons 303
POPUP_TO_DECIDE_LIST – Provides user with several radio buttons 304
POPUP_TO_DECIDE_WITH_MESSAGE – Displays a diagnosis text 305
POPUP_TO_DISPLAY_TEXT – Displays a two-line message 307
POPUP_TO_INFORM – Displays several lines of text 308
POPUP_TO_SELECT_MONTH – Popup to choose a month and year 308
POPUP_WITH_TABLE_DISPLAY – Displays internal table data in a popup table 309
SO_EXPRESS_FLAG_SET – Popup after user performs an action 311
TERM_CONTROL_EDIT – Pops up mini-text editor 312
TH_POPUP – Popup on a specific users screen 315
TXW_TEXTNOTE_EDIT – Pops up mini-text editor 316
WS_MSG – Displays a one-line message 318

10. **Miscellaneous** 321
Jobs 321
BP_JOB_DELETE – Deletes background job(s) 321
BP_JOB_SELECT – Returns a table with job(s) details 321
BP_JOBLOG_READ – Fetches job log executions 324
BP_JOBLOG_SHOW – Displays job log in window 325
JOB_CLOSE – Schedules a background job 325

JOB_OPEN – Creates a background job 326
JOB_SUBMIT – Adds a step (program) to a background job 327

Numbers 328
CLOI_PUT_SIGN_IN_FRONT – Moves negative sign of a number 328
G_DECIMAL_PLACES_GET – Number of decimal places set for currency 329
NUMERIC_CHECK – Returns the format of a number 329
QF05_RANDOM – Returns a random number between 0 and 1 330
QF05_RANDOM_INTEGER – Returns a random number 331

Printing 332
ADDRESS_INTO_PRINTFORM – Formats an address for printing 332
FM_SELECTION_CRITERIA_PRINT – Displays criteria used in selection screen 333
GET_PRINT_PARAMETERS – Reads and changes spool print parameters 334
LOAD_PRINT_PARAMETERS – User default printer settings 336
PRINT_SELECTIONS – Builds criteria table used in selection screen 337
SET_PRINT_PARAMETERS – Sets users print settings for a report 337
STORE_PRINT_PARAMETERS – Saves users current print settings 338

Programs and Transactions 339
BAPI_TRANSACTION_COMMIT – Explicitly commits a BAPI 339
BAPI_TRANSACTION_ROLLBACK – Prevents permanent changes by BAPIs 340
DEQUEUE_ESFUNCTION – Unlocks program so that it can be executed 341
ENQUE_SLEEP – Waits a specified period of time 341
ENQUEUE_ESFUNCTION – Locks program so that it cannot be executed 342
GET_COMPONENT_LIST – Detailed description of fields from programs 343
GET_FIELDTAB – Retrieves table fields with field metadata 344
GET_GLOBAL_SYMBOLS – Returns all components of a program 345
GET_INCLUDETAB – Lists all INCLUDEs in a program 346
RFC_ABAP_INSTALL_AND_RUN – Runs a program that is stored in a table 347
RPY_TRANSACTION_READ – Where used for transactions and programs 348
RS_GET_ALL_INCLUDES – Lists all INCLUDEs in a program 349
RZL_SLEEP – Hangs application from 1 to 5 seconds 350
SAPGUI_SET_FUNCTIONCODE – Simulates a keystroke in an ABAP report 351

Text and Strings 352
CLPB_EXPORT – Loads text table from the clipboard 352
CLPB_IMPORT – Sends text table to the clipboard 353
RKD_WORD_WRAP – Converts a long string into several lines 353
SCP_REPLACE_STRANGE_CHARS – Replaces special letters with normal text 354
SPELL_AMOUNT – Converts numeric amount into characters 356
STRING_CENTER – Centres a string within another 357
STRING_CONCATENATE – Joins two strings together 358
STRING_CONCATENATE_3 – Joins three strings together 359
STRING_LENGTH – Returns the length of a string 360
STRING_MOVE_RIGHT – Shifts a string right 360
STRING_REVERSE – Returns a string in reverse order 361
STRING_SPLIT – Splits a string into smaller strings 362

STRING_UPPER_LOWER_CASE – Converts string to proper case 363

SWA_STRING_SPLIT – Splits a string into smaller strings 364

TEXT_SPLIT – Splits text into smaller strings 365

Various 366

CALL_BROWSER – Calls default web browser or file manger 366

CHANGEDOCUMENT_READ_HEADERS – Gets change document header 367

CHANGEDOCUMENT_READ_POSITIONS – Gets change document details 369

CL_TABLE_EDITOR – Displays and edits internal table data 370

CSAP_MAT_BOM_READ – Displays simple material BOMs 371

DDIF_FIELDINFO_GET – Information about tables 372

FORMAT_MESSAGE – Formats error message for display 373

K_WERKS_OF_BUKRS_FIND – Lists all plants for a given company code 374

MATERIAL_BTCI_SELECTION_NEW – Selects the correct views on material master 375

MATERIAL_BTCI_TEXT – BDC fields and OK codes for materials 377

REGISTRY_GET – Reads an entry from the registry 378

REGISTRY_SET – Sets an entry in the registry 379

RV_ORDER_FLOW_INFORMATION – Reads sales document flow 380

WRITE_MESSAGE – Formats error message for display 381

Appendix – Tables Used in Examples 383

Introduction

This book is a reference guide to the functions provided by the SAP R/3 system.

The SAP R/3 (SAP for short) system provides many built-in functions (approximately 237,000 as of release 4.6C) to assist in the rapid development of ABAP-programming projects, by reducing the amount of "reinventing the wheel" code that would otherwise be required.

Some of the functions are extremely specific, written by SAP to solve a particular problem in a single program. Many of them, however, are generalised enough for repeated use in a variety of circumstances in ABAP programs. These are the foci of this book.

The problem of using SAP's functions is that most of them are either poorly documented or have no documentation at all, and there is almost no information on what functions are actually available, their purpose, or their method of operation. It is often a long and arduous process of investigation, trial and error, and sheer luck to discover a suitable function.

This book intends to change all that by providing a central resource for the most commonly used SAP functions. Each function contains a summary of its purpose, a longer detailed description or other pertinent information (such as if the function has been superseded or is obsolete), an explanation of the most commonly used parameters (input, output, changing, tables) with a list of possible values passed to them (where appropriate), a fully worked example of the function in action, and ending with references to other related functions documented elsewhere in the book.

Contained within these pages are those functions that are most likely to be required in your ABAP-programming projects. They include time, date, and numeric conversions, popup dialogue boxes, uploading and downloading MS Excel and ordinary file data, sending e-mail onto the Internet, date and time calculations, and much more.

Functions are arranged alphabetically within each chapter. So if you need to know on what day Easter will fall for any year, GET_EASTER_DATE will be found in the Date and Time routines chapter. Similarly, to upload Excel data to an ABAP-internal table, look at ALSM_EXCEL_TO_INTERNAL_TABLE in the Office Integration chapter.

Lists describing the most commonly used parameters to a function are also provided. These lists offer a clear textual description of the parameter, which can be of help to the more obscurely named parameters. In some modules, parameter tables list the values that an input parameter takes, and describes each individually.

Each function described also contains a simple but fully working example (4.6B). To offer the reader a more complete understanding of the function, some closely related modules (e.g. the RSPO_* group) are coded into one complete program, demonstrating how the functions interact with each other. Each function ends with references to other related documented functions, if appropriate.

This information often takes years to accumulate. The seasoned ABAPer should have at least seen some of these functions before, and the beginner now has instant access to a host of cross-application functionality, which will be of immense value in any ABAP-programming project, or thumbed through as a reference at leisure, away from the PC.

Layout of Reference Entries

GUI_UPLOAD

Summary
Uploads file from the application server.

Description
Replaces WS_UPLOAD.

Parameters

```
EXPORTING
    FILENAME                    Path and filename to download
    FILETYPE                    File type:
                                Value  Meaning
                                ASC    ASCII (default)
                                BIN    Binary
                                DBF    DBASE
                                IBM    ASCII with IBM code page conversion
                                WK1    Spreadsheet
                                DAT    ASCII data table with column tab
TABLES
    DATA_TAB                    Table of data
```

Example

```
REPORT ZEXAMPLE.
DATA: BEGIN OF ITAB OCCURS 0,
        COLA(10),
        COLB(10),
      END OF ITAB.

  CALL FUNCTION 'GUI_UPLOAD'
      EXPORTING
          FILENAME                 = 'C:\TEMP\zexample.txt'
          FILETYPE                 = 'ASC'
      TABLES
          DATA_TAB                 = ITAB
      EXCEPTIONS
          FILE_OPEN_ERROR          = 1
          FILE_READ_ERROR          = 2
          NO_BATCH                 = 3
          GUI_REFUSE_FILETRANSFER  = 4
          INVALID_TYPE             = 5
          OTHERS                   = 6.

  IF SY-SUBRC NE 0.
    WRITE:/ 'Could not upload file'.
  ELSE.
    WRITE:/ 'File uploaded into internal table.'.
  ENDIF.
```

See Also
UPLOAD, WS_UPLOAD

See also: Names of related functions documented in the book

Example: Working ABAP coding of the function

Parameters: Most commonly used function parameters with input values

Description: Optional. Noteworthy information about the function

Summary: Brief explanation of the function

GUI_UPLOAD: Name of the function

An Introduction to SAP

The SAP name (pronounced S-A-P not "sap") is derived from the German "Systeme, Andwendungen, Produkte in der Datenverarbeitung", or in English, "Systems, Applications, and Products in Data Processing".

SAP AG, the company behind the system, was founded in 1972 by five ex-IBM employees. Their global headquarters is based in Walldorf, Germany and has subsidiaries in over 50 countries around the world. SAP AG is now the third largest software maker in the world with over 17,500 customers, including more than half of the world's 500 top companies.

SAP R/3 is the leading example of an Enterprise Resource Planning (ERP) system, used by medium to large companies to track and manage in real time, business information, such as sales, production, and financial data. The R/3 system is known simply as SAP. It consists of suites of major business applications, which can be viewed as a tightly integrated collection of logical business modules. A module is a set of programs (or transactions) that deal with the same area of business functionality, such as Financial Accounting, Materials Management, and Human Resource Management. The software was developed with this idea of componentisation of business functions in mind.

Each module, which is based on detailed analyses of industry best practices, implements a specific segment of enterprise operations and are in themselves, extremely complex. The modules work in close cooperation and this comprehensive integration offers complete harmonisation across all business functions. For example, when a vendor completes a purchase order, inventory levels are adjusted in Materials Management, and triggers the issuing of an invoice from Financial Accounting.

There are 11 modules in SAP, usually referred to by a two-letter acronym. The BASIS system could also be considered a module, but is the heart of the SAP system and is not normally evident to users. All these modules need not be implemented in a company:

AM   Asset Management – track, value, and depreciate assets, including:
- Purchase
- Depreciation
- Sale

CO   Controlling – internal cost management accounting, including:
- Overhead cost
- Product cost
- Profitability analysis

FI   Financial Accounting – normal accounting books, including:
- General ledger
- Special purpose ledger
- Accounts receivable and payable

HR   Human Resources – people management, including:
- Payroll
- Recruitment
- Personnel development

MM   Materials Management – anything to do with goods, including:
- Inventory management
- Consumption-based planning
- Purchasing

PM   Plant Maintenance – equipment maintenance record, including:
- Maintenance order management
- Equipment inventory
- Down time

PP   Production Planning – manages the production process, including:
- Production orders execution
- Material requirements planning
- Capacity planning

PS   Project System – standard tools for project management, including:
- Progress analysis
- Time sheets
- Costs and forecasts

QM   Quality Management – controls material quality, including:
- Planning
- Inspections
- Certificates

SD   Sales and Distribution – controls the order lifecycle, including:
- Sales promotions
- Pricing
- Billing

CA   Cross-Application – enhances the individual modules, including:
- Workflow (WF)
- Business information warehouse (BW)
- Industry solutions (IS)

SAP is delivered to customers with selected standard processes turned on and it is the process of configuration which gives SAP its great flexibility. This configuration is done by business analysts, people experienced in identifying and mapping (or where necessary, changing) business processes. They customise the modules by adjusting the thousands of possible values within each module. This phase precedes going live and no programming is normally required at this stage.

The SAP R/2 system, that was released into the German market in 1979, was designed purely to operate as a mainframe system, and was the first integrated, enterprise-wide computer system. In line with the trends in technology towards the end of the 1980s, SAP AG launched R/3 in 1992, which runs under the three-tier client/server paradigm. These tiers include:

Presentation server: The local PC that has SAPGUI installed.
Application server: Loads and runs programs from the database server.
Database server: Stores SAP's application programs and data.

The software-orientated, client/server architecture of the R/3 system enables real-time enterprise-wide information management and runs contrary to the central-processing design of R/2. In mid-2001, there were approximately 644 installations of R/2. The number dropped to below 200 by 2002 and is expected to be close to zero by mid/end-2004. Maintenance for all remaining SAP R/2 systems ends by December 2004.

R/3 is hardware and operating-system neutral, and operates in a wide variety of environments which has helped it to grow, in just 10 years, to over 44,500 installations with an estimated 10 million users in 120 countries. Today, SAP is available in 46 country-specific versions, incorporating 28 languages including Japanese Kanji and other double-byte character languages.

With each release, the system has been developed to meet the increasing commercial and technological needs of organisations around the globe. Each release is assigned a version number and the higher the version number, the later the release. The current release of R/3 is 4.7, called "Enterprise". From version to version, bugs have been fixed and the scope of the system has been expanded to include new functionality, however subsequent releases and revisions are downward compatible.

Using Function Modules

The programming language ABAP/4 (or now officially just called ABAP, "Advanced Business Application Language") originated in the R/2 system, and was used exclusively for reporting. With each release of SAP, the scope of the language has expanded to include new features, and is now a modern fourth-generation language with object-oriented functionality.

Basic programs and reports are written entirely in ABAP and do not require any additional assistance from the numerous tools and utilities within SAP. Usually, the ABAP editor (Transaction SE38) is enough. Complex programs, called Transactions, require several development tools, such as Screen Painter (Transaction SE51) to create and design interactive screens and Menu Painter (Transaction SE41) to create custom screen titles and menu bars for each screen.

As with all modern-programming languages, SAP comes with a host of pre-written procedures available for reuse in ABAP programs, called Function Modules, which can be accessed from Transaction SE37. A function module is an independent routine that can be called from within an ABAP program (using the CALL FUNCTION statement) to perform a specific task. Examples include determining the IP address of a terminal, to finding the number of seconds, hours, days, months and years between two dates.

Each function module is unique and is global to all ABAP programs, which is to say that no special "include" statements need be inserted into the beginning of ABAP programs, unlike for some functions in the C language, for example. Each module forms part of a function group (pool), which is a way of grouping together modules with similar functionality. These can be accessed from Transaction SE80.

Most function modules can be tested independently of the calling program, within Transaction SE37. Exceptions defined in the module can be used to flag error conditions. These errors are not necessarily ABAP coding errors, but could be a legitimate response coded in the function module to certain conditions.

For example, if the date 31 September is passed into a function, the module can determine that this is an invalid date and raise it as an exception, to be handled by the calling program. Usually, each exception is given a unique (per module) numerical value, which is placed in the system variable SY-SUBRC. The calling program can then examine the contents of this variable to determine whether or not an exception has been triggered and, if so, which exception, and take the appropriate action. A value of zero in this variable signifies that no errors occurred in the function module.

A program snippet calling a function and handling errors would typically look something like this:

```
REPORT ZEXAMPLE.
DATA V_YEARS TYPE I.

PARAMETERS: BIRTHDAY LIKE SY-DATUM.
```

```
CALL FUNCTION 'COMPUTE_YEARS_BETWEEN_DATES'
     EXPORTING
          FIRST_DATE                    = BIRTHDAY
          SECOND_DATE                   = SY-DATUM
     IMPORTING
          YEARS_BETWEEN_DATES           = V_YEARS
     EXCEPTIONS
          SEQUENCE_OF_DATES_NOT_VALID   = 1
          OTHERS                        = 2.

CASE SY-SUBRC.
  WHEN 0.
    WRITE:/ 'YOU ARE', V_YEARS, 'YEARS OLD'.
  WHEN 1.
    WRITE:/ 'INPUT DATE IS NOT VALID'.
  WHEN OTHERS.
    WRITE:/ 'COULD NOT CALCULATE AGE FROM INPUT DATES'.
ENDCASE.
```

There is no guarantee that a desired function module exists, but SAP has developed a module to cover almost every conceivable requirement, sometimes more than one to do a similar job. There is no sure fire way of finding the module you need either, but generally the best method is to enter a string containing the likely text of the function module in the function name box in SE37, surrounded by asterisks (*) for wild-card characters.

If a list of functions is returned, simply double click on the function name, click the test button, and enter appropriate input values. Check the results to determine if it suits your requirements. The function module can be easily copied into a program by selecting the Pattern button in Transaction SE38 and entering the function's name. All import, export, and exception parameters are automatically pasted into the program. Optional parameters are commented out (usually in a blue colour), while required parameters are coloured black, ready to be assigned a value.

System

1

This chapter contains functions that could be associated with BASIS type of operations, such as finding the IP address of a terminal and opening FTP sessions.

ABAP4_CALL_TRANSACTION

Summary

Initiates a transaction in a separate window.

Description

Basically a wrapper to CALL TRANSACTION. Within an ABAP program, this will start an additional transaction. The normal rules of authorisation to run the transaction naturally still apply.

Parameters

```
EXPORTING
        TCODE          Contains the transaction code to be called.
        SKIP_SCREEN    If set, will skip the first screen of the transaction.
        MODE_VAL       Display mode:
                       Value           Meaning
                       A (default)     Display the screens
                       E               Only display screens if an error occurs
                       N               Do not display (background mode)
        UPDATE_VAL     Update mode:
                       Value           Meaning
                       A (default)     Asynchronous update
                       S               Synchronous update
                       L               Local update
TABLES
        USING_TAB      BDC data for the transaction
        SPAGPA_TAB     Holds SPA\GPA parameters to fill input fields
        MESS_TAB       Contains any error messages from the transaction
```

1

Example

```
REPORT ZEXAMPLE.
DATA: BEGIN OF IMESS OCCURS 0.
        INCLUDE STRUCTURE BDCMSGCOLL.
DATA: END OF IMESS.


CALL FUNCTION 'ABAP4_CALL_TRANSACTION' STARTING NEW TASK 'ZTSK'
        EXPORTING
          TCODE                   = 'SE38'       "START ABAP DEVELOPMENT
        TABLES
          MESS_TAB                = IMESS
        EXCEPTIONS
          CALL_TRANSACTION_DENIED = 1
          TCODE_INVALID           = 2
          OTHERS                  = 3.


IF SY-SUBRC <> 0.
  LOOP AT IMESS.
    WRITE:/ IMESS-MSGV1,
            IMESS-MSGV2,
            IMESS-MSGV3.
  ENDLOOP.
ENDIF.
```

See Also

HLP_MODE_CREATE, TH_REMOTE_TRANSACTION, TRANSACTION_CALL

ARFC_GET_TID

Summary

Returns the IP address of the server in hexadecimal.

Description

The IP address is returned from the function in hexadecimal, so this should be formatted to the normal dotted notation of an IP address before being displayed to the user. The example will do this for you.

Parameters

```
IMPORTING
        TID   Contains the IP address of the user's computer that runs the function.
```

Example

```
REPORT ZEXAMPLE.
DATA: TERM_IP        LIKE ARFCTID,
      IP_ADDR(20)    TYPE C,
      IP_BIT(3)      TYPE C,
      HOSTADDR(4)    TYPE X,
      HEX_CHAR       TYPE X,
      HADDR_X(8)     TYPE X,
      IP_LEN         TYPE I,
      HEXIP_LEN      TYPE I VALUE 0,
      HEXIP          TYPE I,
      CHAR_HEX       TYPE I.

CALL FUNCTION 'ARFC_GET_TID'
     IMPORTING
          TID = TERM_IP.

HOSTADDR = TERM_IP(8).
HADDR_X = HOSTADDR.

DESCRIBE FIELD HOSTADDR LENGTH HEXIP_LEN.
HEXIP_LEN = HEXIP_LEN - 1.

DO HEXIP_LEN TIMES.
  HEX_CHAR = HADDR_X + HEXIP(1).
  CHAR_HEX = HEX_CHAR.
  IP_BIT = CHAR_HEX.
  CONDENSE IP_BIT.
  IP_LEN = STRLEN(IP_ADDR).
  IP_ADDR + IP_LEN = IP_BIT.
  IP_LEN = STRLEN(IP_ADDR).
  IP_ADDR + IP_LEN = '.'.
  HEXIP = HEXIP + 1.
ENDDO.

HEX_CHAR = HADDR_X + HEXIP(1).
CHAR_HEX = HEX_CHAR.
IP_BIT = CHAR_HEX.
CONDENSE IP_BIT.
IP_LEN = STRLEN(IP_ADDR).
IP_ADDR + IP_LEN = IP_BIT.

WRITE:/ 'SERVER IP ADDRESS IS:', IP_ADDR.
```

See Also

TERMINAL_ID_GET, TH_USER_INFO

AUTHORITY_CHECK_DATASET

Summary

Checks file access authorisation.

Description

This function module allows you to check the user's authorisation to access files (with commands OPEN DATASET, READ DATASET, TRANSFER and DELETE DATASET). A check should be performed before opening a file. This function is well documented.

Parameters

```
EXPORTING
        PROGRAM      Program containing file access command (default: current program)
        ACTIVITY     Access type required to file:
                     Value                   Meaning
                     READ                    Read file
                     WRITE                   Change file
                     READ_WITH_FILTER        Read file with filter function
                     WRITE_WITH_FILTER       Change file with filter function
                     DELETE                  Delete file
        FILENAME     Name of accessed file
```

Example

```
REPORT ZEXAMPLE.
DATA: BEGIN OF ITAB OCCURS 0,
        ATYPE(20),
     END OF ITAB.

PARAMETER  P_FNAME LIKE AUTHB-FILENAME.
PARAMETERS:P_READ AS CHECKBOX DEFAULT 'X',
           P_WRITE AS CHECKBOX DEFAULT 'X',
           P_RWF AS CHECKBOX DEFAULT 'X',
           P_WWF AS CHECKBOX DEFAULT 'X',
           P_DELETE AS CHECKBOX DEFAULT 'X'.

CLEAR: ITAB, ITAB[].

IF P_READ EQ 'X'.
  ITAB-ATYPE = 'READ'.
  APPEND ITAB.
ENDIF.

IF P_WRITE EQ 'X'.
  ITAB-ATYPE = 'WRITE'.
  APPEND ITAB.
ENDIF.

IF P_RWF EQ 'X'.
  ITAB-ATYPE = 'READ_WITH_FILTER'.
  APPEND ITAB.
ENDIF.

IF P_WWF EQ 'X'.
  ITAB-ATYPE = 'WRITE_WITH_FILTER'.
  APPEND ITAB.
ENDIF.
```

```
IF P_DELETE EQ 'X'.
  ITAB-ATYPE = 'DELETE'.
  APPEND ITAB.
ENDIF.

LOOP AT ITAB.
  CALL FUNCTION 'AUTHORITY_CHECK_DATASET'
      EXPORTING
            ACTIVITY            = ITAB-ATYPE
            FILENAME            = P_FNAME
      EXCEPTIONS
            NO_AUTHORITY        = 1
            ACTIVITY_UNKNOWN    = 2
            OTHERS              = 3.
  CASE SY-SUBRC.
    WHEN 0.
      WRITE:/ 'You have', ITAB-ATYPE, 'access to', P_FNAME.
    WHEN 1.
      WRITE:/ 'You do not have', ITAB-ATYPE, 'access to', P_FNAME.
    WHEN OTHERS.
      WRITE:/ 'Error with function'.
  ENDCASE.
ENDLOOP.
```

BP_EVENT_RAISE

Summary

Triggers an event in the background-processing system from an ABAP program.

Description

Events let you start background jobs under defined conditions. The event IDs are defined in transaction SM62 (event arguments are specified when the job is scheduled).

When you define a new event, a transport request must be manually created if it is to be transported to another system.

Parameters

```
EXPORTING
      EVENTID    The event name, defined in SM62
      EVENTPARM  Job can be scheduled to wait for an EVENTID or combination of EVENTID
                 and EVENTPARM
```

Example

```
REPORT ZEXAMPLE.
DATA: Q_EVENT     LIKE TBTCJOB-EVENTID    VALUE 'SAP_QEVENT',
      Q_EVENTPARM LIKE TBTCJOB-EVENTPARM.
```

```
CALL FUNCTION 'BP_EVENT_RAISE'
        EXPORTING
                EVENTID                 = Q_EVENT
                EVENTPARM               = Q_EVENTPARM
        EXCEPTIONS
                BAD_EVENTID             = 1
                EVENTID_DOES_NOT_EXIST  = 2
                EVENTID_MISSING         = 3
                RAISE_FAILED            = 4
                OTHERS                  = 5.

IF SY-SUBRC NE 0.
        WRITE:/ 'EVENT', Q_EVENT, 'NOT RAISED'.
ELSE.
        WRITE:/ 'EVENT', Q_EVENT, 'RAISED SUCCESSFULLY'.
ENDIF.
```

See Also

GET_JOB_RUNTIME_INFO

CAT_CHECK_RFC_DESTINATION

Summary

Checks for the RFC destinations and connections on a client.

Description

RFC destinations are defined within SAP using transaction code SM59.

Parameters

```
EXPORTING
        RFCDESTINATION      System to be tested
IMPORTING
        MSGV1               RFC message
        MSGV2               RFC message
        RFC_SUBRC           RFC return code
```

Example

```
REPORT ZEXAMPLE.
DATA:   RFCDESTINATION   LIKE  RSCAT-RFCDEST,
        V_MSGV1          LIKE  SY-MSGV1,
        V_MSGV2          LIKE  SY-MSGV2,
        V_SUBRC          LIKE  SYST-SUBRC.
```

```
CALL FUNCTION 'CAT_CHECK_RFC_DESTINATION'
      EXPORTING
            RFCDESTINATION  = RFCDESTINATION
      IMPORTING
            MSGV1           = V_MSGV1
            MSGV2           = V_MSGV2
            RFC_SUBRC       = V_SUBRC.

IF V_SUBRC NE 0.
      WRITE:/ 'ERROR:', V_MSGV1, V_MSGV2.
ELSE.
      SET PARAMETER ID 'RFC' FIELD RFCDESTINATION.
      WRITE:/ 'CONNECTION TO', RFCDESTINATION, 'IS WORKING'.
ENDIF.
```

See Also

CAT_PING, TH_SERVER_LIST

CAT_PING

Summary

Checks RFC system and configuration.

Description

Tests if an RFC system is reachable and returns configuration data if possible.

Parameters

```
EXPORTING
      RFCDESTINATION   System to be tested
IMPORTING
      SYSINFO          Structure with RFC system configuration information
```

Example

```
REPORT ZEXAMPLE.
DATA: BEGIN OF SYSINFO.
        INCLUDE STRUCTURE CATFR.
DATA: END OF SYSINFO.
DATA RFC_DESTINATION LIKE RFCDES-RFCDEST.

SYSINFO = SPACE.

CALL FUNCTION 'CAT_PING' DESTINATION RFC_DESTINATION
      IMPORTING
            SYSINFO = SYSINFO
```

```
     EXCEPTIONS
               COMMUNICATION_FAILURE  = 1
               SYSTEM_FAILURE         = 2.

IF SY-SUBRC NE 0.
    WRITE:/ 'COULD NOT CONNECT TO', RFC_DESTINATION.
ELSE.
    WRITE:/ SYSINFO.
ENDIF.
```

See Also

CAT_CHECK_RFC_DESTINATION

DEQUEUE_ES_PROG

Summary

Releases program locks.

Description

This function releases a lock in a program that has been set by ENQUEUE_ES_PROG.

Parameters

```
EXPORTING
    NAME    Program name to lock
```

Example

```
REPORT ZEXAMPLE.
DATA V_PGM TYPE PROGRAMM.

CALL FUNCTION 'DEQUEUE_ES_PROG'
    EXPORTING
            NAME  = V_PGM.

    WRITE:/ 'PROGRAM', V_PGM, 'IS UNLOCKED'.
```

See Also

DEQUEUE_ESFUNCTION, ENQUEUE_ES_PROG

ENQUEUE_ES_PROG

Summary

Prevents the parallel execution of a program.

Description

This function creates a lock in a program that should not be processed more than once, simultaneously. The lock remains in place until either the DEQUEUE_ES_PROG function module is called or the transaction is completed (with an implicit DEQUEUE_ALL call).

Parameters

```
EXPORTING
        NAME        Program name to lock
        SCOPE       Controls how the lock is passed to the update program:
                    Value       Meaning
                    1           The lock is not passed to the update program. The lock
                                is removed when the transaction ends.
                    2 (default) The lock is passed to the update program. The update
                                program is responsible for removing the lock.
                    3           The lock is passed to the update program. The lock must
                                be removed in both the interactive program and in the
                                update program.
```

Example

```
REPORT ZEXAMPLE.
DATA V_PGM TYPE PROGRAMM.

CALL FUNCTION 'ENQUEUE_ES_PROG'
     EXPORTING
          NAME            = V_PGM
          SCOPE           = '3'
     EXCEPTIONS
          FOREIGN_LOCK    = 1
          SYSTEM_FAILURE  = 2
          OTHERS          = 3.

IF SY-SUBRC NE 0.
     WRITE:/ 'LOCK FAILED ON PROGRAM ZPROGRAM'.
ELSE.
     WRITE:/ V_PGM, 'SUCCESSFULLY LOCKED AGAINST SIMULTANEOUS PROCESSING'.
ENDIF.
```

See Also

DEQUEUE_ES_PROG, ENQUEUE_ESFUNCTION

FTP_COMMAND

Summary

Executes a command on an FTP server.

Description

Passes an FTP command to an FTP server for processing.

Parameters

```
EXPORTING
      HANDLE      Unique ID identifying FTP session (from FTP_CONNECT)
      COMMAND     Any FTP command. For example, DIR lists files in a directory
TABLES
      DATA        Results from FTP command. For example, filenames in a directory
```

Example

See FTP_CONNECT

See Also

FTP_CONNECT

FTP_CONNECT

Summary

Opens a connection to the FTP server.

Description

FTP_CONNECT requires an encrypted password to work. It returns a unique ID (handle) that can be used with other FTP functions (e.g. FTP_COMMAND).

For the RFC_DESTINATION value, you can use CAT_CHECK_RFC_DESTINATION to determine the FTP server as defined in SAP.

Parameters

```
EXPORTING
    USER                Username to the FTP server
    PASSWORD            Password valid for the FTP server (encrypted)
    HOST               FTP server name
    RFC_DESTINATION    The server name as configured in SAP
IMPORTING
    HANDLE             Unique ID created for this FTP session
```

Example

```
REPORT ZEXAMPLE.
DATA: FTP_USER(64)      VALUE 'FTPUSER',
```

```
            FTP_PWD(64)          VALUE 'FTPPWD',
            FTP_HOST(50)         VALUE 'FTPSERVER',
            RFC_DEST             LIKE RSCAT-RFCDEST VALUE 'RFC_SERVER'.

DATA: HDL TYPE I,
      KEY TYPE I VALUE 26101957,
      DSTLEN TYPE I.

DATA: BEGIN OF FTP_DATA OCCURS 0,
         LINE(132) TYPE C,
      END OF FTP_DATA.

DESCRIBE FIELD FTP_PWD LENGTH DSTLEN.

CALL 'AB_RFC_X_SCRAMBLE_STRING'
      ID 'SOURCE'           FIELD FTP_PWD
      ID 'KEY'              FIELD KEY
      ID 'SCR'              FIELD 'X'
      ID 'DESTINATION'      FIELD FTP_PWD
      ID 'DSTLEN'           FIELD DSTLEN.

CALL FUNCTION 'FTP_CONNECT'
      EXPORTING
            USER              = FTP_USER
            PASSWORD          = FTP_PWD
            HOST              = FTP_HOST
            RFC_DESTINATION   = RFC_DEST
      IMPORTING
            HANDLE            = HDL
      EXCEPTIONS
            NOT_CONNECTED     = 1
            OTHERS            = 2.

IF SY-SUBRC NE 0.
      WRITE:/ 'COULD NOT CONNECT TO', FTP_HOST.
ELSE.
      WRITE:/ 'CONNECTED SUCCESSFULLY. SESSION HANDLE IS', HDL.

      CALL FUNCTION 'FTP_COMMAND'
              EXPORTING
                      HANDLE        = HDL
                      COMMAND       = 'DIR'
              TABLES
                      DATA          = FTP_DATA
              EXCEPTIONS
                      TCPIP_ERROR   = 1
                      COMMAND_ERROR = 2
                      DATA_ERROR    = 3
                      OTHERS        = 4.

   IF SY-SUBRC NE 0.
      WRITE:/ 'COULD NOT EXECUTE FTP COMMAND'.
```

```
 ELSE.
      LOOP AT FTP_DATA.
      WRITE: / FTP_DATA.
      ENDLOOP.

      CALL FUNCTION 'FTP_DISCONNECT'
              EXPORTING
                      HANDLE          = HDL
              EXCEPTIONS
                      OTHERS          = 1.
     IF SY-SUBRC NE 0.
      WRITE:/ 'COULD NOT DISCONNECT FROM FTP SERVER'.
   ELSE.
      WRITE:/ 'DISCONNECTED FROM FTP SERVER'.
   ENDIF.
  ENDIF.
ENDIF.
```

See Also

CAT_CHECK_RFC_DESTINATION, FTP_COMMAND, FTP_DISCONNECT

FTP_DISCONNECT

Summary

Closes the connection and logs off the FTP server.

Description

This function also destroys the handle created by FTP_CONNECT, so it is no longer valid for subsequent commands.

Parameters

```
EXPORTING
      HANDLE     Unique ID created by FTP_CONNECT to identify the FTP session
```

Example

See FTP_CONNECT

See Also

FTP_CONNECT, FTP_COMMAND

GET_JOB_RUNTIME_INFO

Summary

Gets information about a job.

Description

This function can also determine what event and argument triggered the start of a background job from within the background job. This is possible only in job steps that start ABAP programs.

Parameters

```
IMPORTING
        EVENTID                 Event that started the job (if any)
        EVENTPARM               Event parameters
        JOBNAME                 Job returned by function
```

Example

```
REPORT ZEXAMPLE.
PARAMETERS:V_EVTID    LIKE TBTCM-EVENTID,
           V_EVTPRM   LIKE TBTCM-EVENTPARM,
           V_JOBNAM   LIKE TBTCM-JOBNAME.

CALL FUNCTION 'GET_JOB_RUNTIME_INFO'
     IMPORTING
           EVENTID            = V_EVTID
           EVENTPARM          = V_EVTPRM
           JOBNAME            = V_JOBNAM
     EXCEPTIONS
           NO_RUNTIME_INFO    = 1
           OTHERS             = 2.

IF SY-SUBRC NE 0.
     WRITE:/ 'ERROR IN FUNCTION'.
ELSE.
     WRITE:/ 'JOB', V_JOBNAM, 'STARTED WITH EVENT', V_EVTID, 'AND PARAMETER', V_EVTPRM.
ENDIF.
```

See Also

BP_EVENT_ RAISE

GUI_EXEC

Summary

Starts an external program asynchronously.

Description

Replaces WS_EXECUTE to start an external application. This function is only available for Windows 32-bit clients and does not associate applications with file extensions.

Parameters

```
EXPORTING
        COMMAND         Program name
        PARAMETER       Optional field for parameters (if not specified in COMMAND)
IMPORTING
        RETURNCODE      Function return code, assigned by Windows system
```

Example

```
REPORT ZEXAMPLE.
DATA: PROGRAM(255) TYPE C VALUE 'NOTEPAD',
      PARAMETER(255) TYPE C VALUE 'C:\DATAFILE.TXT',
RETCODE TYPE I.

CALL FUNCTION 'GUI_EXEC'
        EXPORTING
                COMMAND     = PROGRAM
                PARAMETER   = PARAMETER
        IMPORTING
                RETURNCODE  = RETCODE.

IF RETCODE NE 0.
  WRITE:/ 'PROGRAM', PROGRAM, 'NOT FOUND OR COULD NOT BE STARTED'.
ENDIF.
```

See Also

GUI_RUN, EXECUTE_WINWORD, WS_EXECUTE, WS_EXCEL

GUI_GET_DESKTOP_INFO

Summary

Returns information about the end-users client (the desktop).

Description

This function is platform specific. Replaces WS_QUERY.

Parameters

```
EXPORTING
      TYPE:   Indicates the information to be returned:
              Value       Meaning
              -2          SAP system directory
              1           Computer name
              2           Windows directory
              3           Windows system directory
              4           Temporary directory
              5           Windows user name
              6           Windows OS
              7           Windows build number
              8           Windows version
              9           SAP GUI program name
              10          SAP GUI program path
              11          SAP current directory
              12          Desktop directory
CHANGING
      RETURN Text information from function
```

Example

```
REPORT ZEXAMPLE.
DATA: V_VALU(255)    TYPE C,
      INFOREQ        TYPE I VALUE '-2'.

WHILE INFOREQ NE 13.
  CALL FUNCTION 'GUI_GET_DESKTOP_INFO'
        EXPORTING
              TYPE    = INFOREQ
        CHANGING
              RETURN  = V_VALU.

  CASE INFOREQ.
    WHEN '-2'.
      WRITE:/ 'SAP SYSTEM DIRECTORY:', V_VALU.
    WHEN '1'.
      WRITE:/ 'COMPUTER NAME:', V_VALU.
    WHEN '2'.
      WRITE:/ 'WINDOWS DIRECTORY:', V_VALU.
    WHEN '3'.
      WRITE:/ 'WINDOWS SYSTEM DIRECTORY:', V_VALU.
    WHEN '4'.
      WRITE:/ 'TEMPORARY DIRECTORY:', V_VALU.
    WHEN '5'.
      WRITE:/ 'WINDOWS USER NAME:', V_VALU.
    WHEN '6'.
      WRITE:/ 'WINDOWS OS:', V_VALU.
    WHEN '7'.
      WRITE:/ 'WINDOWS BUILD NUMBER:', V_VALU.
    WHEN '8'.
      WRITE:/ 'WINDOWS VERSION:', V_VALU.
```

```
  WHEN '9'.
    WRITE:/ 'SAP GUI PROGRAM NAME:', V_VALU.
  WHEN '10'.
    WRITE:/ 'SAP GUI PROGRAM PATH:', V_VALU.
  WHEN '11'.
    WRITE:/ 'SAP CURRENT DIRECTORY:', V_VALU.
  WHEN '12'.
    WRITE:/ 'DESKTOP DIRECTORY:', V_VALU.
  ENDCASE.

  INFOREQ = INFOREQ + 1.
ENDWHILE.
```

See Also

IW_C_GET_FRONTEND_VERSION, WS_QUERY

GUI_RUN

Summary

Starts program asynchronously with ShellExecute.

Description

This function is only available for Windows 32-bit clients. If you enter a document name for COMMAND, the document is displayed in its corresponding application.

Parameters

```
EXPORTING
      COMMAND       File or program name
      PARAMETER     Optional field for parameters (if not specified in COMMAND)
IMPORTING
      RETURNCODE    Function return code, assigned by the Windows system
```

Example

```
REPORT ZEXAMPLE.
DATA:   PROGRAM(255)    TYPE C VALUE 'NOTEPAD',
        PARAMETER(255)  TYPE C VALUE 'C:\DATAFILE.TXT',
RETCODE TYPE I.

CALL FUNCTION 'GUI_RUN'
      EXPORTING
            COMMAND    = PROGRAM
            PARAMETER  = PARAMETER
      IMPORTING
            RETURNCODE = RETCODE.
```

```
IF RETCODE NE 0.
  WRITE:/ 'PROGRAM', PROGRAM, 'NOT FOUND OR COULD NOT BE STARTED'.
ENDIF.
```

See Also

GUI_EXEC

GWY_READ_CONNECTIONS

Summary

Checks if the gateway connection is open.

Description

When the connection is broken, the entry is still in the connection tables. The length of time this takes to clear (usually a few seconds) is defined in R/3.

Parameters

```
EXPORTING
    GWHOST              Local host
    GWSERV              Remote server
TABLES
    CONNECTIONS         List of gateway connections
```

Example

```
REPORT ZEXAMPLE.
DATA:  GW_HOST          LIKE  GWY_STRUCT-GWHOST,
       GW_SERV          LIKE  GWY_STRUCT-GWSERV,
       SAPSYS(2),
       CONVERSATION_ID(8).

DATA: BEGIN OF GWCONN OCCURS 0.
      INCLUDE STRUCTURE GWY_CONN.
DATA: END OF GWCONN.

* 1 GET HOST AND SERVICE
CALL 'C_SAPGPARAM' ID 'NAME'  FIELD 'SAPLOCALHOST'
                   ID 'VALUE' FIELD GW_HOST.

CALL 'C_SAPGPARAM' ID 'NAME'  FIELD 'SAPSYSTEM'
                   ID 'VALUE' FIELD SAPSYS.

GW_SERV     = 'SAPGW'.
GW_SERV + 5 = SAPSYS.
```

```
CALL  FUNCTION 'GWY_READ_CONNECTIONS'
     EXPORTING
          GWHOST                       = GW_HOST
          GWSERV                       = GW_SERV
     TABLES
          CONNECTIONS                  = GWCONN
     EXCEPTIONS
          GWY_UNKNOWN_OPCODE           = 01
          GWY_COMMUNICATION_FAILURE    = 02
          GWY_GET_TAB_FAILED           = 03
          GWY_NEWLINE_FAILED           = 04
          GWY_TABLEN_TOO_SHORT         = 05
          GWY_GET_OPCODE_FAILED        = 06
          GWY_GET_GWHOST_FAILED        = 07
          GWY_GET_GWSERV_FAILED        = 08.
IF SY-SUBRC NE 0.
  WRITE:/ 'ERROR IN FUNCTION'.
ELSE.
  WRITE:/2 'UNIT', 11 'PROGRAM', 20 'USER', 33 'SYSTEM', 50 'LAST REQUEST'.
  ULINE AT /1(70).

  LOOP AT GWCONN.
    WRITE:   /2 GWCONN-LU,
             11 GWCONN-TP,
             20 GWCONN-GWUSER,
             33 GWCONN-SYMDEST,
             50 GWCONN-LAST_REQ.
  ENDLOOP.
ENDIF.
```

HLP_MODE_CREATE

Summary

Creates another session in the system.

Description

This function creates another session in your system with the transaction passed as parameter to the function module.

Parameters

```
EXPORTING
     TCODE   Transaction to call in new session
```

Example

```
REPORT ZEXAMPLE.
```

```
CALL  FUNCTION    'HLP_MODE_CREATE'
      EXPORTING
                TCODE = 'SE38'.       "ABAP DEVELOPMENT
```

See Also

ABAP4_CALL_TRANSACTION, TH_REMOTE_TRANSACTION, TRANSACTION_CALL

IW_C_GET_FRONTEND_VERSION

Summary

Version of the SAP frontend installed on a PC.

Description

Display the SAP logon screen (where you choose the server you want to logon), select the vend diagram (top right). Then choose "About Frontend". There is a file version number: 4640.2.0.2071 (as an example). The function returns this value.

Find the path and name by clicking on "Loaded DLLs" pushbutton on the popup box. On scrolling to the bottom of this list, you will see the path to the FRONT.EXE application.

Parameters

```
EXPORTING
      COMPPATH                  Path to the SAP GUI
      COMPNAME                  Name of the SAP GUI program
IMPORTING
      FILEVERSION               Release version of the GUI
```

Example

```
REPORT ZEXAMPLE.
DATA FILEVERSION LIKE CNTLSTRINF-VERSION.

CALL FUNCTION 'IW_C_GET_FRONTEND_VERSION'
      EXPORTING
          COMPPATH       = 'C:\PROGRAM FILES\SAPPC\SAPGUI\'
          COMPNAME       = 'FRONT.EXE'
      IMPORTING
          FILEVERSION    = FILEVERSION.

WRITE:/ 'THE FRONT-END PROGRAM VERSION IS:', FILEVERSION.
```

See Also

GUI_GET_DESKTOP_INFO

RFC_MAIL

Summary

Sends an e-mail to another SAP system.

Description

To view the function (as it cannot be seen in SE37), go to SM59, select "TCP/IP connections", select and open "SERVER_EXEC" or "LOCAL_EXEC", look on the pull down menu SYSTEM INFORMATION->FUNCTION LIST.

Parameters

```
EXPORTING
     USER              E-mail address of recipient
TABLES
     MAIL              E-mail message
```

Example

```
REPORT ZEXAMPLE.
DATA V_EMAIL(200) TYPE C OCCURS O WITH HEADER LINE.

V_EMAIL = 'MESSAGE BODY LINE 1'.     APPEND V_EMAIL.
V_EMAIL = 'MESSAGE BODY LINE 2'.     APPEND V_EMAIL.

CALL FUNCTION 'RFC_MAIL' DESTINATION 'LOCAL_EXEC'
      EXPORTING
            USER = 'USERNAME@SOMEWHERE.COM'
      TABLES
            MAIL = V_EMAIL.

IF SY-SUBRC EQ O.
      WRITE 'E-MAIL SENT SUCCESSFULLY.'.
ELSE.
      WRITE 'ERROR SENDING E-MAIL.'.
ENDIF.
```

See Also

CAT_CHECK_RFC_DESTINATION, SO_NEW_DOCUMENT_ATT_SEND_API1, SO_ NEW_DOCUMENT_SEND_API1

RSPO_FIND_SPOOL_REQUESTS

Summary

Finds a spool number.

Description

Returns spool number(s) for a user, SAP client, and\or printer ID.

Parameters

```
EXPORTING
     RQOWNER          Spool owner
     ALLCLIENTS       SAP clients
     RQDEST           Printer name
TABLES
     SPOOLREQUESTS    List of spool(s) information
```

Example

```
REPORT ZEXAMPLE.
TYPE-POOLS:SLIS,
          SP01R.
DATA: SPOOL_OWNER    LIKE SY-UNAME,
      PRN            LIKE TSP03-PADEST VALUE 'LOCL',
      SPOOL_NUMBER   LIKE TSP01-RQIDENT.

DATA: BEGIN OF IRQTAB OCCURS 0.
        INCLUDE STRUCTURE RSPORQ.
DATA: END OF IRQTAB.

DATA: LTAB TYPE SP01R_TVIEW WITH HEADER LINE,
      RS_SELFIELD TYPE SLIS_SELFIELD.
SPOOL_OWNER = SY-UNAME.
CALL FUNCTION 'RSPO_FIND_SPOOL_REQUESTS'
     EXPORTING
          RQOWNER           = SPOOL_OWNER
          RQDEST            = PRN
     TABLES
          SPOOLREQUESTS     = IRQTAB.

WRITE:/ 'PRINTING SPOOLS OF', SPOOL_OWNER, 'ON PRINTER', PRN, 'NOW.'.
LOOP AT IRQTAB.
  SPOOL_NUMBER = IRQTAB-RQIDENT.

  CALL FUNCTION 'RSPO_OUTPUT_SPOOL_REQUEST'
     EXPORTING
          DEVICE            = PRN
          SPOOL_REQUEST_ID  = SPOOL_NUMBER
     EXCEPTIONS
          OTHERS            = 1.

  SKIP.
  IF SY-SUBRC EQ 0.
     WRITE: IRQTAB-RQIDENT,'PRINTED ON', PRN.
     EXIT.                      "ONLY PRINT ONE IN THIS EXAMPLE
```

```
ELSE.
      WRITE: IRQTAB-RQIDENT, 'NOT PRINTED ON', PRN.
  ENDIF.
ENDLOOP.

* PRINT THE LAST ONE, WITH NO PRINT DIALOG BOX
MOVE-CORRESPONDING IRQTAB TO LTAB.
APPEND LTAB.

CALL  FUNCTION 'RSPO_RPRINT_SPOOLREQ'
      EXPORTING
          TEND         = SPOOL_NUMBER
          POPUP        = ' '
      TABLES
          REQ_VIEW     = LTAB
      CHANGING
          RS_SELFIELD  = RS_SELFIELD
      EXCEPTIONS
          OTHERS       = 1.

IF SY-SUBRC EQ 0.
  WRITE:/ LTAB-RQIDENT, 'PRINTED ON DEFAULT PRINTER'.
ELSE.
  WRITE:/ LTAB-RQIDENT, 'NOT PRINTED'.
ENDIF.

* DOWNLOAD A SPOOLJOB TO A FILE
CALL  FUNCTION 'RSPO_DOWNLOAD_SPOOLJOB'
      EXPORTING
          ID    = LTAB-RQIDENT
          FNAME = 'C:\TEMP\SPOOLFILE.TXT'.

WRITE:/ LTAB-RQIDENT, 'DOWNLOADED TO C:\TEMP\SPOOLFILE.TXT'.
```

RSPO_OUTPUT_SPOOL_REQUEST

Summary

Outputs the same request on a different printer.

Description

Picks up a spool on one printer and sends it to another for printing.

Parameters

```
EXPORTING
      DEVICE             Printer name
      SPOOL_REQUEST_ID   Spool number
```

Example

See RSPO_FIND_SPOOL_REQUESTS

See Also

GET_PRINT_PARAMETERS, RSPO_FIND_SPOOL_REQUESTS

RSPO_RPRINT_SPOOLREQ

Summary

Triggers spool to print automatically.

Description

Prints the data from the spool number which is passed into it.

Parameters

```
EXPORTING
    TEND          Spool request number
    POPUP         Display print parameters (default X = Yes)
TABLES
    REQ_VIEW      Spool information
CHANGING
    RS_SELFIELD   Spool ALV display information
```

Example

See RSPO_FIND_SPOOL_REQUESTS

See Also

RSPO_FIND_SPOOL_REQUESTS, GET_PRINT_PARAMETERS

SAPWL_GET_SUMMARY_STATISTIC

Summary

Object usage statistics summary.

Description

Returns summary of usage statistics on a variety of objects, such as users of transactions and reports.

Parameters

```
EXPORTING
    PERIODTYPE              Period to report:
                            Value      Meaning
                            D          Daily
                            W          Weekly
                            M          Monthly
                            Y          Yearly
    HOSTID                  Client
    STARTDATE               Start date to calculate statistics
TABLES
    SUMMARY                 Statistical summary
```

Example

```
REPORT ZEXAMPLE.
DATA: BEGIN OF SUMMARY OCCURS 0.
        INCLUDE STRUCTURE SAPWLSUMRY.
DATA: END OF SUMMARY.

DATA: PERIODTYPE LIKE  SAPWLACCTP-PERIODTYPE VALUE 'D',
      HOSTID     LIKE  SAPWLSERV-HOSTSHORT,
      STARTDAT   LIKE  SAPWLACCTP-STARTDATE.

DATA AVG(5).

STARTDAT = SY-DATUM.
HOSTID   = SY-HOST.

CALL  FUNCTION 'SAPWL_GET_SUMMARY_STATISTIC'
      EXPORTING
          PERIODTYPE  = PERIODTYPE
          HOSTID      = HOSTID
          STARTDATE   = STARTDAT
      TABLES
          SUMMARY     = SUMMARY.

LOOP AT SUMMARY.
  IF SUMMARY-TASKTYPE = 'DIALOG'.
    AVG = SUMMARY-RESPTI / SUMMARY-COUNT.
    EXIT.
  ENDIF.
ENDLOOP.

WRITE:/ 'AVERAGE RESPONSE TIME:', AVG.
```

See Also

SAPWL_WORKLOAD_GET_DIRECTORY, SAPWL_WORKLOAD_GET_STATISTIC

SAPWL_WORKLOAD_GET_DIRECTORY

Summary

Timeframe of statistics on SAP database.

Parameters

```
TABLES
    DIRECTORY                Table of contents
```

Example

```
REPORT ZEXAMPLE.
DATA: WL_DIR LIKE SAPWLDIR OCCURS 1 WITH HEADER LINE,
      NUM_LINES LIKE SYST-INDEX.

DATA: BEGIN OF ITIME_FRAME OCCURS 1,
         FILLER(14) TYPE C,
         VALUE(7)   TYPE C,
END OF ITIME_FRAME.

CALL  FUNCTION 'SAPWL_WORKLOAD_GET_DIRECTORY'
      TABLES
         DIRECTORY = WL_DIR.

DESCRIBE TABLE WL_DIR LINES NUM_LINES.
IF NUM_LINES > 0.
  LOOP AT WL_DIR WHERE PERIODTYPE = 'M' AND HOSTID <> 'TOTAL'.
    CONCATENATE  WL_DIR-STARTDATE + 4(2)
                 WL_DIR-STARTDATE + 0(4)
    INTO ITIME_FRAME-VALUE SEPARATED BY '/'.
    APPEND ITIME_FRAME.
  ENDLOOP.
ELSE.
  CONCATENATE SYST-DATUM + 4(2) SYST-DATUM + 0(4)
  INTO ITIME_FRAME-VALUE SEPARATED BY '/'.
  APPEND ITIME_FRAME.
ENDIF.

* DELETE DUPLICATE INFO FROM MULTIPLE APP. SERVERS
SORT ITIME_FRAME BY VALUE + 3(4) VALUE(2) ASCENDING.
DELETE ADJACENT DUPLICATES FROM ITIME_FRAME COMPARING VALUE.

LOOP AT ITIME_FRAME.
  WRITE:/ ITIME_FRAME-VALUE.
ENDLOOP.
```

See Also

SAPWL_GET_SUMMARY_STATISTIC, SAPWL_WORKLOAD_GET_STATISTIC

SAPWL_WORKLOAD_GET_STATISTIC

Summary

Object usage statistics.

Description

Returns usage statistics on a variety of objects, such as users of transactions and reports.

Parameters

```
EXPORTING
    PERIODTYPE              Period to report:
                            Value     Meaning
                            D         Daily
                            W         Weekly
                            M         Monthly
                            Y         Yearly
    HOSTID                  Client
    STARTDATE               Start date to calculate statistics
TABLES
    USER_STATISTIC          Users of transactions and reports
```

Example

```
REPORT ZEXAMPLE.
DATA: BEGIN OF USER_STATISTIC OCCURS 0.
        INCLUDE STRUCTURE SAPWLUENTI.
DATA: END OF USER_STATISTIC.

DATA: PERIODTYPE LIKE  SAPWLACCTP-PERIODTYPE VALUE 'D',
      HOSTID     LIKE  SAPWLSERV-HOSTSHORT,
      STARTDAT   LIKE  SAPWLACCTP-STARTDATE.

STARTDAT = SY-DATUM.
HOSTID   = SY-HOST.
CALL  FUNCTION 'SAPWL_WORKLOAD_GET_STATISTIC'
    EXPORTING
        PERIODTYPE      = PERIODTYPE
        HOSTID          = HOSTID
        STARTDATE       = STARTDAT
    TABLES
        USER_STATISTIC  = USER_STATISTIC
    EXCEPTIONS
        NO_DATA_FOUND   = 1.

IF SY-SUBRC EQ 0.
  LOOP AT USER_STATISTIC.
    WRITE:/  USER_STATISTIC-TTYPE,
             USER_STATISTIC-ENTRY_ID,
```

```
                    USER_STATISTIC-ACCOUNT.
  ENDLOOP.
ELSE.
  WRITE:/ 'NO USER STATISTICS'.
ENDIF.
```

See Also

SAPWL_GET_SUMMARY_STATISTIC, SAPWL_WORKLOAD_GET_STATISTIC

SHOW_JOBSTATE

Summary

Checks the status of a job.

Parameters

```
EXPORTING
     JOBCOUNT          ID number of job
     JOBNAME           Job name
IMPORTING
     ABORTED           Job terminated abnormally
     FINISHED          Job completed successfully
     PRELIMINARY       Job not released to run or no start condition
     READY             Job scheduled, released, start condition fulfilled, but job not
                       yet started
     RUNNING           Job in progress
     SCHEDULED         Job scheduled and released, waiting for start condition to be
                       fulfilled
```

Example

```
REPORT ZEXAMPLE.
TABLES: TBIST, TBIER.

DATA: BEGIN OF I_TJOBS OCCURS 0.
        INCLUDE STRUCTURE TBIER_S.
DATA: END OF I_TJOBS.
DATA: I_TBIZU LIKE TBIZU OCCURS 0 WITH HEADER LINE.

DATA: ABORTED,FINISHED,PRELIMINARY,READY,RUNNING,SCHEDULED.

* JOB NAMES
SELECT * FROM TBIZU INTO TABLE I_TBIZU.

* CURRENT JOBS
SELECT * FROM TBIST.
  MOVE-CORRESPONDING TBIST TO I_TJOBS.
  I_TJOBS-JOBID = TBIST-JOBNAME.
```

```
  APPEND I_TJOBS.
ENDSELECT.

* COMPLETED JOBS
SELECT * FROM TBIER.
  MOVE-CORRESPONDING TBIER TO I_TJOBS.
  I_TJOBS-JOBID = TBIER-JOBNAME.
  APPEND I_TJOBS.
ENDSELECT.

LOOP AT I_TJOBS.
  READ TABLE I_TBIZU WITH KEY JOBID = I_TJOBS-JOBID BINARY SEARCH.
  IF SY-SUBRC        = 0.
    I_TJOBS-JOBTEXT  = I_TBIZU-JOBTEXT.
    I_TJOBS-BTCJOB   = I_TBIZU-BTCJOB.
  ENDIF.

  CALL FUNCTION 'SHOW_JOBSTATE'
       EXPORTING
           JOBCOUNT          = I_TJOBS-JOBCOUNT
           JOBNAME           = I_TJOBS-BTCJOB
       IMPORTING
           ABORTED           = ABORTED
           FINISHED          = FINISHED
           PRELIMINARY       = PRELIMINARY
           READY             = READY
           RUNNING           = RUNNING
           SCHEDULED         = SCHEDULED
       EXCEPTIONS
           JOBCOUNT_MISSING  = 01
           JOBNAME_MISSING   = 02
           JOB_NOTEX         = 03
           OTHERS            = 99.
  IF SY-SUBRC <> 0.
    I_TJOBS-STATUSTEXT = 'ERROR IN FUNCTION CALL'.
  ELSE.
    IF ABORTED = 'X'.
      I_TJOBS-STATUSTEXT   = 'JOB ABORTED'.
    ELSEIF FINISHED        = 'X'.
      I_TJOBS-STATUSTEXT   = 'JOB FINISHED'.
    ELSEIF SCHEDULED       = 'X'.
      I_TJOBS-STATUSTEXT   = 'JOB SCHEDULED'.
    ELSEIF RUNNING         = 'X'.
      I_TJOBS-STATUSTEXT   = 'JOB RUNNING'.
    ELSEIF READY           = 'X'.
      I_TJOBS-STATUSTEXT   = 'JOB READY'.
    ELSE.
      I_TJOBS-STATUSTEXT   = 'JOB UNKNOWN'.
    ENDIF.
    MODIFY I_TJOBS.
  ENDIF.
ENDLOOP.

WRITE:/'JOB ID', 10 'JOB STATUS'.
LOOP AT I_TJOBS.
```

```
  WRITE:/ I_TJOBS-JOBID,
         I_TJOBS-STATUSTEXT.
ENDLOOP.
```

SO_SPOOL_READ

Summary

Returns printer spool information.

Description

Retrieves data from a spool.

Parameters

```
EXPORTING
     SPOOL_NUMBER              Printer spool number
TABLES
     OBJCONT                   Data from printer spool
```

Example

```
REPORT ZEXAMPLE.
DATA: BEGIN OF OBJCONT OCCURS 0.
        INCLUDE STRUCTURE SOLI.
DATA: END OF OBJCONT.

DATA: SPOOL_NUMBER    LIKE  RSPOTYPE-RQNUMBER,
      OWNER           LIKE  SOUD-USRNAM,
      CONT_SIZE       LIKE  RSTSTYPE-LINELENGTH.

OWNER = SY-UNAME.
CALL  FUNCTION 'SO_WIND_SPOOL_LIST' "DISPLAY ALL SPOOL NUMBERS FOR OWNER
     EXPORTING
          OWNER        = OWNER
     IMPORTING
          SPOOL_NUMBER = SPOOL_NUMBER.

CALL  FUNCTION 'SO_SPOOL_READ'        "GET SPOOL INFOMATION
     EXPORTING
          SPOOL_NUMBER               = SPOOL_NUMBER
     TABLES
          OBJCONT                    = OBJCONT
     EXCEPTIONS
          CONVERT_ERROR              = 1
          OBJECT_NOT_EXIST           = 2
          OPERATION_NO_AUTHORIZATION = 3
          SPOOL_CLOSE_ERROR          = 4
```

```
            SPOOL_OPEN_ERROR              = 5
            SPOOL_READ_ERROR             = 6
            OTHERS                       = 7.

IF SY-SUBRC EQ 0.
  CALL FUNCTION 'RSPO_SPOOLDATA_WRITE_INIT'.

  LOOP AT OBJCONT.
    CONT_SIZE = STRLEN(OBJCONT).
    CALL FUNCTION 'RSPO_SPOOLDATA_WRITE' "DISPLAY SPOOL
         EXPORTING
             SPOOL_DATA  = OBJCONT
             DATA_LENGTH = CONT_SIZE
             START_POS   = 1
         EXCEPTIONS
             OTHERS      = 1.
  ENDLOOP.
ELSE.
  WRITE:/ 'COULD NOT DISPLAY SPOOL:', SPOOL_NUMBER.
ENDIF.
```

See Also

RSPO_RETURN_ABAP_SPOOLJOB, SO_WIND_SPOOL_LIST

SO_WIND_SPOOL_LIST

Summary

Popup dialogue to browse printer spool numbers.

Parameters

```
EXPORTING
      OWNER                    Name of printer spool creator
IMPORTING
      SPOOL_NUMBER             Printer spool number
```

Example

See SO_SPOOL_READ

See Also

SO_SPOOL_READ

SXPG_CALL_SYSTEM

Summary

Calls a command external to the SAP system.

Description

The function checks the user's authorisation to run a command and runs the command on the system on which the function module is executed. Internally, it calls SXPG_COMMAND_LIST_GET and SXPG_COMMAND_EXECUTE. Use with caution!!

Parameters

```
IMPORTING
     COMMANDNAME          Name of the external command, as defined in the maintenance
                          function (transaction SM69)
     PARAMETERS           Arguments for the external command
EXPORTING
     STATUS               Returns the final execution status of the external command:
                          Value     Meaning
                          0         Command started and completed successfully
                          E         Command failed
TABLES
     EXEC_PROTOCOL        Contains output of the command and host system
```

Example

```
REPORT ZEXAMPLE.
DATA: BEGIN OF COMMAND_LIST OCCURS 0.
        INCLUDE STRUCTURE SXPGCOLIST.
DATA: END OF COMMAND_LIST .

DATA: BEGIN OF EXEC_PROTOCOL OCCURS 0.
        INCLUDE STRUCTURE BTCXPM.
DATA: END OF EXEC_PROTOCOL.

DATA: STATUS LIKE BTCXP3-EXITSTAT,
      COMMANDNAME LIKE SXPGCOLIST-NAME VALUE '*',
      SEL_NO LIKE SY-TABIX.

* GET LIST OF EXTERNAL COMMANDS
CALL FUNCTION 'SXPG_COMMAND_LIST_GET'
     EXPORTING
         COMMANDNAME      = COMMANDNAME
         OPERATINGSYSTEM  = SY-OPSYS
     TABLES
         COMMAND_LIST     = COMMAND_LIST
```

```
        EXCEPTIONS
            OTHERS              = 1.


IF SY-SUBRC EQ 0.
   CALL FUNCTION 'POPUP_WITH_TABLE_DISPLAY'
         EXPORTING
             ENDPOS_COL    = 100
             ENDPOS_ROW    = 20
             STARTPOS_COL  = 2
             STARTPOS_ROW  = 2
             TITLETEXT     = 'CHOOSE A COMMAND TO EXECUTE:'
         IMPORTING
             CHOISE        = SEL_NO
         TABLES
             VALUETAB      = COMMAND_LIST
         EXCEPTIONS
             BREAK_OFF     = 1
             OTHERS        = 2.


   IF SY-SUBRC EQ 0.
     READ TABLE COMMAND_LIST INDEX SEL_NO.

* CHECK AUTHORIZATION
     CALL FUNCTION 'SXPG_COMMAND_CHECK'
           EXPORTING
               COMMANDNAME                 = COMMAND_LIST-NAME
               OPERATINGSYSTEM             = SY-OPSYS
           EXCEPTIONS
               NO_PERMISSION               = 1
               COMMAND_NOT_FOUND           = 2
               PARAMETERS_TOO_LONG         = 3
               SECURITY_RISK               = 4
               WRONG_CHECK_CALL_INTERFACE  = 5
               X_ERROR                     = 6
               TOO_MANY_PARAMETERS         = 7
               PARAMETER_EXPECTED          = 8
               ILLEGAL_COMMAND             = 9
               COMMUNICATION_FAILURE       = 10
               SYSTEM_FAILURE              = 11
               OTHERS                      = 12.

   CASE SY-SUBRC.
     WHEN 0.
       CALL FUNCTION 'SXPG_COMMAND_EXECUTE'
             EXPORTING
                 COMMANDNAME                 = COMMAND_LIST-NAME
             TABLES
                 EXEC_PROTOCOL               = EXEC_PROTOCOL
             EXCEPTIONS
                 NO_PERMISSION               = 1
                 COMMAND_NOT_FOUND           = 2
                 PARAMETERS_TOO_LONG         = 3
                 SECURITY_RISK               = 4
                 WRONG_CHECK_CALL_INTERFACE  = 5
                 PROGRAM_START_ERROR         = 6
```

```
                PROGRAM_TERMINATION_ERROR        = 7
                X_ERROR                          = 8
                PARAMETER_EXPECTED               = 9
                TOO_MANY_PARAMETERS              = 10
                ILLEGAL_COMMAND                  = 11
                WRONG_ASYNCHRONOUS_PARAMETERS    = 12
                CANT_ENQ_TBTCO_ENTRY             = 13
                JOBCOUNT_GENERATION_ERROR        = 14
                OTHERS                           = 15.

        IF SY-SUBRC EQ 0.
          WRITE:/ COMMAND_LIST-NAME, 'RAN SUCCESSFULLY'.
        ELSE.
          WRITE:/ 'ERROR WITH COMMAND', COMMAND_LIST-NAME.
        ENDIF.

        WHEN 1.
          WRITE:/'YOU ARE NOT AUTHORIZED TO RUN', COMMAND_LIST-NAME.

         WHEN OTHERS.
          WRITE:/'ERROR WITH FUNCTION WITH COMMAND', COMMAND_LIST-NAME.
        ENDCASE.
      ENDIF. "POPUP_WITH_TABLE_DISPLAY
  ENDIF.    "SXPG_COMMAND_LIST_GET
```

See Also

SXPG_COMMAND_EXECUTE

SXPG_COMMAND_CHECK

Summary

Checks authorisation to run a command.

Description

Checks user's authorisation to execute the command on the host system with the specified arguments, and then carry out the command.

Parameters

```
IMPORTING
    ADDITIONAL_PARAMETERS     Arguments for the external command
    COMMANDNAME               Name of the external command, as defined in the maintenance
                              function (transaction SM69)
    OPERATINGSYSTEM           The host system on which the command is to be executed
                              OPERATINGSYSTEM value is defined as part of the command
                              definition (transaction SM69)
    TARGETSYSTEM              System upon which the command is to run
```

EXPORTING
    PROGRAMNAME   Name and path to the command to be executed. Arguments are not included
    DEFINED_PARAMETERS   Returns argument string from the command definition
    ALL_PARAMETERS   Returns complete argument string for the command, consisting of ADDITIONAL_PARAMETERS and DEFINED_PARAMETERS

Example

See SXPG_CALL_SYSTEM

SXPG_COMMAND_EXECUTE

Summary

Executes a command on remote system.

Description

Checks user's authorisation to run the command and if the authorisation check is successful, then the command is executed on the target host system. Commands are defined with SM69 and can be tested with SM49. Use with caution!

Parameters

IMPORTING
    COMMANDNAME   Name of the external command, as defined in the maintenance function (transaction SM69)
    OPERATINGSYSTEM   The host system on which the command is to be executed OPERATINGSYSTEM value is defined as part of the command definition (transaction SM69)
    TARGETSYSTEM   System upon which the command is to run
    STDOUT   Log STDOUT output from the external command in parameter EXEC_PROTOCOL
    STDERR   Log STDERR output from the external command in parameter EXEC_PROTOCOL
    TERMINATIONWAIT   Wait for termination of external command and event log
    TRACE   Trace execution through CALL "writetrace" and through the local trace function of the command
    ADDITIONAL_PARAMETERS   Arguments for the external command
    ABAPPROG   ABAP program name
    ABAPFORM   ABAP procedure (FORM) in program ABAPPROG
EXPORTING
    STATUS   Returns the final status of the execution of the external command:

Value	Meaning
0	Command started and completed successfully
E	Command failed

TABLES
    EXEC_PROTOCOL   Contains output of the command and host system.

Example

See SXPG_CALL_SYSTEM

See Also

SXPG_CALL_SYSTEM

SXPG_COMMAND_LIST_GET

Summary

Reads a list of the external commands that have been defined in R/3 into an internal table.

Description

You can loop through the table to select a command, or offer the list to your user for selection. You can pass the selection onto SXPG_COMMAND_EXECUTE for an authorisation check and execution of the command.

Parameters

```
IMPORTING
    COMMANDNAME            Name of the external command, as defined in the maintenance
                           function (transaction SM69).
    OPERATINGSYSTEM        The host system on which the command is to be executed.
                           OPERATINGSYSTEM value is defined as part of the command
                           definition (transaction SM69).
    TARGETSYSTEM           System upon which the command is to run.
TABLES
    COMMAND_LIST           Contains list of selected commands in the format shown in
                           transaction SM49 or SM69.
```

Example

See SXPG_CALL_SYSTEM

TERMINAL_ID_GET

Summary

Returns the IP address and terminal ID.

Parameters

```
EXPORTING
    USERNAME           SAP user
```

```
IMPORTING
    TERMINAL                IP address and terminal information
```

Example

```
REPORT ZEXAMPLE.
DATA TERMINAL LIKE USR41-TERMINAL.

CALL FUNCTION 'TERMINAL_ID_GET'
    EXPORTING
        USERNAME                = SY-UNAME
    IMPORTING
        TERMINAL                = TERMINAL
    EXCEPTIONS
        MULTIPLE_TERMINAL_ID    = 1
        NO_TERMINAL_FOUND       = 2
        OTHERS                  = 3.

IF SY-SUBRC EQ 0.
  WRITE:/'USER', SY-UNAME, 'IS USING TERMINAL', TERMINAL.
ELSE.
  WRITE:/'ERROR IN FUNCTION'.
ENDIF.
```

See Also

ARFC_GET_TID, TH_USER_INFO

TH_DELETE_USER

Summary

Logoffs a user.

Description

Results are similar to using transaction SM04. Does not actually delete the user's ID from SAP!

Parameters

```
EXPORTING
    USER                    SAP username to logoff the system
    CLIENT                  SAP client to log users off
```

Example

```
REPORT ZEXAMPLE.

PARAMETERS V_BNAME LIKE SY-UNAME.
```

```
CALL FUNCTION 'TH_DELETE_USER'
    EXPORTING
        USER            = V_BNAME
        CLIENT          = SY-MANDT
    EXCEPTIONS
        AUTHORITY_ERROR = 1
        OTHERS          = 2.

IF SY-SUBRC EQ 0.
  WRITE:/ V_BNAME, 'LOGGED OFF THE SYSTEM'.
ELSE.
  WRITE:/ V_BNAME, 'NOT LOGGED OFF THE SYSTEM'.
ENDIF.
```

TH_ENVIRONMENT

Summary

Gets values in SAP environment variables.

Description

Returns the values of SAP systems environment variables.

Parameters

```
TABLES

    ENVIRONMENT  Holds names and values of environment variables.
```

Example

```
REPORT ZEXAMPLE.
DATA: BEGIN OF IENV OCCURS 0.
      INCLUDE STRUCTURE THENV.
DATA: END OF IENV.

DATA: V_VAR(20), V_VALUE(235).

CALL FUNCTION 'TH_ENVIRONMENT'
     TABLES
     ENVIRONMENT = IENV.

WRITE:/ 'VARIABLE', 30 'VALUE'.
ULINE.
LOOP AT IENV.
  SPLIT IENV-LINE AT '=' INTO V_VAR V_VALUE.
  WRITE:/ V_VAR, 30 V_VALUE.
  CLEAR: V_VAR, V_VALUE.
ENDLOOP.
```

TH_REMOTE_TRANSACTION

Summary

Runs a transaction on a remote server.

Description

The transaction may be run as a BDC by filling in the BDCTAB table parameter.

Parameters

```
EXPORTING
    TCODE                   Transaction code to be run
    DEST                    RFC-capable server on which to run transaction
IMPORTING
    COMM_MESSAGE            Error messages
    SYST_MESSAGE            Success messages
TABLES
    BDCTAB                  BDC data
```

Example

```
REPORT ZEXAMPLE.
DATA: BEGIN OF SERVER_LIST OCCURS 0 .
        INCLUDE STRUCTURE MSXXLIST .
DATA: END OF SERVER_LIST .

DATA: MESSAGE_SERVER LIKE MSXXLIST-HOST,
      V_LINE TYPE I,
      COMM_MESSAGE(256),
      SYST_MESSAGE(256).

CALL FUNCTION 'TH_SERVER_LIST'
     TABLES
         LIST    = SERVER_LIST
     EXCEPTIONS
         OTHERS  = 1.

IF SY-SUBRC NE 0.
  CALL 'C_SAPGPARAM' ID 'NAME'  FIELD 'RDISP/MSHOST'
                     ID 'VALUE' FIELD MESSAGE_SERVER.

  SERVER_LIST-NAME = MESSAGE_SERVER.
  APPEND SERVER_LIST.
ENDIF.

DESCRIBE TABLE SERVER_LIST LINES V_LINE.
IF V_LINE GE 1.
  READ TABLE SERVER_LIST INDEX 1.       "RUN TXN ON FIRST SERVER FOUND
```

```
CALL FUNCTION 'TH_REMOTE_TRANSACTION'
      EXPORTING
           TCODE         = 'SE37'
           DEST          = SERVER_LIST-NAME
      IMPORTING
           COMM_MESSAGE  = COMM_MESSAGE
           SYST_MESSAGE  = SYST_MESSAGE.

IF COMM_MESSAGE <> SPACE.
  WRITE:/ COMM_MESSAGE.
ELSE.
  WRITE:/ SYST_MESSAGE.
ENDIF.
ELSE.
  WRITE:/ 'NO SERVERS FOUND'.
ENDIF.
```

See Also

ABAP4_CALL_TRANSACTION, HLP_MODE_CREATE, TRANSACTION_CALL

TH_SERVER_LIST

Summary

List of RFC servers.

Parameters

```
TABLES
   LIST                    List of servers
```

Example

See TH_REMOTE_TRANSACTION

See Also

CAT_CHECK_RFC_DESTINATION

TH_USER_INFO

Summary

Returns information about user.

Parameters

```
IMPORTING
     HOSTADDR                    IP address of the frontend computer
     TERMINAL                    Terminal name of the user
     ACT_SESSIONS                Current number of open sessions
     MAX_SESSIONS                Maximum number of sessions allowed
     MY_SESSION                  Currently active session
     MY_INTERNAL_SESSION         Current internal session
     TASK_STATE                  Task state
```

Example

```
REPORT ZEXAMPLE.
TABLES: MSXXLIST.

DATA:  HOSTADDR                 LIKE   MSXXLIST-HOSTADR,
       TERMINAL(255),
       ACT_SESSIONS             LIKE   SM04DIC-COUNTER,
       MAX_SESSIONS             LIKE   SM04DIC-COUNTER,
       MY_SESSION               LIKE   SM04DIC-COUNTER,
       MY_INTERNAL_SESSION      LIKE   SM04DIC-COUNTER,
       TASK_STATE               LIKE   SM04DIC-COUNTER.

DATA:    DOT          VALUE '.',
         IP1          TYPE I,
         IP2          TYPE I,
         IP3          TYPE I,
         IP4          TYPE I,
         C_IP1(3)     TYPE C,
         C_IP2(3)     TYPE C,
         C_IP3(3)     TYPE C,
         C_IP4(3)     TYPE C,
         V_IPADDR(15).

CALL  FUNCTION 'TH_USER_INFO'
     IMPORTING
          HOSTADDR             = HOSTADDR
          TERMINAL             = TERMINAL
          ACT_SESSIONS         = ACT_SESSIONS
          MAX_SESSIONS         = MAX_SESSIONS
          MY_SESSION           = MY_SESSION
          MY_INTERNAL_SESSION  = MY_INTERNAL_SESSION
          TASK_STATE           = TASK_STATE.

* FORMAT THE IP ADDRESS
C_IP1 = IP1 = HOSTADDR(1).
C_IP2 = IP2 = HOSTADDR + 1(1).
C_IP3 = IP3 = HOSTADDR + 2(1).
C_IP4 = IP4 = HOSTADDR + 3(1).
CONCATENATE C_IP1 DOT C_IP2 DOT C_IP3 DOT C_IP4 INTO V_IPADDR.
CONDENSE V_IPADDR NO-GAPS.
```

```
WRITE:/ SY-UNAME, 'INFORMATION:'.
ULINE.

WRITE:/ 'IP ADDRESS:', 20 V_IPADDR,
     / 'TERMINAL:', 20 TERMINAL,
     / 'OPEN SESSIONS:', 20 ACT_SESSIONS,
     / 'MAXIMUM SESSIONS:', 20 MAX_SESSIONS,
     / 'CURRENT SESSION:', 20 MY_SESSION,
     / 'INTERNAL SESSION:', 20 MY_INTERNAL_SESSION,
     / 'TASK STATE:', 20 TASK_STATE.
```

See Also

ARFC_GET_TID, TERMINAL_ID_GET, TH_USER_LIST

TH_USER_LIST

Summary

Displays users logged onto a server.

Parameters

```
TABLES
    LIST                    List of users logged into the system
```

Example

```
REPORT ZEXAMPLE.
DATA: BEGIN OF IUSRTBL OCCURS 0.
        INCLUDE STRUCTURE UINFO.
DATA: END OF IUSRTBL.

DATA NUMBER_OF_USERS TYPE I.

CALL  FUNCTION 'TH_USER_LIST'
     TABLES
         LIST    = IUSRTBL
     EXCEPTIONS
         OTHERS  = 1.

DESCRIBE TABLE IUSRTBL LINES NUMBER_OF_USERS.
WRITE:/ NUMBER_OF_USERS, 'ARE LOGGED IN NOW'.

LOOP AT IUSRTBL.
  WRITE:/ IUSRTBL-BNAME.
ENDLOOP.
```

See Also

TH_USER_INFO

TRANSACTION_CALL

Summary

Initiates a transaction in a separate window.

Description

An extremely simple function, which issues a CALL TRANSACTION command. This function cannot process exceptions (so will crash if a non-existent transaction code is passed into it). Use one of the alternative functions in the "See Also:" section instead.

Parameters

```
EXPORTING
    TRANSACTION_NAME          Transaction code to call
```

Example

```
REPORT ZEXAMPLE.

CALL FUNCTION 'TRANSACTION_CALL'
    EXPORTING
        TRANSACTION_NAME = 'SE37'        "FUNCTION MODULES
    EXCEPTIONS
        OTHERS           = 1.

WRITE:/ 'FUNCTION CALLED'.
```

See Also

ABAP4_CALL_TRANSACTION, HLP_MODE_CREATE, TH_REMOTE_TRANSACTION

USER_EXISTS

Summary

Checks whether user ID is valid.

Parameters

```
EXPORTING
    BNAME              User ID
    CLIENT             Client to check for user ID
IMPORTING
    LOCKED             Flag whether user ID is locked
```

Example

See F4_USER

See Also

F4_USER

WS_EXECUTE

Summary

Calls an external program from ABAP.

Description

Replaced by GUI_EXEC.

Parameters

```
EXPORTING
    COMMANDLINE        File to load with external application
    PROGRAM            Path and name of external application
```

Example

```
REPORT ZEXAMPLE.
DATA: V_PGM(100)    VALUE 'C:\PROGRAM FILES\MICROSOFT OFFICE\OFFICE\WINWORD.EXE',
      V_FNAME       LIKE RLGRAP-FILENAME VALUE 'C:\DOCUMENT.DOC'.

CALL FUNCTION 'WS_EXECUTE'
    EXPORTING
        COMMANDLINE       = V_FNAME
        PROGRAM           = V_PGM
    EXCEPTIONS
        FRONTEND_ERROR    = 1
        NO_BATCH          = 2
        PROG_NOT_FOUND    = 3
        ILLEGAL_OPTION    = 4
        GUI_REFUSE_EXECUTE = 5
        OTHERS            = 6.
```

```
IF SY-SUBRC NE 0.
  WRITE:/ V_FNAME, 'NOT OPENED WITH', V_PGM.
ELSE.
  WRITE:/ 'EXTERNAL APPLICATION CALLED SUCCESSFULLY'.
ENDIF.
```

See Also

SXPG_COMMAND_EXECUTE, GUI_RUN, GUI_EXEC

WS_QUERY

Summary

Executes query function on frontend.

Description

Replaced by GUI_GET_DESKTOP_INFO. The query command "OS" under UNIX returns the output of the UNIX command "uname".

Parameters

```
EXPORTING
        ENVIRONMENT             Environment variable for EN query, e.g. TEMP
        FILENAME                Variable requirement for FC\FE\FL\FT\DE queries
        QUERY                   Query command:
                                Value       Meaning
                                CD          Current directory
                                DE          Directory exists
                                EN          Value of environment variable
                                FC          Filename creator (Apple only)
                                FE          Filename exists
                                FL          File length
                                FT          Filetype and status (UNIX only)
                                GM          GMUX version (internal use only)
                                LF          Linefeed code
                                OS          Operating system of presentation server
                                RC          Last return code
                                WI          Window ID graphics program
                                WS          Windows System of presentation server
                                XP          Execution path (UNIX only)
                                WINID       Variable requirement for WI query
IMPORTING
        RETURN                  Result of the query:
                                Command     Return value (non-exhaustive)
                                OS          AIX
                                DOS
                                            HP-UX
                                            MAC
                                            NT
                                            OS2
```

```
                                    OS\2
                                    OSF1
                                    SINIX
                                    SunOS
                                    ULTRIX
                                    VMS
                        WS          MC              (Macintosh)
                                    MF              (UNIX-Motif)
                        NT          (Windows NT)
                        PM          (OS/2)
                        WN          (DOS\Windows 3.xx)
                                    WN32   (32-bit Windows)
                                    WN32_95
                                    WN32_98
                                    WN32_S
```

Example

```
REPORT ZEXAMPLE.
DATA: WINSYS(20),
      OSSYS(20).

START-OF-SELECTION.
  CALL FUNCTION 'WS_QUERY'
        EXPORTING
              QUERY               = 'WS'
        IMPORTING
              RETURN              = WINSYS
        EXCEPTIONS
              INV_QUERY           = 1
              NO_BATCH            = 2
              FRONTEND_ERROR      = 3
              OTHERS              = 4.

  CALL FUNCTION 'WS_QUERY'
        EXPORTING
              QUERY               = 'OS'
        IMPORTING
              RETURN              = OSSYS
        EXCEPTIONS
              INV_QUERY           = 1
              NO_BATCH            = 2
              FRONTEND_ERROR      = 3
              OTHERS              = 4.

  PERFORM WSQUERY_CODE CHANGING WINSYS OSSYS.

  WRITE:/ 'RUNNING', WINSYS, 'ON THE', OSSYS, 'OPERATING SYSTEM'.

*&---------------------------------------------------------------------*
*& FORM WSQUERY_CODE
*&---------------------------------------------------------------------*
FORM WSQUERY_CODE CHANGING  P_WINSYS
                            P_OSSYS.
```

```
* READABLE TEXTS:
  CASE P_WINSYS.
    WHEN 'MC'.
      P_WINSYS = 'MACINTOSH'.
    WHEN 'MF'.
      P_WINSYS = 'UNIX'.
    WHEN 'NT'.
      P_WINSYS = 'WINDOWS NT'.
    WHEN 'PM'.
      P_WINSYS = 'OS\2'.
    WHEN 'WN'.
      P_WINSYS = 'WINDOWS 3.XX'.
    WHEN 'WN32'.
      P_WINSYS = '32-BIT WINDOWS'.
    WHEN 'WN32_95'.
      P_WINSYS = 'WINDOWS 95'.
    WHEN 'WN32_98'.
      P_WINSYS = 'WINDOWS 98'.
    WHEN OTHERS.
      P_WINSYS = 'UNKNOWN'.
  ENDCASE.

  CASE P_OSSYS.
    WHEN 'AIX'.
      P_OSSYS = 'AIX'.
    WHEN 'DOS'.
      P_OSSYS = 'DOS'.
    WHEN 'HP-UX'.
      P_OSSYS = 'HP-UX'.
    WHEN 'MAC'.
      P_OSSYS = 'MAC'.
    WHEN 'NT'.
      P_OSSYS = 'NT'.
    WHEN 'OS2' OR 'OS\2'.
      P_OSSYS = 'OS\2'.
    WHEN 'OSF1'.
      P_OSSYS = 'OSF1'.
    WHEN 'SINIX'.
      P_OSSYS = 'SINIX'.
    WHEN 'SUNOS'.
      P_OSSYS = 'SUNOS'.
    WHEN 'ULTRIX'.
      P_OSSYS = 'ULTRIX'.
    WHEN 'VMS'.
      P_OSSYS = 'VMS'.
    WHEN OTHERS.
      P_OSSYS = 'UNKNOWN'.
  ENDCASE.
ENDFORM. " WSQUERY_CODE
```

See Also

GUI_GET_DESKTOP_INFO

Conversions 2

This chapter lists conversion routines for currencies, strings, numbers, dates, and data.

BAPI_CURRENCY_CONV_TO_EXTERNAL

Summary

Converts currency amounts from SAP data formats into external data formats.

Parameters

```
EXPORTING
    CURRENCY            Currency to format amount into
    AMOUNT_INTERNAL     Amount to convert
IMPORTING
    AMOUNT_EXTERNAL     Amount formatted after conversion
```

Example

```
REPORT ZEXAMPLE.

DATA:  R_TABIX     LIKE ACCBAPIFD1-TABIX,
       R_WAERS     LIKE TCURC-WAERS VALUE 'JPY',
       R_INTERNAL  LIKE BAPICURR-BAPICURR,
       R_EXTERNAL  LIKE BAPICURR-BAPICURR VALUE '1500'.

DATA:  LD_LENGTH   TYPE I,
       LD_TYPE,
       LD_DIGITS   TYPE I,
       LD_RETURN   LIKE BAPIRETURN,
       V_MSG(255).

* CONVERT INTO SAP INTERNAL FORMAT
DESCRIBE FIELD R_INTERNAL LENGTH LD_LENGTH TYPE LD_TYPE.
```

```
IF LD_TYPE = 'P'.
  LD_DIGITS = 2 * LD_LENGTH - 1.
ELSE.
  LD_DIGITS = LD_LENGTH.
ENDIF.

CALL FUNCTION 'BAPI_CURRENCY_CONV_TO_INTERNAL'
     EXPORTING
          CURRENCY            = R_WAERS
          AMOUNT_EXTERNAL     = R_EXTERNAL
          MAX_NUMBER_OF_DIGITS = LD_DIGITS
     IMPORTING
          AMOUNT_INTERNAL     = R_INTERNAL
          RETURN              = LD_RETURN.

CALL FUNCTION 'MESSAGE_TEXT_BUILD'
     EXPORTING
          MSGID               = LD_RETURN-CODE(2)
          MSGNR               = LD_RETURN-CODE + 2(3)
          MSGV1               = LD_RETURN-MESSAGE_V1
          MSGV2               = LD_RETURN-MESSAGE_V2
          MSGV3               = LD_RETURN-MESSAGE_V3
          MSGV4               = LD_RETURN-MESSAGE_V4
     IMPORTING
          MESSAGE_TEXT_OUTPUT = V_MSG.

IF V_MSG EQ '*** NO MESSAGE FOUND IN T100 ***'.
  WRITE:/ R_EXTERNAL, 'FORMATTED INTO', R_INTERNAL, 'USING CURRENCY', R_WAERS.

* CONVERT INTO EXTERNAL FORMAT
  CALL FUNCTION 'BAPI_CURRENCY_CONV_TO_EXTERNAL'
       EXPORTING
            CURRENCY         = R_WAERS
            AMOUNT_INTERNAL = R_INTERNAL
       IMPORTING
            AMOUNT_EXTERNAL = R_EXTERNAL.

  WRITE:/ R_INTERNAL, 'FORMATTED BACK INTO', R_EXTERNAL, 'USING CURRENCY', R_WAERS.
ELSE.
  WRITE:/ V_MSG.
ENDIF.
```

See Also

BAPI_CURRENCY_CONV_TO_INTERNAL

BAPI_CURRENCY_CONV_TO_INTERNAL

Summary

Converts currency amounts from external data formats into SAP data formats.

Parameters

```
EXPORTING
      CURRENCY                        Currency ID
      AMOUNT_EXTERNAL                 Quantity to convert
      MAX_NUMBER_OF_DIGITS            Number of decimals
IMPORTING
      AMOUNT_INTERNAL                 Amount after conversion
      RETURN                          Return value from function
```

Example

See BAPI_CURRENCY_CONV_TO_EXTERNAL

See Also

BAPI_CURRENCY_CONV_TO_EXTERNAL

CF_UT_UNIT_CONVERSION

Summary

Converts material unit quantities.

Description

Converts quantities from one unit of measure to another.

Parameters

```
EXPORTING
      MATNR_IMP                  Material number
      MEINS_IMP                  Material unit
      UNIT_NEW_IMP               New material unit of measure
      UNIT_OLD_IMP               Old material unit of measure
      VALUE_OLD_IMP              Material quantity
IMPORTING
      VALUE_NEW_EXP              Material quantity in new unit of measure
```

Example

```
REPORT ZEXAMPLE.

TABLES MARA.
FIELD-SYMBOLS <FIELD>.

DATA: RETURN_VALUE LIKE PLFH-MGVGW,
      UNIT_VALUE LIKE PLFH-MGVGW.

SELECT SINGLE * FROM MARA INTO MARA WHERE GEWEI NE 'KG' AND BRGEW GT 0.
```

```
ASSIGN ('MARA-BRGEW') TO <FIELD>.
MOVE: <FIELD> TO UNIT_VALUE.

CALL FUNCTION 'CF_UT_UNIT_CONVERSION'
    EXPORTING
        MATNR_IMP         = MARA-MATNR
        MEINS_IMP         = MARA-MEINS
        UNIT_NEW_IMP      = 'KG'
        UNIT_OLD_IMP      = MARA-GEWEI
        VALUE_OLD_IMP     = UNIT_VALUE
    IMPORTING
        VALUE_NEW_EXP     = RETURN_VALUE
    EXCEPTIONS
        OVERFLOW          = 1
        OTHERS            = 2.

IF SY-SUBRC EQ 0.
  WRITE:/ 'MATERIAL', MARA-MATNR, MARA-BRGEW, MARA-GEWEI,
        / 'MATERIAL', MARA-MATNR, RETURN_VALUE, 'KG'.
ELSE.
  WRITE:/ 'COULD NOT CONVERT UNIT', MARA-GEWEI, 'AMOUNT', UNIT_VALUE, 'OF MATERIAL',
  MARA-MATNR, 'INTO KG'.
ENDIF.
```

See Also

MD_CONVERT_MATERIAL_UNIT, MATERIAL_UNIT_CONVERSION,
CONVERSION_FACTOR_GET

CONVERSION_EXIT_ALPHA_INPUT

Summary

Converts any number into a string filled with zeroes.

Description

The number appears on the extreme right.

Parameters

```
EXPORTING
      INPUT           String
IMPORTING
      OUTPUT          String with zeroes after conversion
```

Example

```
REPORT ZEXAMPLE.

DATA V_NUM(10) TYPE C VALUE '1234'.
```

```
CALL FUNCTION 'CONVERSION_EXIT_ALPHA_INPUT'
     EXPORTING
         INPUT    = V_NUM
     IMPORTING
         OUTPUT   = V_NUM.

WRITE:/ V_NUM.

CALL FUNCTION 'CONVERSION_EXIT_ALPHA_OUTPUT'
     EXPORTING
         INPUT    = V_NUM
     IMPORTING
         OUTPUT   = V_NUM.

WRITE:/ V_NUM.
```

See Also

CONVERSION_EXIT_ALPHA_OUTPUT

CONVERSION_EXIT_ALPHA_OUTPUT

Summary

Converts any number with zeroes right into a simple integer.

Parameters

```
EXPORTING
     INPUT         String
IMPORTING
     OUTPUT        String without zeroes after conversion
```

Example

See CONVERSION_EXIT_ALPHA_INPUT

See Also

CONVERSION_EXIT_ALPHA_INPUT

CONVERSION_EXIT_AUART_INPUT

Summary

Converts sales document-type code.

Description

Function which converts sales document code display format to SAP's internal format.

Parameters

```
EXPORTING
    INPUT           External formatted document code
IMPORTING
    OUTPUT          SAP formatted document code
```

Example

```
REPORT ZEXAMPLE.
TABLES TVAKT.

DATA: V_AUART LIKE TVAKT-AUART,
      V_AUART_IN1(4),
      V_AUART_IN2(4).

WRITE:/ 'INTERNAL FORMAT', 20 'OUTPUT FORMAT', 40 'BACK TO INTERNAL FORMAT'.
ULINE.

SELECT * FROM TVAKT WHERE SPRAS EQ SY-LANGU.
  CALL FUNCTION 'CONVERSION_EXIT_AUART_OUTPUT'
       EXPORTING
         INPUT    = TVAKT-AUART
       IMPORTING
         OUTPUT   = V_AUART.

  CALL FUNCTION 'CONVERSION_EXIT_AUART_INPUT'
       EXPORTING
         INPUT    = V_AUART
       IMPORTING
         OUTPUT   = V_AUART_IN2.

  IF TVAKT-AUART NE V_AUART.
    MOVE TVAKT-AUART TO V_AUART_IN1.
    WRITE:/ V_AUART_IN1, 20 V_AUART, 40 V_AUART_IN2.
  ENDIF.
ENDSELECT.

WRITE:/ 'END OF REPORT'.
```

See Also

CONVERSION_EXIT_AUART_OUTPUT

CONVERSION_EXIT_AUART_OUTPUT

Summary

Converts sales document type.

Description

Function which converts sales document code from SAP's internal format to display format.

Parameters

```
EXPORTING
     INPUT    SAP formatted document code
IMPORTING
     OUTPUT   Display formatted document code
```

Example

See CONVERSION_EXIT_AUART_INPUT

See Also

CONVERSION_EXIT_AUART_INPUT

CONVERSION_EXIT_CUNIT_INPUT

Summary

Converts external measurement unit for SAP's internal unit.

Description

Specifies the internal measurement unit for a commercial measurement unit.

Parameters

```
EXPORTING
     INPUT       Input unit
     LANGUAGE    Unit language
IMPORTING
     OUTPUT      SAP unit
```

Example

```
REPORT ZEXAMPLE.
TABLES T006A.

DATA: V_MSEHI(5),
      V_MSEHI1(5),
      V_MSEHI2(5).
WRITE:/ 'INTERNAL FORMAT', 20 'OUTPUT FORMAT', 40 'BACK TO INTERNAL FORMAT'.
ULINE.
```

```
SELECT * FROM T006A WHERE SPRAS EQ SY-LANGU.

  CALL FUNCTION 'CONVERSION_EXIT_CUNIT_OUTPUT'
      EXPORTING
          INPUT              = T006A-MSEHI
      IMPORTING
          OUTPUT             = V_MSEHI
      EXCEPTIONS
          UNIT_NOT_FOUND     = 1
          OTHERS             = 2.

  CALL FUNCTION 'CONVERSION_EXIT_CUNIT_INPUT'
      EXPORTING
          INPUT              = V_MSEHI
      IMPORTING
          OUTPUT             = V_MSEHI2
      EXCEPTIONS
          UNIT_NOT_FOUND     = 1
          OTHERS             = 2.

  IF T006A-MSEHI NE V_MSEHI.
    MOVE T006A-MSEHI TO V_MSEHI1.
    WRITE:/ V_MSEHI1, 20 V_MSEHI, 40 V_MSEHI2.
  ENDIF.
ENDSELECT.

WRITE:/ 'END OF REPORT'.
```

See Also

CONVERSION_EXIT_CUNIT_OUTPUT

CONVERSION_EXIT_CUNIT_OUTPUT

Summary

Converts SAP's internal measurement unit to external measurement unit.

Description

Specifies the language-dependent commercial measurement unit and the associated short and long text for an internal measurement unit. It is automatically called when measurement units are output to the screen, and by the WRITE command.

Parameters

```
EXPORTING
    INPUT        Input unit
    LANGUAGE     Unit language
IMPORTING
    LONG_TEXT    Full text description of unit
```

```
OUTPUT     Converted unit
SHORT_TEXT Shortened text description of unit
```

Example

See CONVERSION_EXIT_CUNIT_INPUT

See Also

CONVERSION_EXIT_CUNIT_INPUT

CONVERSION_EXIT_LUNIT_INPUT

Summary

Converts technical unit to internal unit.

Description

Specifies the internal measurement unit associated with a technical measurement unit (six-character external measurement unit).

Parameters

```
EXPORTING
      LANGUAGE    Language of unit
      INPUT       Unit to convert to SAP
IMPORTING
      OUTPUT      Converted unit
```

Example

```
REPORT ZEXAMPLE.

TABLES: MARA, T006, T006T.

DATA:  UNIT_INT LIKE T006-MSEHI,
       UNIT_EXT LIKE T006A-MSEH6,
       NO_UNIT(60) VALUE 'NO ENTRY MAINTAINED FOR UNIT &1 IN LANGUAGE &2',
                          NO_UNIT_MSG(60).

WRITE:/ 'INTERNAL UNIT', 20 'EXTERNAL UNIT', 40 'DIMENSION'.

SELECT * FROM T006.

  CALL FUNCTION 'CONVERSION_EXIT_LUNIT_OUTPUT'
      EXPORTING
            INPUT         = T006-MSEHI
      IMPORTING
```

```
                OUTPUT        = UNIT_EXT
          EXCEPTIONS
                UNIT_NOT_FOUND = 1.

   IF SY-SUBRC NE 0.
     NO_UNIT_MSG = NO_UNIT.
     REPLACE '&1' WITH T006-MSEHI INTO NO_UNIT_MSG.
     REPLACE '&2' WITH SY-LANGU INTO NO_UNIT_MSG.
     WRITE:/5 T006-MSEHI, 25 NO_UNIT_MSG.
   ELSE.
     CALL FUNCTION 'CONVERSION_EXIT_LUNIT_INPUT'
          EXPORTING
                INPUT         = UNIT_EXT
          IMPORTING
                OUTPUT        = UNIT_INT
          EXCEPTIONS
                UNIT_NOT_FOUND = 1.

     IF SY-SUBRC NE 0.
       NO_UNIT_MSG = NO_UNIT.
       REPLACE '&1' WITH UNIT_EXT INTO NO_UNIT_MSG.
       REPLACE '&2' WITH SY-LANGU INTO NO_UNIT_MSG.
       WRITE:/5 UNIT_EXT, 25 NO_UNIT_MSG.
     ELSE.
       SELECT SINGLE * FROM T006T WHERE SPRAS = SY-LANGU AND DIMID = T006-DIMID.
       WRITE:/5 UNIT_INT, 25 UNIT_EXT, 45 T006T-TXDIM.
     ENDIF.
   ENDIF.
ENDSELECT.
```

See Also

CONVERSION_EXIT_LUNIT_OUTPUT

CONVERSION_EXIT_LUNIT_OUTPUT

Summary

Converts internal measurement unit to technical measurement unit.

Description

Specifies the language-dependent technical measurement unit (six-character external measurement unit) and its associated short and long text for an internal measurement unit.

Parameters

```
EXPORTING
   LANGUAGE    Language of unit
   INPUT       Unit to convert from SAP
IMPORTING
   OUTPUT      Converted unit
```

Example

See CONVERSION_EXIT_LUNIT_INPUT

See Also

CONVERSION_EXIT_LUNIT_INPUT

CONVERSION_FACTOR_GET

Summary

Conversion factors for a measurement unit.

Description

Determines the conversion factors for the conversion of a measurement unit into another. Also returns the number of decimal places to which the values in the unit UNIT_OUT are to be rounded. The following formula applies for the conversion:

$$\left[\begin{array}{c} \text{value in the unit} \\ \text{UNIT\_OUT} \end{array} \right] = \left[\begin{array}{c} \text{value in the unit} \\ \text{UNIT\_IN} \end{array} \right] \times \frac{\text{numerator}}{\text{denominator}}$$

Parameters

```
EXPORTING
     UNIT_IN          Unit to convert
     UNIT_OUT         Unit to be converted into
IMPORTING
     ADD_CONST        Constant value for unit
     DENOMINATOR      The denominator
     NUMERATOR        The numerator
     DECIMALS         Number of decimals in unit
     DIMENSION        Dimension of unit
```

Example

```
REPORT ZEXAMPLE.

TABLES: MARA, MARM.

DATA: BEGIN OF IMEINS OCCURS 0,
     MEINS LIKE MARA-MEINS,
     MEINH LIKE MARM-MEINH,
     END OF IMEINS.
```

```
DATA: ADD_CONST       TYPE F,
      DENOMINATOR     TYPE F,
      NUMERATOR       TYPE F,
      DECIMALS        LIKE T006-ANDEC,
      DIMENSION       LIKE T006-DIMID,
      FACT            TYPE F.

WRITE:/ 'BASE UNIT', 20 'ALTERNATIVE UNIT', 40 'FACTOR'.
ULINE.

SELECT * FROM MARA.
  SELECT SINGLE * FROM MARM WHERE MATNR = MARA-MATNR.
  IF SY-SUBRC EQ 0.
    IF MARA-MEINS NE MARM-MEINH.
      READ TABLE IMEINS WITH KEY MEINS     = MARA-MEINS
                                 MEINH     = MARM-MEINH
                            BINARY SEARCH.
      IF SY-SUBRC NE 0.
        IMEINS-MEINS = MARA-MEINS.
        IMEINS-MEINH = MARM-MEINH.
        APPEND IMEINS.
        SORT IMEINS.

        CALL FUNCTION 'CONVERSION_FACTOR_GET'
             EXPORTING
                  UNIT_IN              = MARA-MEINS
                  UNIT_OUT             = MARM-MEINH
             IMPORTING
                  ADD_CONST            = ADD_CONST
                  DENOMINATOR          = DENOMINATOR
                  NUMERATOR            = NUMERATOR
                  DECIMALS             = DECIMALS
                  DIMENSION            = DIMENSION
             EXCEPTIONS
                  CONVERSION_NOT_FOUND = 01
                  OVERFLOW             = 02
                  TYPE_INVALID         = 03
                  UNITS_MISSING        = 04
                  UNIT_IN_NOT_FOUND    = 05
                  UNIT_OUT_NOT_FOUND   = 06.

        IF SY-SUBRC EQ 0.
           FACT = (NUMERATOR / DENOMINATOR) + ADD_CONST.
           WRITE:/ MARA-MEINS, 20 MARM-MEINH, 40 FACT.
        ENDIF.
      ENDIF.
    ENDIF.
  ENDIF.
ENDSELECT.
```

See Also

CF_UT_UNIT_CONVERSION, MATERIAL_UNIT_CONVERSION,
MD_CONVERT_MATERIAL_UNIT

CONVERT_ABAPSPOOLJOB_2_PDF

Summary

Converts ABAP spool output to PDF.

Parameters

```
EXPORTING
     SRC_SPOOLID       Spool number
     NO_DIALOG         Display popup dialogue box
     DST_DEVICE        Printer name
IMPORTING
     PDF_BYTECOUNT     Size of PDF file
TABLES
     PDF               PDF formatting data
```

Example

```
REPORT ZEXAMPLE.
TABLES TSP01.

DATA:   MTAB_PDF      LIKE TLINE OCCURS 0 WITH HEADER LINE,
        MC_FILENAME   LIKE RLGRAP-FILENAME.

DATA:   MSTR_PRINT_PARMS  LIKE PRI_PARAMS,
        MC_VALID(1)       TYPE C,
        MI_BYTECOUNT      TYPE I.

PARAMETERS:  P_RQIDET  LIKE TSP01-RQIDENT,  "SPOOL TO CONVERT
             P_PDFILE  LIKE SY-REPID.       " PDF FILENAME

START-OF-SELECTION.

  CONCATENATE 'C:\' P_PDFILE '.PDF' INTO MC_FILENAME.

  CALL FUNCTION 'GET_PRINT_PARAMETERS'
       EXPORTING
            COPIES              = '1'
            COVER_PAGE          = SPACE
            DESTINATION         = SPACE
            EXPIRATION          = '1'
            IMMEDIATELY         = SPACE
            LAYOUT              = SPACE
            MODE                = SPACE
            NEW_LIST_ID         = 'X'
            NO_DIALOG           = 'X'
            USER                = SY-UNAME
       IMPORTING
            OUT_PARAMETERS      = MSTR_PRINT_PARMS
            VALID               = MC_VALID
```

```
        EXCEPTIONS
             ARCHIVE_INFO_NOT_FOUND = 1
             INVALID_PRINT_PARAMS   = 2
             INVALID_ARCHIVE_PARAMS = 3
             OTHERS                 = 4.
  IF SY-SUBRC EQ 0.
     CALL FUNCTION 'CONVERT_ABAPSPOOLJOB_2_PDF'
          EXPORTING
             SRC_SPOOLID              = P_RQIDET
             NO_DIALOG                = SPACE
             DST_DEVICE               = MSTR_PRINT_PARMS-PDEST
          IMPORTING
             PDF_BYTECOUNT            = MI_BYTECOUNT
          TABLES
             PDF                      = MTAB_PDF
          EXCEPTIONS
             ERR_NO_ABAP_SPOOLJOB     = 1
             ERR_NO_SPOOLJOB          = 2
             ERR_NO_PERMISSION        = 3
             ERR_CONV_NOT_POSSIBLE    = 4
             ERR_BAD_DESTDEVICE       = 5
             USER_CANCELLED           = 6
             ERR_SPOOLERROR           = 7
             ERR_TEMSEERROR           = 8
             ERR_BTCJOB_OPEN_FAILED   = 9
             ERR_BTCJOB_SUBMIT_FAILED = 10
             ERR_BTCJOB_CLOSE_FAILED  = 11
             OTHERS                   = 12.
     IF SY-SUBRC EQ 0.
        CALL FUNCTION 'DOWNLOAD'
             EXPORTING
                BIN_FILESIZE          = MI_BYTECOUNT
                FILENAME              = MC_FILENAME
                FILETYPE              = 'BIN'
             IMPORTING
                ACT_FILENAME          = MC_FILENAME
             TABLES
                DATA_TAB              = MTAB_PDF
             EXCEPTIONS
                INVALID_FILESIZE      = 1
                INVALID_TABLE_WIDTH   = 2
                INVALID_TYPE          = 3
                NO_BATCH              = 4
                UNKNOWN_ERROR         = 5
                GUI_REFUSE_FILETRANSFER = 6
                CUSTOMER_ERROR        = 7
                OTHERS                = 8.
     IF SY-SUBRC EQ 0.
        WRITE:/ MC_FILENAME, 'CONVERTED TO PDF AND DOWNLOADED'.
     ELSE.
        WRITE:/ 'PROBLEM WITH DOWNLOAD'.
     ENDIF.
  ELSE.
     WRITE:/ 'PROBLEM WITH PDF CONVERSION'.
  ENDIF.
```

```
ELSE.
   WRITE:/ 'PROBLEM GETTING PRINT PARAMETERS'.
ENDIF.
```

See Also

CONVERT_OTFSPOOLJOB_2_PDF

CONVERT_OTFSPOOLJOB_2_PDF

Summary

Converts an OTF (SAPscript) spool to PDF.

Parameters

```
EXPORTING
       SRC_SPOOLID          Spool number
       NO_DIALOG            Popup dialogue box (' ' value means no dialogue box)
IMPORTING
       PDF_BYTECOUNT        Number of bytes in download file
       PDF_SPOOLID          PDF spool number
TABLES
       PDF                  Format data for PDF file
```

Example

```
REPORT ZEXAMPLE.

TABLES TSP01.

DATA:  OTF LIKE ITCOO OCCURS 100 WITH HEADER LINE,
       PDF LIKE TLINE OCCURS 100 WITH HEADER LINE.

DATA:  NUMBYTES TYPE I,
       PDFSPOOLID LIKE TSP01-RQIDENT,
       OBJTYPE LIKE RSTSTYPE-TYPE,
       TYPE LIKE RSTSTYPE-TYPE,
       CANCEL.

PARAMETERS:  SPOOLNO LIKE TSP01-RQIDENT,
             P_FILE  LIKE RLGRAP-FILENAME DEFAULT 'C:\TEMP\DATA.PDF'.

SELECT SINGLE * FROM TSP01 WHERE RQIDENT = SPOOLNO.
IF SY-SUBRC <> 0.
  WRITE: / 'SPOOL', SPOOLNO, 'DOES NOT EXIST'.
  EXIT.
ENDIF.

CALL FUNCTION 'RSTS_GET_ATTRIBUTES'
     EXPORTING
         AUTHORITY      = 'SP01'
```

```
        CLIENT        = TSP01-RQCLIENT
        NAME          = TSP01-RQ01NAME
        PART          = 1
    IMPORTING
        TYPE          = TYPE
        OBJTYPE       = OBJTYPE
    EXCEPTIONS
        FB_ERROR      = 1
        FB_RSTS_OTHER = 2
        NO_OBJECT     = 3
     .  NO_PERMISSION = 4.

IF SY-SUBRC EQ 0.
  IF OBJTYPE(3) = 'OTF'.
    CALL FUNCTION 'CONVERT_OTFSPOOLJOB_2_PDF'
        EXPORTING
            SRC_SPOOLID             = SPOOLNO
            NO_DIALOG               = ' '
        IMPORTING
            PDF_BYTECOUNT           = NUMBYTES
            PDF_SPOOLID             = PDFSPOOLID
        TABLES
            PDF                     = PDF
        EXCEPTIONS
            ERR_NO_OTF_SPOOLJOB     = 1
            ERR_NO_SPOOLJOB         = 2
            ERR_NO_PERMISSION       = 3
            ERR_CONV_NOT_POSSIBLE   = 4
            ERR_BAD_DSTDEVICE       = 5
            USER_CANCELLED          = 6
            ERR_SPOOLERROR          = 7
            ERR_TEMSEERROR          = 8
            ERR_BTCJOB_OPEN_FAILED  = 9
            ERR_BTCJOB_SUBMIT_FAILED = 10
            ERR_BTCJOB_CLOSE_FAILED = 11.

    IF SY-SUBRC NE 0.
      WRITE:/ SPOOLNO, 'NOT CONVERTED TO PDF'.
      EXIT.
    ENDIF.
  ELSE.
    WRITE:/ SPOOLNO, 'IS NOT AN OTF'.
  ENDIF.

  CALL FUNCTION 'DOWNLOAD'
      EXPORTING
          BIN_FILESIZE = NUMBYTES
          FILENAME     = P_FILE
          FILETYPE     = 'BIN'
      IMPORTING
          ACT_FILENAME = P_FILE
          FILESIZE     = NUMBYTES
          CANCEL       = CANCEL
      TABLES
          DATA_TAB     = PDF.
```

```
   IF CANCEL = SPACE.
     WRITE: / NUMBYTES, 'BYTES DOWNLOADED TO FILE', P_FILE.
   ENDIF.
ELSE.
   WRITE:/ 'ATTRIBUTES OF SPOOL', SPOOLNO, 'NOT FOUND'.
ENDIF.
```

See Also

CONVERT_ABAPSPOOLJOB_2_PDF, SX_OBJECT_CONVERT_OTF_PDF

CONVERT_TO_FOREIGN_CURRENCY

Summary

Translates local currency amount into foreign currency.

Description

An amount in foreign currency is calculated from a specified local currency amount. When Table TCURR is read, the foreign currency key is always taken as the first part of the key and the local currency as the second part.

Parameters

```
EXPORTING
        DATE
        FOREIGN_CURRENCY         Currency to convert amount into
        LOCAL_AMOUNT             Amount to convert
        LOCAL_CURRENCY           Currency of local amount
        RATE                     Exchange rate
        TYPE_OF_RATE             Type of exchange rate:
                                 Value   Meaning
                                 M       Average exchange rate (default)
                                 G       Buying rate
                                 B       Selling rate
                                 Other values in TCURV-KURST
        TCURR                    Read database Table TCURR
IMPORTING
        EXCHANGE_RATE            Exchange rate used during conversion
        FOREIGN_AMOUNT           Local amount after conversion
        FOREIGN_FACTOR           Factor for the foreign currency units
        LOCAL_FACTOR             Factor for the local currency units
```

Example

```
REPORT ZEXAMPLE.

DATA: XRATE   TYPE F,
      FAMT    TYPE P,
```

```
        FFACT  TYPE F,
        LFACT  TYPE F.

PARAMETERS: FCURR  LIKE TCURC-WAERS,
            LCURR  LIKE TCURC-WAERS,
            LAMT   TYPE P.

CALL FUNCTION 'CONVERT_TO_FOREIGN_CURRENCY'
    EXPORTING
          DATE             = SY-DATUM
          FOREIGN_CURRENCY = FCURR
          LOCAL_AMOUNT     = LAMT
          LOCAL_CURRENCY   = LCURR
    IMPORTING
          EXCHANGE_RATE    = XRATE
          FOREIGN_AMOUNT   = FAMT
          FOREIGN_FACTOR   = FFACT
          LOCAL_FACTOR     = LFACT
    EXCEPTIONS
          NO_RATE_FOUND    = 1
          OVERFLOW         = 2
          NO_FACTORS_FOUND = 3
          NO_SPREAD_FOUND  = 4
          DERIVED_2_TIMES  = 5
          OTHERS           = 6.

IF SY-SUBRC EQ 0.
  WRITE:/ LAMT, 'CONVERTED FROM', LCURR, 'TO', FCURR, 'IS:', FAMT.
  WRITE:/ 'EXCHANGE RATE:', XRATE,
       / 'FOREIGN FACTOR:', FFACT,
       / 'LOCAL FACTOR:', LFACT.
ELSE.
  WRITE:/ LAMT, 'NOT CONVERTED'.
ENDIF.
```

See Also

CONVERT_TO_LOCAL_CURRENCY

CONVERT_TO_LOCAL_CURRENCY

Summary

Converts from foreign currency to local currency.

Description

When Table TCURR is read, the foreign currency key is always taken as the first part of the key and the local currency as the second part.

Parameters

```
EXPORTING
      DATE
      FOREIGN_AMOUNT      Amount to convert
      FOREIGN_CURRENCY    Currency of foreign amount
      LOCAL_CURRENCY      Currency to convert amount into
      RATE                Exchange rate
      TYPE_OF_RATE        Type of exchange rate:
                          Value   Meaning
                          M       Average exchange rate (default)
                          G       Buying rate
                          B       Selling rate
                          Other values in TCURV-KURST
      TCURR               Read database Table TCURR
IMPORTING
      EXCHANGE_RATE       Exchange rate used during conversion
      FOREIGN_FACTOR      Factor for the foreign currency units
      LOCAL_AMOUNT        Local amount after conversion
      LOCAL_FACTOR        Factor for the local currency units
```

Example

```
REPORT ZEXAMPLE.

DATA: XRATE  TYPE F,
      LAMT   TYPE P,
      FFACT  TYPE F,
      LFACT  TYPE F.

PARAMETERS:  FCURR LIKE TCURC-WAERS,
             LCURR LIKE TCURC-WAERS,
             FAMT  TYPE P.

CALL FUNCTION 'CONVERT_TO_LOCAL_CURRENCY'
     EXPORTING
           DATE             = SY-DATUM
           FOREIGN_AMOUNT   = FAMT
           FOREIGN_CURRENCY = FCURR
           LOCAL_CURRENCY   = LCURR
     IMPORTING
           EXCHANGE_RATE    = XRATE
           FOREIGN_FACTOR   = FFACT
           LOCAL_AMOUNT     = LAMT
           LOCAL_FACTOR     = LFACT
     EXCEPTIONS
           NO_RATE_FOUND    = 1
           OVERFLOW         = 2
           NO_FACTORS_FOUND = 3
           NO_SPREAD_FOUND  = 4
           DERIVED_2_TIMES  = 5
           OTHERS           = 6.
```

```
IF SY-SUBRC EQ 0.
  WRITE:/ FAMT, 'CONVERTED FROM', FCURR, 'TO', LCURR, 'IS:', LAMT.
  WRITE:/ 'EXCHANGE RATE:', XRATE,
        / 'FOREIGN FACTOR:', FFACT,
        / 'LOCAL FACTOR:', LFACT.
ELSE.
  WRITE:/ FAMT, 'NOT CONVERTED'.
ENDIF.
```

See Also

CONVERT_TO_FOREIGN_CURRENCY

CURRENCY_AMOUNT_SAP_TO_IDOC

Summary

Converts currency to IDOC format.

Parameters

```
EXPORTING
      CURRENCY              Convert amount to this currency
      SAP_AMOUNT            Amount to convert
IMPORTING
      IDOC_AMOUNT           Amount after conversion
```

Example

```
REPORT ZEXAMPLE.

TABLES TCURC.
DATA P_IDOCAMT(16).

PARAMETERS: P_AMT LIKE BSEG-DMBTR.

WRITE:/ 'AMOUNT', 20 'CURRENCY', 30 'IDOC AMOUNT'.
ULINE.

SELECT * FROM TCURC.
  CALL FUNCTION 'CURRENCY_AMOUNT_SAP_TO_IDOC'
      EXPORTING
            CURRENCY     = TCURC-WAERS
            SAP_AMOUNT   = P_AMT
      IMPORTING
            IDOC_AMOUNT  = P_IDOCAMT
      EXCEPTIONS
            OTHERS       = 1.

  IF SY-SUBRC EQ 0.
    WRITE:/ P_AMT, 20 TCURC-WAERS, 30 P_IDOCAMT.
```

```
  ELSE.
    WRITE:/ P_AMT, 20 TCURC-WAERS, 30 'NO CONVERSION'.
  ENDIF.
ENDSELECT.
```

CURRENCY_CODE_ISO_TO_SAP

Summary

Converts ISO currency code to SAP's currency code.

Parameters

```
EXPORTING
       ISO_CODE               ISO standard currency code
IMPORTING
       SAP_CODE               SAP's code for the ISO standard
```

Example

```
REPORT ZEXAMPLE.

TABLES TCURC.
DATA: SAP_CODE LIKE TCURC-WAERS,
      ISO_CODE LIKE TCURC-ISOCD.

WRITE:/ 'ISO CODE', 15 'SAP CODE', 30 'ISO CODE'.
ULINE.

SELECT * FROM TCURC.
  CALL FUNCTION 'CURRENCY_CODE_ISO_TO_SAP'
       EXPORTING
            ISO_CODE  = TCURC-ISOCD
       IMPORTING
            SAP_CODE  = SAP_CODE
       EXCEPTIONS
            NOT_FOUND = 1
            OTHERS    = 2.

  IF SY-SUBRC EQ 0.
    IF TCURC-ISOCD NE SAP_CODE.
      FORMAT COLOR COL_TOTAL.
    ENDIF.
    WRITE:/ TCURC-ISOCD, 15 SAP_CODE.
    FORMAT RESET.

    CALL FUNCTION 'CURRENCY_CODE_SAP_TO_ISO'
         EXPORTING
              SAP_CODE  = SAP_CODE
         IMPORTING
              ISO_CODE  = ISO_CODE
```

```
        EXCEPTIONS
             NOT_FOUND = 1
             OTHERS    = 2.

   IF SY-SUBRC EQ 0.
     WRITE: 30 ISO_CODE.
   ENDIF.
 ELSE.
   WRITE:/ TCURC-ISOCD, 15 'SAP CODE NOT FOUND'.
 ENDIF.
ENDSELECT.
```

See Also

CURRENCY_CODE_SAP_TO_ISO

CURRENCY_CODE_SAP_TO_ISO

Summary

Converts SAP's currency code to ISO currency code.

Parameters

```
EXPORTING
   SAP_CODE   SAP standard currency code
IMPORTING
   ISO_CODE   ISO's code
```

Example

See CURRENCY_CODE_ISO_TO_SAP

See Also

CURRENCY_CODE_ISO_TO_SAP

DATE_STRING_CONVERT

Summary

Converts a string date into DATE type.

Description

Changes a date in CHAR-type format into DATE-type format.

Parameters

```
EXPORTING
        DATE_FORMAT                    Format for resulting date
                                       Value    Meaning
                                       1        DD.MM.YYYY
                                       4        YYYY.MM.DD
                                       5        YYYY/MM/DD
                                       Others   MM/DD/YYYY
                                                MM-DD-YYYY
        DATE_STRING                    Date to convert
        START_DATE                     Base date
IMPORTING
        RESULT_DATE                    String date in DATE format
```

Example

```
REPORT ZEXAMPLE.

DATA: V_DATE LIKE SY-DATUM,
      V_DATE_O(10).

CALL FUNCTION 'DATE_STRING_CONVERT'
    EXPORTING
        DATE_FORMAT = '5'
        DATE_STRING = SY-DATUM
    IMPORTING
        RESULT_DATE = V_DATE.

V_DATE_O = V_DATE.

WRITE:/ V_DATE_O.
```

DIMENSION_CHECK

Summary

Checks internal measurement unit of specified dimension.

Description

Checks whether the internal measurement unit corresponds to the specified dimension.

Parameters

```
EXPORTING
        DIMID                  Dimension key
        MSEHI                  Internal unit of measurement
```

Example

```
REPORT ZEXAMPLE.

DATA: DIM_ID   LIKE T006D-DIMID,
      DIM_TEXT LIKE T006T-TXDIM.

PARAMETER: DIM_UNIT LIKE T006-MSEHI DEFAULT 'H'. "ENTER UNIT FOR TIME

WRITE:/ 'DIMENSION ID', 15 'DESCRIPTION', 30 'DIMENSION UNIT'.
ULINE.

* CHECKING DIMENSIONS VALID FOR TIME:
CALL FUNCTION 'DIMENSION_GET'
    EXPORTING
        AMOUNT_OF_SUBSTANCE = 0
        ELECTRIC_CURRENT    = 0
        LANGUAGE            = SY-LANGU
        LENGTH              = 0
        LUMINOUS_INTENSITY  = 0
        MASS                = 0
        TEMPERATURE         = 0
        TIME                = 1
    IMPORTING
        DIMID               = DIM_ID
        TEXT                = DIM_TEXT
    EXCEPTIONS
        DIMENSION_NOT_FOUND = 1
        OTHERS              = 2.

IF SY-SUBRC EQ 0.
  CALL FUNCTION 'DIMENSION_CHECK'
      EXPORTING
          DIMID                 = DIM_ID
          MSEHI                 = DIM_UNIT
      EXCEPTIONS
          DIMENSION_CHECK_FAILED = 01
          UNIT_NOT_VALID         = 02.

  IF SY-SUBRC EQ 0.
    CALL FUNCTION 'DIMENSION_GET_FOR_UNIT'
        EXPORTING
            LANGUAGE    = SY-LANGU
            UNIT        = DIM_UNIT
        IMPORTING
            DIMENSION   = DIM_ID
            TEXT        = DIM_TEXT
        EXCEPTIONS
            UNIT_NOT_FOUND = 1
            OTHERS         = 2.

  WRITE:/ DIM_ID, 15 DIM_TEXT, 30 DIM_UNIT.
  ELSE.
    WRITE:/ DIM_UNIT, 'IS NOT A VALID DIMENSION FOR', DIM_TEXT.
  ENDIF.
```

```
ELSE.
  WRITE:/ DIM_ID, 15 'ERROR WITH GETTING TIME DIMENSION'.
ENDIF.
```

See Also

DIMENSION_GET

DIMENSION_GET

Summary

Retrieves dimension key of specified dimension.

Description

Combination of input values returns the dimension. These are defined in Table T006D_TAB. For example, LENGTH set to 1 gives the base unit "LENGTH". However, LENGTH set to 1 and TIME set to 2 will give the dimension ACCELERATION.

Parameters

```
EXPORTING
        AMOUNT_OF_SUBSTANCE          Value to the mole quantity
        ELECTRIC_CURRENT             Value for the voltage
        LANGUAGE                     Language indicator (default: logon language)
        LENGTH                       Value for the length
        LUMINOUS_INTENSITY           Value for the brightness
        MASS                         Value for mass
        TEMPERATURE                  Value for the temperature
        TIME                         Value for the time
IMPORTING
        DIMID                        Dimension key
        TEXT                         Text for the dimension
```

Example

See DIMENSION_CHECK

See Also

DIMENSION_CHECK, DIMENSION_GET_FOR_UNIT, SI_UNIT_GET

DIMENSION_GET_FOR_UNIT

Summary

Textual description of dimension.

Description

Determines the text of the dimension to which the unit belongs.

Parameters

```
EXPORTING
        LANGUAGE                Language of unit
        UNIT                    Unit to get description
IMPORTING
        DIMENSION               ID of dimension
        TEXT                    Textual description of unit
```

Example

See DIMENSION_CHECK

See Also

DIMENSION_CHECK, DIMENSION_GET

HR_ROUND_NUMBER

Summary

Rounds a number according to rules.

Description

Rules are defined in Database Table T559R.

Parameters

```
EXPORTING
        RND_RDTYP               Rounding rule
CHANGING
        RND_NUMBER              Number after rule has been applied
```

Example

```
REPORT ZEXAMPLE.
TABLES T559R.
DATA V_NUM LIKE PC207-BETRG.
PARAMETER P_NUM LIKE PC207-BETRG.

WRITE:/ 'SEE THE EFFECT OF ROUNDING RULES ON NUMBERS:',
        'INITIAL NUMBER:', P_NUM,
        'RULE', 10 'NUMBER'.
ULINE.
```

```
SELECT DISTINCT * FROM T559R.
  V_NUM = P_NUM.

  CALL FUNCTION 'HR_ROUND_NUMBER'
      EXPORTING
            RND_RDTYP      = T559R-RDTYP
      CHANGING
            RND_NUMBER     = V_NUM
      EXCEPTIONS
            RULE_NOT_FOUND = 1
            OTHERS         = 2.

  IF SY-SUBRC EQ O.
    WRITE:/ T559R-RDTYP, 10 V_NUM.
  ELSE.
    WRITE:/ T559R-RDTYP, 10 'RULE NOT FOUND'.
  ENDIF.
ENDSELECT.
```

See Also

ROUND, ROUND_AMOUNT

HRCM_AMOUNT_TO_STRING_CONVERT

Summary

Converts an amount to a character string.

Parameters

```
EXPORTING
      BETRG                          Amount to convert
      WAERS                          Convert using this currency format
      NEW_DECIMAL_SEPARATOR          Change decimal separator in amount
      NEW_THOUSANDS_SEPARATOR        Change thousands separator in amount
IMPORTING
      STRING                         String format of amount after conversion
```

Example

```
REPORT ZEXAMPLE.
DATA: V_AMT(10), V_AMT2(10).

PARAMETER: P_BETRG LIKE T5G15-AMUNT.

CALL FUNCTION 'HRCM_AMOUNT_TO_STRING_CONVERT'
    EXPORTING
        BETRG                   = P_BETRG
```

```
          NEW_DECIMAL_SEPARATOR   = '.'
          NEW_THOUSANDS_SEPARATOR = ','
     IMPORTING
          STRING                  = V_AMT.

WRITE:/ P_BETRG, 'AFTER CONVERSION IS:', V_AMT.

CALL FUNCTION 'HRCM_STRING_TO_AMOUNT_CONVERT'
     EXPORTING
          STRING              = V_AMT
          DECIMAL_SEPARATOR   = ','
          THOUSANDS_SEPARATOR = '.'
     IMPORTING
          BETRG               = V_AMT2
     EXCEPTIONS
          CONVERT_ERROR       = 1
          OTHERS              = 2.

IF SY-SUBRC EQ 0.
  WRITE:/ V_AMT, 'AFTER CONVERSION IS:', V_AMT2.
ELSE.
  WRITE:/ 'COULD NOT CONVERT STRING', V_AMT, 'INTO AMOUNT'.
ENDIF.
```

See Also

HRCM_STRING_TO_AMOUNT_CONVERT, SPELL_AMOUNT

HRCM_STRING_TO_AMOUNT_CONVERT

Summary

Converts a character string to an amount.

Parameters

```
EXPORTING
    STRING                      String amount to convert
    NEW_DECIMAL_SEPARATOR       Change decimal separator in amount
    NEW_THOUSANDS_SEPARATOR     Change thousands separator in amount
    WAERS                       Currency (format) to use for conversion
IMPORTING
    BETRG                       Amount after conversion
```

Example

See HRCM_AMOUNT_TO_STRING_CONVERT

See Also

HRCM_AMOUNT_TO_STRING_CONVERT, SPELL_AMOUNT

MATERIAL_UNIT_CONVERSION

Summary

Converts base unit of measure to alternative unit and vice versa.

Description

For dimensionless units of measure (box, each, etc.), conversion depends on the material (see Table MARM). For other units (length, weight, etc.), conversion can be calculated via function module CONVERSION_FACTOR_GET.

Parameters

```
EXPORTING
        MATNR                   Material number
        MEINH                   Alternative unit of measure
        MEINS                   Base unit of measure
IMPORTING
        UMREN                   Denominator
        UMREZ                   Numerator
        OUTPUT                  Output value
```

Example

```
REPORT ZEXAMPLE.

TABLES: MARA, MARM.

DATA: BEGIN OF IMEINS OCCURS 0,
        MEINS LIKE MARA-MEINS,
        MEINH LIKE MARM-MEINH,
      END OF IMEINS.

DATA: OUTPUT TYPE I,
      UMREN  TYPE I,
      UMREZ  TYPE I,
      FACT   TYPE F.

WRITE:/ 'MATERIAL', 30 'ALT UOM', 40 'BUOM', 50 'FACTOR'.
ULINE.

SELECT * FROM MARA UP TO 10 ROWS.
  SELECT SINGLE * FROM MARM WHERE MATNR = MARA-MATNR.
  IF SY-SUBRC EQ 0.
    IF MARA-MEINS NE MARM-MEINH.
      READ TABLE IMEINS WITH KEY MEINS = MARA-MEINS
                                 MEINH = MARM-MEINH
                        BINARY SEARCH.
      IF SY-SUBRC NE 0.
        IMEINS-MEINS = MARA-MEINS.
        IMEINS-MEINH = MARM-MEINH.
```

```
          APPEND IMEINS.
          SORT IMEINS.

          CALL FUNCTION 'MATERIAL_UNIT_CONVERSION'
               EXPORTING
                      MATNR            = MARA-MATNR
                      MEINH            = MARM-MEINH
                      MEINS            = MARA-MEINS
               IMPORTING
                      UMREN            = UMREN
                      UMREZ            = UMREZ
                      OUTPUT           = OUTPUT
               EXCEPTIONS
                      CONVERSION_NOT_FOUND = 01
                      INPUT_INVALID    = 02.

       IF NOT SY-SUBRC IS INITIAL OR UMREZ IS INITIAL OR UMREN IS INITIAL.

          WRITE:/ MARA-MATNR, 30 MARM-MEINH, 40 'CANNOT BE CONVERTED TO UNIT', MARA-MEINS.
          ELSE.
          FACT = UMREZ / UMREN.
          WRITE:/ MARA-MATNR, 30 MARM-MEINH, 40 MARA-MEINS, 50 FACT.
          ENDIF.
        ENDIF.
      ENDIF.
    ENDIF.
ENDSELECT.
```

See Also

CONVERSION_FACTOR_GET, CT_UT_UNIT_CONVERSION, MD_CONVERT_
MATERIAL_ UNIT

MD_CONVERT_MATERIAL_UNIT

Summary

Conversion of material units.

Parameters

```
EXPORTING
     I_MATNR    Material number
     I_IN_ME    Input unit
     I_OUT_ME   Output unit
     I_MENGE    Output quantity
IMPORTING
     E_MENGE    Output quantity in output unit
```

Example

```
REPORT ZEXAMPLE.
```

```
TABLES: MARA, MARM.
DATA: BEGIN OF IMEINS OCCURS 0,
        MEINS LIKE MARA-MEINS,
        MEINH LIKE MARM-MEINH,
      END OF IMEINS.

DATA: IN_MENGE LIKE MDRR-BDMNG VALUE '1000',
      OUT_MENGE LIKE MDRR-BDMNG.

WRITE:/ 'MATERIAL', 20 'BUOM', 30 'AUOM', 40 'INVALU', 60 'OUTVALU'.
ULINE.

SELECT * FROM MARA UP TO 10 ROWS.
  SELECT SINGLE * FROM MARM WHERE MATNR = MARA-MATNR.
  IF SY-SUBRC EQ 0.
    IF MARA-MEINS NE MARM-MEINH.
      READ TABLE IMEINS WITH KEY MEINS = MARA-MEINS
                                 MEINH = MARM-MEINH
                            BINARY SEARCH.
      IF SY-SUBRC NE 0.
        IMEINS-MEINS = MARA-MEINS.
        IMEINS-MEINH = MARM-MEINH.
        APPEND IMEINS.
        SORT IMEINS.

        CALL FUNCTION 'MD_CONVERT_MATERIAL_UNIT'
             EXPORTING
                  I_MATNR            = MARA-MATNR
                  I_IN_ME            = MARA-MEINS
                  I_OUT_ME           = MARM-MEINH
                  I_MENGE            = IN_MENGE
             IMPORTING
                  E_MENGE            = OUT_MENGE
             EXCEPTIONS
                  ERROR_IN_APPLICATION = 1
                  ERROR              = 2
                  OTHERS             = 3.

        IF SY-SUBRC EQ 0.
          WRITE:/ MARA-MATNR, 20 MARA-MEINS, 30 MARM-MEINH, 40 IN_MENGE, 60 OUT_MENGE.
        ENDIF.
      ENDIF.
    ENDIF.
  ENDIF.
ENDSELECT.
```

See Also

CONVERSION_FACTOR_GET, CT_UT_UNIT_CONVERSION, MD_CONVERT_
MATERIAL_UNIT

ROUND

Summary

Rounds to a specified number of decimal places.

Description

Rounds a value to the specified number of decimal places. You can choose between three rounding types: rounding up (+), rounding down (−), or commercial rounding (X). If SIGN = SPACE, there is no rounding (OUTPUT = INPUT).

Parameters

```
EXPORTING
        DECIMALS              Number of decimals places in output
        INPUT                 Input quantity
        SIGN                  Rounding type:
                              Value     Meaning
                              +         Round up (10.55 => 10.60)
                              -         Round down (10.55 => 10.50)
                              X         Commercial (10.55 => 10.60)
                              ' '       No rounding (10.55 => 10.55)
IMPORTING
        OUTPUT                Output quantity after rounding
```

Example

```
REPORT ZEXAMPLE.
DATA: BEGIN OF ISIGNS,
        C_DOWN VALUE '-',
        C_UP VALUE '+',
        C_COMM VALUE 'X',
        C_NONE VALUE ' ',
     END OF ISIGNS.

DATA: V_OUT TYPE P DECIMALS 2,
      V_SIGN.

PARAMETERS: V_IN TYPE P DECIMALS 2.

WRITE:/ 'INITIAL AMT', 20 'TYPE', 30 'ROUNDED AMT'.
ULINE.

DO VARYING V_SIGN FROM ISIGNS-C_DOWN NEXT ISIGNS-C_UP.
  CALL FUNCTION 'ROUND'
      EXPORTING
          DECIMALS      = 1
          INPUT         = V_IN
          SIGN          = V_SIGN
      IMPORTING
          OUTPUT        = V_OUT
      EXCEPTIONS
          INPUT_INVALID = 1
          OVERFLOW      = 2
          TYPE_INVALID  = 3
          OTHERS        = 4.

  IF SY-SUBRC EQ 0.
    WRITE:/ V_IN, 20 V_SIGN, 30 V_OUT.
```

```
  ELSE.
    WRITE:/ V_IN, 20 'COULD NOT ROUND'.
  ENDIF.
  IF V_SIGN EQ ' '.
    EXIT.
  ENDIF.
ENDDO.
```

See Also

HR_ROUND_NUMBER, ROUND_AMOUNT

ROUND_AMOUNT

Summary

Rounding based on company code and currency.

Description

Rounds a value based on a company's rounding rules and currency.

Parameters

```
EXPORTING
    AMOUNT_IN       Amount to be rounded
    COMPANY         Company code
    CURRENCY        Currency code
IMPORTING
    AMOUNT_OUT      Amount after rounding
    DIFFERENCE      Difference between Amount In and Amount Out
    NO_ROUNDING     Flag: no rounding setup for this company code and currency
    ROUNDING_UNIT   Unit to round up to
```

Example

```
REPORT ZEXAMPLE.
TABLES T001R.
DATA V_AMTOUT LIKE BSEG-WSKTO.

PARAMETERS P_AMTIN LIKE BSEG-WSKTO.
WRITE:/ 'Original amount:', P_AMTIN,
     / 'Company', 15 'Currency', 35 'Amount'.
ULINE.

LOOP AT T001R.
  CALL FUNCTION 'ROUND_AMOUNT'
       EXPORTING
            AMOUNT_IN  = P_AMTIN
```

```
              COMPANY    = T001R-BUKRS
              CURRENCY   = T001R-WAERS
          IMPORTING
              AMOUNT_OUT = V_AMTOUT.


  WRITE:/ T001R-BUKRS, 15 T001R-WAERS, 25 V_AMTOUT.
ENDLOOP.
```

See Also

HR_ROUND_NUMBER, ROUND

SI_UNIT_GET

Summary

Retrieves the international system unit of measure.

Description

You pass either a unit or a dimension to this function module to get the "systeme international" (SI) unit. If you pass both a unit and a dimension, the SI unit for the dimension is returned. For example, the SI unit for length is the metre, the SI unit for time is the second, etc. Check <http://www.bipm.org/enus/3_SI/base_units.html> for the definitive list of SI units, and <http://physics.nist.gov/cuu/units/units.html> for an extended list of units.

Parameters

```
EXPORTING
      DIMENSION                  Dimension key of unit
      UNIT                       Unit of measure
IMPORTING
      SI_UNIT                    SI unit of measure
```

Example

```
REPORT ZEXAMPLE.
TABLES: T006, T006D.

DATA SI_UNIT LIKE T006-MSEHI.
WRITE:/ 'DIMENSION', 20 'UNIT', 30 'SI UNIT'.
ULINE.

SELECT * FROM T006D.
  SELECT * FROM T006 WHERE DIMID = T006D-DIMID.
    CALL FUNCTION 'SI_UNIT_GET'
        EXPORTING
              DIMENSION              = T006D-DIMID
              UNIT                   = T006-MSEHI
```

```
        IMPORTING
              SI_UNIT              = SI_UNIT
        EXCEPTIONS
              DIMENSION_NOT_FOUND = 1
              UNIT_NOT_FOUND      = 2
              OTHERS              = 3.

    IF SY-SUBRC EQ 0.
      WRITE:/ T006D-DIMID, 20 T006-MSEHI, 30 SI_UNIT.
    ELSE.
      WRITE:/ T006D-DIMID, 20 T006-MSEHI, 30 'SI UNIT NOT FOUND'.
    ENDIF.
  ENDSELECT.
ENDSELECT.
```

SX_OBJECT_CONVERT_OTF_PDF

Summary

Conversion from OTF (SAPscript) to PDF.

Parameters

```
EXPORTING
        FORMAT_SRC            Input format of data (ignored – always converted from OTF)
        FORMAT_DST            Output format of data (ignored – always converted to PDF)
        DEVTYPE              SAPscript device type for conversion
        LEN_IN              Number of bytes in input file
IMPORTING
        LEN_OUT              Number of bytes in output file
TABLES
        CONTENT_IN            Object contents in current format
        CONTENT_OUT          Object contents in required format
```

Example

```
REPORT ZEXAMPLE.

TABLES TSP01.

DATA: OTF             LIKE ITCOO OCCURS 0 WITH HEADER LINE,
      CONTENT_OUT     LIKE SOLISTI1 OCCURS 0 WITH HEADER LINE,
      T_COMPRESSED_LIST LIKE SOLI OCCURS 0.

DATA: NUMBYTES LIKE SOOD-OBJLEN,
      PDFSPOOLID LIKE TSP01-RQIDENT,
      OBJTYPE LIKE RSTSTYPE-TYPE,
      TYPE LIKE RSTSTYPE-TYPE,
      CANCEL.

PARAMETERS: SPOOLNO LIKE TSP01-RQIDENT,
            P_FILE LIKE RLGRAP-FILENAME DEFAULT 'C:\',
```

```
                 P_PDF TYPE C RADIOBUTTON GROUP RAD1,
                 P_PRT TYPE C RADIOBUTTON GROUP RAD1,
                 P_RAW TYPE C RADIOBUTTON GROUP RAD1.


SELECT SINGLE * FROM TSP01 WHERE RQIDENT = SPOOLNO.
IF SY-SUBRC <> 0.
  WRITE: / 'SPOOL', SPOOLNO, 'DOES NOT EXIST'.
  EXIT.
ENDIF.


CALL FUNCTION 'RSTS_GET_ATTRIBUTES'
     EXPORTING
          AUTHORITY     = 'SP01'
          CLIENT        = TSP01-RQCLIENT
          NAME          = TSP01-RQO1NAME
          PART          = 1
     IMPORTING
          TYPE          = TYPE
          OBJTYPE       = OBJTYPE
     EXCEPTIONS
          FB_ERROR      = 1
          FB_RSTS_OTHER = 2
          NO_OBJECT     = 3
          NO_PERMISSION = 4.


IF SY-SUBRC EQ 0.
  IF OBJTYPE(3) = 'OTF'.

    CALL FUNCTION 'RSPO_RETURN_SPOOLJOB'
         EXPORTING
              RQIDENT = SPOOLNO
         TABLES
              BUFFER  = T_COMPRESSED_LIST.

    IF P_PDF EQ 'X'.
      CALL FUNCTION 'SX_OBJECT_CONVERT_OTF_PDF'
           EXPORTING
                FORMAT_SRC      = 'OTF'
                FORMAT_DST      = 'PDF'
                DEVTYPE         = 'ASCIIPRI'
                LEN_IN          = NUMBYTES
           IMPORTING
                LEN_OUT         = NUMBYTES
           TABLES
                CONTENT_IN      = T_COMPRESSED_LIST
                CONTENT_OUT     = CONTENT_OUT
           EXCEPTIONS
                ERR_CONV_FAILED = 1
                OTHERS          = 2.

    IF SY-SUBRC NE 0.
      WRITE:/ SPOOLNO, 'NOT CONVERTED TO PDF'.
      EXIT.
    ENDIF.
```

```
      ELSEIF P_PRT EQ 'X'.
        CALL FUNCTION 'SX_OBJECT_CONVERT_OTF_PRT'
             EXPORTING
                    FORMAT_SRC      = 'OTF'
                    FORMAT_DST      = 'PRT'
                    DEVTYPE         = 'ASCIIPRI'
                    FUNCPARA        = ''
                    LEN_IN          = NUMBYTES
             IMPORTING
                    LEN_OUT         = NUMBYTES
             TABLES
                    CONTENT_IN      = T_COMPRESSED_LIST
                    CONTENT_OUT     = CONTENT_OUT
             EXCEPTIONS
                    ERR_CONV_FAILED = 1
                    OTHERS          = 2.

        IF SY-SUBRC NE 0.
          WRITE:/ SPOOLNO, 'NOT CONVERTED TO PRT'.
          EXIT.
        ENDIF.

      ELSEIF P_RAW EQ 'X'.
        CALL FUNCTION 'SX_OBJECT_CONVERT_OTF_RAW'
             EXPORTING
                    FORMAT_SRC      = 'OTF'
                    FORMAT_DST      = 'RAW'
                    DEVTYPE         = 'ASCIIPRI'
                    LEN_IN          = NUMBYTES
             IMPORTING
                    LEN_OUT         = NUMBYTES
             TABLES
                    CONTENT_IN      = T_COMPRESSED_LIST
                    CONTENT_OUT     = CONTENT_OUT
             EXCEPTIONS
                    ERR_CONV_FAILED = 1
                    OTHERS          = 2.

        IF SY-SUBRC NE 0.
          WRITE:/ SPOOLNO, 'NOT CONVERTED TO RAW'.
          EXIT.
        ENDIF.
      ENDIF.       "CONVERSION TYPE
    ELSE.
      WRITE:/ SPOOLNO, 'IS NOT AN OTF'.
    ENDIF.

* OUTPUT:
  CALL FUNCTION 'DOWNLOAD'
       EXPORTING
            BIN_FILESIZE = NUMBYTES
            FILENAME     = P_FILE
            FILETYPE     = 'BIN'
       IMPORTING
            ACT_FILENAME = P_FILE
```

```
                FILESIZE    = NUMBYTES
                CANCEL      = CANCEL
        TABLES
                DATA_TAB    = CONTENT_OUT.

  IF CANCEL = SPACE.
    WRITE: / NUMBYTES, 'BYTES DOWNLOADED TO FILE', P_FILE.
  ENDIF.
ELSE.
  WRITE:/ 'ATTRIBUTES OF SPOOL', SPOOLNO, 'NOT FOUND'.
ENDIF.
```

See Also

CONVERT_OTFSPOOLJOB_2_PDF

SX_OBJECT_CONVERT_OTF_PRT

Summary

Conversion from OTF (SAPscript) to PRT (printer format).

Parameters

```
EXPORTING
        FORMAT_SRC          Input format of data (ignored - always converted from OTF)
        FORMAT_DST          Output format of data (ignored - always converted to PRT)
        DEVTYPE             SAPscript device type for conversion
        LEN_IN              Number of bytes in input file
IMPORTING
        LEN_OUT             Number of bytes in output file
TABLES
        CONTENT_IN          Object contents in current format
        CONTENT_OUT         Object contents in required format
```

Example

See SX_OBJECT_CONVERT_OTF_PDF

See Also

SX_OBJECT_CONVERT_OTF_PDF

SX_OBJECT_CONVERT_OTF_RAW

Summary

Conversion from OTF (SAPscript) to ASCII.

Parameters

```
EXPORTING
        FORMAT_SRC              Input format of data (ignored - always converted from OTF)
        FORMAT_DST              Output format of data (ignored - always converted to RAW)
        DEVTYPE                 SAPscript device type for conversion
        LEN_IN                  Number of bytes in input file
IMPORTING
        LEN_OUT                 Number of bytes in output file
TABLES
        CONTENT_IN              Object contents in current format
        CONTENT_OUT             Object contents in required format
```

Example

See SX_OBJECT_CONVERT_OTF_PDF

See Also

SX_OBJECT_CONVERT_OTF_PDF

UNIT_CONVERSION_SIMPLE

Summary

Converts measurement unit values and rounds the values.

Description

Converts values from one measurement unit to another and rounds the result to the number of decimal places maintained in the measurement unit table, if necessary. The rounding is up (+), down (−), commercial (X), or no rounding (SPACE), depending on the parameter ROUND_SIGN.

Parameters

```
EXPORTING
        INPUT                   Quantity to convert
        ROUND_SIGN              Rounding type:
                                Value   Meaning
                                +       Round up (10.55 => 10.60)
                                -       Round down (10.55 => 10.50)
                                X       Commercial (10.55 => 10.60)
                                ' '     No rounding (10.55 => 10.55)
        UNIT_IN                 Unit of quantity in
        UNIT_OUT                Unit of quantity out
IMPORTING
        OUTPUT                  Quantity after conversion
```

Example

```
REPORT ZEXAMPLE.

DATA: SECS TYPE I,
      HOURS_OUT TYPE I.

PARAMETERS P_STRDTE LIKE SY-DATUM.

CALL FUNCTION 'SWI_DURATION_DETERMINE'
    EXPORTING
        START_DATE = P_STRDTE
        END_DATE   = SY-DATUM
        START_TIME = SY-UZEIT
        END_TIME   = SY-UZEIT
    IMPORTING
        DURATION   = SECS.

CALL FUNCTION 'UNIT_CONVERSION_SIMPLE'
    EXPORTING
        INPUT                 = SECS
        ROUND_SIGN            = ' '
        UNIT_IN               = 'S'
        UNIT_OUT              = 'H'
    IMPORTING
        OUTPUT                = HOURS_OUT
    EXCEPTIONS
        CONVERSION_NOT_FOUND = 1
        DIVISION_BY_ZERO     = 2
        INPUT_INVALID        = 3
        OUTPUT_INVALID       = 4
        OVERFLOW             = 5
        TYPE_INVALID         = 6
        UNITS_MISSING        = 7
        UNIT_IN_NOT_FOUND    = 8
        UNIT_OUT_NOT_FOUND   = 9
        OTHERS               = 10.

IF SY-SUBRC EQ 0.
  WRITE:/ HOURS_OUT, 'HOURS HAVE PASSED SINCE', P_STRDTE.
ELSE.
  WRITE:/ 'ERROR IN FUNCTION'.
ENDIF.
```

See Also

ROUND, HR_ROUND_NUMBER

UNIT_CONVERSION_WITH_FACTOR

Summary

Converts a value according to the factor passed.

Parameters

```
EXPORTING
        ADD_CONST                     A constant value to add to result
        DENOMINATOR                   Denominator factor
        INPUT                         Input quantity
        NUMERATOR                     Numerator factor
IMPORTING
        OUTPUT                        Output quantity after factor calculation
```

Example

```
REPORT ZEXAMPLE.

TABLES LIPS.

DATA MENGE LIKE EKPO-MENGE.

WRITE:/ 'QUANTITY', 20 'DENOMINATOR', 40 'NUMERATOR', 60 'OUTPUT'.
ULINE.

SELECT * FROM LIPS UP TO 1000 ROWS WHERE LGMNG GT 0.
  CALL FUNCTION 'UNIT_CONVERSION_WITH_FACTOR'
       EXPORTING
            ADD_CONST        = 0
            DENOMINATOR      = LIPS-UMVKN
            INPUT            = LIPS-LGMNG
            NUMERATOR        = LIPS-UMVKZ
       IMPORTING
            OUTPUT           = MENGE
       EXCEPTIONS
            DIVISION_BY_ZERO = 01
            OVERFLOW         = 02
            TYPE_INVALID     = 03.

  IF SY-SUBRC EQ 0.
    WRITE:/ LIPS-LGMNG, 20 LIPS-UMVKN, 40 LIPS-UMVKZ, 60 MENGE.
  ELSE.
    WRITE:/ LIPS-LGMNG, 20 LIPS-UMVKN, 40 LIPS-UMVKZ, 60 'NO CONVERSION'.
  ENDIF.
ENDSELECT.
```

UNIT_CORRESPONDENCE_CHECK

Summary

Checks if the two units belong to the same dimension.

Parameters

```
EXPORTING
        UNIT_IN                       Unit to compare with UNIT_OUT
        UNIT_OUT                      Unit to convert to
```

Example

```
REPORT ZEXAMPLE.

TABLES MARA.

SELECT * FROM MARA UP TO 100 ROWS.

* TRY CONVERT TO KG
  CALL FUNCTION 'UNIT_CORRESPONDENCE_CHECK'
       EXPORTING
            UNIT_IN                 = MARA-MEINS
            UNIT_OUT                = 'KG'
       EXCEPTIONS
            DIMENSIONS_ARE_DIFFERENT = 1
            UNIT_IN_NOT_FOUND       = 2
            UNIT_OUT_NOT_FOUND      = 3
            OTHERS                  = 4.

  IF SY-SUBRC EQ 0.
    WRITE:/ 'CONVERSION FROM UNIT', MARA-MEINS, 'TO UNIT KG IS POSSIBLE'.
  ELSE.
    WRITE:/ 'CONVERSION FROM UNIT', MARA-MEINS, 'TO UNIT KG IS NOT POSSIBLE'.
  ENDIF.
ENDSELECT.
```

UNIT_GET

Summary

Returns unit for the specified dimension and conversion factor.

Parameters

```
EXPORTING
      DIMENSION                 Dimension of unit
      NUMERATOR                 Numerator
      DENOMINATOR               Denominator
IMPORTING
      UNIT                      Unit of dimension entered
```

Example

```
REPORT ZEXAMPLE.

DATA DIMID LIKE T006D-DIMID.
DATA: BEGIN OF TIME_UNITS,
      SECOND LIKE T006-MSEHI,
      MINUTE LIKE T006-MSEHI,
      HOUR   LIKE T006-MSEHI,
      DAY    LIKE T006-MSEHI,
    END OF TIME_UNITS.
```

```
PARAMETERS: P_MINUTE  RADIOBUTTON GROUP RAD1,
            P_HOUR     RADIOBUTTON GROUP RAD1,
            P_DAY      RADIOBUTTON GROUP RAD1.


CALL FUNCTION 'DIMENSION_GET'
     EXPORTING
         TIME              = 1
     IMPORTING
         DIMID             = DIMID
     EXCEPTIONS
         DIMENSION_NOT_FOUND = 01.
IF SY-SUBRC <> 0.
  WRITE:/ 'TIME DIMENSION MISSING'.
ENDIF.


IF P_MINUTE EQ 'X'.
  CALL FUNCTION 'UNIT_GET'
     EXPORTING
         DIMENSION      = DIMID
         NUMERATOR      = 60
         DENOMINATOR    = 1
     IMPORTING
         UNIT           = TIME_UNITS-MINUTE
     EXCEPTIONS
         UNIT_NOT_FOUND = 01.
  IF SY-SUBRC <> 0.
    WRITE:/ 'MINUTE MISSING'.
  ELSE.
    WRITE:/ 'UNIT OF MINUTE IS:', TIME_UNITS-MINUTE.
  ENDIF.
ENDIF.


IF P_HOUR EQ 'X'.
  CALL FUNCTION 'UNIT_GET'
     EXPORTING
         DIMENSION      = DIMID
         NUMERATOR      = 3600
         DENOMINATOR    = 1
     IMPORTING
         UNIT           = TIME_UNITS-HOUR
     EXCEPTIONS
         UNIT_NOT_FOUND = 01.
  IF SY-SUBRC <> 0.
    WRITE:/ 'HOUR MISSING'.
  ELSE.
    WRITE:/ 'UNIT OF HOUR IS:', TIME_UNITS-HOUR.
  ENDIF.
ENDIF.


IF P_DAY EQ 'X'.
  CALL FUNCTION 'UNIT_GET'
     EXPORTING
         DIMENSION      = DIMID
         NUMERATOR      = 86400
```

```
            DENOMINATOR   = 1
      IMPORTING
            UNIT          = TIME_UNITS-DAY
      EXCEPTIONS
            UNIT_NOT_FOUND = 01.
  IF SY-SUBRC <> 0.
    WRITE:/ 'DAY MISSING'.
  ELSE.
    WRITE:/ 'UNIT OF DAY IS:', TIME_UNITS-DAY.
  ENDIF.
ENDIF.
```

See Also

SI_UNIT_GET, DIMENSION_GET

UNIT_OF_MEASURE_ISO_TO_SAP

Summary

Converts ISO unit to SAP unit of measure.

Description

This function module converts the international ISO code for measurement units into the SAP's internal measurement unit code.

Parameters

```
EXPORTING
      ISO_CODE                ISO code
IMPORTING
      SAP_CODE                SAP's internal code
```

Example

```
REPORT ZEXAMPLE.

TABLES T006.
DATA: SAP_CODE LIKE T006-MSEHI,
      ISO_CODE LIKE T006-ISOCODE.

WRITE:/ 'ISO UOM', 15 'SAP UOM', 30 'ISO UOM'.
ULINE.
SELECT * FROM T006.
  CALL FUNCTION 'UNIT_OF_MEASURE_ISO_TO_SAP'
      EXPORTING
            ISO_CODE  = T006-ISOCODE
      IMPORTING
            SAP_CODE  = SAP_CODE
```

```
        EXCEPTIONS
            NOT_FOUND = 1.

  IF SY-SUBRC EQ 0.
    WRITE:/ T006-ISOCODE, 15 SAP_CODE.

    CALL FUNCTION 'UNIT_OF_MEASURE_SAP_TO_ISO'
        EXPORTING
            SAP_CODE     = SAP_CODE
        IMPORTING
            ISO_CODE     = ISO_CODE
        EXCEPTIONS
            NOT_FOUND    = 1
            NO_ISO_CODE  = 2
            OTHERS       = 3.

    IF SY-SUBRC EQ 0.
      WRITE: 30 ISO_CODE.
    ENDIF.
  ENDIF.
ENDSELECT.
```

See Also

UNIT_OF_MEASURE_SAP_TO_ISO

UNIT_OF_MEASURE_SAP_TO_ISO

Summary

Converts SAP unit to ISO unit of measure.

Description

This function module converts the SAP's internal measurement unit code into international ISO code for measurement units.

Parameters

```
EXPORTING
      SAP_CODE                SAP's internal code
IMPORTING
      ISO_CODE                ISO code
```

Example

See UNIT_OF_MEASURE_ISO_TO_SAP

See Also

UNIT_OF_MEASURE_SAP_TO_ISO

UNIT_OF_MEASUREMENT_HELP

Summary

Displays all units of a specified dimension.

Description

Displays in a dialogue box either all measurement units or all commercial measurement units of a specified dimension (external measurement unit and associated long text). If you do not specify a dimension, all measurement units are displayed.

Parameters

```
EXPORTING
      CUCOL                         Column position of dialogue box
      CUROW                         Row position of dialogue box
      DIMID                         Restrict display to this dimension key
      LANGUAGE                      Logon language
IMPORTING
      SELECT_UNIT                   Unit selected from dialogue box
```

Example

```
REPORT ZEXAMPLE.

DATA UNIT(6).

* DISPLAY DIALOG BOX OF ALL MEASURE TYPES IN LOGON LANGUAGE
CALL FUNCTION 'UNIT_OF_MEASUREMENT_HELP'
     EXPORTING
          CUCOL      = 30
          CUROW      = 5
          LANGUAGE   = SY-LANGU
     IMPORTING
          SELECT_UNIT = UNIT

IF NOT UNIT IS INITIAL.
  WRITE:/ 'YOU HAVE CHOSEN UNIT', UNIT.
ELSE.
  WRITE:/ 'DIALOG BOX CANCELLED'.
ENDIF.
```

Dates and Times

3

This chapter contains functions you can use to manipulate date and time information in ABAP programs.

Most applications store and manipulate dates and times. Dates are quite complicated: not only are they highly formatted, but also there are a myriad of rules for determining valid values in calculations (leap days and years, national and company (factory) holidays, date ranges, etc.). Fortunately, SAP provides many functions to handle this information.

ADD_TIME_TO_DATE

Summary

Adds months/days/years to a date.

Description

Entering a negative value will subtract from the date.

Parameters

```
EXPORTING
      I_IDATE                 Initial date
      I_TIME                  Quantity to add to date
      I_IPRKZ                 Unit of I_TIME:
                              Value     Meaning
                              D         Day
                              M         Month
                              W         Week
                              Y         Year
                              ' '       No calculation
IMPORTING
      O_IDATE                 Output date
```

Example

```
REPORT ZEXAMPLE.

DATA: O_IDATE LIKE MCHA-VFDAT,
      I_IPRKZ LIKE MARA-IPRKZ.

PARAMETERS:  P_TIME   LIKE MARA-MHDHB.
PARAMETERS:  P_DAY    RADIOBUTTON GROUP RAD1,
             P_MONTH RADIOBUTTON GROUP RAD1,
             P_WEEK   RADIOBUTTON GROUP RAD1,
             P_YEAR   RADIOBUTTON GROUP RAD1.

IF P_DAY EQ 'X'.
  I_IPRKZ = 'D'.
ELSEIF P_MONTH EQ 'X'.
  I_IPRKZ = 'M'.
ELSEIF P_WEEK EQ 'X'.
  I_IPRKZ = 'W'.
ELSEIF P_YEAR EQ 'X'.
  I_IPRKZ = 'Y'.
ENDIF.

*   CONVERT TO INTERNAL REPRESENTATION
CALL FUNCTION 'CONVERSION_EXIT_PERKZ_INPUT'
     EXPORTING
          INPUT                = I_IPRKZ
     IMPORTING
          OUTPUT               = I_IPRKZ.

CALL FUNCTION 'ADD_TIME_TO_DATE'
     EXPORTING
          I_IDATE              = SY-DATUM
          I_TIME               = P_TIME
     I_IPRKZ                   = I_IPRKZ
     IMPORTING
          O_IDATE              = O_IDATE
     EXCEPTIONS
          INVALID_PERIOD        = 1
          INVALID_ROUND_UP_RULE = 2
          INTERNAL_ERROR        = 3
          OTHERS                = 4.
IF SY-SUBRC EQ 0.
  WRITE:/ P_TIME, 'ADDED TO', SY-DATUM, 'IS', O_IDATE.
ELSE.
     WRITE:/ 'COULD NOT CONVERT'.
ENDIF.
```

See Also

DATE_IN_FUTURE, MONTH_PLUS_DETERMINE, RE_ADD_MONTH_TO_DATE, RP_CALC_DATE_IN_INTERVAL, SUBTRACT_TIME_FROM_DATE

C14B_ADD_TIME

Summary

Adds time to a date and time.

Parameters

```
EXPORTING
      I_STARTTIME             Start time value in STARTDATE
      I_STARTDATE             Start date value
      I_ADDTIME               Time value added to STARTTIME
IMPORTING
      E_ENDTIME               Time after calculation
      E_ENDDATE               Date after calculation
```

Example

```
REPORT ZEXAMPLE.

DATA: CLOCK_OUT_DATE LIKE SY-DATUM,
      CLOCK_OUT_TIME LIKE SY-UZEIT.

PARAMETERS:P_CI_DAT LIKE SY-DATUM,
           P_CN_TIM LIKE SY-UZEIT,
           P_WK_TIM LIKE SY-UZEIT.

WRITE:/ 'CLOCK IN DATE', 15 'CLOCK IN TIME', 30 'WORKING TIME', 45
        'CLOCK OUT DATE', 60 'CLOCK OUT TIME'.
ULINE.

CALL FUNCTION 'C14B_ADD_TIME'
     EXPORTING
           I_STARTTIME             = P_CN_TIM
           I_STARTDATE             = P_CI_DAT
           I_ADDTIME               = P_WK_TIM
     IMPORTING
           E_ENDTIME               = CLOCK_OUT_TIME
           E_ENDDATE               = CLOCK_OUT_DATE.

WRITE:/ P_CI_DAT, 15 P_CN_TIM, 30 P_WK_TIM, 45 CLOCK_OUT_DATE, 60 CLOCK_OUT_TIME.
```

COMPUTE_YEARS_BETWEEN_DATES

Summary

Computes number of years between two dates.

Parameters

```
EXPORTING
        FIRST_DATE                 Start date
        SECOND_DATE                End date
IMPORTING
        YEARS_BETWEEN_DATES        Years difference between dates
```

Example

```
REPORT ZEXAMPLE.

DATA AGE TYPE I.
PARAMETERS P_BIRTHD LIKE SY-DATUM.

CALL FUNCTION 'COMPUTE_YEARS_BETWEEN_DATES'
     EXPORTING
            FIRST_DATE                 = P_BIRTHD
            SECOND_DATE                = SY-DATUM
     IMPORTING
            YEARS_BETWEEN_DATES        = AGE
     EXCEPTIONS
            SEQUENCE_OF_DATES_NOT_VALID = 1
            OTHERS                     = 2.

IF SY-SUBRC EQ 0.
  WRITE:/ 'YOU ARE', AGE, 'YEARS OLD'.
ELSE.
  WRITE:/ 'COULD NOT COMPUTE'.
ENDIF.
```

See Also

DAYS_BETWEEN_TWO_DATES, HR_HK_DIFF_BT_2_DATES,
HR_IE_NUM_PRSI_WEEKS, SD_DATETIME_DIFFERENCE,
SWI_DURATION_DETERMINE, FIMA_DAYS_AND_MONTHS_AND_YEARS

CONVERSION_EXIT_LDATE_OUTPUT

Summary

Converts date format.

Description

Converts date with format of YYYYMMDD to DD.MMMM.YYYY.

Parameters

```
EXPORTING
      INPUT                     Date in YYYYMMDD format
IMPORTING
      OUTPUT                    Date in DD.MMMM.YYYY format
```

Example

```
REPORT ZEXAMPLE.

DATA V_MONTH(11).

CALL FUNCTION 'CONVERSION_EXIT_LDATE_OUTPUT'
     EXPORTING
          INPUT               = SY-DATUM
     IMPORTING
          OUTPUT              = V_MONTH.

WRITE:/ 'CURRENT MONTH IN WORDS:', V_MONTH+3(8).
```

CONVERT_DATE_INPUT

Summary

Conversion exit routine for inverted date.

Description

This (obsolete) function module converts a date from the externally formatted user input into the internal SAP system format. There is no function module CONVERT_DATE_OUTPUT as this is done via the WRITE statement, using parameter DD/MM/YYYY.

Parameters

```
EXPORTING
      INPUT                     External date format DD.MM.YYYY
      PLAUSIBILITY_CHECK        Check validity of input date
IMPORTING
      OUTPUT                    Output of a data field in the format YYYYMMDD
```

Example

```
REPORT ZEXAMPLE.
DATA: V_DATE LIKE SY-DATUM,
      V_DATE2(10).
```

```
CALL FUNCTION 'CONVERT_DATE_INPUT'
     EXPORTING
          INPUT                      = '21102002'   "DD.MM.YYYY
          PLAUSIBILITY_CHECK         = 'X'
     IMPORTING
          OUTPUT                     = V_DATE       "YYYY.MM.DD
     EXCEPTIONS
          PLAUSIBILITY_CHECK_FAILED = 1
          WRONG_FORMAT_IN_INPUT     = 2
          OTHERS                    = 3.

V_DATE2 = V_DATE.
WRITE:/ V_DATE2.
```

See Also

CONVERT_DATE_TO_INTERNAL

CONVERT_DATE_TO_EXTERNAL

Summary

Changes format of date from display to internal.

Description

Can be configured through transaction SU50 or menu System > User profile > User defaults.

Parameters

```
EXPORTING
       DATE_INTERNAL              Date in internal format
IMPORTING
       DATE_EXTERNAL              Date converted to external format
```

Example

```
REPORT ZEXAMPLE.
TABLES: MARA, MDKP.

DATA V_DATE(30).

SELECT * FROM MARA UP TO 100 ROWS.
   SELECT SINGLE * FROM MDKP WHERE MATNR EQ MARA-MATNR AND
                                  BEADA NE '00000000'.

   IF SY-SUBRC EQ 0.
     V_DATE = MDKP-BEADA.
     WRITE:/ 'DATE IN INTERNAL FORMAT:', V_DATE.
```

```
    CALL FUNCTION 'CONVERT_DATE_TO_EXTERNAL'
         EXPORTING
              DATE_INTERNAL            = MDKP-BEADA
         IMPORTING
              DATE_EXTERNAL            = V_DATE
         EXCEPTIONS
              DATE_INTERNAL_IS_INVALID = 1
              OTHERS                   = 2.


    IF SY-SUBRC EQ 0.
      WRITE:/ 'DATE NOW IN EXTERNAL FORMAT:', V_DATE.
    ENDIF.


    CALL FUNCTION 'CONVERT_DATE_TO_INTERNAL'
         EXPORTING
              DATE_EXTERNAL            = V_DATE
         IMPORTING
              DATE_INTERNAL            = V_DATE
         EXCEPTIONS
              DATE_EXTERNAL_IS_INVALID = 1
              OTHERS                   = 2.
    IF SY-SUBRC EQ 0.
      WRITE:/ 'DATE NOW BACK IN INTERNAL FORMAT:', V_DATE.
      ULINE.
    ENDIF.
  ENDIF.
ENDSELECT.
```

See Also

CONVERT_DATE_TO_INTERNAL, CONVERT_DATE_INPUT

CONVERT_DATE_TO_INTERNAL

Summary

Changes format of date from internal to display.

Description

Can be configured through transaction SU50 or menu System > User profile > User defaults.

Parameters

```
EXPORTING
    DATE_EXTERNAL            Date in external format
IMPORTING
    DATE_INTERNAL            Date converted to internal format
```

Example

See CONVERT_DATE_TO_EXTERNAL

See Also

CONVERT_DATE_TO_EXTERNAL, CONVERT_DATE_INPUT

COPF_DETERMINE_DURATION

Summary

Calculates the difference between two dates and times.

Description

Calculates the difference between two date and time in minutes or hours. Specifies the time unit in which the difference is calculated and a specific factory calendar.

Parameters

```
EXPORTING
        I_START_DATE          The start date of the time interval
        I_START_TIME          The start time of the time interval
        I_END_DATE            The end date of the time interval
        I_END_TIME            The end time of the time interval
        I_UNIT_OF_DURATION    Time unit of the duration if not to be calculated in days:
                              Value      Meaning
                              ' '        Day (default)
                              D          Days
                              H          Hours
                              MIN        Minute
                              MON        Months
                              S          Seconds
                              WK         Weeks
                              YR         Years
        I_FACTORY_CALENDAR    A factory calendar if not using the Gregorian calendar
IMPORTING
        E_DURATION            Time difference in unit specified
```

Example

```
REPORT ZEXAMPLE.

DATA I_DUR TYPE F.

PARAMETERS:  P_CI_DAT LIKE SY-DATUM,
```

```
                    P_CI_TIM LIKE SY-UZEIT,
                    P_CO_DAT LIKE SY-DATUM,
                    P_CO_TIM LIKE SY-UZEIT.

WRITE:/ 'CLOCK IN DATE', 15 'CLOCK IN TIME', 30 'CLOCK OUT DATE',
          45 'CLOCK OUT TIME', 60 'WORKING TIME'.
ULINE.

CALL FUNCTION 'COPF_DETERMINE_DURATION'
     EXPORTING
            I_START_DATE              = P_CI_DAT
            I_START_TIME              = P_CI_TIM
            I_END_DATE                = P_CO_DAT
            I_END_TIME                = P_CO_TIM
            I_UNIT_OF_DURATION        = 'H'
     IMPORTING
            E_DURATION                = I_DUR
     EXCEPTIONS
            EXCEPTION_RAISED          = 1
            OTHERS                    = 2.

IF SY-SUBRC EQ 0.
  WRITE:/ P_CI_DAT, 15 P_CI_TIM, 30 P_CO_DAT, 45 P_CO_TIM, 60 I_DUR, 'IN HOURS'.
ELSE.
  WRITE:/ 'COULD NOT CALCULATE'.
ENDIF.
```

See Also

COMPUTE_YEARS_BETWEEN_DATES, DAYS_BETWEEN_TWO_DATES,
HR_HK_DIFF_BT_2_DATES, HR_IE_NUM_PRSI_WEEKS, SD_DATETIME_DIFFERENCE,
SWI_DURATION_DETERMINE, FIMA_DAYS_AND_MONTHS_AND_YEARS

DATE_CHECK_PLAUSIBILITY

Summary

Checks if the value of a field is a date format (YYYYMMDD).

Description

Ideally suited to validating dates being passed in from other systems.

Parameters

```
EXPORTING
      DATE          Date to be checked
```

Example

```
REPORT ZEXAMPLE.
PARAMETERS P_DATE LIKE SY-DATUM.

CALL FUNCTION 'DATE_CHECK_PLAUSIBILITY'
     EXPORTING
          DATE                        = P_DATE
     EXCEPTIONS
          PLAUSIBILITY_CHECK_FAILED = 1
          OTHERS                      = 2.

IF SY-SUBRC  <> 0.
  WRITE:/ P_DATE, 'IS NOT A VALID DATE'.
ELSE.
  WRITE:/ P_DATE, 'IS A VALID DATE'.
ENDIF.
```

See Also

RP_CHECK_DATE

DATE_CHECK_WORKINGDAY

Summary

Determines if a date is a working day.

Description

You can decide the level of error message (information, warning, etc.) if the date turns out not to be a working day.

Parameters

```
EXPORTING
      DATE                        Date to check
      FACTORY_CALENDAR_ID         Factory calendar
      MESSAGE_TYPE                Type of message, if not a working day
                                  Value   Meaning
                                  I       Information
                                  W       Warning
                                  E       Error
                                  A       Abend
                                  S       Status
```

Example

```
REPORT ZEXAMPLE.
TABLES T001W.

PARAMETERS:P_DATE LIKE SY-DATUM,
           P_PLANT LIKE T001W-WERKS.

SELECT SINGLE * FROM T001W WHERE WERKS = P_PLANT.

CALL FUNCTION 'DATE_CHECK_WORKINGDAY'
     EXPORTING
          DATE                       = P_DATE
          FACTORY_CALENDAR_ID        = T001W-FABKL
          MESSAGE_TYPE               = 'E'
     EXCEPTIONS
          DATE_AFTER_RANGE          = 1
          DATE_BEFORE_RANGE         = 2
          DATE_INVALID              = 3
          DATE_NO_WORKINGDAY        = 4
          FACTORY_CALENDAR_NOT_FOUND = 5
          MESSAGE_TYPE_INVALID      = 6
          OTHERS                    = 7.

IF SY-SUBRC EQ 0.
  WRITE:/ P_DATE, 'IS A WORKING DAY IN', P_PLANT.
ELSE.
  IF SY-SUBRC EQ 4.
    WRITE:/ P_DATE, 'IS A HOLIDAY IN', P_PLANT.
  ELSE.
    WRITE:/ 'COULD NOT DETERMINE DATE'.
  ENDIF.
ENDIF.
```

See Also

DATE_CHECK_WORKINGDAY_MULIPLE, DATE_CONVERT_TO_FACTORYDATE, DATE_CONVERT_TO_WORKINGDAY

DATE_CHECK_WORKINGDAY_MULTIPLE

Summary

Checks date across multiple factory calendars.

Parameters

```
EXPORTING
     DATE                  Input date to check
```

```
        MESSAGE_TYPE              Type of message, if not a working day:
                                  Value      Meaning
                                  I          Information
                                  W          Warning
                                  E          Error
                                  A          Abend
                                  S          Status
TABLES
        FACTORY_CALENDARS         Range of factory calendars to check date
```

Example

```
REPORT ZEXAMPLE.

DATA BEGIN OF I_CALENDARS OCCURS 0.
      INCLUDE STRUCTURE VTBFCAL.
DATA END OF I_CALENDARS.

PARAMETERS: VDATE LIKE SY-DATUM OBLIGATORY,
            CAL1 LIKE TFACD-IDENT OBLIGATORY DEFAULT 'OC',
            CAL2 LIKE TFACD-IDENT OBLIGATORY DEFAULT 'OD'.

CLEAR: I_CALENDARS, I_CALENDARS[].

I_CALENDARS-IDENT   = CAL1.
APPEND I_CALENDARS.
I_CALENDARS-IDENT   = CAL2.
APPEND I_CALENDARS.

CALL FUNCTION 'DATE_CHECK_WORKINGDAY_MULTIPLE'
     EXPORTING
          DATE                    = VDATE
          MESSAGE_TYPE            = 'I'
     TABLES
          FACTORY_CALENDARS       = I_CALENDARS
     EXCEPTIONS
          DATE_AFTER_RANGE        = 1
          DATE_BEFORE_RANGE       = 2
          DATE_INVALID            = 3
          DATE_NO_WORKINGDAY      = 4
          FACTORY_CALENDAR_NOT_FOUND = 5
          MESSAGE_TYPE_INVALID    = 6
          OTHERS                  = 7.

CASE SY-SUBRC.
  WHEN 0.
    WRITE:/ VDATE, 'IS A WORKING DAY IN ALL CALENDARS.'.
  WHEN 4..
    WRITE:/ VDATE, 'IS A HOLIDAY IN AT LEAST ONE CALENDAR.'.
  WHEN OTHERS.
    WRITE:/ 'ERROR WITH FUNCTION.'.
ENDCASE.
```

See Also

DATE_CHECK_WORKINGDAY, DATE_CONVERT_TO_WORKINGDATE

DATE_COMPUTE_DAY

Summary

Determines the day of the week for a date.

Parameters

```
EXPORTING
        DATE              Valid date
IMPORTING
        DAY               A number representing a day of the week:
                          Value      Meaning
                          1          Monday
                          2          Tuesday
                          3          Wednesday
                          4          Thursday
                          5          Friday
                          6          Saturday
                          7          Sunday
```

Example

```
REPORT ZEXAMPLE.
DATA: WEEKDAY     LIKE SCAL-INDICATOR,
      MSG(30)     TYPE C VALUE 'WAS A &1',
      DOW(10)     TYPE C.

PARAMETERS: P_DATE LIKE SY-DATUM.

CALL FUNCTION 'DATE_COMPUTE_DAY'
     EXPORTING
         DATE                = P_DATE
     IMPORTING
         DAY                 = WEEKDAY.

CASE WEEKDAY.
  WHEN    '1'.
    DOW  = 'MONDAY'.
  WHEN    '2'.
    DOW  = 'TUESDAY'.
  WHEN    '3'.
    DOW  = 'WEDNESDAY'.
  WHEN    '4'.
    DOW  = 'THURSDAY'.
```

```
WHEN   '5'.
   DOW  = 'FRIDAY'.
WHEN   '6'.
   DOW  = 'SATURDAY'.
WHEN   '7'.
   DOW  = 'SUNDAY'.
ENDCASE.

REPLACE '&1' WITH DOW INTO MSG.
CONDENSE MSG.
WRITE:/ P_DATE, MSG.
```

See Also

DAY_IN_WEEK, WEEKDAY_GET

DATE_CONV_EXT_TO_INT

Summary

Conversion of dates to SAP's internal format.

Description

Can also be used to check if a date is valid.

Parameters

```
EXPORTING
      I_DATE_EXT                       Date in external format
IMPORTING
      E_DATE_INT                       Date converted to internal format
```

Example

```
REPORT ZEXAMPLE.
DATA: V_DATE LIKE MDKP-BEADA,
      V_DISP(10).

CALL FUNCTION 'DATE_CONV_EXT_TO_INT'
     EXPORTING
          I_DATE_EXT            = SY-DATUM
     IMPORTING
          E_DATE_INT            = V_DATE
     EXCEPTIONS
          ERROR                 = 1
          OTHERS                = 2.
```

```
IF SY-SUBRC EQ 0.
  V_DISP = V_DATE.
  WRITE:/ SY-DATUM, 'NOW IN INTERNAL FORMAT:', V_DISP.
ELSE.
  WRITE:/ 'ERROR IN CONVERSION'.
ENDIF.
```

See Also

CONVERT_DATE_TO_INTERNAL, CONVERT_DATE_INPUT,
DATE_CHECK_PLAUSIBILITY

DATE_CONVERT_TO_FACTORYDATE

Summary

Converts a calendar date into factory date.

Description

Table TFACD contains the factory calendar definitions. In the factory calendar, the working days are numbered sequentially from the first working day. The working day numbers are called the factory days. This function module calculates the factory date for a calendar date. If the date passed is not a working day, the next or previous working day is calculated.

Parameters

```
EXPORTING
      CORRECT_OPTION          Flag how workday should be calculated:
                              Value   Meaning
                              +       If the specified date is not a working day, the first
                                      working day after the date is returned (default)
                              -       If the specified date is not a working day, the first
                                      working day before the date is returned
      DATE                    Date to be converted into factory calendar date.
      FACTORY_CALENDAR_ID     Factory calendar key
IMPORTING
      DATE                    Date format of the factory calendar date
      FACTORYDATE             Number of the workday in the specified calendar
      WORKINGDAY_INDICATOR    Flag whether date is a workday
```

Example

```
REPORT ZEXAMPLE.
TABLES: T001W, MDCAL.
```

```
PARAMETERS:P_DATE LIKE SY-DATUM,
           P_PLANT LIKE T001W-WERKS.

SELECT SINGLE * FROM T001W WHERE WERKS = P_PLANT.
IF SY-SUBRC EQ 0.
   CALL FUNCTION 'DATE_CONVERT_TO_FACTORYDATE'
         EXPORTING
               CORRECT_OPTION                 = '+'
               DATE                           = P_DATE
               FACTORY_CALENDAR_ID            = T001W-FABKL
         IMPORTING
               DATE                           = MDCAL-GKDAY
               FACTORYDATE                    = MDCAL-FKDAY
               WORKINGDAY_INDICATOR           = MDCAL-WORKI
         EXCEPTIONS
               CALENDAR_BUFFER_NOT_LOADABLE = 1
               CORRECT_OPTION_INVALID         = 2
               DATE_AFTER_RANGE               = 3
               DATE_BEFORE_RANGE              = 4
               DATE_INVALID                   = 5
               FACTORY_CALENDAR_NOT_FOUND   = 6
               OTHERS                         = 7.

   IF SY-SUBRC EQ 0.
     IF MDCAL-WORKI EQ 'X'.
       WRITE:/ P_DATE, 'IS A WORKING DAY IN', P_PLANT.
     ELSE.
       WRITE:/ P_DATE, 'IS NOT A WORKING DAY IN', P_PLANT.
     ENDIF.

     CALL FUNCTION 'FACTORYDATE_CONVERT_TO_DATE'
           EXPORTING
                 FACTORYDATE                    = MDCAL-FKDAY
                 FACTORY_CALENDAR_ID            = T001W-FABKL
           IMPORTING
                 DATE                           = MDCAL-GKDAY
           EXCEPTIONS
                 CALENDAR_BUFFER_NOT_LOADABLE = 01
                 FACTORYDATE_AFTER_RANGE        = 02
                 FACTORYDATE_BEFORE_RANGE       = 03
                 FACTORYDATE_INVALID            = 04
                 FACTORY_CALENDAR_ID_MISSING  = 05
                 FACTORY_CALENDAR_NOT_FOUND   = 06.
     IF SY-SUBRC EQ 0.
       WRITE:/ 'FACTORY DATE', MDCAL-FKDAY, 'IS THE DATE', MDCAL-GKDAY.
     ELSE.
       WRITE:/ 'COULD NOT CONVERT', MDCAL-FKDAY.
     ENDIF.
   ENDIF.
ENDIF.
ENDIF.
```

See Also

FACTORYDATE_CONVERT_TO_DATE, DATE_CONVERT_TO_WORKINGDAY

DATE_CONVERT_TO_WORKINGDAY

Summary

Converts a calendar date into working day.

Parameters

```
EXPORTING
        DATE                 Date to convert to factory date
        DIRECTION            How working day is calculated:
                             Value    Meaning
                             +        If the specified date is not a working day, the first
                                      working day after the date is returned (default)
                             -        If the specified date is not a working day, the first
                                      working day before the date is returned
IMPORTING
        WORKINGDAY           Nearest working day to DATE
TABLES
        FACTORY_CALENDARS Factory calendar ID
```

Example

```
REPORT ZEXAMPLE.
TABLES T001W.

DATA: BEGIN OF FCAL OCCURS 0.
        INCLUDE STRUCTURE VTBFCAL.
DATA: END OF FCAL.

DATA V_DATE LIKE SY-DATUM.

PARAMETERS:P_DATE LIKE SY-DATUM,
           P_PLANT LIKE T001W-WERKS.

SELECT SINGLE * FROM T001W WHERE WERKS = P_PLANT.
FCAL-IDENT = T001W-FABKL.
APPEND FCAL.
CALL FUNCTION 'DATE_CONVERT_TO_WORKINGDAY'
     EXPORTING
          DATE                 = P_DATE
     IMPORTING
          WORKINGDAY           = V_DATE
     TABLES
          FACTORY_CALENDARS    = FCAL.

WRITE:/ 'THE NEAREST WORKING DAY TO', P_DATE, 'IN', P_PLANT, 'IS', V_DATE.
```

See Also

DATE_CHECK_WORKINGDAY, DATE_CONVERT_TO_WORKINGDATE

DATE_CREATE

Summary

Calculates a date from the input parameters.

Parameters

```
EXPORTING
        ANZAHL_JAHRE                Number of years to add to initial date
        ANZAHL_KALTAGE              Number of dates to add to initial date
        ANZAHL_MONATE               Number of months to add to initial date
        ANZAHL_TAGE                 Number of days to add to initial date
        DATUM_EIN                   Initial date
IMPORTING
        DATUM_AUS                   Date calculated from inputs
```

Example

```
REPORT ZEXAMPLE.
DATA V_DATE LIKE SY-DATUM.

PARAMETERS: P_YEAR TYPE I,
            P_MONTH TYPE I,
            P_DAY TYPE I.

CALL FUNCTION 'DATE_CREATE'
    EXPORTING
        ANZAHL_JAHRE   = P_YEAR
        ANZAHL_MONATE  = P_MONTH
        ANZAHL_TAGE    = P_DAY
        DATUM_EIN      = SY-DATUM
    IMPORTING
        DATUM_AUS      = V_DATE.

WRITE:/ 'INPUT DATE', 15 'YEARS ADDED', 30 'MONTHS ADDED', 45 'DAYS ADDED',
        60 'OUTPUT DATE'.
ULINE.
WRITE:/ SY-DATUM, 15 P_YEAR, 30 P_MONTH, 45 P_DAY, 60 V_DATE.
```

See Also

DATE_IN_FUTURE, MONTH_PLUS_DETERMINE, RE_ADD_MONTH_TO_DATE, RP_CALC_DATE_IN_INTERVAL, SUBTRACT_TIME_FROM_DATE

DATE_GET_WEEK

Summary

Determines the week in a year for a date.

Description

Import: YYYYMMDD; Export: YYYYWW, where WW is the week number.

Parameters

```
EXPORTING
       DATE                Date for which the week should be calculated
IMPORTING
       WEEK                Week for date (format: YYYYWW)
```

Example

```
REPORT ZEXAMPLE.
DATA: BEGIN OF DAYNAMES OCCURS 0.
        INCLUDE STRUCTURE T246.
DATA: END OF DAYNAMES.

DATA: V_WEEK LIKE SCAL-WEEK,
      WOTNR TYPE P,
      V_MONDAY LIKE SCAL-DATE.

*   GET THE CURRENT WEEK OF A DATE
CALL FUNCTION 'DATE_GET_WEEK'
     EXPORTING
          DATE                = SY-DATUM
     IMPORTING
          WEEK                = V_WEEK "YYYYWW
     EXCEPTIONS
          DATE_INVALID        = 1
          OTHERS              = 2.

*   GET THE DATE OF THE FIRST MONDAY OF THE WEEK
CALL FUNCTION 'WEEK_GET_FIRST_DAY'
     EXPORTING
          WEEK        = V_WEEK
     IMPORTING
          DATE        = V_MONDAY
     EXCEPTIONS
          WEEK_INVALID = 1
          OTHERS       = 2.

*   DAY NUMBER OF A DATE
CALL FUNCTION 'DAY_IN_WEEK'
     EXPORTING
          DATUM = SY-DATUM
     IMPORTING
          WOTNR = WOTNR.

*   NAMES OF THE DAYS
CALL FUNCTION 'WEEKDAY_GET'
     EXPORTING
          LANGUAGE = SY-LANGU
```

```
      TABLES
          WEEKDAY = DAYNAMES.

READ TABLE DAYNAMES WITH KEY WOTNR = WOTNR.
WRITE: / 'DATE:', SY-DATUM,
       / 'WEEK NUMBER:', V_WEEK+4,
       / 'FIRST DAY OF WEEK:', V_MONDAY,
       / 'CURRENT DAY OF WEEK:', DAYNAMES-LANGT.
```

DATE_IN_FUTURE

Summary

Calculates a future or past date.

Description

Entering a negative value will return the number of days in the past.

Parameters

```
EXPORTING
        ANZAHL_TAGE                  Number of days that are added/subtracted
        IMPORT_DATUM                 Initial date (DDMMYYYY)
IMPORTING
        EXPORT_DATUM_EXT_FORMAT       Future date in external format
        EXPORT_DATUM_INT_FORMAT       Future date in internal format (YYYYMMDD)
```

Example

```
REPORT ZEXAMPLE.

DATA: V_DATE_IN(10),
      V_DATE_OUT_INT  LIKE SY-DATUM,
      V_DATE_OUT_EXT(10).

PARAMETERS:P_DATE LIKE SY-DATUM,
           P_DAYS(3).

V_DATE_IN+0  = P_DATE+6(2).  "DD
V_DATE_IN+2  = P_DATE+4(2).  "MM
V_DATE_IN+4  = P_DATE(4).    "YYYY

CALL FUNCTION 'DATE_IN_FUTURE'
    EXPORTING
        ANZAHL_TAGE              = P_DAYS
    IMPORT_DATUM                 = V_DATE_IN
```

```
      IMPORTING
          EXPORT_DATUM_INT_FORMAT = V_DATE_OUT_INT
          EXPORT_DATUM_EXT_FORMAT = V_DATE_OUT_EXT.

WRITE:/ 'IN', P_DAYS, 'DAYS TIME, IT WILL BE THE', V_DATE_OUT_EXT.
```

See Also

ADD_TIME_TO_DATE, DATE_IN_FUTURE, MONTH_PLUS_DETERMINE, RE_ADD_MONTH_TO_DATE, RP_CALC_DATE_IN_INTERVAL, SUBTRACT_TIME_FROM_DATE

DATE_TO_PERIOD_CONVERT

Summary

Returns the period of a date.

Parameters

```
EXPORTING
        I_DATE          Date to retrieve periods
        I_PERIV         Period version
IMPORTING
        E_BUPER         Calculated posting period
        E_GJAHR         Calculated fiscal year
```

Example

```
REPORT ZEXAMPLE.
TABLES T009.

DATA: V_GJAHR   LIKE   T009B-BDATJ,   "FISCAL YEAR
      V_POPER   LIKE   T009B-POPER,   "POSTING PERIOD
      F_DAY     LIKE   SY-DATUM,
      L_DAY     LIKE   SY-DATUM,
      C_PERIO   LIKE   CEST1-PERIO,   "CURRENT PERIOD
      N_PERIO   LIKE   CEST1-PERIO.   "NEXT PERIOD

WRITE: / 'PERIOD INFORMATION'.
ULINE.
WRITE: / 'PERIOD', 10 'DATE', 30 'FIRST DAY', 50 'LAST DAY', 70 'NEXT PERIOD'.
ULINE.

SELECT * FROM T009.
  CALL FUNCTION 'DATE_TO_PERIOD_CONVERT'
      EXPORTING
            I_DATE          = SY-DATUM
            I_PERIV         = T009-PERIV
```

```
         IMPORTING
             E_BUPER          = V_POPER
             E_GJAHR          = V_GJAHR
             EXCEPTIONS
             INPUT_FALSE      = 1
             T009_NOTFOUND    = 2
             T009B_NOTFOUND   = 3
             OTHERS           = 4.
IF SY-SUBRC EQ 0.
  CALL FUNCTION 'FIRST_DAY_IN_PERIOD_GET'
         EXPORTING
             I_GJAHR          = V_GJAHR
             I_PERIV          = T009-PERIV
             I_POPER          = V_POPER
         IMPORTING
             E_DATE           = F_DAY
         EXCEPTIONS
             INPUT_FALSE      = 1
             T009_NOTFOUND    = 2
             T009B_NOTFOUND   = 3
             OTHERS           = 4.

IF SY-SUBRC EQ 0.
  CALL FUNCTION 'LAST_DAY_IN_PERIOD_GET'
         EXPORTING
             I_GJAHR          = V_GJAHR
             I_PERIV          = T009-PERIV
             I_POPER          = V_POPER
         IMPORTING
             E_DATE           = L_DAY
         EXCEPTIONS
             INPUT_FALSE      = 1
             T009_NOTFOUND    = 2
             T009B_NOTFOUND   = 3
             OTHERS           = 4.

  IF SY-SUBRC EQ 0.
    CONCATENATE V_GJAHR V_POPER INTO C_PERIO.
    CALL FUNCTION 'RKE_ADD_TO_PERIOD'
         EXPORTING
             DELTA            = T009-ANZBP
             PERIO            = C_PERIO
             PERIV            = T009-PERIV
         IMPORTING
             PERIO            = N_PERIO
         EXCEPTIONS
             I_ERROR          = 1
             I_PERFLAG_INVALID = 2
             I_PERIV_NOTFOUND = 3
             OTHERS           = 4.
  CLEAR C_PERIO.
  IF SY-SUBRC EQ 0.
    WRITE:/ T009-PERIV, 10 SY-DATUM, 30 F_DAY, 50 L_DAY, 70 N_PERIO.
  ELSE.
    WRITE:/ T009-PERIV, 10 SY-DATUM, 30 F_DAY, 50 L_DAY,
```

```
                        70 'NEXT PERIOD COULD NOT BE CALCULATED'.
              ENDIF.
          ELSE.
            WRITE:/ T009-PERIV, 10 SY-DATUM, 30 F_DAY, 50 'LAST DAY COULD NOT BE CALCULATED'.
          ENDIF.
        ELSE.
          WRITE:/ T009-PERIV, 10 SY-DATUM, 30 'FIRST DAY COULD NOT BE CALCULATED'.
        ENDIF.
      ELSE.
        WRITE:/ T009-PERIV, 10 'COULD NOT CONVERT TO DATE'.
      ENDIF.
ENDSELECT.
```

See Also

HR_PAYROLL_PERIOD_GET

DATUMSAUFBEREITUNG

Summary

Formats date per the user settings.

Parameters

```
EXPORTING
        IDATE        Date in the form YYYYMMDD
        IMONT        Date in the form YYYYMM
        IWEEK        Date in the form YYYYWW
IMPORTING
        MDAT4        Month four digit, example 01/98
        MDAT6        Month six digit, example 01/1998
        TDAT6        Day six digit, example 1/1/1998
        TDAT8        Day eight digit, example 01/01/1998
        WDAT4        Week four digit, example 05/98
        WDAT6        Week six digit, example 05/1998
```

Example

```
REPORT ZEXAMPLE.

DATA: TDAT6(10),
      TDAT8(10).

CALL FUNCTION 'DATUMSAUFBEREITUNG'
    EXPORTING
        IDATE          = SY-DATUM
```

```
     IMPORTING
          TDAT6            = TDAT6
          TDAT8            = TDAT8
     EXCEPTIONS
          DATFM_UNGUELTIG = 1
          DATUM_UNGUELTIG = 2
          OTHERS          = 3.

IF SY-SUBRC EQ 0.
  WRITE:/ 'YYYYMMDD', 15 'DMYYYY', 30 'DDMMYYYY'.
  ULINE.
  WRITE:/ SY-DATUM, 15 TDAT6, 30 TDAT8.
ELSE.
  WRITE:/ 'DATE IS INVALID'.
ENDIF.
```

DAY_ATTRIBUTES_GET

Summary

Returns information about a day.

Parameters

```
EXPORTING
        DATE_FROM                Start date range
        DATE_TO                  End date range
        LANGUAGE                 Language of texts
TABLES
        DAY_ATTRIBUTES           Attributes of each day in range
```

Example

```
REPORT ZEXAMPLE.

DATA: BEGIN OF DAY_ATTRIBUTES OCCURS 0.
      INCLUDE STRUCTURE SCSDAYATTR.
DATA: END OF DAY_ATTRIBUTES.

DATA V_FUTURE LIKE SY-DATUM.

V_FUTURE = SY-DATUM+30. "DATA FOR NEXT 30 DAYS

CALL FUNCTION 'DAY_ATTRIBUTES_GET'
     EXPORTING
          DATE_FROM                = SY-DATUM
          DATE_TO                  = V_FUTURE
          LANGUAGE                 = SY-LANGU
```

```
        TABLES
              DAY_ATTRIBUTES              = DAY_ATTRIBUTES
        EXCEPTIONS
              FACTORY_CALENDAR_NOT_FOUND = 1
              HOLIDAY_CALENDAR_NOT_FOUND = 2
              DATE_HAS_INVALID_FORMAT    = 3
              DATE_INCONSISTENCY         = 4
              OTHERS                     = 5.

IF SY-SUBRC EQ 0.
  WRITE:/ 'DATE', 15 'DATE STRING'.
  ULINE.
  LOOP AT DAY_ATTRIBUTES.
    WRITE:/ DAY_ATTRIBUTES-DATE, 15 DAY_ATTRIBUTES-DAY_STRING.
  ENDLOOP.
ELSE.
  WRITE:/ 'ERROR IN FUNCTION'.
ENDIF.
```

DAY_IN_WEEK

Summary

Returns the day of the week for a date.

Parameters

```
EXPORTING
      DATUM        Date
IMPORTING
      WOTNR        Number representing the day of the week
                   Value   Meaning
                   1       Monday
                   2       Tuesday
                   3       Wednesday
                   4       Thursday
                   5       Friday
                   6       Saturday
                   7       Sunday
```

Example

See DATE_GET_WEEK

See Also

DATE_COMPUTE_DAY, WEEKDAY_GET

DAYS_BETWEEN_TWO_DATES

Summary

Calculates the number of days between given dates.

Parameters

```
EXPORTING
      I_DATUM_BIS              End date
      I_DATUM_VON              Start date
IMPORTING
      E_TAGE                   Number of days in the time interval
```

Example

```
REPORT ZEXAMPLE.
DATA V_DIFF TYPE I.

PARAMETERS P_BIRTHD LIKE SY-DATUM.

CALL FUNCTION 'DAYS_BETWEEN_TWO_DATES'
    EXPORTING
        I_DATUM_BIS             = SY-DATUM
        I_DATUM_VON             = P_BIRTHD
    IMPORTING
        E_TAGE                  = V_DIFF
    EXCEPTIONS
        DAYS_METHOD_NOT_DEFINED = 1
        OTHERS                  = 2.

IF SY-SUBRC EQ 0.
  WRITE:/ V_DIFF, 'DAYS HAVE PASSED SINCE', P_BIRTHD.
ELSE.
  WRITE:/ 'ERROR IN CALCULATION'.
ENDIF.
```

See Also

COMPUTE_YEARS_BETWEEN_DATES, HR_HK_DIFF_BT_2_DATES,
HR_IE_NUM_PRSI_WEEKS, SD_DATETIME_DIFFERENCE,
SWI_DURATION_DETERMINE, FIMA_DAYS_AND_MONTHS_AND_YEARS

EASTER_GET_DATE

Summary

The date of Easter Sunday.

Parameters

```
EXPORTING
      YEAR                        Year for which Easter date is to be returned
IMPORTING
      EASTERDATE                  Date of Easter Sunday for inputted year
```

Example

```
REPORT ZEXAMPLE.

DATA DATE          LIKE SCAL-DATE.

PARAMETERS P_YEAR  LIKE SCAL-YEAR.

CALL FUNCTION 'EASTER_GET_DATE'
    EXPORTING
        YEAR         = P_YEAR
    IMPORTING
        EASTERDATE   = DATE
    EXCEPTIONS
        YEAR_INVALID = 1
        OTHERS       = 2.

IF SY-SUBRC EQ 0.
  WRITE:/ 'EASTER SUNDAY WILL FALL ON THE', DATE.
ELSE.
  WRITE:/ 'EASTER SUNDAY COULD NOT BE DETERMINED FOR', P_YEAR.
ENDIF.
```

FACTORYDATE_CONVERT_TO_DATE

Summary

Converts factory day into calendar date.

Description

In the factory calendar the working days are numbered sequentially from the first working day. The numbers of the working days are called factory dates.

Parameters

```
EXPORTING
      FACTORYDATE           Serial number of working day in factory calendar
      FACTORY_CALENDAR_ID   Factory calendar key
IMPORTING
      DATE                  Date format of the factory calendar date
```

Example

See DATE_CONVERT_TO_FACTORYDATE

See Also

DATE_CONVERT_TO_FACTORYDATE, DATE_CONVERT_TO_WORKINGDAY

FIMA_DAYS_AND_MONTHS_AND_YEARS

Summary

Calculates the difference between two dates.

Description

Returns the number of days, months, and years between two dates.

Parameters

```
EXPORTING
        I_DATE_FROM                 First date
        I_DATE_TO                   Last date
IMPORTING
        E_DAYS                      Difference in days
        E_MONTHS                    Difference in months
        E_YEARS                     Difference in years
```

Example

```
REPORT ZEXAMPLE.

DATA:  VDAYS     LIKE VTBBEWE-ATAGE,
       VMONTHS   LIKE VTBBEWE-ATAGE,
       VYEARS    LIKE VTBBEWE-ATAGE.

PARAMETERS:  DATEFROM   LIKE VTBBEWE-DBERVON,
             DATETO     LIKE VTBBEWE-DBERBIS DEFAULT SY-DATUM.

CALL FUNCTION 'FIMA_DAYS_AND_MONTHS_AND_YEARS'
     EXPORTING
          I_DATE_FROM = DATEFROM
          I_DATE_TO   = DATETO
     IMPORTING
          E_DAYS      = VDAYS
          E_MONTHS    = VMONTHS
          E_YEARS     = VYEARS.
```

```
WRITE: / 'DIFFERENCE IN DAYS:    ', VDAYS,
       / 'DIFFERENCE IN MONTHS: ', VMONTHS,
       / 'DIFFERENCE IN YEARS:   ', VYEARS.
```

See Also

COMPUTE_YEARS_BETWEEN_DATES, DAYS_BETWEEN_TWO_DATES,
HR_HK_DIFF_BT_2_DATES, HR_IE_NUM_PRSI_WEEKS, SD_DATETIME_DIFFERENCE,
SWI_DURATION_DETERMINE

FIRST_AND_LAST_DAY_IN_YEAR_GET

Summary

Gets first and last day of a period.

Parameters

```
EXPORTING
        I_GJAHR                   Year
        I_PERIV                   Period
IMPORTING
        E_FIRST_DAY               First day of period
        E_LAST_DAY                Last day of period
```

Example

```
REPORT ZEXAMPLE.

DATA: V_FIRST LIKE SY-DATUM,
      V_LAST LIKE SY-DATUM.

PARAMETERS:P_GJAHR LIKE T009B-BDATJ,
           P_PERIV LIKE T009B-PERIV.

CALL FUNCTION 'FIRST_AND_LAST_DAY_IN_YEAR_GET'
     EXPORTING
         I_GJAHR          = P_GJAHR
         I_PERIV          = P_PERIV
     IMPORTING
         E_FIRST_DAY      = V_FIRST
         E_LAST_DAY       = V_LAST
     EXCEPTIONS
         INPUT_FALSE      = 1
         T009_NOTFOUND    = 2
         T009B_NOTFOUND   = 3
         OTHERS           = 4.
```

```
IF SY-SUBRC EQ 0.
  WRITE: / P_GJAHR, '\', P_PERIV,
         / 'FIRST DAY:', V_FIRST,
         / 'LAST DAY:', V_LAST.
ELSE.
  WRITE:/ 'COULD NOT DETERMINE DATES FOR', P_GJAHR, P_PERIV.
ENDIF.
```

See Also

DATE_TO_PERIOD_CONVERT, LAST_DAY_IN_PERIOD_GET, PERIOD_DAY_DETERMINE

FIRST_DAY_IN_PERIOD_GET

Summary

Gets first day of the required period.

Parameters

```
EXPORTING
        I_GJAHR             Fiscal year
        I_PERIV             Period version
        I_POPER             Fiscal period
IMPORTING
        E_DATE              First calendar day in the fiscal period
```

Example

See DATE_TO_PERIOD_CONVERT

See Also

DATE_TO_PERIOD_CONVERT, LAST_DAY_IN_PERIOD_GET

GET_CURRENT_YEAR

Summary

Gets the current fiscal year for a company.

Parameters

```
EXPORTING
        BUKRS               Company code
        DATE                Date to find fiscal year for
```

```
IMPORTING
        CURRM                Current fiscal month
        CURRY                Current fiscal year
        PREVM                Previous fiscal month
        PREVY                Previous fiscal year
```

Example

```
REPORT ZEXAMPLE.

DATA:  CURRM  LIKE  BKPF-MONAT,
       CURRY  LIKE  BKPF-GJAHR,
       PREVM  LIKE  BKPF-MONAT,
       PREVY  LIKE  BKPF-GJAHR.

PARAMETERS P_BUKRS LIKE T001-BUKRS.

CALL FUNCTION 'GET_CURRENT_YEAR'
     EXPORTING
         BUKRS  = P_BUKRS
         DATE   = SY-DATUM
     IMPORTING
         CURRM  = CURRM
         CURRY  = CURRY
         PREVM  = PREVM
         PREVY  = PREVY.

WRITE:/ 'COMPANY', 20 'CURRENT MONTH YEAR', 60 'PREVIOUS MONTH YEAR'.
ULINE.
WRITE:/ P_BUKRS, 29 CURRM, 33 CURRY, 70 PREVM, 75 PREVY.
```

HOLIDAY_CHECK_AND_GET_INFO

Summary

Determines whether or not a date is a holiday.

Description

As several holidays can occur on one date, the attributes are passed in a table.

Parameters

```
EXPORTING
        DATE                 Date to be checked
        HOLIDAY_CALENDAR_ID  Public holiday calendar ID
IMPORTING
        HOLIDAY_FOUND        Flag whether the date is a public holiday
TABLES
        HOLIDAY_ATTRIBUTES   Attributes of the found public holidays
```

Example

```
REPORT ZEXAMPLE.
TABLES TFACD.

DATA: H_ID      LIKE  SCAL-FCALID,
      H_FOUND   LIKE  SCAL-INDICATOR.
DATA: BEGIN OF H_ATTRIBUTES OCCURS 0.
        INCLUDE STRUCTURE THOL.
DATA: END OF H_ATTRIBUTES.

PARAMETERS: H_DATE LIKE SCAL-DATE.

WRITE:/ 'HOLIDAY ID', 15 'DATE', 30 'DAYS TO EASTER'.
ULINE.

SELECT * FROM TFACD WHERE VJAHR GE H_DATE(4).
  CALL FUNCTION 'HOLIDAY_CHECK_AND_GET_INFO'
      EXPORTING
          DATE                        = H_DATE
          HOLIDAY_CALENDAR_ID         = TFACD-IDENT
      IMPORTING
          HOLIDAY_FOUND               = H_FOUND
      TABLES
          HOLIDAY_ATTRIBUTES          = H_ATTRIBUTES
      EXCEPTIONS
          HOLIDAY_CALENDAR_ID_MISSING = 1
          DATE_AFTER_RANGE            = 2
          DATE_BEFORE_RANGE           = 3
          DATE_INVALID                = 4
          HOLIDAY_CALENDAR_NOT_FOUND  = 5.

  IF SY-SUBRC EQ 0.
    IF H_FOUND EQ 'X'.
      LOOP AT H_ATTRIBUTES.
        WRITE:/ TFACD-IDENT, 15 H_DATE, 30 H_ATTRIBUTES-ABSTD.
      ENDLOOP.
      CLEAR: H_ATTRIBUTES, H_ATTRIBUTES[].
    ELSE.
      WRITE:/ TFACD-IDENT, 15 H_DATE, 'IS NOT A HOLIDAY'.
    ENDIF.
  ELSE.
    WRITE:/ TFACD-IDENT, 15 'COULD NOT CHECK DATE'.
  ENDIF.
ENDSELECT.
```

See Also

HOLIDAY_GET

HOLIDAY_GET

Summary

Returns all the holidays based upon a factory calendar.

Parameters

```
EXPORTING
        FACTORY_CALENDAR           Factory calendar ID
        DATE_FROM                  Starting date range
        DATE_TO                    Ending date range
IMPORTING
        RETURNCODE                 Return value
TABLES
        HOLIDAYS                   Table of holiday data
```

Example

```
REPORT ZEXAMPLE.
TABLES TFACD.
DATA: RETURNCODE   LIKE SY-SUBRC,
      HOLIDAYS     TYPE STANDARD TABLE OF ISCAL_DAY WITH HEADER LINE.

PARAMETER P_IDENT LIKE TFACD-IDENT.
WRITE: / 'HOLIDAYS IN 2003 FOR CALENDAR', P_IDENT.
ULINE.
WRITE: / 'CALENDAR ID', 15 'DATE', 30 'NAME OF HOLIDAY'.
ULINE.

CALL FUNCTION 'HOLIDAY_GET'
    EXPORTING
        FACTORY_CALENDAR              = P_IDENT
        DATE_FROM                     = '20030101'
        DATE_TO                       = '20031231'
    IMPORTING
        RETURNCODE                    = RETURNCODE
    TABLES
        HOLIDAYS                      = HOLIDAYS
    EXCEPTIONS
        FACTORY_CALENDAR_NOT_FOUND = 1
        HOLIDAY_CALENDAR_NOT_FOUND = 2
        DATE_HAS_INVALID_FORMAT    = 3
        DATE_INCONSISTENCY         = 4
        OTHERS                     = 5.

IF SY-SUBRC NE 0 OR RETURNCODE NE 0.
  WRITE:/ 'HOLIDAY CANNOT BE DETERMINED WITH CALENDER', P_IDENT.
ELSE.
  LOOP AT HOLIDAYS.
    WRITE:/ P_IDENT, 15 HOLIDAYS-DATE, 30 HOLIDAYS-TXT_LONG.
  ENDLOOP.
ENDIF.
```

See Also

HOLIDAY_CHECK_AND_GET_INFO

HR_BEN_GET_DATE_INTERSECTION

Summary

Determines if a date range overlaps another date range.

Description

In the illustration, there is a flight available between 2003.01.01 and 2003.01.04 inclusive, but not between 2003.01.05 and 2003.01.06.

Parameters

```
EXPORTING
        BEGDA1                  First date in range 1
        ENDDA1                  Last date in range 1
        BEGDA2                  First date in range 2
        ENDDA2                  Last date in range 2
        REACTION                Message handling - display error message if any of these occur:
                                Value     Meaning
                                ' '       Record error in error table only (default)
                                E         Error
                                W         Warning
                                I         Information
                                S         Success
                                A         Abort
                                N         No log
                                L         Log
IMPORTING
        INTERSECTION_BEGDA Start date of intersection
        INTERSECTION_ENDDA End date of intersection
        SUBRC              Return value from function
TABLES
        ERROR_TABLE        Error messages
```

Example

```
REPORT ZEXAMPLE.
DATA: V_BEGDATE  LIKE  SY-DATUM,
      V_ENDDATE  LIKE  SY-DATUM,
      V_DEPART1  LIKE  SY-DATUM,  "EARLIEST FLIGHT DEPARTURE DATE
      V_DEPART2  LIKE  SY-DATUM,  "LATEST FLIGHT DEPARTURE DATE
      V_SUBRC    LIKE  SY-SUBRC,
      P_MONTH(2),
      IERRTAB    LIKE  RPBENERR OCCURS 0 WITH HEADER LINE.

*  FILL TABLE WITH FLIGHT DEPARTURE INFORMATION FOR 2003
DATA: BEGIN OF FLIGHT_DEPARTS OCCURS 0,
        MONTH(2),
        DEPART1  LIKE SY-DATUM,   "EARLIEST FLIGHT DEPARTURE DATE
```

```
            DEPART2  LIKE SY-DATUM,   "LATEST FLIGHT DEPARTURE DATE
END OF FLIGHT_DEPARTS.

*  CHECK IF ANY FLIGHTS BETWEEN DATES
PARAMETERS:
      P_DEPAR1 LIKE SY-DATUM DEFAULT '20030101', "EARLIEST DEPART DATE (FOR PASSENGER)
      P_DEPAR2 LIKE SY-DATUM DEFAULT '20030104'. "LATEST DEPART DATE (FOR PASSENGER)

P_MONTH = P_DEPAR1+4.
PERFORM FILL_FLIGHT_DEPARTS.  "FILL WITH SAMPLE DATA

PERFORM GET_FLIGHT_DATES  USING P_MONTH
                          CHANGING V_DEPART1
                                   V_DEPART2.

IF V_DEPART1 IS INITIAL OR V_DEPART2 IS INITIAL.
  WRITE:/ 'NO FLIGHTS DURING MONTH', P_MONTH.
ELSE.
  CALL FUNCTION 'HR_BEN_GET_DATE_INTERSECTION'
       EXPORTING
            BEGDA1              = V_DEPART1
            ENDDA1              = V_DEPART2
            BEGDA2              = P_DEPAR1
            ENDDA2              = P_DEPAR2
            REACTION            = ' '
       IMPORTING
            INTERSECTION_BEGDA  = V_BEGDATE
            INTERSECTION_ENDDA  = V_ENDDATE
            SUBRC               = V_SUBRC
       TABLES
            ERROR_TABLE         = IERRTAB.

  IF SY-SUBRC EQ 0.
    IF V_BEGDATE IS INITIAL.
      WRITE: 'NO FLIGHTS AVAILABLE BETWEEN  REQUESTED DATES'.
    ELSE.
      WRITE: 'A FLIGHT IS AVAILABLE BETWEEN', V_BEGDATE, 'AND',V_ENDDATE.
    ENDIF.
  ENDIF.
ENDIF.

*————————————————————————————————-*
* FORM FILL_FLIGHT_DEPARTS         *
*————————————————————————————————-*
FORM FILL_FLIGHT_DEPARTS.
CLEAR: FLIGHT_DEPARTS, FLIGHT_DEPARTS[].

FLIGHT_DEPARTS-MONTH = '01'.
FLIGHT_DEPARTS-DEPART1 = '20030101'.
FLIGHT_DEPARTS-DEPART2 = '20030117'.

APPEND FLIGHT_DEPARTS.
FLIGHT_DEPARTS-MONTH = '04'.
FLIGHT_DEPARTS-DEPART1 = '20030407'.
FLIGHT_DEPARTS-DEPART2 = '20030417'.
```

```
APPEND FLIGHT_DEPARTS.
FLIGHT_DEPARTS-MONTH   = '05'.
FLIGHT_DEPARTS-DEPART1 = '20030515'.
FLIGHT_DEPARTS-DEPART2 = '20030520'.

APPEND FLIGHT_DEPARTS.
FLIGHT_DEPARTS-MONT  H = '10'.
FLIGHT_DEPARTS-DEPART1 = '20031021'.
FLIGHT_DEPARTS-DEPART2 = '20031031'.

APPEND FLIGHT_DEPARTS.
FLIGHT_DEPARTS-MONTH   = '12'.
FLIGHT_DEPARTS-DEPART1 = '20031201'.
FLIGHT_DEPARTS-DEPART2 = '20031231'.
APPEND FLIGHT_DEPARTS.
ENDFORM.

*─────────────────────────────── - *
* FORM GET_FLIGHT_DATES             *
*─────────────────────────────── - *
* -> P_MONTH                        *
* -> V_DEPART1                      *
* -> V_DEPART2                      *
*─────────────────────────────── - *
FORM GET_FLIGHT_DATES USING P_MONTH
                      CHANGING  V_DEPART1
                                V_DEPART2.

  LOOP AT FLIGHT_DEPARTS WHERE MONTH EQ P_MONTH.
    V_DEPART1 = FLIGHT_DEPARTS-DEPART1.
    V_DEPART2 = FLIGHT_DEPARTS-DEPART2.
  ENDLOOP.
ENDFORM.
```

HR_GET_LEAVE_DATA

Summary

Gets all leave information.

Description

Information returned includes leave entitlement and used/paid holidays.

Parameters

```
EXPORTING
        PERNR              Personnel number
        UBEGD              Start of deduction period
        UENDD              End of deduction period
```

```
        BEGDA_0005         From date (infotype 0005)
        ENDDA_0005         To date (infotype 0005)
        SEL_MOD            Selection mode:
                           Value      Meaning
                           S          Cumulate values for all leave years
                           B          Calculate values for individual leave year
        OBJPS_0005         Object identification
IMPORTING
        ENTITLE            Entitlement up to key date (cumulated)
        ACCOUNT            Accounted up to key date (cumulated)
        ORDERED            Requested up to key date (cumulated)
        REDUCED            Compensated up to key date (cumulated)
TABLES
        URART_SEL          Selection options for leave types
```

Example

```
REPORT ZEXAMPLE.
INFOTYPES 0005.
TYPE-POOLS TPTIM.
SELECT-OPTIONS URSEL FOR P0005-UAR01.
PARAMETERS: PERNR   LIKE   PERNR-PERNR,
            UBEGD   LIKE   P0005-BEGDA DEFAULT '20030101',
            UENDD   LIKE   P0005-ENDDA DEFAULT SY-DATUM,
            BEGDA   LIKE   P0005-BEGDA DEFAULT '20030101',
            ENDDA   LIKE   P0005-ENDDA DEFAULT '99991231',
            SEL_M   DEFAULT 'S',
            OBJPS   LIKE   P0005-OBJPS.

DATA: ENTITLE TYPE TPTIM_ENTITLE,
      ACCOUNT TYPE TPTIM_ACCOUNT,
      ORDERED TYPE TPTIM_ORDERED,
      REDUCED TYPE TPTIM_REDUCE.

CALL FUNCTION 'HR_GET_LEAVE_DATA'
    EXPORTING
        PERNR                    = PERNR
        UBEGD                    = UBEGD
        UENDD                    = UENDD
        BEGDA_0005               = BEGDA
        ENDDA_0005               = ENDDA
        SEL_MOD                  = SEL_M
        OBJPS_0005               = OBJPS
    IMPORTING
        ENTITLE                  = ENTITLE
        ACCOUNT                  = ACCOUNT
        ORDERED                  = ORDERED
        REDUCED                  = REDUCED
    TABLES
        URART_SEL                = URSEL
    EXCEPTIONS
        INFTY_0005_NOT_DEFINED   = 1
        INFTY_0083_NOT_DEFINED   = 2
```

```
                   MISSING_AUTHORITY          = 3
                   OLD_NE_NEW_PC_VERSION_NR = 4
                   OTHERS                     = 5.

IF SY-SUBRC NE 0.
  WRITE: 'ERROR READING DATA FOR', PERNR.
ELSE.
  WRITE:/'PERSONNEL', 15 'ENTITLEMENT', 30 'ACCOUNTED', 45 'REQUESTED',
         60 'COMPENSATED', 75 'LEAVE TYPES'.
  ULINE.
  WRITE:/ PERNR, 15 ENTITLE, 30 ACCOUNT, 45 ORDERED, 60 REDUCED.
  LOOP AT URSEL.
    WRITE:/75 URSEL-SIGN,
           77 URSEL-OPTION,
           79 URSEL-LOW,
           82 URSEL-HIGH.
  ENDLOOP.
ENDIF.
```

HR_HK_DIFF_BT_2_DATES

Summary

Calculates the days, months and years between two dates.

Parameters

```
EXPORTING
        DATE1                Begin date
        DATE2                End date
        OUTPUT_FORMAT        Format to display the output
                             Value   Meaning
                             01      Years with decimals (default)
                             02      Days
                             03      Days and years
                             04      Months with decimals
                             05      Years, months, and days
                             06      Years and months
                             07      Anniversary years
                             08      Anniversary months
IMPORTING
        YEARS                Years between the begin and end date
        MONTHS               Months between the begin and end date
        DAYS                 Days between the begin and end date
```

Example

```
REPORT ZEXAMPLE.
DATA: V_YEARS  LIKE PO347-SCRYY,
      V_MONTHS LIKE PO347-SCRMM,
      V_DAYS   LIKE PO347-SCRDD.
```

```
PARAMETERS: P_SDATE  LIKE SY-DATUM,
            P_EDATE  LIKE SY-DATUM.

CALL FUNCTION 'HR_HK_DIFF_BT_2_DATES'
     EXPORTING
             DATE1                    = P_EDATE
             DATE2                    = P_SDATE
             OUTPUT_FORMAT            = '05'
     IMPORTING
             YEARS                    = V_YEARS
             MONTHS                   = V_MONTHS
             DAYS                     = V_DAYS
     EXCEPTIONS
             INVALID_DATES_SPECIFIED  = 1
             OTHERS                   = 2.

IF SY-SUBRC EQ 0.
     WRITE:/ V_YEARS, 'YEARS,', V_MONTHS, 'MONTHS, AND', V_DAYS, 'DAYS HAVE PASSED'.
ELSE.
     WRITE:/ 'COULD NOT CALCULATE THE DIFFERENCE BETWEEN', P_SDATE, 'AND', P_EDATE.
ENDIF.
```

See Also

COMPUTE_YEARS_BETWEEN_DATES, DAYS_BETWEEN_TWO_DATES,
HR_IE_NUM_PRSI_WEEKS, SD_DATETIME_DIFFERENCE,
SWI_DURATION_DETERMINE, FIMA_DAYS_AND_MONTHS_AND_YEARS

HR_IE_NUM_PRSI_WEEKS

Summary

Returns the number of weeks between two dates.

Description

Can be used to check if any PRSI contributions belong to previous tax year and should not be included in the current tax year.

Parameters

```
EXPORTING
        TAX_YEAR_BEGIN          Tax year
        PERIOD_BEGIN            First date of period in tax year
        PERIOD_END             Last date of period in tax year
IMPORTING
        NUM_WEEKS              Number of weeks between dates
```

Example

```
REPORT ZEXAMPLE.
DATA: NUM_WEEKS LIKE PC26W-WEEKS,
      V_SPERIOD LIKE SY-DATUM,
      V_EPERIOD LIKE SY-DATUM.

PARAMETERS: P_TYEAR LIKE SY-DATUM.

CONCATENATE P_TYEAR(4)'0101' INTO V_SPERIOD.
CONCATENATE P_TYEAR(4)'1231' INTO V_EPERIOD.

CALL FUNCTION 'HR_IE_NUM_PRSI_WEEKS'
    EXPORTING
        TAX_YEAR_BEGIN       = P_TYEAR
        PERIOD_BEGIN         = V_SPERIOD
        PERIOD_END           = V_EPERIOD
    IMPORTING
        NUM_WEEKS            = NUM_WEEKS
    EXCEPTIONS
        END_LT_START         = 1
        END_LT_YEAR_START    = 2
        START_LT_YEAR_START  = 3
        OTHERS               = 4.

IF SY-SUBRC EQ 0.
  WRITE:/ 'THERE ARE', NUM_WEEKS, 'WEEKS BETWEEN', V_SPERIOD, 'AND', V_EPERIOD.
ELSE.
  WRITE:/ 'COULD NOT CALCULATE THE NUMBER OF WEEKS BETWEEN', V_SPERIOD, 'AND', V_EPERIOD.
ENDIF.
```

See Also

COMPUTE_YEARS_BETWEEN_DATES, DAYS_BETWEEN_TWO_DATES,
HR_HK_DIFF_BT_2_DATES, HR_IE_NUM_PRSI_WEEKS,
SD_DATETIME_DIFFERENCE, SWI_DURATION_DETERMINE,
FIMA_DAYS_AND_MONTHS_AND_YEARS

HR_PAYROLL_PERIODS_GET

Summary

Gets the payroll period for a particular date.

Parameters

```
EXPORTING
        GET_BEGDA                 Start date of payroll period
        GET_ENDDA                 End date of payroll period
TABLES
        GET_PERIODS               Table of all payroll periods
```

Example

```
REPORT ZEXAMPLE.
DATA:   IPERIODS TYPE T549Q OCCURS 0 WITH HEADER LINE,
ITIME     TYPE PC2BF OCCURS 0 WITH HEADER LINE,
        V_IFTYP(10).

PARAMETERS: P_PERNR LIKE PERNR-PERNR,
            P_SDATE LIKE SY-DATUM,
            P_EDATE LIKE SY-DATUM.

WRITE:/ 'PERSONNEL', 20 'PERIOD START', 40 'PERIOD END', 60 'WAGE DATE',
        80 'ABSENT\WORK'.
ULINE.
CALL FUNCTION 'HR_PAYROLL_PERIODS_GET'
    EXPORTING
         GET_BEGDA      = P_SDATE
         GET_ENDDA      = P_EDATE
    TABLES
         GET_PERIODS    = IPERIODS
    EXCEPTIONS
         NO_PERIOD_FOUND = 1
         NO_VALID_PERMO  = 2.

IF SY-SUBRC EQ 0.
  LOOP AT IPERIODS.
    CALL FUNCTION 'HR_TIME_RESULTS_GET'
        EXPORTING
             GET_PERNR           = P_PERNR
             GET_PABRJ           = IPERIODS-PABRJ
             GET_PABRP           = IPERIODS-PABRP
        TABLES
             GET_ZL              = ITIME
        EXCEPTIONS
             NO_PERIOD_SPECIFIED   = 1
             WRONG_CLUSTER_VERSION = 2
             NO_READ_AUTHORITY     = 3
             CLUSTER_ARCHIVED      = 4
             TECHNICAL_ERROR       = 5.

    IF SY-SUBRC EQ 0.
      LOOP AT ITIME.
        CASE ITIME-IFTYP.
          WHEN 'A'.
            V_IFTYP = 'ABSENT'.
          WHEN 'S'.
            V_IFTYP = 'AT WORK'.
        ENDCASE.
        WRITE:/ P_PERNR, 20 IPERIODS-BEGDA, 40 IPERIODS-ENDDA, 60 ITIME-DATUM,
                80 V_IFTYP.
      ENDLOOP.
    ELSE.
      WRITE:/ P_PERNR, 20 IPERIODS-BEGDA, 40 IPERIODS-ENDDA,
              60 'COULD NOT GET PAYROLL RESULTS'.
```

```
    ENDIF.
  ENDLOOP.
ELSE.
  WRITE:/ P_PERNR, 20 'COULD NOT GET PAYROLL PERIODS'.
ENDIF.
```

See Also

HR_TIME_RESULTS_GET, DATE_TO_PERIOD_CONVERT

HR_TIME_RESULTS_GET

Summary

Gets the time results for a payroll period.

Parameters

```
EXPORTING
        GET_PERNR               Personnel number
        GET_PABRJ               Payroll year
        GET_PABRP               Payroll period
TABLES
        GET_WPBP                Work centre data
        GET_ALP                 Alternative payment
        GET_AB                  Absences
        GET_SKO                 Time transfers
        GET_VERT                Substitutions
        GET_SALDO               Period balances
        GET_ZES                 Time accounts
        GET_ZKO                 Time quotas
        GET_FEHLER              Error
        GET_ABWKONTI            Absence quotas
        GET_PSP                 Personal work schedule
        GET_ANWKONTI            Attendance quotas
        GET_MEHR                Overtime
        GET_ANWES               Attendance
        GET_RUFB                On call data
        GET_ZL                  Time wage types
        GET_URLAN               Automatic leave accrual
        GET_VS                  Variable balances
        GET_CVS                 Cumulated variable balances
        GET_C1                  Cost distribution
        GET_AT                  Link pairs/time tickets
        GET_PT                  Time pairs
        GET_WST                 Time tickets, other documents
        GET_CWST                Cumulated time tickets
```

Example

See HR_PAYROLL_PERIODS_GET

See Also

HR_PAYROLL_PERIODS_GET

LAST_DAY_IN_PERIOD_GET

Summary

Returns the last day of the required period.

Parameters

```
EXPORTING
      I_GJAHR           Fiscal year
      I_PERIV           Period version
      I_POPER           Fiscal period
IMPORTING
      E_DATE            Last calendar day in the fiscal period
```

Example

See DATE_TO_PERIOD_CONVERT

See Also

DATE_TO_PERIOD_CONVERT, FIRST_DAY_IN_PERIOD_GET

MONTH_NAMES_GET

Summary

Returns the names of the months.

Description

The names can be in multiple languages.

Parameters

```
EXPORTING
      LANGUAGE                  Language of the month names
TABLES
      MONTH_NAMES               Table holding the names of the month
```

Example

```
REPORT ZEXAMPLE.

DATA: BEGIN OF MONTH_NAMES OCCURS 0.
        INCLUDE STRUCTURE T247.
DATA: END OF MONTH_NAMES.

DATA: V_LASTDAY      LIKE SY-DATUM,
      V_NEXTMONTH    LIKE SY-DATUM,
      V_DAYTXT(15).

CALL FUNCTION 'MONTH_NAMES_GET'
    EXPORTING
        LANGUAGE              = SY-LANGU
    TABLES
        MONTH_NAMES           = MONTH_NAMES
    EXCEPTIONS
        MONTH_NAMES_NOT_FOUND = 1
        OTHERS                = 2.

CALL FUNCTION 'RP_LAST_DAY_OF_MONTHS'
    EXPORTING
        DAY_IN            = SY-DATUM
    IMPORTING
        LAST_DAY_OF_MONTH = V_LASTDAY.

CALL FUNCTION 'RH_GET_DATE_DAYNAME'
    EXPORTING
        LANGU  = SY-LANGU
        DATE   = V_LASTDAY
    IMPORTING
        DAYTXT = V_DAYTXT.

READ TABLE MONTH_NAMES WITH KEY MNR = SY-DATUM+4(2).
WRITE:/'THE LAST DAY OF', MONTH_NAMES-LTX, 'IS THE', V_LASTDAY, 'WHICH IS A', V_DAYTXT.

CALL FUNCTION 'MONTH_PLUS_DETERMINE'
    EXPORTING
        MONTHS  = '1'
        OLDDATE = SY-DATUM
    IMPORTING
        NEWDATE = V_NEXTMONTH.

READ TABLE MONTH_NAMES WITH KEY MNR = V_NEXTMONTH+4(2).
WRITE:/'NEXT MONTH IS', MONTH_NAMES-LTX.

CALL FUNCTION 'RE_ADD_MONTH_TO_DATE'
    EXPORTING
        MONTHS  = '1'
        OLDDATE = V_NEXTMONTH
    IMPORTING
        NEWDATE = V_NEXTMONTH.

READ TABLE MONTH_NAMES WITH KEY MNR = V_NEXTMONTH+4(2).
WRITE:/'THE MONTH AFTER THAT IS', MONTH_NAMES-LTX.
```

MONTH_PLUS_DETERMINE

Summary

Adds or subtracts months from a date.

Description

Enters a negative value for the 'months' parameter to subtract a month.

Parameters

```
EXPORTING
      MONTHS                    Number of months to add or subtract
      OLDDATE                   Initial date
IMPORTING
      NEWDATE                   New date after adding\subtracting months
```

Example

See MONTH_NAMES_GET

See Also

DATE_IN_FUTURE, MONTH_PLUS_DETERMINE, RE_ADD_MONTH_TO_DATE, RP_CALC_DATE_IN_INTERVAL, SUBTRACT_TIME_FROM_DATE

PERIOD_DAY_DETERMINE

Summary

Returns start and finish date for a given year and period.

Parameters

```
EXPORTING
      I_GJAHR                   Fiscal year
      I_MONAT                   Posting period
      I_PERIV                   Period version
IMPORTING
      E_FDAY                    First period day
      E_LDAY                    Last period day
```

Example

```
REPORT ZEXAMPLE.

TABLES: T009.
DATA: V_FDAY LIKE SY-DATUM, V_LDAY LIKE SY-DATUM.

WRITE:/ 'Period', 10 'First Day', 30 'Last Day'.
ULINE.
SELECT * FROM T009.
  CALL FUNCTION 'PERIOD_DAY_DETERMINE'
       EXPORTING
            I_GJAHR              = SY-DATUM(4)
            I_MONAT              = SY-DATUM+4(2)
            I_PERIV              = T009-PERIV
       IMPORTING
            E_FDAY               = V_FDAY
            E_LDAY               = V_LDAY
       EXCEPTIONS
            ERROR_PERIOD         = 1
            ERROR_PERIOD_VERSION = 2
            FIRSTDAY_NOT_DEFINED = 3
            PERIOD_NOT_DEFINED   = 4
            YEAR_INVALID         = 5
            OTHERS               = 6.
  IF SY-SUBRC EQ 0.
    WRITE:/ T009-PERIV, 10 V_FDAY, 30 V_LDAY.
  ELSE.
    WRITE:/ T009-PERIV, 10 'Could not determine dates'.
  ENDIF.
ENDSELECT.
```

See Also

FIRST_AND_LAST_DAY_IN_YEAR_GET

RE_ADD_MONTH_TO_DATE

Summary

Calculates a new month.

Description

Adds (positive value) and subtracts (negative value).

Parameters

```
EXPORTING
        MONTHS                   Number of months to add
        OLDDATE                  Current date
```

```
IMPORTING
        NEWDATE                      New date after months added
```

Example

See MONTH_NAMES_GET

See Also

DATE_IN_FUTURE, MONTH_PLUS_DETERMINE, RE_ADD_MONTH_TO_DATE, RP_CALC_DATE_IN_INTERVAL, SUBTRACT_TIME_FROM_DATE

RH_GET_DATE_DAYNAME

Summary

Returns the day based on the input date.

Parameters

```
EXPORTING
        LANGU                        Language of the day
        DATE                         Date
        CALID                        Factory calendar (optional)
IMPORTING
        DAYNR                        Number of the day
        DAYTXT                       Weekday name (in Language)
        DAYFREE                      Flag, if holiday according to factory calendar
```

Example

See MONTH_NAMES_GET

See Also

WEEKDAY_GET

RKE_ADD_TO_PERIOD

Summary

Calculates period from any period.

Parameters

```
EXPORTING
        DELTA                   Number of periods that are added
        PERIO                   Period in the format YYYYPPP
        PERIV                   Period version
IMPORTING
        PERIO                   New period in the format YYYYPPP
```

Example

See DATE_TO_PERIOD_CONVERT

RKE_TIMESTAMP_CONVERT_INPUT

Summary

Converts display to TIMESTAMP fields.

Description

Can be used to generate a timestamp.

Parameters

```
EXPORTING
        I_DATE                  Date
        I_DAYST                 Active daylight savings time indicator
        I_TIME                  Time
        I_TZONE                 Time difference to GMT in seconds
IMPORTING
        E_TIMESTMP              Point in time in GMT (seconds since 1/1/1970)
```

Example

```
REPORT ZEXAMPLE.

DATA: BIS_TIMESTMP LIKE ZABP_DLP-TIMESTAMP,
      RANDOM_VAR   TYPE SY-UZEIT,
      E_DATE       LIKE SY-DATUM,
      E_TIME       LIKE SY-UZEIT.

DO 10 TIMES.
  RANDOM_VAR = SY-UZEIT+SY-INDEX.
```

```
CALL FUNCTION 'RKE_TIMESTAMP_CONVERT_INPUT'
     EXPORTING
          I_DAT    = SY-DATUM
          I_DAYS   = SY-DAYST
          I_TIM    = RANDOM_VAR
          I_TZON   = SY-TZONE
     IMPORTING
          E_TIMESTM = BIS_TIMESTMP.

WRITE:/ 'GENERATED TIMESTAMP:', BIS_TIMESTMP.

CALL FUNCTION 'RKE_TIMESTAMP_CONVERT_OUTPUT'
     EXPORTING
          I_DAYST    = SY-DAYST
          I_TIMESTMP = BIS_TIMESTMP
          I_TZONE    = SY-TZONE
     IMPORTING
          E_DATE     = E_DATE
          E_TIME     = E_TIME.

  WRITE:/ 'TIMESTAMP', BIS_TIMESTMP, 'WAS GENERATED FROM', E_DATE, E_TIME.
  ULINE.
ENDDO.
```

See Also

RKE_TIMESTAMP_CONVERT_OUTPUT

RKE_TIMESTAMP_CONVERT_OUTPUT

Summary

Converts TIMESTAMP field for display.

Parameters

```
EXPORTING
     I_DAYST                Active daylight savings time indicator
     I_TIMESTMP             Point in time in GMT (seconds since 1/1/1970)
     I_TZONE                Time difference to GMT in seconds
IMPORTING
     E_DATE                 Date
     E_TIME                 Time
```


Example

See RKE_TIMESTAMP_CONVERT_INPUT

See Also

RKE_TIMESTAMP_CONVERT_INPUT

RP_CALC_DATE_IN_INTERVAL

Summary

Adds or subtracts years/months/days to/from a date.

Parameters

```
EXPORTING
        DATE            Initial date
        DAYS            Number of days to add/subtract
        MONTHS          Number of months to add/subtract
        SIGNUM          Flag to Add or subtract
                        Value     Meaning
                        +         Add values to DATE (default)
                        -         Subtract values from DATE
        YEARS           Number of years to add/subtract
IMPORTING
        CALC_DATE       Date after calculations
```

Example

See RP_CHECK_DATE

See Also

DATE_IN_FUTURE, MONTH_PLUS_DETERMINE, RE_ADD_MONTH_TO_DATE,
SUBTRACT_TIME_FROM_DATE

RP_CHECK_DATE

Summary

Checks if the value of a field is in date format.

Parameters

```
EXPORTING
        DATE                Date to check for validity
```

Example

```
REPORT ZEXAMPLE.
DATA V_SIGN.

PARAMETERS:   P_DATE    LIKE SY-DATUM DEFAULT SY-DATUM,
              P_DAYS    LIKE T5A4A-DLYDY DEFAULT 0,
              P_MONTHS  LIKE T5A4A-DLYMO DEFAULT 0,
              P_YEARS   LIKE T5A4A-DLYYR DEFAULT 0,
              P_PLUS    RADIOBUTTON GROUP RADI,
              P_MINUS   RADIOBUTTON GROUP RADI.

IF P_PLUS EQ 'X'.
  V_SIGN = '+'.
ELSE.
  V_SIGN = '-'.
ENDIF.

CALL FUNCTION 'RP_CHECK_DATE'
    EXPORTING
         DATE         = P_DATE
    EXCEPTIONS
         DATE_INVALID = 1
         OTHERS       = 2.

IF SY-SUBRC EQ 0.
  WRITE:/ P_DATE, 'IS A VALID DATE'.

CALL FUNCTION 'RP_CALC_DATE_IN_INTERVAL'
    EXPORTING
         DATE      = P_DATE
         DAYS      = P_DAYS
         MONTHS    = P_MONTHS
         SIGNUM    = V_SIGN
         YEARS     = P_YEARS
    IMPORTING
         CALC_DATE = P_DATE.

  WRITE:/ 'THE NEW DATE IS:', P_DATE.
ELSE.
  WRITE:/ P_DATE, 'IS AN INVALID DATE'.
ENDIF.
```

See Also

DATE_CHECK_PLAUSIBILITY

RP_LAST_DAY_OF_MONTHS

Summary

Gets the last day of the month.

Parameters

```
EXPORTING
        DAY_IN                    Date
IMPORTING
        LAST_DAY_OF_MONTH         Date of last day of the month
```

Example

See MONTH_NAMES_GET

SD_DATETIME_DIFFERENCE

Summary

Returns the difference in days and time for two dates.

Parameters

```
EXPORTING
        DATE1                     First date
        TIME1                     First time
        DATE2                     Second date
        TIME2                     Second time
IMPORTING
        DATEDIFF                  Full day difference between first date and second date
        TIMEDIFF                  Difference in hours between first time and second time
        EARLIEST                  Index of the earlier time ("1", "2" or "0")
```

Example

```
REPORT ZEXAMPLE LINE-SIZE 120.
DATA: DDIFF  TYPE P,
      TDIFF  TYPE P,
      EDATE.

PARAMETERS: P_STARTD  LIKE SY-DATUM DEFAULT SY-DATUM,
            P_STARTT  LIKE SY-UZEIT DEFAULT SY-UZEIT,
            P_ENDD    LIKE SY-DATUM,
            P_ENDT    LIKE SY-UZEIT.

WRITE:/ 'START DATE', 15 'START TIME', 30 'END DATE', 45 'END TIME', 60 'DAYS DIFF', 75
        'HOURS DIFF', 90 'EARLIEST'.
ULINE.

CALL FUNCTION 'SD_DATETIME_DIFFERENCE'
    EXPORTING
        DATE1             = P_STARTD
        TIME1             = P_STARTT
```

```
        DATE2            = P_ENDD
        TIME2            = P_ENDT
    IMPORTING
        DATEDIFF         = DDIFF
        TIMEDIFF         = TDIFF
        EARLIEST         = EDATE
    EXCEPTIONS
        INVALID_DATETIME = 1
        OTHERS           = 2.


IF SY-SUBRC EQ 0.
  WRITE:/ P_STARTD, 15 P_STARTT, 30 P_ENDD, 45 P_ENDT, 50 DDIFF, 65 TDIFF, 95 EDATE.
ELSE.
  WRITE:/ 'COULD NOT CALCULATE THE DIFFERENCE'.
ENDIF.
```

SUBTRACT_TIME_FROM_DATE

Summary

Subtracts months/days/years from a given date.

Parameters

```
EXPORTING
        I_IDATE          Initial date
        I_TIME           Time to subtract
        I_IPRKZ          Unit of time
                         Value     Meaning
                         D         Day
                         M         Month
                         W         Week
                         Y         Year
IMPORTING
        O_IDATE          Date after calculations
```

Example

```
REPORT ZEXAMPLE.

DATA: V_DATE  LIKE SY-DATUM,
      V_IPRKZ LIKE MARA-IPRKZ.

PARAMETERS:  P_DATE   LIKE SY-DATUM,
             P_TIME   LIKE MARA-MHDHB,
             P_DAY    RADIOBUTTON GROUP RADI,
             P_MONTH  RADIOBUTTON GROUP RADI,
```

```
              P_WEEK   RADIOBUTTON GROUP RADI,
              P_YEAR   RADIOBUTTON GROUP RADI.

IF P_DAY EQ 'X'.
  V_IPRKZ = 'D'.
ELSEIF P_MONTH EQ 'X'.
  V_IPRKZ = 'M'.
ELSEIF P_WEEK EQ 'X'.
  V_IPRKZ = 'W'.
ELSEIF P_YEAR EQ 'X'.
  V_IPRKZ = 'Y'.
ENDIF.

*  CONVERT TO INTERNAL REPRESENTATION
CALL FUNCTION 'CONVERSION_EXIT_PERKZ_INPUT'
     EXPORTING
         INPUT                 = V_IPRKZ
     IMPORTING
         OUTPUT                = V_IPRKZ

CALL FUNCTION 'SUBTRACT_TIME_FROM_DATE'
     EXPORTING
         I_IDATE               = P_DATE
         I_TIME                = P_TIME
         I_IPRKZ               = V_IPRKZ
     IMPORTING
         O_IDATE               = V_DATE
     EXCEPTIONS
         INVALID_PERIOD        = 1
         INVALID_ROUND_UP_RULE = 2
         INTERNAL_ERROR        = 3
         OTHERS                = 4.

IF SY-SUBRC EQ 0.
  WRITE:/ 'NEW DATE:', V_DATE.
ELSE.
  WRITE:/ 'COULD NOT CALCULATE THE DATE'.
ENDIF.
```

See Also

ADD_TIME_TO_DATE, COMPUTE_YEARS_BETWEEN_DATES,
DAYS_BETWEEN_TWO_DATES, HR_HK_DIFF_BT_2_DATES,
HR_IE_NUM_PRSI_WEEKS, RP_CALC_DATE_IN_INTERVAL,
SD_DATETIME_DIFFERENCE, SWI_DURATION_DETERMINE,
FIMA_DAYS_AND_MONTHS_AND_YEARS

SWI_DURATION_DETERMINE

Summary

The time between two events in seconds.

Parameters

```
EXPORTING
      START_DATE            Initial date of event
      END_DATE              Final date of event
      START_TIME            Initial time of event
      END_TIME              Final time of event
IMPORTING
      DURATION              Duration of event in seconds
```

Example

See UNIT_CONVERSION_SIMPLE

See Also

COMPUTE_YEARS_BETWEEN_DATES, DAYS_BETWEEN_TWO_DATES,
HR_HK_DIFF_BT_2_DATES, HR_IE_NUM_PRSI_WEEKS,
SD_DATETIME_DIFFERENCE, SWI_DURATION_DETERMINE,
FIMA_DAYS_AND_MONTHS_AND_YEARS

WDKAL_DATE_ADD_FKDAYS

Summary

Number of working days in a date range.

Description

Number of working days in a factory calendar between two dates.

Parameters

```
EXPORTING
      I_DATE                Input date
      I_FKDAY               Number of working days
      I_FABKL               Factory calendar key
IMPORTING
      E_DATE                Working day date = input date + working days
      E_FKDAY               Working days
```

Example

```
REPORT ZEXAMPLE.

TABLES TFACD.
```

```
DATA: E_DATE LIKE SY-DATLO, E_FKDAY LIKE MDCAL-FKDAY.

WRITE:/ 'FACTORY ID', 15 'LAST WORKING DAY', 40 'DAY'.
ULINE.
LOOP AT TFACD.
  CALL FUNCTION 'WDKAL_DATE_ADD_FKDAYS'
       EXPORTING
               I_DATE  = SY-DATUM
               I_FKDAY = 0
               I_FABKL = TFACD-IDENT
       IMPORTING
               E_DATE  = E_DATE
               E_FKDAY = E_FKDAY
       EXCEPTIONS
               ERROR   = 1
               OTHERS  = 2.


  IF SY-SUBRC EQ 0.
    WRITE:/ TFACD-IDENT, 15 E_DATE, 40 E_FKDAY.
  ELSE.
    WRITE:/ TFACD-IDENT, 15 'COULD NOT CALCULATE WORKING DAYS'.
  ENDIF.
ENDLOOP.
```

See Also

WEEK_GET_NR_OF_WORKDAYS

WEEK_GET_FIRST_DAY

Summary

Returns the date of the Monday of a given week.

Description

Returns the first day of the week passed, which is always a Monday, regardless of whether it is a working day or a holiday. Input is in the form YYYYWW, where WW is the week number.

Parameters

```
EXPORTING
      WEEK                 Week for which the date is to be determined (YYYYWW)
IMPORTING
      DATE                 Date of the first day of the week
```

Example

See DATE_GET_WEEK

WEEK_GET_NR_OF_WORKDAYS

Summary

The number of workable days in a week for a factory calendar.

Parameters

```
EXPORTING
      WEEK                      Week to calculate number of working days
      DAY                       Day to calculate number of working days
      FABKL                     Factory calendar ID
      REST_OF_WEEK              Only days until the end of the week
IMPORTING
      NR_OF_WORKDAYS            Number of working days in the calendar
```

Example

```
REPORT ZEXAMPLE.
TABLES T001W.
DATA WDAYS LIKE MDCAL-ANZFD.

WRITE:/ 'CALENDAR', 20 'WORKING DAYS'.
ULINE.
LOOP AT T001W.
  CALL FUNCTION 'WEEK_GET_NR_OF_WORKDAYS'
      EXPORTING
            DAY            = SY-DATUM
            FABKL          = T001W-FABKL
      IMPORTING
            NR_OF_WORKDAYS = WDAYS
      EXCEPTIONS
            WEEK_INVALID   = 1
            DAY_INVALID    = 2
            FABKL_INVALID  = 3
            FABKL_EMPTY    = 4
            OTHERS         = 5.

  IF SY-SUBRC EQ 0.
    WRITE:/ T001W-FABKL, 20 WDAYS.
  ELSE.
    WRITE:/ T001W-FABKL, 20 'COULD NOT CALCULATE WORKING DAYS'.
  ENDIF.
ENDLOOP.
```

See Also

WDKAL_DATE_ADD_FKDAYS

WEEKDAY_GET

Summary

Names of all the days of the week.

Parameters

```
EXPORTING
        LANGUAGE              Language of the days of the week
TABLES
        WEEKDAY               Table of the days of the week
```

Example

See DATE_GET_WEEK

See Also

DAY_IN_WEEK, RH_GET_DATE_DAYNAME

4

Files

An SAP system normally consists of Application and Presentation servers. How files are uploaded, downloaded, created, and deleted depends on its location on these servers and in which mode (background\foreground) the program is running.

C13Z_FILE_DOWNLOAD_ASCII

Summary

Downloads a file in ASCII format.

Description

Takes a file on the application server and writes it to a file on the frontend.

Parameters

```
EXPORTING
        I_FILE_FRONT_END            Filename on frontend
        I_FILE_APPL                 Filename on application server
        I_FILE_OVERWRITE            Flag to overwrite existing file (default: No)
IMPORTING
        E_FLG_OPEN_ERROR            Error opening the flag file
        E_OS_MESSAGE                Error message from the operating system
```

Example

```
REPORT ZEXAMPLE.

CONSTANTS: TRUE  TYPE BOOLEAN VALUE 'X',
           FALSE TYPE BOOLEAN VALUE ' '.

DATA: I_FLG_OVERWRITE      LIKE RCGFILETR-IEFOW,
      L_FLG_OPEN_ERROR     TYPE BOOLEAN,
      L_OS_MESSAGE(100)    TYPE C,
      L_FLG_CONTINUE       TYPE BOOLEAN.
```

```
PARAMETERS:   P_LFNAME  LIKE RCGFILETR-FTFRONT, "FRONT-END FILENAME
              P_SFNAME  LIKE RCGFILETR-FTAPPL,  "SERVER FILENAME
              P_ASCII   RADIOBUTTON GROUP RAD1,
              P_BINARY  RADIOBUTTON GROUP RAD1.

*   TRANSFER FILE FROM APPLICATION SERVER TO FRONT-END
IF P_ASCII EQ 'X'.
  CALL FUNCTION 'C13Z_FILE_DOWNLOAD_ASCII'
       EXPORTING
            I_FILE_FRONT_END   = P_LFNAME
            I_FILE_APPL        = P_SFNAME
       IMPORTING
            E_FLG_OPEN_ERROR   = L_FLG_OPEN_ERROR
            E_OS_MESSAGE       = L_OS_MESSAGE
       EXCEPTIONS
            FE_FILE_OPEN_ERROR = 1
            FE_FILE_EXISTS     = 2
            FE_FILE_WRITE_ERROR = 3
            AP_NO_AUTHORITY    = 4
            AP_FILE_OPEN_ERROR = 5
            AP_FILE_EMPTY      = 6
            OTHERS             = 7.
  IF SY-SUBRC NE 0.
    CASE SY-SUBRC.
      WHEN 2.
        CALL FUNCTION 'C14A_POPUP_ASK_FILE_OVERWRITE'
             IMPORTING
                  E_FLG_CONTINUE       = L_FLG_CONTINUE
             EXCEPTIONS
                  OTHERS               = 1.

        IF L_FLG_CONTINUE EQ TRUE.
          CALL FUNCTION 'C13Z_FILE_DOWNLOAD_ASCII'
               EXPORTING
                    I_FILE_FRONT_END   = P_LFNAME
                    I_FILE_APPL        = P_SFNAME
               IMPORTING
                    E_FLG_OPEN_ERROR   = L_FLG_OPEN_ERROR
                    E_OS_MESSAGE       = L_OS_MESSAGE
               EXCEPTIONS
                    FE_FILE_OPEN_ERROR   = 1
                    FE_FILE_EXISTS       = 2
                    FE_FILE_WRITE_ERROR  = 3
                    AP_NO_AUTHORITY      = 4
                    AP_FILE_OPEN_ERROR   = 5
                    AP_FILE_EMPTY        = 6
                    OTHERS               = 7.
          IF SY-SUBRC NE 0.
            WRITE:/ 'CANNOT DOWNLOAD FILE', P_SFNAME, '(', L_OS_MESSAGE, ')'.
          ENDIF.
        ENDIF.
      WHEN OTHERS.
        WRITE:/ 'CANNOT DOWNLOAD FILE', P_SFNAME, '(', L_OS_MESSAGE, ')'.
    ENDCASE.
  ENDIF.
ELSE.
```

```
      CALL FUNCTION 'C13Z_FILE_DOWNLOAD_BINARY'
            EXPORTING
                  I_FILE_FRONT_END        = P_LFNAME
                  I_FILE_APPL             = P_SFNAME
            IMPORTING
                  E_FLG_OPEN_ERROR        = L_FLG_OPEN_ERROR
                  E_OS_MESSAGE            = L_OS_MESSAGE
            EXCEPTIONS
                  FE_FILE_OPEN_ERROR     = 1
                  FE_FILE_EXISTS         = 2
                  FE_FILE_WRITE_ERROR    = 3
                  AP_NO_AUTHORITY        = 4
                  AP_FILE_OPEN_ERROR     = 5
                  AP_FILE_EMPTY          = 6
                  OTHERS                 = 7.
  IF SY-SUBRC NE 0.
    CASE SY-SUBRC.
      WHEN 2.
        CALL FUNCTION 'C14A_POPUP_ASK_FILE_OVERWRITE'
              IMPORTING
                  E_FLG_CONTINUE = L_FLG_CONTINUE
              EXCEPTIONS
                  OTHERS         = 1.

        IF L_FLG_CONTINUE EQ TRUE.
          CALL FUNCTION 'C13Z_FILE_DOWNLOAD_BINARY'
                EXPORTING
                    I_FILE_FRONT_END        = P_LFNAME
                    I_FILE_APPL             = P_SFNAME
                IMPORTING
                    E_FLG_OPEN_ERROR        = L_FLG_OPEN_ERROR
                    E_OS_MESSAGE            = L_OS_MESSAGE
                EXCEPTIONS
                    FE_FILE_OPEN_ERROR     = 1
                    FE_FILE_EXISTS         = 2
                    FE_FILE_WRITE_ERROR    = 3
                    AP_NO_AUTHORITY        = 4
                    AP_FILE_OPEN_ERROR     = 5
                    AP_FILE_EMPTY          = 6
                    OTHERS                 = 7.
          IF SY-SUBRC NE 0.
              WRITE:/ 'CANNOT DOWNLOAD FILE', P_SFNAME, '(', L_OS_MESSAGE, ')'.
          ENDIF.
        ENDIF.
      WHEN OTHERS.
        WRITE:/ 'CANNOT DOWNLOAD FILE', P_SFNAME, '(', L_OS_MESSAGE, ')'.
    ENDCASE.
  ENDIF.
ENDIF.

*  UPLOAD THE FILE
IF P_ASCII EQ 'X'.
  CALL FUNCTION 'C13Z_FILE_UPLOAD_ASCII'
        EXPORTING
            I_FILE_FRONT_END     = P_LFNAME
```

```
              I_FILE_APPL          = P_SFNAME
              I_FILE_OVERWRITE     = I_FLG_OVERWRITE
       IMPORTING
              E_FLG_OPEN_ERROR     = L_FLG_OPEN_ERROR
              E_OS_MESSAGE         = L_OS_MESSAGE
       EXCEPTIONS
              FE_FILE_NOT_EXISTS   = 1
              FE_FILE_READ_ERROR   = 2
              AP_NO_AUTHORITY      = 3
              AP_FILE_OPEN_ERROR   = 4
              AP_FILE_EXISTS       = 5
              OTHERS               = 6.
IF SY-SUBRC NE 0.
   CASE SY-SUBRC.
      WHEN 2.
         CALL FUNCTION 'C14A_POPUP_ASK_FILE_OVERWRITE'
               IMPORTING
                     E_FLG_CONTINUE = L_FLG_CONTINUE
               EXCEPTIONS
                     OTHERS         = 1.

         IF L_FLG_CONTINUE EQ TRUE.
            CALL FUNCTION 'C13Z_FILE_UPLOAD_ASCII'
                  EXPORTING
                        I_FILE_FRONT_END    = P_LFNAME
                        I_FILE_APPL         = P_SFNAME
                  IMPORTING
                        E_FLG_OPEN_ERROR    = L_FLG_OPEN_ERROR
                        E_OS_MESSAGE        = L_OS_MESSAGE
                  EXCEPTIONS
                        FE_FILE_OPEN_ERROR  = 1
                        FE_FILE_EXISTS      = 2
                        FE_FILE_WRITE_ERROR = 3
                        AP_NO_AUTHORITY     = 4
                        AP_FILE_OPEN_ERROR  = 5
                        AP_FILE_EMPTY       = 6
                        OTHERS              = 7.
            IF SY-SUBRC NE 0.
                WRITE:/ 'CANNOT UPLOAD FILE', P_SFNAME, '(', L_OS_MESSAGE, ')'.
            ENDIF.
         ENDIF.
      WHEN OTHERS.
         WRITE:/ 'CANNOT UPLOAD FILE', P_SFNAME, '(', L_OS_MESSAGE, ')'.
   ENDCASE.
  ENDIF.
ELSE.
  CALL FUNCTION 'C13Z_FILE_UPLOAD_BINARY'
       EXPORTING
              I_FILE_FRONT_END    = P_LFNAME
              I_FILE_APPL         = P_SFNAME
              I_FILE_OVERWRITE    = I_FLG_OVERWRITE
       IMPORTING
              E_FLG_OPEN_ERROR    = L_FLG_OPEN_ERROR
              E_OS_MESSAGE        = L_OS_MESSAGE
       EXCEPTIONS
```

```
                    FE_FILE_NOT_EXISTS   = 1
                    FE_FILE_READ_ERROR   = 2
                    AP_NO_AUTHORITY      = 3
                    AP_FILE_OPEN_ERROR   = 4
                    AP_FILE_EXISTS       = 5
                    OTHERS               = 6.
         IF SY-SUBRC NE 0.
           CASE SY-SUBRC.
             WHEN 2.
               CALL FUNCTION 'C14A_POPUP_ASK_FILE_OVERWRITE'
                     IMPORTING
                         E_FLG_CONTINUE = L_FLG_CONTINUE
                     EXCEPTIONS
                         OTHERS        = 1.

               IF L_FLG_CONTINUE EQ TRUE.
                 CALL FUNCTION 'C13Z_FILE_UPLOAD_BINARY'
                       EXPORTING
                           I_FILE_FRONT_END   = P_LFNAME
                           I_FILE_APPL        = P_SFNAME
                       IMPORTING
                           E_FLG_OPEN_ERROR   = L_FLG_OPEN_ERROR
                           E_OS_MESSAGE       = L_OS_MESSAGE
                       EXCEPTIONS
                           FE_FILE_OPEN_ERROR = 1
                           FE_FILE_EXISTS     = 2
                           FE_FILE_WRITE_ERROR = 3
                           AP_NO_AUTHORITY    = 4
                           AP_FILE_OPEN_ERROR = 5
                           AP_FILE_EMPTY      = 6
                           OTHERS             = 7.
                 IF SY-SUBRC NE 0.
                     WRITE:/ 'CANNOT UPLOAD FILE', P_SFNAME, '(', L_OS_MESSAGE, ')'.
                 ENDIF.
               ENDIF.
             WHEN OTHERS.
               WRITE:/ 'CANNOT UPLOAD FILE', P_SFNAME, '(', L_OS_MESSAGE, ')'.
           ENDCASE.
         ENDIF.
       ENDIF.
```

See Also

See C13Z_FILE_DOWNLOAD_BINARY

C13Z_FILE_DOWNLOAD_BINARY

Summary

Downloads a file in binary format.

Description

Takes a file on the application server and writes it to a file on the frontend.

Parameters

```
EXPORTING
        I_FILE_FRONT_END                Filename on frontend
        I_FILE_APPL                     Filename on application server
        I_FILE_OVERWRITE                Flag to overwrite existing file (default: No)
IMPORTING
        E_FLG_OPEN_ERROR                Error opening the flag file
        E_OS_MESSAGE                    Error message from the operating system
```

Example

See C13Z_FILE_DOWNLOAD_ASCII

See Also

See C13Z_FILE_DOWNLOAD_ASCII

C13Z_FILE_UPLOAD_ASCII

Summary

Uploads a file in ASCII format.

Description

Takes a file on the frontend and writes it to a file on the application server.

Parameters

```
EXPORTING
        I_FILE_FRONT_END                Filename on frontend
        I_FILE_APPL                     Filename on application server
        I_FILE_OVERWRITE                Flag to overwrite existing file (default: No)
IMPORTING
        E_FLG_OPEN_ERROR                Error opening the flag file
        E_OS_MESSAGE                    Error message from the operating system
```

Example

See C13Z_FILE_DOWNLOAD_ASCII

See Also

See C13Z_FILE_DOWNLOAD_BINARY

C13Z_FILE_UPLOAD_BINARY

Summary

Uploads a file in binary format.

Description

Takes a file on the frontend and writes it to a file on the application server.

Parameters

```
EXPORTING
      I_FILE_FRONT_END              Filename on frontend
      I_FILE_APPL                   Filename on application server
      I_FILE_OVERWRITE              Flag to overwrite existing file (default: No)
IMPORTING
      E_FLG_OPEN_ERROR              Error opening the flag file
      E_OS_MESSAGE                  Error message from the operating system
```

Example

See C13Z_FILE_DOWNLOAD_ASCII

See Also

See C13Z_FILE_DOWNLOAD_ASCII

DOWNLOAD

Summary

Downloads a file to the presentation server (PC).

Description

Stores an internal table as a file on the presentation server. It uses a dialogue box, and will therefore only work in foreground mode.

Parameters

```
EXPORTING
        BIN_FILESIZE          File length for binary files
        CODEPAGE              Code page for ASCII download
        FILENAME              Name of the file
        FILETYPE              File type
                                  Value    Meaning
                                  ASC      ASCII (default)
                                  BIN      Binary
                                  DBF      DBASE
                                  IBM      ASCII with IBM code page conversion
                                  WK1      Spreadsheet
                                  DAT      ASCII data table with column tab
        ITEM                  Header text for dialogue box
        MODE                  Writing mode (overwrite, append)
        WK1_N_FORMAT          Format for value columns in files of type WK1
        WK1_N_SIZE            Column width for value columns in files of type WK1
        WK1_T_FORMAT          Format for text columns for files of type WK1
        WK1_T_SIZE            Column width for text columns for files of type WK1
        FILEMASK_MASK         Mask for file selection (e.g. "*.txt")
        FILEMASK_TEXT         Mask for file selection (help text)
        FILETYPE_NO_CHANGE    Allow user to select different filetype (X = disable)
        FILEMASK_ALL
        FILETYPE_NO_SHOW      Do not display filetype (X = suppress)
        SILENT                Display download success screen (S = enable, X = disable)
IMPORTING
        ACT_FILENAME          Name of the file (entered value)
        ACT_FILETYPE          File type (entered value)
        FILESIZE              Number of bytes transferred
        CANCEL                Cancel dialogue box
TABLES
        DATA_TAB              Transfer data table
```

Example

```
REPORT ZEXAMPLE.

*   FORMAT OF TEXT FILE USED IN THIS EXAMPLE (COLUMNS SEPARATED BY TAB)
*                      COLUMN A         COLUMN B           COLUMN C
*   ROWS (DATA)    :   WCL123456        02/01/2002
*
DATA: BEGIN OF ITAB OCCURS 0,
        MATNR LIKE MARA-MATNR,  "COLUMN A
        ERSDA LIKE MARA-ERSDA,  "COLUMN B
        CONFIRM(11),            "COLUMN C
      END OF ITAB.

PARAMETERS: P_FNAME LIKE RLGRAP-FILENAME,
            P_FTYPE LIKE RLGRAP-FILETYPE DEFAULT 'DAT'.

WRITE:/ 'MATERIAL NUMBER', 20 'CREATION DATE'.
ULINE.
```

```
CALL FUNCTION 'UPLOAD'
     EXPORTING
          FILENAME                = P_FNAME
          FILETYPE                = P_FTYPE
          FILEMASK_MASK           = '*.TXT'
     TABLES
          DATA_TAB                = ITAB
     EXCEPTIONS
          CONVERSION_ERROR        = 1
          INVALID_TABLE_WIDTH     = 2
          INVALID_TYPE            = 3
          NO_BATCH                = 4
          UNKNOWN_ERROR           = 5
          GUI_REFUSE_FILETRANSFER = 6
          OTHERS                  = 7.

IF SY-SUBRC EQ 0.
  LOOP AT ITAB.
    WRITE:/ ITAB-MATNR, 20 ITAB-ERSDA.
    ITAB-CONFIRM = '*CONFIRMED*'.
    MODIFY ITAB.
  ENDLOOP.

  CALL FUNCTION 'DOWNLOAD'
       EXPORTING
            FILENAME                = P_FNAME
            FILETYPE                = P_FTYPE
            FILEMASK_MASK           = '*.TXT'
       TABLES
            DATA_TAB                = ITAB
       EXCEPTIONS
            INVALID_FILESIZE        = 1
            INVALID_TABLE_WIDTH     = 2
            INVALID_TYPE            = 3
            NO_BATCH                = 4
            UNKNOWN_ERROR           = 5
            GUI_REFUSE_FILETRANSFER = 6
            CUSTOMER_ERROR          = 7
            OTHERS                  = 8.

  IF SY-SUBRC EQ 0.
    ULINE.
    WRITE:/ P_FNAME, 'UPDATED AND DOWNLOADED SUCCESSFULLY'.
  ELSE.
    ULINE.
    WRITE:/ 'COULD NOT DOWNLOAD FILE', P_FNAME.
  ENDIF.
ELSE.
  WRITE:/ 'COULD NOT UPLOAD FILE', P_FNAME.
ENDIF.
```

See Also

UPLOAD, WS_DOWNLOAD, RZL_WRITE_FILE_LOCAL

EPS_GET_DIRECTORY_LISTING

Summary

Returns a list of filenames from the application server.

Parameters

```
EXPORTING
        DIR_NAME                        Directory to query
        FILE_MASK                       Return files of this type (SPACE = all file types)
TABLES
        DIR_LIST                        Tables holding list of files
```

Example

```
REPORT ZEXAMPLE.

CONSTANTS DAYS1980      TYPE I VALUE 3652.

DATA: DLIST            LIKE EPSFILI OCCURS 0 WITH HEADER LINE,
      DPATH            LIKE EPSF-EPSDIRNAM,
      MDATE            LIKE SY-DATUM,
      MTIME            LIKE SY-UZEIT,
      POINT_IN_TIME    TYPE I.

DATA: BEGIN OF FATTR OCCURS 0,
        FILE_NAME  LIKE EPSF-EPSFILNAM,
        FILE_SIZE  LIKE EPSF-EPSFILSIZ,
        FILE_OWNER LIKE EPSF-EPSFILOWN,
        FILE_MODE  LIKE EPSF-EPSFILMOD,
        FILE_TYPE  LIKE EPSF-EPSFILTYP,
        FILE_MTIME(12),
      END OF FATTR.

PARAMETER P_PATH(50) TYPE C DEFAULT '/TMP' LOWER CASE.

DPATH = P_PATH.
CALL FUNCTION 'EPS_GET_DIRECTORY_LISTING'
    EXPORTING
        DIR_NAME                = DPATH
    TABLES
        DIR_LIST                = DLIST
    EXCEPTIONS
        INVALID_EPS_SUBDIR      = 1
        SAPGPARAM_FAILED        = 2
        BUILD_DIRECTORY_FAILED  = 3
        NO_AUTHORIZATION        = 4
        READ_DIRECTORY_FAILED   = 5
        TOO_MANY_READ_ERRORS    = 6
        EMPTY_DIRECTORY_LIST    = 7
        OTHERS                  = 8.
```

```
IF SY-SUBRC EQ 0.
  LOOP AT DLIST.
    CALL FUNCTION 'EPS_GET_FILE_ATTRIBUTES'
          EXPORTING
                FILE_NAME             = DLIST-NAME
                DIR_NAME              = DPATH
          IMPORTING
                FILE_SIZE             = FATTR-FILE_SIZE
                FILE_OWNER            = FATTR-FILE_OWNER
                FILE_MODE             = FATTR-FILE_MODE
                FILE_TYPE             = FATTR-FILE_TYPE
                FILE_MTIME            = FATTR-FILE_MTIME
          EXCEPTIONS
                READ_DIRECTORY_FAILED = 1
                READ_ATTRIBUTES_FAILED = 2
                OTHERS                = 3.

    IF SY-SUBRC EQ 0.
       FATTR-FILE_NAME = DLIST-NAME.
       APPEND FATTR.
    ENDIF.
  ENDLOOP.

  SORT FATTR BY FILE_NAME.
  LOOP AT FATTR.
    POINT_IN_TIME = FATTR-FILE_MTIME.

    CALL FUNCTION 'POINT_IN_TIME_CONVERT'
          EXPORTING
                POINT_IN_TIME = POINT_IN_TIME
          IMPORTING
                DATE          = MDATE
                TIME          = MTIME
          EXCEPTIONS
                OTHERS        = 1.

    SUBTRACT DAYS1980 FROM MDATE.
    WRITE: / FATTR-FILE_NAME,
             FATTR-FILE_SIZE,
             MDATE,
             MTIME.
  ENDLOOP.
ENDIF.
```

See Also

TMP_GUI_DIRECTORY_LIST_FILES, TMP_GUI_READ_DIRECTORY, RZL_READ_DIR

EPS_GET_FILE_ATTRIBUTES

Summary

Returns attributes for a file.

Description

For a file, it returns the size, owner, mode, and type.

Parameters

```
EXPORTING
        FILE_NAME                      File name
        DIR_NAME                       Directory path to file
IMPORTING
        FILE_SIZE                      Size of file in bytes
        FILE_OWNER                     Owner of file
        FILE_MODE                      File mode
        FILE_TYPE                      Type of file
```

Example

See EPS_GET_DIRECTORY_LISTING

GUI_CREATE_DIRECTORY

Summary

Creates a directory on the presentation server.

Description

In Windows, the directory should have a final "\". Note: If the function creates the directory, but sets SY-SUBRC NE 0, check OSS note 0391861.

Parameters

```
EXPORTING
        DIRNAME                        Full path and new directory name
```

Example

```
REPORT ZEXAMPLE.

DATA: BEGIN OF ITAB OCCURS 0,
       COLA(10),
       COLB(10),
     END OF ITAB.

DATA: V_DIR   LIKE RLGRAP-FILENAME,
      V_FNAME LIKE RLGRAP-FILENAME,
      V_DEST  LIKE RLGRAP-FILENAME.
```

```
PARAMETERS: P_DIR   LIKE RLGRAP-FILENAME,
            P_FNAME LIKE RLGRAP-FILENAME.


CALL FUNCTION 'GUI_CREATE_DIRECTORY'
        EXPORTING
                DIRNAME      = P_DIR
        EXCEPTIONS
                FAILED       = 1
                OTHERS       = 2.


IF SY-SUBRC NE 0.
  WRITE:/ 'DIRECTORY', P_DIR, 'NOT CREATED'.
ELSE.
  WRITE:/ 'DIRECTORY CREATED:', P_DIR.

  CALL FUNCTION 'GUI_UPLOAD'
        EXPORTING
                FILENAME              = P_FNAME
                FILETYPE              = 'ASC'
        TABLES
                DATA_TAB              = ITAB
        EXCEPTIONS
                FILE_OPEN_ERROR       = 1
                FILE_READ_ERROR       = 2
                NO_BATCH              = 3
                GUI_REFUSE_FILETRANSFER = 4
                INVALID_TYPE          = 5
                OTHERS                = 6.
  IF SY-SUBRC NE 0.
    WRITE:/ 'COULD NOT UPLOAD', P_FNAME.
  ELSE.
    CALL FUNCTION 'SO_SPLIT_FILE_AND_PATH'
        EXPORTING
                FULL_NAME     = P_FNAME
        IMPORTING
                STRIPPED_NAME = V_FNAME
                FILE_PATH     = V_DIR
        EXCEPTIONS
                X_ERROR       = 1
                OTHERS        = 2.
    IF SY-SUBRC NE 0.
      WRITE:/ 'COULD NOT SPLIT', P_FNAME, 'INTO DIRECTORY AND FILENAME'.
    ELSE.
      CONCATENATE P_DIR V_FNAME INTO V_DEST.

      CALL FUNCTION 'GUI_DOWNLOAD'
            EXPORTING
                    FILENAME              = V_DEST
                    FILETYPE              = 'ASC'
            TABLES
                    DATA_TAB              = ITAB
            EXCEPTIONS
                    FILE_WRITE_ERROR      = 1
                    NO_BATCH              = 2
                    GUI_REFUSE_FILETRANSFER = 3
```

```
                    INVALID_TYPE           = 4
                    OTHERS                 = 5.

        IF SY-SUBRC NE 0.
          WRITE:/ 'COULD NOT DOWNLOAD', V_DEST, 'INTO', P_DIR.
        ELSE.
          WRITE:/ 'FILE', V_FNAME, 'MOVED FROM', V_DIR, 'TO', P_DIR.
        ENDIF.
      ENDIF.
    ENDIF.
  ENDIF.
ENDIF.
```

GUI_DELETE_FILE

Summary

Deletes a file on the presentation server.

Description

Replaces WS_FILE_DELETE.

Parameters

```
EXPORTING
      FILE_NAME                      Delete full path and filename
```

Example

```
REPORT ZEXAMPLE.

PARAMETERS: P_PATH LIKE RLGRAP-FILENAME,
            P_FILE RADIOBUTTON GROUP RAD1,
            P_DIR  RADIOBUTTON GROUP RAD1.

IF P_FILE EQ 'X'.
  CALL FUNCTION 'GUI_DELETE_FILE'
       EXPORTING
            FILE_NAME = P_PATH
       EXCEPTIONS
            FAILED    = 1
            OTHERS    = 2.
  IF SY-SUBRC NE 0.
    WRITE:/ P_PATH, 'DELETED'.
  ELSE.
    WRITE:/ 'COULD NOT DELETE', P_PATH.
  ENDIF.
ELSE.
```

```
  CALL FUNCTION 'GUI_REMOVE_DIRECTORY'
       EXPORTING
             DIRNAME = P_PATH
       EXCEPTIONS
             FAILED  = 1
             OTHERS  = 2.
  IF SY-SUBRC NE 0.
    WRITE:/ P_PATH, 'DELETED'.
  ELSE.
    WRITE:/ 'COULD NOT DELETE', P_PATH.
  ENDIF.
ENDIF.
```

See Also

WS_FILE_DELETE

GUI_DOWNLOAD

Summary

Downloads a file from the application server.

Description

Replaces WS_DOWNLOAD.

Parameters

```
EXPORTING
       FILENAME                 Path and filename to download
       FILETYPE                 File type
                                Value   Meaning
                                ASC     ASCII (default)
                                BIN     Binary
                                DBF     DBASE
                                IBM     ASCII with IBM code page conversion
                                WK1     Spreadsheet
                                DAT     ASCII data table with column tab
TABLES
       DATA_TAB                 Table of data
```

Example

See GUI_CREATE_DIRECTORY

See Also

DOWNLOAD, WS_DOWNLOAD, RZL_WRITE_FILE_LOCAL

GUI_REMOVE_DIRECTORY

Summary

Deletes a directory on the presentation server.

Description

The directory must be empty (no files) before it will delete.

Parameters

```
EXPORTING
        DIRNAME                         Path of directory to delete
```

Example

See GUI_DELETE_FILE

GUI_UPLOAD

Summary

Uploads a file from the presentation server.

Description

Replaces WS_UPLOAD.

Parameters

```
EXPORTING
        FILENAME                        Path and filename to upload
        FILETYPE                        File type
                                        Value    Meaning
                                        ASC      ASCII (default)
                                        BIN      Binary
                                        DBF      DBASE
                                        IBM      ASCII with IBM code page conversion
```

```
                                     WK1     Spreadsheet
                                     DAT     ASCII data table with column tab
IMPORTING
     FILELENGTH                      Number of bytes transferred
TABLES
     DATA_TAB                        Table of data
```

Example

See GUI_CREATE_DIRECTORY

See Also

UPLOAD, WS_UPLOAD, RZL_READ_FILE

LIST_DOWNLOAD

Summary

Downloads ABAP list (report) to local file.

Description

The standard menu for lists (… LIST → SAVE → Local file) provides the same functionality as this module. LIST_DOWNLOAD allows you to bypass the selection dialogue for the file format, and to specify one directly using the METHOD parameter. If you save the list in unconverted form, you can also include a link to a particular list level (LIST_INDEX parameter).

Parameters

```
EXPORTING
     LIST_INDEX                      List index
     METHOD                          Backup method
                                         Value   Meaning
                                         RTF     Rich Text Format
                                         DAT     Tab delimited
                                         NOCO    No conversion
                                         HTML    HTML
```

Example

```
REPORT ZEXAMPLE.

WRITE:/ 'LOOP COUNTER'.
ULINE.

DO 10 TIMES.
  WRITE:/ SY-INDEX.
ENDDO.
```

```
CALL FUNCTION 'LIST_DOWNLOAD'
    EXPORTING
        METHOD              = 'DAT'
    EXCEPTIONS
        LIST_DOWNLOAD_ERROR = 1
        OTHERS              = 2.
IF SY-SUBRC NE 0.
  WRITE:/ 'COULD NOT DOWNLOAD REPORT TO FILE'.
ELSE.
  WRITE:/ 'REPORT DOWNLOADED SUCCESSFULLY'.
ENDIF.
```

See Also

STRR_GET_REPORT

PROFILE_GET

Summary

Reads an entry in an INI file from the frontend.

Parameters

```
EXPORTING
      FILENAME                  Path and name of the .INI file
      KEY                       Key in the .INI file
      SECTION                   Section in the .INI file
IMPORTING
      VALUE                     Current value in the section
```

Example

```
REPORT ZEXAMPLE.
DATA:  INI_FILE        LIKE    RLGRAP-FILENAME VALUE 'C:\TEMP\ZEXAMPLE.INI',
       INI_ULOAD       LIKE    RLGRAP-FILENAME,
       INI_DLOAD       LIKE    RLGRAP-FILENAME,
       V_LASTRUN(30).

*   ZEXAMPLE.INI LAYOUT USED IN THIS EXAMPLE:
*   [FILES]
*   UPLOAD        = 'C:\TEMP\ULOAD.TXT'
*   DOWNLOAD      = 'C:\TEMP\DLOAD.TXT'
*   [HISTORY]
*   LASTRUN       = 20030102 174347

*   RETRIEVE DEFAULT FILENAMES
CALL FUNCTION 'PROFILE_GET'
```

```
      EXPORTING
            FILENAME = INI_FILE
            KEY      = 'UPLOAD'
            SECTION  = 'FILES'
      IMPORTING
            VALUE    = INI_ULOAD.

IF INI_ULOAD IS INITIAL.
  WRITE:/ 'UPLOAD PATH AND FILENAME NOT FOUND'.
ELSE.
  WRITE:/ 'UPLOAD FILENAME AND PATH:', INI_ULOAD.

  CALL FUNCTION 'PROFILE_GET'
      EXPORTING
            FILENAME = INI_FILE
            KEY      = 'DOWNLOAD'
            SECTION  = 'FILES'
      IMPORTING
            VALUE    = INI_DLOAD.

  IF INI_DLOAD IS INITIAL.
    WRITE:/ 'DOWNLOAD PATH AND FILENAME NOT FOUND'.
  ELSE.
    WRITE:/ 'DOWNLOAD FILENAME AND PATH:', INI_DLOAD.
  ENDIF.
ENDIF.

CLEAR V_LASTRUN.
CONCATENATE SY-DATUM SY-UZEIT INTO V_LASTRUN SEPARATED BY SPACE.
CALL FUNCTION 'PROFILE_SET'
     EXPORTING
            FILENAME = INI_FILE
            KEY      = 'LASTRUN'
            SECTION  = 'HISTORY'
            VALUE    = V_LASTRUN.

IF SY-SUBRC EQ 0.
  WRITE:/ INI_FILE, 'HAS BEEN UPDATED'.
ELSE.
  WRITE:/ INI_FILE, 'HAS NOT BEEN UPDATED'.
ENDIF.
```

See Also

PROFILE_SET

PROFILE_SET

Summary

Writes an entry to an INI file to the frontend.

Parameters

```
EXPORTING
        FILENAME                        Path and name of the .INI file
        KEY                             Key in the .INI file
        SECTION                         Section in the .INI file
        VALUE                           Value to write to the section
```

Example

See PROFILE_GET

See Also

PROFILE_GET

RS_DELETE_PROGRAM

Summary

Deletes an ABAP program.

Description

The function includes parameters to delete all associated objects with a program, such as includes and screens. Use with caution!!

Parameters

```
EXPORTING
        PROGRAM                         Program name to delete
        SUPPRESS_CHECKS                 No enqueue in module
        SUPPRESS_COMMIT                 No enqueue in module
        SUPPRESS_POPUP                  Suppress all popups and messages
        WITH_CUA                        Delete CUA (default - yes)
        WITH_DOCUMENTATION              Delete program documentation (default - yes)
        WITH_DYNPRO                     Delete screens (default - yes)
        WITH_INCLUDES                   Delete standard includes (default - yes)
        WITH_TEXTPOOL                   Delete programs textpools (default - yes)
        WITH_VARIANTS                   Delete programs variants (default - yes)
IMPORTING
        CORRNUMBER                      Correction (transport) number if transportable
        PROGRAM                         Program name deleted
```

Example

```
REPORT ZEXAMPLE.
DATA:   V_ANS,
```

```
            CORRNUMBER         LIKE E071-TRKORR,
            V_RPT              LIKE SY-REPID.

PARAMETERS: P_REPID LIKE SY-REPID.

CALL FUNCTION 'POPUP_TO_CONFIRM_STEP'
      EXPORTING
            TEXTLINE1 = 'PERMANENTLY DELETE THIS PROGRAM?'
            TEXTLINE2 = P_REPID
            TITEL     = 'PERMANENTLY DELETE A PROGRAM'
      IMPORTING
            ANSWER    = V_ANS.

IF V_ANS EQ 'J'.
  CALL FUNCTION 'RS_DELETE_PROGRAM'
      EXPORTING
            PROGRAM              = P_REPID
      IMPORTING
            CORRNUMBER           = CORRNUMBER
            PROGRAM              = V_RPT
      EXCEPTIONS
            ENQUEUE_LOCK       = 1
            OBJECT_NOT_FOUND   = 2
            PERMISSION_FAILURE = 3
            REJECT_DELETION    = 4
            OTHERS             = 5.
  IF SY-SUBRC NE 0.
    WRITE:/ 'ERROR DELETING', P_REPID.
  ELSE.
    WRITE:/ 'PROGRAM', V_RPT, 'DELETED. TRANSPORT:', CORRNUMBER.
  ENDIF.
ELSE.
  WRITE:/ 'NOTHING DELETED!'.
ENDIF.
```

RSPO_DOWNLOAD_SPOOLJOB

Summary

Downloads a printer spool to a file.

Parameters

```
EXPORTING
        ID        Spool ID
        FNAME     Filename
```

Example

See RSPO_FIND_SPOOL_REQUESTS

RZL_READ_DIR

Summary

Reads a directory.

Description

If no remote server name is entered, it reads a directory from local presentation server.

Parameters

```
EXPORTING
        FROMLINE                    Start from list index of files
        NAME                        Local filename
        NRLINES                     Number of files to read
        SRVNAME                     Name of application server
TABLES
        FILE_TBL                    List of filenames in a directory
```

Example

```
REPORT ZEXAMPLE LINE-SIZE 255.

PARAMETERS: V_DIR LIKE RLGRAP-FILENAME DEFAULT '/TMP'.

DATA: BEGIN OF FILE_LIST OCCURS 0.
        INCLUDE STRUCTURE SALFLDIR.
DATA: END OF FILE_LIST.

DATA: BEGIN OF FILE_DATA OCCURS 0.
        INCLUDE STRUCTURE SPFLIST.
DATA: END OF FILE_DATA.

DATA: BEGIN OF LOCAL_FILE OCCURS 0,
        LNAME LIKE SALFLDIR-NAME,
        LLINE LIKE SPFLIST-LINE,
      END OF LOCAL_FILE.

WRITE:/ 'FILENAME', 'FILE DATA'.
ULINE.

CALL FUNCTION 'RZL_READ_DIR'
    EXPORTING
        NAME            = V_DIR
    TABLES
        FILE_TBL        = FILE_LIST
    EXCEPTIONS
        ARGUMENT_ERROR  = 1
        NOT_FOUND       = 2
        SEND_ERROR      = 3
        OTHERS          = 4.
```

```
IF SY-SUBRC EQ 0.
  LOOP AT FILE_LIST.
    CALL FUNCTION 'RZL_READ_FILE'
         EXPORTING
              DIRECTORY       = V_DIR
              NAME            = FILE_LIST-NAME
         TABLES
              LINE_TBL        = FILE_DATA
         EXCEPTIONS
              ARGUMENT_ERROR  = 1
              NOT_FOUND       = 2
              SEND_ERROR      = 3
              OTHERS          = 4.
    IF SY-SUBRC NE 0.
      WRITE:/ FILE_LIST-NAME, 'NOT READ'.
    ELSE.
      LOOP AT FILE_DATA.
        WRITE:/ FILE_LIST-NAME, FILE_DATA-LINE.
        MOVE: FILE_LIST-NAME TO LOCAL_FILE-LNAME,
              FILE_DATA-LINE TO LOCAL_FILE-LLINE.
        APPEND LOCAL_FILE.
      ENDLOOP.
    ENDIF.
  ENDLOOP.
ELSE.
  WRITE:/ 'READ DIRECTORY ERROR'.
ENDIF.
CALL FUNCTION 'RZL_WRITE_FILE_LOCAL'
     EXPORTING
          NAME            = 'C:\LOCAL_FILE.TXT'
     TABLES
          LINE_TBL        = LOCAL_FILE
     EXCEPTIONS
          ARGUMENT_ERROR  = 1
          WRITE_ERROR     = 2
          OTHERS          = 3.
IF SY-SUBRC EQ 0.
  WRITE:/ 'DATA DOWNLOADED TO FILE'.
ELSE.
  WRITE:/ 'ERROR DOWNLOADING FILE TO PC'.
ENDIF.
```

See Also

See EPS_GET_DIRECTORY_LISTING

RZL_READ_FILE

Summary

Reads a file.

Description

Reads a file from the presentation server if no server name is given. It does not use the OPEN DATASET statement, therefore avoiding authority checks.

Parameters

```
EXPORTING
        DIRECTORY                       Directory path
        FROMLINE                        Start from list index of files
        NAME                            Name of file to read
        NRLINES                         Number of files to read
        SRVNAME                         Server name
TABLES
        LINE_TBL                        Table to hold file data
```

Example

See RZL_READ_DIR

See Also

UPLOAD, WS_UPLOAD, GUI_UPLOAD

RZL_WRITE_FILE_LOCAL

Summary

Saves internal table to the presentation server.

Description

It does not use the OPEN DATASET statement, therefore avoiding authority checks.

Parameters

```
EXPORTING
        NAME                            Filename and path
TABLES
        LINE_TBL                        Data to download
```

Example

See RZL_READ_DIR

See Also

DOWNLOAD, WS_DOWNLOAD, GUI_DOWNLOAD

SO_SPLIT_FILE_AND_PATH

Summary

Splits a fully formed path into a filename and a path.

Description

The directory path ends with a "\" under Windows.

Parameters

```
EXPORTING
      FULL_NAME                       Full filename and path
IMPORTING
      STRIPPED_NAME                   Filename without path
      FILE_PATH                       Directory path without filename
```

Example

See GUI_CREATE_DIRECTORY

STRR_GET_REPORT

Summary

Downloads ABAP source code.

Description

Downloads ABAP source code to an internal table.

Parameters

```
EXPORTING
      REPORT                          Program name
TABLES
      TAB_OUT                         Table containing all lines from the program
```

Example

```
REPORT ZEXAMPLE.
DATA: BEGIN OF IABAP OCCURS 0.
        INCLUDE STRUCTURE ABAPTEXT.
DATA: END OF IABAP.

PARAMETERS P_ABAP LIKE TFDIR-PNAME.

CALL FUNCTION 'STRR_GET_REPORT'
    EXPORTING
        REPORT      = P_ABAP
    TABLES
        TAB_OUT     = IABAP
    EXCEPTIONS
        TR_NO_REPORT = 1
        OTHERS       = 2.
IF SY-SUBRC EQ 0.
  WRITE:/ 'SOURCE CODE OF THE PROGRAM', P_ABAP.
  ULINE.
  LOOP AT IABAP.
    WRITE:/ IABAP-LINE.
  ENDLOOP.
ELSE.
  WRITE:/ 'COULD NOT DOWNLOAD', P_ABAP.
ENDIF.
```

See Also

LIST_DOWNLOAD

STRUCTURE_EXPORT_TO_MSACCESS

Summary

Downloads data from SAP into Microsoft Access.

Description

Passes SAP data to a Microsoft Access database. Only works with data dictionary tables, and Access only supports tables with up to 255 fields. Read OSS note 443027.

Basic Procedure

1. SALE → Communication → Define RFC Destination (transaction SM59).
2. Setup two RFC destinations: RFC_ACCESS_1 (create tables) and RFC_ACCESS_2 (fill tables).

3. Depending on the version of Access you have, point RFC_ACCESS_1 to program WDSASTR.EXE (Access 7.0), WDPSAS97.EXE (Access 97), or WDPSAS00.EXE (Access 2000).

4. Point RFC_ACCESS_2 to WDPSATAB.EXE (Access 7.0), WDSAT97.EXE (Access97), or WDPSAT00.EXE (Access 2000).

5. Execute ABAP program RIACCESS and choose RFC_ACCESS_1 to generate the tables.

Program RIACCESS generates Access databases automatically. This program is well documented.

Check <http://help.sap.com/saphelp_46c/helpdata/EN/4c/2267e346e611d189470000e829fbbd/frameset.htm> for information on RFC programs available. These programs are delivered on the SAP presentation CD.

Parameters

```
EXPORTING
        DBNAME                          Name of MS Access database on PC
        DEST                            RFC destination
TABLES
        TABNAME                         Name of table in MS Access database
```

Example

```
REPORT ZEXAMPLE.
TABLES DD02L.

DATA: ITAB     LIKE DFIES OCCURS 0 WITH HEADER LINE,
      TABNAME  LIKE DFIES-TABNAME,
      REFTABLE LIKE DFIES-REFTABLE.

START-OF-SELECTION.
  SELECT * FROM DD02L UP TO 100 ROWS.
    ITAB-TABNAME = DD02L-TABNAME.
    COLLECT ITAB.
  ENDSELECT.

  CALL FUNCTION 'STRUCTURE_EXPORT_TO_MSACCESS'
      EXPORTING
          DBNAME         = 'C:\SAPTABLES.MDB'
          DEST           = 'RFC_ACCESS_2'
      TABLES
          TABNAME        = ITAB
      EXCEPTIONS
          SYSTEM_FAILURE = 1
          COMM_FAILURE   = 2
          OTHERS         = 3.

IF SY-SUBRC EQ 0.
  WRITE:/ 'TOP 100 TABLE\STRUCTURES TRANSFERRED INTO SAPTABLES.MDB:'.
  LOOP AT ITAB.
    WRITE: / ITAB-TABNAME.
```

```
CALL FUNCTION 'TABLE_EXPORT_TO_MSACCESS'
     EXPORTING
          DBNAME            = 'C:\SAPTABLES_2.MDB'
          DEST              = 'RFC_ACCESS_2'
          TABNAME           = ITAB-TABNAME
     TABLES
          DTAB              = ITAB
     EXCEPTIONS
          WRONG_FORMAT      = 1
          STRUCT_TOOLONG    = 2
          UNKNOWN_DATATYPE  = 3
          SYSTEM_FAILURE    = 4
          COMM_FAILURE      = 5
          OTHERS            = 6.

  IF SY-SUBRC NE 0.
    WRITE:/ ITAB-TABNAME, 'DATA NOT TRANSFERRED INTO SAPTABLES_2.MDB:'.
  ENDIF.
 ENDLOOP.
ENDIF.
```

See Also

TABLE_EXPORT_TO_MSACCESS

TABLE_EXPORT_TO_MSACCESS

Summary

Downloads data from SAP into Microsoft Access.

Description

See STRUCTURE_EXPORT_TO_MSACCESS.

Parameters

```
EXPORTING
     DBNAME                     Name of MS Access database on PC
     DEST                       RFC destination
     TABNAME                    Name of table in MS Access database
     REFTABLE                   Alternative name of table in MS Access database
TABLES
     DTAB                       SAP table name
```

Example

See STRUCTURE_EXPORT_TO_MSACCESS

See Also

STRUCTURE_EXPORT_TO_MSACCESS

TMP_GUI_DIRECTORY_LIST_FILES

Summary

Retrieves all of the files and subdirectories for a given directory.

Description

Filters such as *.TXT may be used.

Parameters

```
EXPORTING
      DIRECTORY                     List files from this directory
      FILTER                        Type of files to list
IMPORTING
      FILE_COUNT                    Number of files read
      DIR_COUNT                     Number of directories read
TABLES
      FILE_TABLE                    Filename and path of each file
      DIR_TABLE                     Directory name and path of each directory
```

Example

```
REPORT ZEXAMPLE.
DATA: FILE_COUNT TYPE I,
      DIR_COUNT  TYPE I,
      DIR_TABLE  LIKE SDOKPATH OCCURS 0 WITH HEADER LINE,
      FILE_TABLE LIKE SDOKPATH OCCURS 0 WITH HEADER LINE,
      IDXTABLE   LIKE IWMULTI OCCURS 0 WITH HEADER LINE,
      DIR_PATH   LIKE RLGRAP-FILENAME.

PARAMETERS:    P_DIR LIKE RLGRAP-FILENAME DEFAULT 'C:\TEMP\'.

CALL FUNCTION 'TMP_GUI_DIRECTORY_LIST_FILES'
     EXPORTING
         DIRECTORY = P_DIR
         FILTER    = '*.*'
     IMPORTING
         FILE_COUNT = FILE_COUNT
         DIR_COUNT  = DIR_COUNT
     TABLES
         FILE_TABLE = FILE_TABLE
         DIR_TABLE  = DIR_TABLE
```

```
      EXCEPTIONS
          CNTL_ERROR = 1
          OTHERS     = 2.

IF SY-SUBRC EQ 0.
  LOOP AT DIR_TABLE.
    CLEAR DIR_PATH.
    CONCATENATE P_DIR DIR_TABLE-PATHNAME INTO DIR_PATH.
    CALL FUNCTION 'TMP_GUI_READ_DIRECTORY'
        EXPORTING
            DIRECTORY_PATH = DIR_PATH
        TABLES
            INDEX_TABLE    = IDXTABLE.
    APPEND IDXTABLE.
    LOOP AT IDXTABLE.
      WRITE:/ DIR_TABLE-PATHNAME, IDXTABLE-VALUE, IDXTABLE-KEY_FIELD.
    ENDLOOP.
  ENDLOOP.
ELSE.
  WRITE:/ 'ERROR LISTING CONTENTS OF', P_DIR.
ENDIF.
```

See Also

EPS_GET_DIRECTORY_LISTING, TMP_GUI_READ_DIRECTORY, RZL_READ_DIR

TMP_GUI_READ_DIRECTORY

Summary

Lists files in a directory.

Description

Downloads and runs a batch file to write list of files into a temporary file.

Parameters

```
EXPORTING
      EXTENSION                 File types, or space for all files
      DIRECTORY_PATH            Path to produce index
IMPORTING
      ERROR_MSG                 Error message from the OS
TABLES
      INDEX_TABLE               Contents of directory
```

Example

See TMP_GUI_DIRECTORY_LIST_FILES

See Also

EPS_GET_DIRECTORY_LISTING, TMP_GUI_READ_DIRECTORY, RZL_READ_DIR

UPLOAD

Summary

Uploads a file into SAP.

Description

Data that is available in a file on the presentation server is transferred in an internal table. As it uses a dialogue, the function will only work in foreground mode.

Parameters

```
EXPORTING
        CODEPAGE                    Code page for ASCII upload
        FILENAME                    Name of the file (default value)
        FILETYPE                    File type
                                        Value   Meaning
                                        ASC     ASCII (default)
                                        BIN     Binary
                                        DBF     DBASE
                                        IBM     ASCII with IBM code page conversion
                                        WK1     Spreadsheet
                                        DAT     ASCII data table with column tab
        ITEM                        Header text for dialogue box
        FILEMASK_MASK               Mask for file selection (e.g. "*.txt")
        FILEMASK_TEXT               Mask for file selection (help text)
        FILETYPE_NO_CHANGE          Allow user to select different filetype (X = disable)
        FILEMASK_ALL
        FILETYPE_NO_SHOW            Do not display filetype (X = suppress)
        SILENT                      Display download success screen (S = enable, X = disable)
IMPORTING
        FILESIZE                    Number of bytes transferred
        CANCEL                      Cancel dialogue box
        ACT_FILENAME                Name of the file (entered value)
        ACT_FILETYPE                File type (entered value)
TABLES
        DATA_TAB                    Transfer data table
```

Example

See DOWNLOAD

See Also

DOWNLOAD, RZL_WRITE_FILE_LOCAL, UPLOAD_FILES, WS_UPLOAD

UPLOAD_FILES

Summary

Uploads multiple files into SAP.

Parameters

```
EXPORTING
        I_TRUNCLEN                  File length
        I_FILETYPE                  File type
                                        Value    Meaning
                                        ASC      ASCII (default)
                                        BIN      Binary
                                        DBF      DBASE
                                        IBM      ASCII with IBM code page conversion
                                        WK1      Spreadsheet
                                        DAT      ASCII data table with column tab
        I_XPC                       Flag file on application or presentation (default)
        I_CODEPAGE                  Codepage used with IBM
TABLES
        FILE_ALL                    Transfer table for file contents
        TAB_FILE                    File paths
```

Example

```
REPORT ZEXAMPLE.
DATA: I_FILE TYPE C OCCURS 0 WITH HEADER LINE,
      I_TAB  LIKE RLGRAP OCCURS 0 WITH HEADER LINE.

I_TAB-FILENAME = 'D:\TEMP\01.TXT'.
APPEND I_TAB.
I_TAB-FILENAME = 'D:\TEMP\02.TXT'.
APPEND I_TAB.

CALL FUNCTION 'UPLOAD_FILES'
     EXPORTING
        I_FILETYPE = 'ASC'
        I_XPC      = 'X'
     TABLES
        FILE_ALL   = I_FILE
        TAB_FILE   = I_TAB
     EXCEPTIONS
        ERROR_FILE = 1
        OTHERS     = 2.
```

```
IF SY-SUBRC EQ 0.
  LOOP AT I_TAB.
    WRITE:/ I_TAB-FILENAME.
  ENDLOOP.
ELSE.
  WRITE:/ 'COULD NOT LIST FILES'.
ENDIF.
```

See Also

UPLOAD

WS_DOWNLOAD

Summary

Transfers file from internal table to presentation server file.

Description

Uses a dialogue, so can only be used in the foreground.

Parameters

```
EXPORTING
      BIN_FILESIZE        File length for binary files
      CODEPAGE            Code page for ASCII download
      FILENAME            Name of the file
      FILETYPE            File type
                              Value    Meaning
                              ASC      ASCII (default)
                              BIN      Binary
                              DBF      DBASE
                              IBM      ASCII with IBM code page conversion
                              WK1      Spreadsheet
                              DAT      ASCII data table with column tab
      MODE                Writing mode (overwrite, append)
      WK1_N_FORMAT        Format for value columns in files of type WK1
      WK1_N_SIZE          Column width for value columns in files of type WK1
      WK1_T_FORMAT        Format for text columns for files of type WK1
      WK1_T_SIZE          Column width for text columns for files of type WK1
IMPORTING
      FILELENGTH          Length of file in bytes
TABLES
      DATA_TAB            Transfer data table
```

Example

See WS_UPLOAD

See Also

GUI_DOWNLOAD, RZL_WRITE_FILE_LOCAL

WS_FILE_DELETE

Summary

Deletes files from the presentation server.

Description

Use with caution!!

Parameters

```
EXPORTING
        FILE       File to delete
```

Example

See WS_UPLOAD

See Also

GUI_DELETE_FILE

WS_FILENAME_GET

Summary

Call a file selector popup.

Parameters

```
EXPORTING
        DEF_PATH              Full path
        MASK                  File types
        TITLE                 Title of dialogue box
IMPORTING
        FILENAME              Filenames in directory
```

Example

See WS_UPLOAD

WS_UPLOAD

Summary

File transfers from presentation server file to internal table.

Description

Uses a dialogue, so can only be used in the foreground.

Parameters

```
EXPORTING
        CODEPAGE                   Code page for ASC upload
        FILENAME                   Filename
        FILETYPE                   File type to upload
                                       Value    Meaning
                                       ASC      ASCII (default)
                                       BIN      Binary
                                       DBF      DBASE
                                       IBM      ASCII with IBM code page conversion
                                       WK1      Spreadsheet
                                       DAT      ASCII data table with column tab
        DAT_D_FORMAT               Date format; e.g. DD.MM.YYYY
IMPORTING
        FILELENGTH                 Length of file in bytes
TABLES
        DATA_TAB                   File contents
```

Example

```
REPORT ZEXAMPLE.
DATA: BEGIN OF DATA_TAB OCCURS 0,
        TEXT(20),
        VAL TYPE I,
        CHK,
      END OF DATA_TAB.

DATA: P_FNAME LIKE RLGRAP-FILENAME,
      V_ANS.

CALL FUNCTION 'WS_FILENAME_GET'
    EXPORTING
        DEF_PATH        = 'C:\'
        MASK            = ',TEXT FILES,*.TXT;*.DOC,ALL FILES,*.*.'
        TITLE           = 'SELECT FILE'
    IMPORTING
        FILENAME        = P_FNAME
    EXCEPTIONS
        INV_WINSYS      = 1
        NO_BATCH        = 2
```

```
                SELECTION_CANCEL  = 3
                SELECTION_ERROR   = 4
                OTHERS            = 5.

IF SY-SUBRC EQ 0.
  CALL FUNCTION 'WS_UPLOAD'
       EXPORTING
             FILENAME                 = P_FNAME
             FILETYPE                 = 'DAT'
       TABLES
             DATA_TAB                 = DATA_TAB
       EXCEPTIONS
             CONVERSION_ERROR         = 1
             FILE_OPEN_ERROR          = 2
             FILE_READ_ERROR          = 3
             INVALID_TYPE             = 4
             NO_BATCH                 = 5
             UNKNOWN_ERROR            = 6
             INVALID_TABLE_WIDTH      = 7
             GUI_REFUSE_FILETRANSFER  = 8
             CUSTOMER_ERROR           = 9
             OTHERS                   = 10.
  IF SY-SUBRC EQ 0.
    WRITE:/'DATA IN', P_FNAME.
    ULINE.
    LOOP AT DATA_TAB.
      WRITE: / DATA_TAB-TEXT,DATA_TAB-VAL.
      DATA_TAB-CHK         = 'X'.
      MODIFY DATA_TAB.
    ENDLOOP.

    CALL FUNCTION 'WS_DOWNLOAD'
         EXPORTING
               FILENAME                 = P_FNAME
               FILETYPE                 = 'DAT'
         TABLES
               DATA_TAB                 = DATA_TAB
         EXCEPTIONS
               FILE_OPEN_ERROR          = 1
               FILE_WRITE_ERROR         = 2
               INVALID_FILESIZE         = 3
               INVALID_TYPE             = 4
               NO_BATCH                 = 5
               UNKNOWN_ERROR           = 6
               INVALID_TABLE_WIDTH      = 7
               GUI_REFUSE_FILETRANSFER  = 8
               CUSTOMER_ERROR           = 9
               OTHERS                   = 10.
    IF SY-SUBRC EQ 0.
      WRITE:/ P_FNAME, 'UPDATED AND DOWNLOADED'.

      CALL FUNCTION 'POPUP_TO_CONFIRM_STEP'
           EXPORTING
                 TEXTLINE1 = 'PERMANENTLY DELETE THIS FILE?'
                 TEXTLINE2 = P_FNAME
```

```
            TITEL     = 'PERMANENTLY DELETE A FILE'
         IMPORTING
            ANSWER    = V_ANS.

   IF V_ANS EQ 'J'.
     CALL FUNCTION 'WS_FILE_DELETE'
         EXPORTING
            FILE   = P_FNAME.
     WRITE:/ P_FNAME, 'DELETED'.
   ELSE.
     WRITE:/ P_FNAME, 'NOT DELETED'.
   ENDIF.
  ELSE.
    WRITE:/ P_FNAME, 'NOT DOWNLOADED'.
  ENDIF.
 ELSE.
   WRITE:/ 'COULD NOT UPLOAD FILE', P_FNAME.
 ENDIF.
ELSE.
 WRITE:/ 'COULD NOT OPEN FILE', P_FNAME.
ENDIF.
```

See Also

GUI_UPLOAD, RZL_READ_FILE

Lists

5

Functions to do with report lists and selection screens.

DYNP_VALUES_READ

Summary

Reads screen-field values before PAI field transport.

Description

This function reads the values from a report's selection screen.

Parameters

```
EXPORTING
        DYNAME                  Name of program from which the function module is called
        DYNUMB                  Number of screen from which the function module is called
        TRANSLATE_TO_UPPER      Field contents are converted to upper case
TABLES
        DYNPFIELDS              Before calling the module, table contains names of the
                                screen fields to be read. After the call, it also contains
                                the values read and the step loop lines (if it is a step
                                loop screen)
```

Example

```
REPORT ZEXAMPLE.
TABLES TSP01.

TYPES: BEGIN OF ISPOOL,
        RQIDENT LIKE TSP01-RQIDENT,
        RQONAME LIKE TSP01-RQONAME,
        RQ1NAME LIKE TSP01-RQ1NAME,
        RQ2NAME LIKE TSP01-RQ2NAME,
        RQOWNER LIKE TSP01-RQOWNER,
```

```
          RQCRETIME LIKE TSP01-RQCRETIME,
        END OF ISPOOL.

DATA:   TI_SPOOL     TYPE TABLE OF ISPOOL WITH HEADER LINE,
        V_RQOWNER    LIKE TSP01-RQOWNER,
        V_DATUM_FROM LIKE TSP01-RQCRETIME,
        V_DATUM_TO   LIKE TSP01-RQCRETIME,
        V_FIELDVALUE LIKE DYNPREAD-FIELDVALUE,
        V_DATUM      LIKE SY-DATUM,
        V_REPID      LIKE SY-REPID,
        V_DYNNR      LIKE SY-DYNNR.

DATA:   IRETURN TYPE TABLE OF DDSHRETVAL WITH HEADER LINE,
        ISCR    TYPE TABLE OF DYNPREAD WITH HEADER LINE.


PARAMETERS:  RQIDENT LIKE TSP01-RQIDENT,
             RQOWNER LIKE TSP01-RQOWNER DEFAULT SY-UNAME,
             DATUM   LIKE SY-DATUM DEFAULT SY-DATUM.


AT SELECTION-SCREEN ON VALUE-REQUEST FOR RQIDENT.

*   BUILD THE TABLE OF VALUES TO BE DISPLAYED
    CLEAR:     ISCR,    ISCR[].
    ISCR-FIELDNAME = 'RQIDENT'. APPEND ISCR.
    ISCR-FIELDNAME = 'RQOWNER'. APPEND ISCR.
    ISCR-FIELDNAME = 'DATUM'. APPEND ISCR.
    V_REPID = SY-REPID.
    V_DYNNR = SY-DYNNR.

    CALL FUNCTION 'DYNP_VALUES_READ'
        EXPORTING
                DYNAME               = V_REPID
                DYNUMB               = V_DYNNR
                TRANSLATE_TO_UPPER   = 'X'
        TABLES
                DYNPFIELDS           = ISCR
        EXCEPTIONS
                INVALID_ABAPWORKAREA = 1
                INVALID_DYNPROFIELD  = 2
                INVALID_DYNPRONAME   = 3
                INVALID_DYNPRONUMMER = 4
                INVALID_REQUEST      = 5
                NO_FIELDDESCRIPTION  = 6
                INVALID_PARAMETER    = 7
                UNDEFIND_ERROR       = 8
                OTHERS               = 9.

READ TABLE ISCR WITH KEY FIELDNAME = 'RQIDENT'.
IF ISCR-FIELDVALUE IS INITIAL.

  CLEAR ISCR.
  READ TABLE ISCR WITH KEY FIELDNAME = 'RQOWNER'.
  IF ISCR-FIELDVALUE IS INITIAL.
```

```
    V_RQOWNER = '%'. "ALL USERS
  ELSE.
    V_RQOWNER = ISCR-FIELDVALUE.
    TRANSLATE V_RQOWNER USING '*%'.
  ENDIF.

  CLEAR ISCR.
  READ TABLE ISCR WITH KEY FIELDNAME = 'DATUM'.
  IF ISCR-FIELDVALUE IS INITIAL OR ISCR-FIELDVALUE EQ '*'.
    V_DATUM_FROM = '19900101000000'. "ALL DATES FROM 1990
    CONCATENATE SY-DATUM SY-UZEIT INTO V_DATUM_TO.
  ELSE.

    CALL FUNCTION 'CONVERSION_EXIT_PDATE_INPUT'
         EXPORTING
              INPUT    = ISCR-FIELDVALUE
         IMPORTING
              OUTPUT   = V_FIELDVALUE.

    CONCATENATE V_FIELDVALUE '000000' INTO V_DATUM_FROM.
    CONCATENATE V_FIELDVALUE '235959' INTO V_DATUM_TO.
  ENDIF.

  SELECT RQIDENT RQ0NAME RQ1NAME RQ2NAME RQOWNER RQCRETIME
    INTO TABLE TI_SPOOL
    FROM TSP01
    WHERE RQOWNER LIKE V_RQOWNER
    AND RQCRETIME BETWEEN V_DATUM_FROM AND V_DATUM_TO.

  SORT TI_SPOOL.

ELSE.
  TRANSLATE ISCR-FIELDVALUE USING ', '.
  TRANSLATE ISCR-FIELDVALUE USING '. '.
  CONDENSE ISCR-FIELDVALUE NO-GAPS.

  RQIDENT = ISCR-FIELDVALUE.

  SELECT RQIDENT RQ0NAME RQ1NAME RQ2NAME RQOWNER RQCRETIME
    INTO TABLE TI_SPOOL
    FROM TSP01
    WHERE RQIDENT EQ RQIDENT.
ENDIF.

LOOP AT TI_SPOOL.
  CONCATENATE  TI_SPOOL-RQCRETIME+0(8)
               TI_SPOOL-RQCRETIME+8(4)
    INTO TI_SPOOL-RQCRETIME
    SEPARATED BY SPACE.

  MODIFY TI_SPOOL.
ENDLOOP.

*  USING DYNPROG/DYNPNR/DYNPROFIELD TO POPULATE THE SCREEN FIELD RQIDENT
*  ONLY WORKS IN DIALOG MODULE SCREENS; THEREFORE MUST READ SELECTED
```

```
*   ENTRY FROM IRETURN AND FORCIBLY POPULATE RQIDENT
    CALL FUNCTION 'F4IF_INT_TABLE_VALUE_REQUEST'
         EXPORTING
              RETFIELD        = 'RQIDENT'
              VALUE_ORG       = 'S'
         TABLES
              VALUE_TAB       = TI_SPOOL
              RETURN_TAB      = IRETURN.

READ TABLE IRETURN INDEX 1.

TRANSLATE IRETURN-FIELDVAL USING ', '.
TRANSLATE IRETURN-FIELDVAL USING '. '.
CONDENSE IRETURN-FIELDVAL NO-GAPS.

RQIDENT = IRETURN-FIELDVAL.

SELECT SINGLE * FROM TSP01 WHERE RQIDENT EQ RQIDENT.
IF SY-SUBRC EQ 0.

  READ TABLE ISCR WITH KEY FIELDNAME = 'RQOWNER'.
  ISCR-FIELDVALUE = TSP01-RQOWNER.
  MODIFY ISCR INDEX SY-TABIX.

  READ TABLE ISCR WITH KEY FIELDNAME = 'DATUM'.
  V_DATUM = TSP01-RQCRETIME+0(8).
  WRITE V_DATUM TO ISCR-FIELDVALUE.
  MODIFY ISCR INDEX SY-TABIX.


  DELETE ISCR WHERE (FIELDNAME NE 'RQOWNER' AND FIELDNAME NE 'DATUM').

* UPDATE THE SCREEN FIELD VALUES ON THE SCREEN...
  CALL FUNCTION 'DYNP_VALUES_UPDATE'
         EXPORTING
              DYNAME                = V_REPID
              DYNUMB                = V_DYNNR
         TABLES
              DYNPFIELDS  = ISCR
         EXCEPTIONS
              INVALID_ABAPWORKAREA    = 1
              INVALID_DYNPROFIELD     = 2
              INVALID_DYNPRONAME      = 3
              INVALID_DYNPRONUMMER    = 4
              INVALID_REQUEST         = 5
              NO_FIELDDESCRIPTION     = 6
              UNDEFIND_ERROR          = 7
              OTHERS                  = 8.
ENDIF.
```

See Also

DYNP_VALUES_UPDATE, RPY_DYNPRO_READ, RS_COVERPAGE_SELECTIONS

DYNP_VALUES_UPDATE

Summary

Changes screen-field contents without PBO.

Description

Ideal for changing a field based on the value entered in another field.

Parameters

```
EXPORTING
        DYNAME      Name of program from which the function module is called
        DYNUMB      Number of screen from which the function module is called
TABLES
        DYNPFIELDS  Contains name and values of the screen fields to be updated
```

Example

See DYNP_VALUES_READ

See Also

DYNP_VALUES_READ

F4IF_INT_TABLE_VALUE_REQUEST

Summary

Standard help at Process on Value-Request.

Description

This module implements the standard help at Process on Value-Request while passing the values to be displayed in a table. The function is well documented.

Parameters

```
EXPORTING
        RETFIELD      Name of return field in FIELD_TAB
        VALUE_ORG     Value return: C: cell by cell, S: structured
TABLES
        VALUE_TAB     Table of values: entries cell by cell
        RETURN_TAB    Return the selected value
```

Example

See DYNP_VALUES_READ

See Also

HELP_VALUES_GET_NO_DD_NAME

HR_DISPLAY_BASIC_LIST

Summary

Provides a table control for data.

Description

Displays a table control to manipulate data and sends it to MS Word and MS Excel. This function is well documented.

Parameters

```
EXPORTING
        BASIC_LIST_TITLE              Title of the table control
        HEAD_LINE1                    Header line on table control
        CURRENT_REPORT                Name of current report
TABLES
        DATA_TAB                      Table containing data for the control
        FIELDNAME_TAB                 Columns headers for the control
```

Example

```
REPORT ZEXAMPLE.
TABLES MARA.

DATA:   BEGIN OF COLUMN OCCURS 0,
          COL_NAME(40),
        END OF COLUMN.

DATA:   BEGIN OF ITAB OCCURS 0.
          INCLUDE STRUCTURE MARA.
DATA:   END OF ITAB.

SELECT * FROM MARA INTO TABLE ITAB UP TO 100 ROWS.

REFRESH COLUMN.
COLUMN-COL_NAME    = 'CLIENT'.
APPEND COLUMN.
```

```
COLUMN-COL_NAME     = 'MATERIAL NUMBER'.
APPEND COLUMN.

CALL FUNCTION 'HR_DISPLAY_BASIC_LIST'
     EXPORTING
          BASIC_LIST_TITLE   = SY-TITLE
          FILE_NAME          = 'SAPDATA'
          HEAD_LINE1         = SY-TITLE
          CURRENT_REPORT     = 'ZEXAMPLE'
     TABLES
          DATA_TAB           = ITAB
          FIELDNAME_TAB      = COLUMN
     EXCEPTIONS
          OTHERS             = 1.
```

K_ABC_DOKU_SHOW

Summary

Reads program documentation from local program.

Description

Reads program documentation from local program (not interactive using editor).

Parameters

```
EXPORTING
     DOKUOBJ     Documentation object ID
     DOKUID      Document class
```

Example

```
REPORT ZEXAMPLE.
TABLES DOKHL.

PARAMETERS P_OBJ LIKE DOKHL-OBJECT DEFAULT 'ERDOPO00'.

SELECT SINGLE * FROM DOKHL WHERE ID = 'RE'
  AND OBJECT = P_OBJ
  AND LANGU  = SY-LANGU
  AND TYP    = 'E'.

CALL FUNCTION 'K_ABC_DOKU_SHOW'
     EXPORTING
          DOKUOBJ  = DOKHL-OBJECT
          DOKUID   = 'RE'.
```

See Also

RS_TOOL_ACCESS

LIST_FROM_MEMORY

Summary

Retrieves the output of a report from memory.

Description

Retrieves from memory the output of a report. The report was executed using SUBMIT... EXPORTING LIST TO MEMORY and placed in the internal table LISTOBJECT.

Parameters

```
TABLES
    LISTOBJECT        Table containing the report
```

Example

```
REPORT ZEXAMPLE.
TABLES MARA.

DATA:      T_LST LIKE ABAPLIST OCCURS 0 WITH HEADER LINE,
           T_LISTOBJECT LIKE ABAPLIST OCCURS 0 WITH HEADER LINE,
           V_STOCK.

DATA: BEGIN OF T_L,
      LINE(120),
      END OF T_L.
DATA: TLX LIKE T_L OCCURS 0 WITH HEADER LINE.

PARAMETERS:    P_SDATE LIKE SY-DATUM DEFAULT SY-DATUM, "STOCK DATE
               P_MATNR LIKE MARA-MATNR,
               P_WERKS LIKE MARC-WERKS.

WRITE:/ 'MATERIAL', 20 'STOCK DATE', 30 'ANY STOCK?'.
ULINE.

SUBMIT RM07MLBD                "STOCK ON POSTING DATE
        WITH DATUM EQ P_SDATE
        WITH MATNR EQ P_MATNR
        WITH WERKS EQ P_WERKS
        EXPORTING LIST TO MEMORY AND RETURN.

CALL FUNCTION 'LIST_FROM_MEMORY'
    TABLES
        LISTOBJECT = T_LST.

CALL FUNCTION 'LIST_TO_ASCI'
    TABLES
        LISTASCI            = TLX
        LISTOBJECT          = T_LST
```

```
      EXCEPTIONS
            EMPTY_LIST          = 1
            LIST_INDEX_INVALID  = 2
            OTHERS              = 3.

IF SY-SUBRC EQ 0.
  LOOP AT TLX FROM 9 TO 9.
    IF TLX+57(14) CA '123456789'.
      WRITE:/ P_MATNR, 20 P_SDATE, 30 'Y'.
    ELSE.
      WRITE:/ P_MATNR, 20 P_SDATE, 30 'N'.
    ENDIF.
  ENDLOOP.

  WRITE:/ 'FULL REPORT:'.
  ULINE.
  CALL FUNCTION 'WRITE_LIST'
       TABLES
            LISTOBJECT     = T_LST
       EXCEPTIONS
            EMPTY_LIST     = 1
            OTHERS         = 2.
ENDIF.
```

See Also

WRITE_LIST

LIST_TO_ASCI

Summary

Converts an ABAP report (displayed on screen) to ASCII format.

Description

Only the text part of the list is copied line by line to the prepared internal table (LISTASCI) without any attributes (colour, icon, symbol, etc.). There is no line break in this case, i.e. if the internal table line is not long enough, the list line is truncated.

Parameters

```
TABLES
    LISTASCI     Table to receive list (ASCI)
    LISTOBJECT   List object ID
```

Example

See LIST_FROM_MEMORY

RPY_DYNPRO_READ

Summary

Reads screen objects, including screen flow logic.

Parameters

```
EXPORTING
     PROGNAME                     Program name
     DYNNR                        Screen number
TABLES
     CONTAINERS                   Container objects in the screen
     FLOW_LOGIC                   Screen logic
     FIELDS_TO_CONTAINERS         All objects on the screen
```

Example

```
REPORT ZEXAMPLE.
DATA:    BEGIN OF DYNPFIELDS OCCURS 0.
            INCLUDE STRUCTURE RPY_DYFATC.
DATA:    END OF DYNPFIELDS.

PARAMETERS:   S_DYNNR    LIKE    D020S-DNUM DEFAULT '0400',
              L_REPID    LIKE    D020S-PROG DEFAULT 'SAPLS38E'.

WRITE:/ 'CONTAINER', 20 'OBJECT', 35 'INPUT', 45 'OUTPUT'.
ULINE.
CALL  FUNCTION 'RPY_DYNPRO_READ'
     EXPORTING
          PROGNAME                = L_REPID
          DYNNR                   = S_DYNNR
     TABLES
          FIELDS_TO_CONTAINERS  = DYNPFIELDS
     EXCEPTIONS
          CANCELLED               = 1
          NOT_FOUND               = 2
          PERMISSION_ERROR        = 3.

IF SY-SUBRC EQ 0.
  LOOP AT DYNPFIELDS.
    WRITE:/ DYNPFIELDS-CONT_TYPE, 20 DYNPFIELDS-NAME, 37 DYNPFIELDS-INPUT_FLD,
          47 DYNPFIELDS-OUTPUT_FLD.
  ENDLOOP.
ELSE.
    WRITE:/ 'COULD NOT READ DYNPRO', S_DYNNR, 'FOR', L_REPID.
ENDIF.
```

See Also

DYNP_VALUES_READ, RS_COVERPAGE_SELECTIONS

RS_COVERPAGE_SELECTIONS

Summary

Returns the selection parameters for a report.

Description

Returns a printable internal table that contains a list of the selection parameters entered for a report.

Parameters

```
EXPORTING
        REPORT      Report name
        VARIANT     Variant name (SPACE also valid)
TABLES
        INFOTAB     Table with parameter and selection options for printing
```

Example

```
REPORT ZEXAMPLE.

DATA:  BEGIN OF SEL_TAB OCCURS 0,
          LINE(132)            TYPE C,
        END OF SEL_TAB.
DATA      VAR                  LIKE SY-SLSET.

PARAMETERS P_REPID LIKE SY-REPID.

CALL FUNCTION 'RS_COVERPAGE_SELECTIONS'
     EXPORTING
          REPORT      = P_REPID
          VARIANT     = VAR
          NO_IMPORT   = ' '
     TABLES
          INFOTAB = SEL_TAB
     EXCEPTIONS
          ERROR_MESSAGE      = 1
          VARIANT_NOT_FOUND  = 3
          OTHERS             = 4.

IF SY-SUBRC EQ 0.
  LOOP AT SEL_TAB.
    WRITE: / SEL_TAB-LINE+2(130).
    AT LAST.
      NEW-PAGE.
    ENDAT.
  ENDLOOP.
ELSE.
    WRITE:/ 'CANNOT OUTPUT SCREEN SELECTIONS OF', P_REPID.
ENDIF.
```

See Also

DYNP_VALUES_READ, RPY_DYNPRO_READ, RS_REFRESH_FROM_SELECTOPTIONS

RS_CREATE_VARIANT

Summary

For creating dynamic variants.

Parameters

```
EXPORTING
        CURR_REPORT        Report name
        CURR_VARIANT       Name of variant
        VARI_DESC          Short description of variant
TABLES
        VARI_CONTENTS      Contents of variant (data for screen fields)
        VARI_TEXT          Variant short texts
```

Example

```
REPORT ZEXAMPLE.

DATA:    JVARI_DESC LIKE VARID,
         RC LIKE SY-SUBRC,
VARIANT_TEXT LIKE VARIT-VTEXT,
         JVT LIKE VARIT OCCURS 0 WITH HEADER LINE,
         SELPA LIKE RSPARAMS OCCURS 0 WITH HEADER LINE,
         PARMS LIKE RSPARAMS OCCURS 0 WITH HEADER LINE,
         OBJS LIKE VANZ OCCURS 0 WITH HEADER LINE.

PARAMETERS:    P_VAR LIKE RSVAR-VARIANT.         "NAME OF VARIANT

JVARI_DESC-REPORT            = SY-REPID.
JVARI_DESC-VARIANT           = P_VAR.
JVARI_DESC-ENAME             = 'EXAMPLES'.

JVT-REPORT                   = SY-REPID.
JVT-VARIANT                  = P_VAR.
JVT-LANGU                    = SY-LANGU.
JVT-VTEXT                    = 'FUNCTION EXAMPLES'.
APPEND JVT.

CLEAR SELPA.
SELPA-SIGN      = 'I'.
SELPA-OPTION    = 'EQ'.
SELPA-KIND      = 'P'.

SELPA-SELNAME   = 'P_VAR'.
SELPA-LOW       = P_VAR.
APPEND SELPA.
```

```
*   CHECK IF VARIANT EXISTS
CALL FUNCTION 'RS_VARIANT_EXISTS'
     EXPORTING
          REPORT                = JVARI_DESC-REPORT
          VARIANT               = P_VAR
     IMPORTING
          R_C                   = RC
     EXCEPTIONS
          NOT_AUTHORIZED        = 1
          NO_REPORT             = 2
          REPORT_NOT_EXISTENT   = 3
          REPORT_NOT_SUPPLIED   = 4
          OTHERS                = 5.

IF RC = 0 AND SY-SUBRC EQ 0.
*   DELETE OLD VARIANT
    CALL FUNCTION 'RS_VARIANT_DELETE'
        EXPORTING
             REPORT                = JVARI_DESC-REPORT
             VARIANT               = P_VAR
             FLAG_CONFIRMSCREEN    = 'X'
        EXCEPTIONS
             NOT_AUTHORIZED        = 1
             NOT_EXECUTED          = 2
             NO_REPORT             = 3
             REPORT_NOT_EXISTENT   = 4
             REPORT_NOT_SUPPLIED   = 5
             VARIANT_LOCKED        = 6
             VARIANT_NOT_EXISTENT  = 7
             NO_CORR_INSERT        = 8
             VARIANT_PROTECTED     = 9
             OTHERS                = 10.
  IF SY-SUBRC NE 0.
    WRITE: 'UNABLE TO DELETE VARIANT:', P_VAR ,'STATUS=', SY-SUBRC.
    EXIT.
  ELSE.
    WRITE:/ P_VAR, 'DELETED'.
  ENDIF.
ELSE.
  WRITE:/ P_VAR, 'DOES NOT EXIST'.
ENDIF. "ALREADY EXISTS

CALL FUNCTION 'RS_CREATE_VARIANT'
     EXPORTING
          CURR_REPORT              = JVARI_DESC-REPORT
          CURR_VARIANT             = P_VAR
          VARI_DESC                = JVARI_DESC
     TABLES
          VARI_CONTENTS            = SELPA
          VARI_TEXT                = JVT
     EXCEPTIONS
          ILLEGAL_REPORT_OR_VARIANT = 1
          ILLEGAL_VARIANTNAME       = 2
          NOT_AUTHORIZED            = 3
          NOT_EXECUTED              = 4
             REPORT_NOT_EXISTENT    = 5
```

```
          REPORT_NOT_SUPPLIED                    = 6
          VARIANT_EXISTS                         = 7
          VARIANT_LOCKED                         = 8
          OTHERS                                 = 9.
IF SY-SUBRC EQ 0.
  WRITE:/ 'VARIANT', P_VAR, 'CREATED FOR PROGRAM', JVARI_DESC-REPORT.
ELSE.
  WRITE:/ 'VARIANT', P_VAR, 'NOT CREATED FOR PROGRAM', JVARI_DESC-REPORT.
    EXIT.
ENDIF.

CALL FUNCTION 'RS_VARIANT_CONTENTS'
     EXPORTING
          REPORT                      = JVARI_DESC-REPORT
          VARIANT                     = P_VAR
     TABLES
          VALUTAB                     = PARMS
          OBJECTS                     = OBJS
     EXCEPTIONS
          VARIANT_NON_EXISTENT        = 1
          VARIANT_OBSOLETE            = 2
          OTHERS                      = 3.

IF SY-SUBRC NE 0.
  WRITE : / 'ERROR READING VARIANT CONTENTS.'.
ELSE.
  CALL FUNCTION 'RS_VARIANT_TEXT'
       EXPORTING
          LANGU       = SY-LANGU
          CURR_REPORT = JVARI_DESC-REPORT
          VARIANT     = P_VAR
       IMPORTING
          V_TEXT      = VARIANT_TEXT.

  WRITE:/ 'VARIANT DESCRIPTION:', VARIANT_TEXT.

  LOOP AT PARMS.
    CHECK PARMS-LOW NE SPACE OR PARMS-HIGH NE SPACE.
    READ TABLE OBJS WITH KEY NAME = PARMS-SELNAME.
    WRITE :  /2 PARMS-SELNAME, OBJS-TEXT,
             45 PARMS-KIND,
                PARMS-SIGN,
                PARMS-OPTION,
                PARMS-LOW,
                PARMS-HIGH.
    NEW-LINE.
  ENDLOOP.
  SKIP.
ENDIF.
```

RS_REFRESH_FROM_SELECTOPTIONS

Summary

Returns the selection parameters for a report.

Parameters

```
EXPORTING
    CURR_REPORT        Report name
TABLES
    SELECTION_TABLE    Table contained the selection-screen fields and criteria
```

Example

```
REPORT ZEXAMPLE.

DATA  BEGIN OF SEL_TBL OCCURS 0.
        INCLUDE STRUCTURE RSPARAMS.
DATA  END OF SEL_TBL.

PARAMETERS P_RPT LIKE SY-REPID.

CALL FUNCTION 'RS_REFRESH_FROM_SELECTOPTIONS'
    EXPORTING
        CURR_REPORT        = P_RPT
    TABLES
        SELECTION_TABLE    = SEL_TBL
    EXCEPTIONS
        NOT_FOUND          = 01
        NO_REPORT          = 02.

WRITE:/ 'SELECTION CRITERIA USED ON', P_RPT.
WRITE:/ 'FIELD', 10 'KIND', 15 'SIGN', 20 'OPTION', 30 'LOW VALUE', 40 'HIGH VALUE'.
ULINE.
LOOP AT SEL_TBL.
  WRITE:/ SEL_TBL-SELNAME, 10 SEL_TBL-KIND, 15 SEL_TBL-SIGN, 20 SEL_TBL-OPTION,
            30 SEL_TBL-LOW, 40 SEL_TBL-HIGH.
ENDLOOP.
```

See Also

RS_COVERPAGE_SELECTIONS

RS_SET_SELSCREEN_STATUS

Summary

Allows you to deactivate function codes on a selection screen.

Description

Usually you build an internal table of type SY-UCOMM with the codes you want to deactivate and call the function with it. So, for example you could deactivate the Print button on a sensitive report. There is a lot of documentation for this function!

Parameters

```
EXPORTING
        P_STATUS              Menu status of program
TABLES
        P_EXCLUDE             Table of function codes to disable from menu
```

Example

```
REPORT ZEXAMPLE.
DATA:   BEGIN OF P_EXTAB OCCURS 0,
          FCODE LIKE SY-PFKEY,
          END OF P_EXTAB.

PARAMETERS P_FCODE LIKE SY-PFKEY.

P_EXTAB-FCODE = P_FCODE.
APPEND P_EXTAB.

CALL FUNCTION 'RS_SET_SELSCREEN_STATUS'
     EXPORTING
          P_STATUS  = SY-PFKEY
     TABLES
          P_EXCLUDE = P_EXTAB
     EXCEPTIONS
          OTHERS    = 1.

IF SY-SUBRC EQ 0.
  WRITE:/ 'FUNCTION', P_FCODE, 'HAS BEEN DISABLED'.
ELSE.
  WRITE:/ 'COULD NOT DISABLE', P_FCODE.
ENDIF.
```

RS_TOOL_ACCESS

Summary

Reads program documentation from another program (not interactive using editor).

Parameters

```
EXPORTING
  OPERATION            Tool operation:
                         Value                    Meaning
    For multiple objects:
                         BOR_SET                  BOR browser
                         CLIF_SET                 Class browsers
                         CROSSREF                 Object cross-references
                         ENVIRONMENT              Object environment settings
                         GRAPHIC                  Display database table info
```

MODSHOW	Show modifications (obsolete)
MOVE	Move to development class
PRINT	Print object code
SRC_SEARCH	Search in object for string
TRANSPORT_SET	Call transport system
TRANSPORT	Place objects in request

For single object:

ACTINT	Activate internal object
ACTIVATE	Activate dialogue objects
ADD OR ADDX	Create object
BATCH	Run (executable) object
CHECK	Syntax check of object
EXTENDED_CHECK	Extended syntax check
COPY	Copy object to another
DEBUG	Debug object
DELETE	Delete object
DOCS	Display documentation
DOCU	Edit documentation
EDIT	Edit object
GENERATE	Generate object
PRINT	Print object
PROFILE	Run time analysis
RENAME	Rename object
SHOW	Display object (e.g. source)
TAB_ADD	Make table entry
TAB_CONT	Table contents
TADIR	Transportation features
TEST	Test run of object
VERSION_NEW	Create new object version
VERSION_OVERVIEW	Display object versions

OBJECT_NAME	Name of object for tool
OBJECT_TYPE	Object type

Example

```
REPORT ZEXAMPLE.

PARAMETERS P_REP LIKE SY-REPID. "PROGRAM NAME

CALL FUNCTION 'RS_TOOL_ACCESS'
    EXPORTING
        OPERATION              = 'DOCS'
        OBJECT_NAME            = P_REP
        OBJECT_TYPE            = 'PROG'
    EXCEPTIONS
        NOT_EXECUTED           = 1
        INVALID_OBJECT_TYPE    = 2
        OTHERS                 = 3.

IF SY-SUBRC NE 0.
  WRITE:/ 'CANNOT DISPLAY DOCUMENTATION FOR', P_REP.
ENDIF.
```

See Also

K_ABC_DOKU_SHOW

RS_VARIANT_CONTENTS

Summary

Values of a variant returned in a table.

Description

This function module checks whether any parameters or select options of the variant have changed. If they have, it outputs the error message "variant obsolete". There is some documentation with this function.

Parameters

```
EXPORTING
       REPORT      Report name
       VARIANT     Name of variant
TABLES
       VALUTAB     Parameter and select-options values
       OBJECTS     Parameter and select-options display information
```

Example

See RS_CREATE_VARIANT

See Also

See RS_CREATE_VARIANT

RS_VARIANT_DELETE

Summary

Deletes a variant from a program.

Description

By default, it will delete the variant from just the current client. Use with caution!!

Parameters

```
EXPORTING
      REPORT                 Report name
      VARIANT                Variant name
      FLAG_CONFIRMSCREEN     Display popup to confirm deletion (default)
```

Example

See RS_CREATE_VARIANT

RS_VARIANT_EXISTS

Summary

Checks whether a variant exists for a report.

Parameters

```
EXPORTING
      REPORT       Report name
      VARIANT      Name of variant
IMPORTING
      R_C          Return code from function
```

Example

See RS_CREATE_VARIANT

RS_VARIANT_TEXT

Summary

Returns short description of a variant.

Parameters

```
EXPORTING
      LANGU        Description in language
      CURR_REPORT  Name of report
      VARIANT      Name of variant
IMPORTING
      V_TEXT       Short text of variant in language
```

Example

See RS_CREATE_VARIANT

See Also

See RS_CREATE_VARIANT

RS_VARIANT_VALUES_TECH_DATA

Summary

Reads variant parameters of a report.

Parameters

```
EXPORTING
        REPORT                  Report name
        VARIANT                 Name of variant
IMPORTING
        TECHN_DATA              Description of the variant in VARID format
TABLES
        VARIANT_VALUES    Names and values of parameters and select-options
```

Example

```
REPORT ZEXAMPLE.

DATA:   BEGIN OF VARIANT_VALUES OCCURS 0.
           INCLUDE STRUCTURE RSPARAMS.
DATA:   END OF VARIANT_VALUES.

DATA:   BEGIN OF TECHN_DATA.
           INCLUDE STRUCTURE VARID.
DATA:   END OF TECHN_DATA.

PARAMETERS:  P_REPT LIKE SY-REPID.
             P_VAR LIKE RSVAR-VARIANT.

CALL  FUNCTION 'RS_VARIANT_VALUES_TECH_DATA'
     EXPORTING
           REPORT                 = P_REPT
           VARIANT                = P_VAR
     IMPORTING
           TECHN_DATA             = TECHN_DATA
     TABLES
           VARIANT_VALUES         = VARIANT_VALUES
     EXCEPTIONS
           VARIANT_NON_EXISTENT   = 01
           VARIANT_OBSOLETE       = 02.
```

```
IF SY-SUBRC EQ 0.
WRITE:/ 'REPORT:', TECHN_DATA-REPORT, 30 'VARIANT:', TECHN_DATA-VARIANT.
  LOOP AT VARIANT_VALUES.
    WRITE:/VARIANT_VALUES-SELNAME, VARIANT_VALUES-OPTION,
          VARIANT_VALUES-LOW, VARIANT_VALUES-HIGH.
  ENDLOOP.
ELSE.
  WRITE:/ 'COULD NOT RETRIEVE INFORMATION'.
ENDIF.
```

RZL_SUBMIT

Summary

Submits a remote report for execution.

Parameters

```
EXPORTING
      REPID           Report to execute
```

Example

```
REPORT ZEXAMPLE.

PARAMETERS P_RPT LIKE SY-REPID.

CALL FUNCTION 'RZL_SUBMIT'
      EXPORTING
            REPID = P_RPT.
```

SAPGUI_PROGRESS_INDICATOR

Summary

Displays a progress bar on the SAP GUI.

Parameters

```
EXPORTING
      PERCENTAGE      Size of bar
      TEXT            Text to be displayed
```

Example

```
REPORT ZEXAMPLE.
TABLES BKPF.
```

```
CONSTANTS:   C_STEP TYPE I VALUE '4',    "% STEP INCREASE
             C_MSGLNS TYPE I VALUE 20.

DATA:    BEGIN OF IBKPF OCCURS 0.
             INCLUDE STRUCTURE BKPF.
DATA:    END OF IBKPF.

DATA:    V_LNS      TYPE I,
         V_REST     TYPE I,
         V_LOOP(4)  TYPE C,
         V_MSG(30)  TYPE C,
         V_PER      TYPE I,
         V_LINES(4) TYPE C.

SELECT * FROM BKPF INTO TABLE IBKPF UP TO 50 ROWS.

DESCRIBE TABLE IBKPF LINES V_LNS.
V_LINES = V_LNS.

LOOP AT IBKPF.
  IF V_LNS GE C_MSGLNS.
    V_LOOP = SY-TABIX.
    V_REST = SY-TABIX MOD (V_LNS / C_MSGLNS).
    IF V_REST EQ 0.
      V_PER = SY-TABIX / (V_LNS / C_MSGLNS) * C_STEP.
      CLEAR V_MSG.
      CONCATENATE 'PROCESSING' V_LOOP 'OF' V_LINES INTO V_MSG SEPARATED BY SPACE.

      CALL FUNCTION 'SAPGUI_PROGRESS_INDICATOR'
            EXPORTING
                  PERCENTAGE  = V_PER
                  TEXT        = V_MSG.
    ENDIF.
  ENDIF.
ENDLOOP.                          "IBKPF
```

See Also

EPS_PROGRESS_POPUP

SAVE_LIST

Summary

Saves report as list container.

Description

The specified list is returned to LISTOBJECT and can be processed like an internal table. SAVE_LIST is not suitable for saving lists produced during background processing.

Parameters

```
EXPORTING
     LIST_INDEX              Index of list report
TABLES
     LISTOBJECT              Container for list object
```

Example

```
REPORT ZEXAMPLE.

DATA:   BEGIN OF LISTOBJECT OCCURS 0.
          INCLUDE STRUCTURE ABAPLIST.
DATA:   END OF LISTOBJECT.

*   GENERATE A LIST
DO 10 TIMES.
  WRITE:/ SY-INDEX.
ENDDO.

CALL FUNCTION 'SAVE_LIST'
     EXPORTING
          LIST_INDEX          = SY-LSIND
     TABLES
          LISTOBJECT          = LISTOBJECT
     EXCEPTIONS
          LIST_INDEX_INVALID  = 1
          OTHERS              = 2.

IF SY-SUBRC EQ 0.
  WRITE:/ 'LIST SAVED'.
ELSE.
  WRITE:/ 'COULD NOT SAVE LIST'.
ENDIF.
```

VRM_SET_VALUES

Summary

Customises values on a drop-down field.

Description

Popup your own set of values when you do a drop down on a field on a selection screen.

Parameters

```
EXPORTING
     ID                Name of the value list
     VALUES            Values in the drop-down list
```

Example

```
REPORT ZEXAMPLE.
TYPE-POOLS VRM.

DATA:    IVRM TYPE VRM_VALUES,
         IVRM_DATA LIKE LINE OF IVRM.

PARAMETERS P_SPRAS LIKE T002T-SPRAS AS LISTBOX
                   VISIBLE LENGTH 10 OBLIGATORY.

INITIALIZATION.
  CLEAR: IVRM, IVRM[].

  SELECT SPRAS SPTXT FROM T002T INTO (IVRM_DATA-KEY, IVRM_DATA-TEXT).
    APPEND IVRM_DATA TO IVRM.
  ENDSELECT.
  P_SPRAS = SY-LANGU.

AT SELECTION-SCREEN OUTPUT.
  CALL FUNCTION 'VRM_SET_VALUES'
       EXPORTING
            ID      = 'P_SPRAS'
            VALUES  = IVRM.

END-OF-SELECTION.
  WRITE: / P_SPRAS.
```

WRITE_LIST

Summary

Writes out the list contents that result from the function LIST_FROM_MEMORY.

Parameters

```
EXPORTING
      WRITE_ONLY      Indicator: list is displayed or displayed in different list
TABLES
      LISTOBJECT      List information
```

Example

See LIST_FROM_MEMORY

See Also

LIST_FROM_MEMORY

WWW_ITAB_TO_HTML

Summary

Converts internal table to HTML format.

Description

This function is well documented.

Parameters

```
EXPORTING
  TABLE_ATTRIBUTES  General table settings
  TABLE_HEADER      Table header format
  ALL_FIELDS        Format all fields (default)
TABLES
  HTML              Source data in HTML
  FIELDS            Formatted fields
  ITABLE            Source data
```

Example

```
REPORT ZEXAMPLE.

TABLES: MARA, MAKT.

DATA: IFLDS LIKE W3FIELDS OCCURS 0,
    IHTML LIKE W3HTML OCCURS 0 WITH HEADER LINE.
DATA: BEGIN OF ITAB OCCURS 0,
     MATNR LIKE MARA-MATNR,
     MAKTX LIKE MAKT-MAKTX,
    END OF ITAB.

PERFORM GET_SOME_DATA.

IF NOT ITAB[] IS INITIAL.
  CALL FUNCTION 'WWW_ITAB_TO_HTML'
     TABLES
       HTML   = IHTML
       FIELDS = IFLDS
       ITABLE = ITAB.
  IF SY-SUBRC NE 0.
   WRITE:/ 'ERROR IN GENERATING HTML'.
   EXIT.
  ENDIF.
```

```
CALL FUNCTION 'WS_DOWNLOAD'
   EXPORTING
     FILENAME = 'c:\materials.html'
     MODE     = 'BIN'
   TABLES
     DATA_TAB = IHTML
   EXCEPTIONS
     OTHERS   = 1.


IF SY-SUBRC <> 0.
  WRITE:/ 'ERROR DOWNLOADING C:\MATERIALS.HTML'.
ELSE.
  WRITE:/ 'OUTPUT SAVED IN FILE C:\MATERIALS.HTML'.
ENDIF.
ENDIF.


*&---------------------------------------------------------------------*
*&      Form  GET_SOME_DATA
*&---------------------------------------------------------------------*
*       Collect data for purpose of demostrating example
*----------------------------------------------------------------------*
FORM GET_SOME_DATA.
* K = MARA
* G = MAKT

  SELECT K~MATNR G~MAKTX
    INTO CORRESPONDING FIELDS OF TABLE ITAB
    FROM MARA AS K INNER JOIN MAKT AS G
    ON K~MATNR = G~MATNR
    UP TO 20 ROWS.

ENDFORM.        " GET_SOME_DATA
```

See Also

WWW_LIST_TO_HTML

WWW_LIST_TO_HTML

Summary

Converts report output to HTML format.

Description

It is not possible to run this function in background because the function needs to read whatever is on the screen (list).

Parameters

```
TABLES
     HTML      List to be converted into HTML
```

Example

```
REPORT ZEXAMPLE.

DATA: ICOA_LIST LIKE ABAPLIST OCCURS O WITH HEADER LINE,
      ICOA_HTML LIKE W3HTML OCCURS O WITH HEADER LINE.

PERFORM GET_SOME_DATA.

IF NOT ICOA_LIST[] IS INITIAL.
  CALL FUNCTION 'WWW_LIST_TO_HTML'
     TABLES
       HTML   = ICOA_HTML
     EXCEPTIONS
       OTHERS = 1.

  IF SY-SUBRC NE O.
    WRITE:/ 'ERROR GENERATING HTML FORMAT'.
  ELSE.
    CALL FUNCTION 'WS_DOWNLOAD'
      EXPORTING
        FILENAME = 'c:\coa.html'
        MODE     = 'BIN'
      TABLES
        DATA_TAB = ICOA_HTML
      EXCEPTIONS
        OTHERS   = 1.

    IF SY-SUBRC <> O.
      WRITE:/ 'ERROR DOWNLOADING C:\COA.HTML'.
    ELSE.
      WRITE:/ 'OUTPUT SAVED IN FILE C:\COA.HTML'.
    ENDIF.
  ENDIF.
ENDIF.
```

```
*&---------------------------------------------------------------*
*&      Form  GET_SOME_DATA
*&---------------------------------------------------------------*
*       Collect data for purpose of demostrating example
*----------------------------------------------------------------*
FORM GET_SOME_DATA.

  SUBMIT RFSKPL00         "CHART OF ACCOUNTS
    EXPORTING LIST TO MEMORY
    AND RETURN.

  CALL FUNCTION 'LIST_FROM_MEMORY'
       TABLES
         LISTOBJECT = ICOA_LIST
       EXCEPTIONS
         OTHERS    = 1.

  CALL FUNCTION 'WRITE_LIST'
       TABLES
         LISTOBJECT = ICOA_LIST
       EXCEPTIONS
         OTHERS    = 1.

ENDFORM.         " GET_SOME_DATA
```

See Also

WWW_ITAB_TO_HTML

Long Texts 6

In table STXH you can find the parameters for the function module in fields.

- TDOBJECT for parameter OBJECT
- TDIS for parameter ID
- TDNAME for parameter NAME
- TDSPRAS for parameter LANGUAGE

The NAME parameter is the key for the text, e.g. Customer Number and Order Number.

COMMIT_TEXT

Summary

Moves long texts from memory into log file.

Description

This function is well documented.

Parameters

```
EXPORTING
      OBJECT          Text object name
      NAME            Short text
      ID              Text ID
      LANGUAGE        Language of text
      KEEP            Indicates whether to keep updated texts in the text memory
```

Example

See CREATE_TEXT

See Also

SAVE_TEXT

CREATE_TEXT

Summary

Create header text.

Description

This function is well documented.

Parameters

```
EXPORTING
        FID              Text ID
        FLANGUAGE        Language of text
        FNAME            Short text
        FOBJECT          Text object name
TABLES
        FLINES              Table containing text
```

Example

```
REPORT ZEXAMPLE.
TABLES: TTXID, ITCPO.

DATA:   LANGUAGE     LIKE    T002-SPRAS VALUE 'E',
        ACTION       LIKE    TTXCT-FUNCTION,
        TEXTTITLE    LIKE    TTXIT-TDTEXT.

DATA BEGIN OF TEXTHEADER.
     INCLUDE STRUCTURE THEAD.
DATA END OF TEXTHEADER.

DATA BEGIN OF TEXTLINES OCCURS 0.
     INCLUDE STRUCTURE TLINE.
DATA END OF TEXTLINES.

*  CREATE A ONE-LINE TEXT ELEMENT
PARAMETERS: P_OBJ     LIKE  TTXID-TDOBJECT DEFAULT 'DOKU' OBLIGATORY,
            P_ID      LIKE  TTXID-TDID DEFAULT 'TB' OBLIGATORY,
            P_NAME    LIKE  STXH-TDNAME DEFAULT 'MARA' OBLIGATORY.
PARAMETERS: P_LINE    LIKE  TLINE-TDLINE,
            P_PRNFMT  LIKE  THEAD-TDTEXTTYPE,
            P_DEL     AS CHECKBOX.

CLEAR: TEXTLINES, TEXTLINES[].
TEXTLINES-TDLINE  = P_LINE.
APPEND TEXTLINES.

SELECT SINGLE * FROM TTXID WHERE TDOBJECT EQ P_OBJ
                             AND TDID EQ P_ID.
```

```
IF SY-SUBRC EQ 0.
  CALL FUNCTION 'READ_TEXT'
        EXPORTING
           ID          = P_ID
           LANGUAGE    = LANGUAGE
           NAME        = P_NAME
           OBJECT      = P_OBJ
        IMPORTING
           HEADER      = TEXTHEADER
        TABLES
           LINES       = TEXTLINES
        EXCEPTIONS
           OTHERS      = 1.

  IF SY-SUBRC = 0.
    MOVE 'LOCL' TO ITCPO-TDDEST.
    MOVE 1 TO ITCPO-TDCOPIES.

    IF P_PRNFMT = 'ITF'.
      CALL FUNCTION 'PRINT_TEXT_ITF'
           EXPORTING
              HEADER      = TEXTHEADER
              OPTIONS     = ITCPO
           TABLES
              LINES       = TEXTLINES.
    ELSE.
      CALL FUNCTION 'PRINT_TEXT'
           EXPORTING
              HEADER      = TEXTHEADER
              OPTIONS     = ITCPO
           TABLES
              LINES       = TEXTLINES
           EXCEPTIONS
              OTHERS      = 1.
    ENDIF.

    IF SY-SUBRC EQ 0.
      CALL FUNCTION 'INIT_TEXT'
           EXPORTING
              ID          = P_ID
              LANGUAGE    = LANGUAGE
              NAME        = P_NAME
              OBJECT      = P_OBJ
           IMPORTING
              HEADER      = TEXTHEADER
           TABLES
              LINES       = TEXTLINES.

    CALL FUNCTION 'EDIT_TEXT'
         EXPORTING
            EDITOR_TITLE  = TEXTTITLE
            HEADER        = TEXTHEADER
            SAVE          = SPACE
         IMPORTING
            FUNCTION      = ACTION
```

```
                NEWHEADER     = TEXTHEADER
          TABLES
                LINES         = TEXTLINES.

    CALL FUNCTION 'CREATE_TEXT'
          EXPORTING
                FID       = P_ID
                FLANGUAGE = LANGUAGE
                FNAME     = P_NAME
                FOBJECT   = P_OBJ
          TABLES
                FLINES    = TEXTLINES
          EXCEPTIONS
                NO_INIT   = 1
                NO_SAVE   = 2
                OTHERS    = 3.

    IF SY-SUBRC EQ 0.
      CALL FUNCTION 'SAVE_TEXT'
          EXPORTING
                HEADER        = TEXTHEADER
          IMPORTING
                NEWHEADER     = TEXTHEADER
          TABLES
                LINES         = TEXTLINES.

      CALL FUNCTION 'COMMIT_TEXT'
          EXPORTING
                OBJECT    = P_OBJ
                NAME      = P_NAME
                ID        = P_ID
                LANGUAGE  = LANGUAGE.
    ELSE.
      IF P_DEL EQ 'X'.
        CALL FUNCTION 'DELETE_TEXT'
            EXPORTING
                OBJECT        = P_OBJ
                ID            = P_ID
                NAME          = P_NAME
                LANGUAGE      = LANGUAGE.
        WRITE:/ P_OBJ, 'DELETED'.
      ELSE.
        WRITE:/ P_OBJ, 'EXISTS'.
      ENDIF.
    ENDIF.
    ENDIF.
  ENDIF.
ENDIF.
```

DELETE_TEXT

Summary

Deletes long text(s) from SAP.

Description

If the TEXTMEMORY_ONLY parameter contains "X", the system does not delete the text itself from the text memory but only its entry (valid only for texts stored in the text memory). This allows the rollback of all changes made to a text during a transaction. This function is well documented. Use with caution!!

Parameters

```
EXPORTING
      OBJECT                   Text object name
      NAME                     Short text
      ID                       Text ID
      LANGUAGE                 Language of text
      TEXTMEMORY_ONLY          Delete to apply to text memory only
```

Example

See CREATE_TEXT

EDIT_TEXT

Summary

Edits text in fullscreen text editor.

Description

The system implicitly calls the function module SAVE_TEXT if you leave the editor choosing SAVE, provided the text is stored in the text file according to the allocated text object. To deactivate this call, use the parameter SAVE. This function is well documented.

Parameters

```
EXPORTING
      DISPLAY                  Call editor in Display ('X') or Change ('') mode
      EDITOR_TITLE             Text for editor title line
      HEADER                   Text header of the text to be edited
      SAVE                     Indicator: Saving by editor
IMPORTING
      FUNCTION                 Indicator: Editing status
      NEWHEADER                Text header (changed)
```

Example

See CREATE_TEXT

INIT_TEXT

Summary

Initialises text header and line table.

Description

This function is well documented.

Parameters

```
EXPORTING
      OBJECT                  Text object name
      NAME                    Short text
      ID                      Text ID
      LANGUAGE                Language of text
IMPORTING
      HEADER                  Initialised work area for text header
TABLES
      LINES                   Initialised table for lines
```

Example

See CREATE_TEXT

PRINT_TEXT

Summary

Formats SAPscript text.

Description

The function module PRINT_TEXT internally calls the function modules OPEN_FORM, WRITE_FORM_LINES, and CLOSE_FORM. Therefore, you cannot call PRINT_TEXT after a form has been opened using OPEN_FORM. The system then ends the function module with the exception UNCLOSED. See the "BC SAPscript: printing with forms" help file for detailed information.

Parameters

```
EXPORTING
      APPLICATION             Application code for interface:
                              Value    Meaning
                              CL       User folders
                              TA       Integrated application texts; without 'Save' key
                              TN       Application texts; with 'Save' key
```

	TD	Documentation
	TO	SAPoffice
	TX	Standard texts (default)
	TY	Forms
	WF	Workflow
	HR	Human Resources
	DEVICE	Output device type:

	Value	Meaning
	PRINTER	To Printer (default)
	SCREEN	To Screen as list
	TELEX	To Telex machine
	TELEFAX	To Telefax machine
	ABAP	To Screen as list
	OTF_MEM	To OTF format and into SAP memory

	MAIL	To an e-mail address
	DIALOG	Flag to display print parameters dialogue
	HEADER	Text header of text to be output
	OPTIONS	Print options
IMPORTING		
	RESULT	Print options from user
TABLES		
	LINES	Lines of text to be output
	OTFDATA	OTF data table

Example

See CREATE_TEXT

See Also

PRINT_TEXT_ITF

PRINT_TEXT_ITF

Summary

Formats SAPscript text to the internal ITF format.

Description

The contents of an SAPscript text line only fit into a layout set line up to column 72. If the text line is longer, it is divided into two parts. The character "." in the tag column indicates that this line contains columns 73–132 of the preceding text line.

Parameters

```
EXPORTING
      HEADER      Text header of text to be output
      OPTIONS     Print options
```

```
IMPORTING
      RESULT          Print options from user
TABLES
      LINES           Lines of text to be output
```

Example

See CREATE_TEXT

See Also

PRINT_TEXT

READ_TEXT

Summary

Reads text module into SAP.

Description

This function is well documented.

Parameters

```
EXPORTING
      OBJECT          Text object name
      NAME            Short text
      ID              Text ID
      LANGUAGE        Language of text
IMPORTING
      HEADER          Initialised work area for text header
TABLES
      LINES           Initialised table for lines
```

Example

See CREATE_TEXT

SAVE_TEXT

Summary

Saves long text in SAP.

Description

You can use this module either to change existing texts or to create new texts. If the lines table passed with the function module is empty, the system deletes the text from the text file. This function is well documented.

Parameters

```
EXPORTING
      HEADER          Text header of text to be saved
      INSERT          Indicates that text module is new
IMPORTING
      NEWHEADER       Text header (changed)
TABLES
      LINES           Lines of text to be saved
```

Example

See CREATE_TEXT

See Also

CREATE_TEXT

Number Ranges 7

Function group SNR2. The function modules in this group perform all read and maintenance accesses to number range objects in the database. Use Transaction SNRO to create one. I would not use an SAP number range for customer objects but rather create my own number range (with Transaction SNUM). Each function is very well documented.

NUMBER_GET_NEXT

Summary

To obtain next number from number range object.

Parameters

```
EXPORTING
        NR_RANGE_NR       Number range number
        OBJECT            Name of number range object
IMPORTING
        NUMBER            Next free number
```

Example

See NUMBER_RANGE_OBJECT_LIST

NUMBER_RANGE_DEQUEUE

Summary

Unlocks the number range object that has been maintained.

Parameters

```
EXPORTING
        OBJECT            Number range object to unlock
```

Example

See NUMBER_RANGE_OBJECT_MAINTAIN

See Also

NUMBER_RANGE_ENQUEUE

NUMBER_RANGE_ENQUEUE

Summary

Locks the number range object that has been maintained.

Description

With this function module, you lock the number range object that is to be maintained.

Parameters

```
EXPORTING
    OBJECT   Number range object to lock
```

Example

See NUMBER_RANGE_OBJECT_MAINTAIN

See Also

NUMBER_RANGE_DEQUEUE

NUMBER_RANGE_INTERVAL_LIST

Summary

Gets the existing intervals to a given number range object.

Description

This function module gets the existing intervals to a given number range object, and puts them in a table.

Parameters

```
EXPORTING
      NR_RANGE_NR1          Internal or external number range object number
      NR_RANGE_NR2          External number range object number
      OBJECT                Number object ID
TABLES
      INTERVAL              Table of number ranges
```

Example

See NUMBER_RANGE_OBJECT_LIST

NUMBER_RANGE_OBJECT_CLOSE

Summary

Writes all changes to a number range object to the database.

Description

Writes all changes to a given number range object, which were put in local memory with NUMBER_RANGE_OBJECT_UPDATE, to the database.

Parameters

```
EXPORTING
      OBJECT          Number range object to close
```

Example

See NUMBER_RANGE_OBJECT_MAINTAIN

NUMBER_RANGE_OBJECT_DELETE

Summary

Deletes the definition of a number range object.

Description

The deletion is performed directly in the database and provides no connection to the correction and transport system.

Parameters

```
EXPORTING
    INDICATOR       Processing flag
                            Value       Meaning
                            Space       Examine if number range in object
                            T           Delete text in input language
                            A           Delete all texts in input language
    OBJECT          Number range object to close
```

Example

See NUMBER_RANGE_OBJECT_MAINTAIN

NUMBER_RANGE_OBJECT_GET_INFO

Summary

Gets information for a given number range object.

Description

Information returned includes long, medium, and short textual descriptions of the object. Displays a popup box if object information not found.

Parameters

```
EXPORTING
        OBJECT          Number object ID
IMPORTING
        INFO            Information on number object
```

Example

See NUMBER_RANGE_OBJECT_LIST

See Also

NUMBER_RANGE_OBJECT_READ

NUMBER_RANGE_OBJECT_INIT

Summary

Initialises local memory for a number object.

Description

Initialises local memory for a given number range object.

Parameters

```
EXPORTING
       OBJECT              Number object ID
```

Example

See NUMBER_RANGE_OBJECT_MAINTAIN

NUMBER_RANGE_OBJECT_LIST

Summary

Lists all number objects with their attributes.

Description

Lists all number range objects with their texts and attributes in a table.

Parameters

```
TABLES
       OBJECTS_ATTRIBUTES      Table containing the attributes of each number range
       OBJECTS_TEXTS           Table containing textual descriptions
```

Example

```
REPORT ZEXAMPLE LINE-SIZE 120.

DATA:  NR1 LIKE NRIV-NRRANGENR,
       NR2 LIKE NRIV-NRRANGENR,
       V_INT,
       V_NUM TYPE I.

DATA:  BEGIN OF IRPT OCCURS 0,
          OBJ LIKE TNRO-OBJECT,
          LTEXT(40),
          INTERVAL,
          FNUMBER LIKE INRIV-FROMNUMBER,
          TNUMBER LIKE INRIV-TONUMBER,
          NEXTNUM TYPE I,
  END OF IRPT.

DATA:  BEGIN OF IINTS OCCURS 0.
          INCLUDE STRUCTURE INRIV.
DATA:  END OF IINTS.
```

```
DATA:  BEGIN OF IATTR OCCURS 0.
          INCLUDE STRUCTURE TNRO.
DATA:  END OF IATTR.

DATA:  BEGIN OF ITXTS OCCURS 0.
          INCLUDE STRUCTURE TNROT.
DATA:  END OF ITXTS.

DATA:  BEGIN OF IINFO OCCURS 0.
          INCLUDE STRUCTURE INROI.
DATA:  END OF IINFO.

CALL FUNCTION 'NUMBER_RANGE_OBJECT_LIST'
    TABLES
        OBJECTS_ATTRIBUTES = IATTR
        OBJECTS_TEXTS      = ITXTS
    EXCEPTIONS
        NO_OBJECTS_FOUND   = 1.
IF SY-SUBRC EQ 0.
  LOOP AT IATTR.
    IRPT-OBJ = IATTR-OBJECT.

    CALL  FUNCTION 'NUMBER_RANGE_OBJECT_GET_INFO'
        EXPORTING
            OBJECT                = IATTR-OBJECT
        IMPORTING
            INFO                  = IINFO
        EXCEPTIONS
            OBJECT_NOT_FOUND      = 1.
    IF SY-SUBRC EQ 0.
      IRPT-LTEXT = IINFO-SOBJTXT_L.

      CALL  FUNCTION 'NUMBER_RANGE_OBJECT_READ'
          EXPORTING
              OBJECT            = IATTR-OBJECT
          IMPORTING
              INTERVAL_EXISTS   = V_INT
          EXCEPTIONS
              OTHERS            = 1.
      IF SY-SUBRC EQ 0.
        IRPT-INTERVAL = V_INT.

        IF V_INT EQ 'X'.
          CALL FUNCTION 'NUMBER_RANGE_INTERVAL_LIST'
              EXPORTING
                  NR_RANGE_NR1  = NR1
                  NR_RANGE_NR2  = NR2
                  OBJECT        = IATTR-OBJECT
              TABLES
                  INTERVAL      = IINTS
              EXCEPTIONS
                  OTHERS        = 1.
          IF SY-SUBRC EQ 0.
            READ TABLE IINTS INDEX 1.
```

```
            IRPT-FNUMBER = IINTS-FROMNUMBER.
            IRPT-TNUMBER = IINTS-TONUMBER.

               CALL  FUNCTION 'NUMBER_GET_NEXT'
                     EXPORTING
                          NR_RANGE_NR        = NR1
                          OBJECT             = IATTR-OBJECT
                     IMPORTING
                          NUMBER             = V_NUM
                     EXCEPTIONS
                          INTERVAL_NOT_FOUND        = 1
                          NUMBER_RANGE_NOT_INTERN   = 2
                          OBJECT_NOT_FOUND          = 3
                          QUANTITY_IS_0             = 4
                          QUANTITY_IS_NOT_1         = 5
                          INTERVAL_OVERFLOW         = 6
                          OTHERS                    = 7.
               IF SY-SUBRC EQ 0.
                 IRPT-NEXTNUM = V_NUM.
               ENDIF.
           ENDIF.
         ENDIF.
         APPEND IRPT.
       ENDIF.
     ENDIF.
   ENDLOOP.
 ELSE.
   WRITE:/ 'NO NUMBER RANGES IN SYSTEM'.
 ENDIF.
 WRITE:/ 'OBJECT', 20 'DESCRIPTION', 50 'INTERVAL?', 60 'START RANGE',
          80 'END RANGE', 100 'NEXT NUMBER'.
 ULINE.
 LOOP AT IRPT.
   WRITE:/  IRPT-OBJ,
            20  IRPT-LTEXT,
            50  IRPT-INTERVAL,
            60  IRPT-FNUMBER,
            80  IRPT-TNUMBER,
            100 IRPT-NEXTNUM.
 ENDLOOP.
```

NUMBER_RANGE_OBJECT_MAINTAIN

Summary

Provides screens to maintain number object.

Description

Provides all the screens needed to maintain a number range object.

Parameters

```
EXPORTING
        DISPLAY_ONLY            Flag whether the object is display only
            INSERT              Flag whether an object is be inserted
            OBJECT              Name of object
IMPORTING
        OBJECTS_ATTRIBUTES      Table containing the attributes of each number range
        OBJECTS_TEXTS           Table containing textual descriptions
```

Example

```
REPORT ZEXAMPLE.

DATA:   BEGIN OF IATTR OCCURS 0.
            INCLUDE STRUCTURE TNRO.
DATA:   END OF IATTR.

DATA:   BEGIN OF ITXTS OCCURS 0.
            INCLUDE STRUCTURE TNROT.
DATA:   END OF ITXTS.

DATA:   BEGIN OF IERRS OCCURS 0.
            INCLUDE STRUCTURE INOER.
DATA:   END OF IERRS.

PARAMETERS:    P_OBJ LIKE TNRO-OBJECT,
               P_DEL AS CHECKBOX DEFAULT 'X'.

CALL FUNCTION 'NUMBER_RANGE_ENQUEUE'
     EXPORTING
          OBJECT            = P_OBJ
     EXCEPTIONS
          FOREIGN_LOCK      = 1
          OBJECT_NOT_FOUND  = 2
          SYSTEM_FAILURE    = 3
          OTHERS            = 4.
IF SY-SUBRC EQ 0.

  CALL FUNCTION 'NUMBER_RANGE_OBJECT_INIT'
       EXPORTING
            OBJECT = P_OBJ.

  CALL FUNCTION 'NUMBER_RANGE_OBJECT_MAINTAIN'
       EXPORTING
            OBJECT            = P_OBJ
       IMPORTING
            OBJECT_ATTRIBUTES = IATTR
            OBJECT_TEXT       = ITXTS.

  CALL FUNCTION 'NUMBER_RANGE_OBJECT_UPDATE'
       EXPORTING
            OBJECT_ATTRIBUTES      = IATTR
            OBJECT_TEXT            = ITXTS
```

```
      TABLES
            ERRORS                      = IERRS
      EXCEPTIONS
            OBJECT_ALREADY_EXISTS      = 1
            OBJECT_ATTRIBUTES_MISSING  = 2
            OBJECT_NOT_FOUND           = 3
            OBJECT_TEXT_MISSING        = 4
            WRONG_INDICATOR            = 5
            OTHERS                     = 6.
IF SY-SUBRC EQ 0.
  CALL FUNCTION 'NUMBER_RANGE_OBJECT_CLOSE'
      EXPORTING
            OBJECT = P_OBJ.
ELSE.
  WRITE:/ 'CANNOT UPDATE', P_OBJ.
ENDIF.

CALL FUNCTION 'NUMBER_RANGE_DEQUEUE'
      EXPORTING
            OBJECT             = P_OBJ
      EXCEPTIONS
            OBJECT_NOT_FOUND   = 1
            OTHERS             = 2.
IF SY-SUBRC EQ 0.
  WRITE:/ P_OBJ, 'UNLOCKED'.
  IF P_DEL EQ 'X'.

    CALL FUNCTION 'NUMBER_RANGE_OBJECT_DELETE'
        EXPORTING
            OBJECT                = P_OBJ
        EXCEPTIONS
            DELETE_NOT_ALLOWED    = 1
            OBJECT_NOT_FOUND      = 2
            WRONG_INDICATOR       = 3
            OTHERS                = 4.
    IF SY-SUBRC EQ 0.
      WRITE:/ P_OBJ, 'DELETED'.
    ELSE.
      WRITE:/ 'CANNOT DELETE', P_OBJ.
    ENDIF.
  ENDIF.
ELSE.
  WRITE:/ 'CANNOT UNLOCK', P_OBJ.
ENDIF.
ELSE.
  WRITE:/ 'CANNOT LOCK', P_OBJ.
ENDIF.
```

NUMBER_RANGE_OBJECT_READ

Summary

Gets texts and attributes of number object.

Description

Gets the texts and attributes of a given number range object.

Parameters

```
EXPORTING
      OBJECT                Number object ID
IMPORTING
      INTERVAL_EXISTS       Flag whether intervals exist
      OBJECTS_ATTRIBUTES    Table containing the attributes of each number range
      OBJECTS_TEXTS         Table containing textual descriptions
```

Example

See NUMBER_RANGE_OBJECT_LIST

See Also

NUMBER_RANGE_OBJECT_GET_INFO

NUMBER_RANGE_OBJECT_UPDATE

Summary

Copies and changes number range objects.

Description

Copies new number range objects or changes to existing number range objects into local memory. No connection to the correction and transport system is provided.

Parameters

```
EXPORTING
      INDICATOR             Processing flag
      OBJECT_ATTRIBUTES     Attributes to change
      OBJECT_TEXT           Object texts to change
TABLES
      ERRORS                Error messages from function
```

Example

See NUMBER_RANGE_OBJECT_MAINTAIN

Office Integration 8

Getting data from SAP to external office programs allows the use of the specialised features of these programs. The resulting data can then be uploaded back into SAP.

ALSM_EXCEL_TO_INTERNAL_TABLE

Summary

Uploads Excel spreadsheet to internal table.

Parameters

```
EXPORTING
        FILENAME         Filename and path to excel file
        I_BEGIN_COL      Excel column number to begin reading
        I_BEGIN_ROW      Excel row number to begin reading
        I_END_COL        Excel column number to end reading
        I_END_ROW        Excel row number to end reading
TABLES
        INTERN           Data from Excel file
```

Example

```
REPORT ZEXAMPLE.

FIELD-SYMBOLS: <FS1>.

DATA: BEGIN OF IEXCEL OCCURS 0.
        INCLUDE STRUCTURE KCDE_CELLS.
DATA: END OF IEXCEL.

DATA: BEGIN OF EXCEL_DATA OCCURS 0,
        VALUE_0001(50),
        VALUE_0002(50),
        VALUE_0003(50),
        VALUE_0004(50),
END OF EXCEL_DATA.
```

```
DATA: VINDX(4) TYPE N,
      XLDATA(21).         "EXCEL_DATA-VALUE_....

PARAMETERS: P_FNAME LIKE RLGRAP-FILENAME DEFAULT 'C:\TEMP\TEST.XLS',
            NOHEADER AS CHECKBOX.

CALL FUNCTION 'ALSM_EXCEL_TO_INTERNAL_TABLE'
     EXPORTING
            FILENAME               = P_FNAME
            I_BEGIN_COL            = 1
            I_BEGIN_ROW            = 1
            I_END_COL              = 10
            I_END_ROW              = 100
     TABLES
            INTERN                 = IEXCEL
     EXCEPTIONS
            INCONSISTENT_PARAMETERS = 1
            UPLOAD_OLE              = 2
            OTHERS                  = 3.

SORT IEXCEL BY ROW COL.
LOOP AT IEXCEL.
  IF NOHEADER = 'X' AND IEXCEL-ROW = 1.
    CONTINUE.
  ENDIF.

  VINDX = IEXCEL-COL.
  CONCATENATE 'EXCEL_DATA-VALUE_' VINDX INTO XLDATA.
  ASSIGN (XLDATA) TO <FS1>.
  <FS1> = IEXCEL-VALUE.

  AT END OF ROW.
    APPEND EXCEL_DATA.
  ENDAT.
ENDLOOP.

WRITE:/ 'COLUMN A', 20 'COLUMN B', 40 'COLUMN C', 60 'COLUMN D'.
ULINE.
LOOP AT EXCEL_DATA.
  WRITE:/ EXCEL_DATA-VALUE_0001, 20 EXCEL_DATA-VALUE_0002,
         40 EXCEL_DATA-VALUE_0003, 60 EXCEL_DATA-VALUE_0004.
ENDLOOP.
```

See Also

EXCEL_OLE_STANDARD_DAT, KCD_EXCEL_OLE_TO_INT_CONVERT,
SAP_CONVERT_ TO_XLS_FORMAT

EXCEL_OLE_STANDARD_DAT

Summary

Starts Excel and transfers internal table data.

Description

Starts Excel with a new sheet and transfers data from an internal table to the sheet.

Parameters

```
EXPORTING
        FILE_NAME              Name of the Excel file to download
        CREATE_PIVOT           Create a pivot table sheet
        DATA_SHEET_NAME        Title on Excel sheet
        PIVOT_SHEET_NAME       Title of pivot table sheet
        PASSWORD               Password to protect file
        PASSWORD_OPTION        Password protect the file:
                               Value      Meaning
                               0          No password
                               1          Save with password from PASSWORD parameter
                               2          Create a new password
TABLES
        PIVOT_FIELD_TAB        Pivot data for Excel file
        DATA_TAB               Data for the Excel file
        FIELDNAMES             Table with column headers
```

Example

```
REPORT ZEXAMPLE.

DATA: T_LST LIKE ABAPLIST OCCURS 0 WITH HEADER LINE.
DATA: BEGIN OF T_L,
      LINE(120),
      END OF T_L.
DATA: TLX LIKE T_L OCCURS 0 WITH HEADER LINE.

DATA V_SHEET_NAME LIKE RLGRAP-FILENAME.

PARAMETERS: P_FNAME LIKE RLGRAP-FILENAME,
            P_DATUM LIKE SY-DATUM,
            P_WERKS LIKE T001W-WERKS.

SUBMIT RM07MLBD                         "REPORT OF STOCK LEVELS
        WITH DATUM EQ P_DATUM
        WITH WERKS EQ P_WERKS
        EXPORTING LIST TO MEMORY AND RETURN.

CALL FUNCTION 'LIST_FROM_MEMORY'
    TABLES
        LISTOBJECT = T_LST.

CALL FUNCTION 'LIST_TO_ASCI'
    TABLES
        LISTASCI          = TLX
        LISTOBJECT        = T_LST
    EXCEPTIONS
        EMPTY_LIST        = 1
        LIST_INDEX_INVALID = 2
        OTHERS            = 3.
```

```
IF SY-SUBRC EQ 0 AND NOT T_LST IS INITIAL.
  CONCATENATE 'MATERIAL STOCK FOR' P_DATUM INTO V_SHEET_NAME.

  CALL FUNCTION 'EXCEL_OLE_STANDARD_DAT'
       EXPORTING
            FILE_NAME                 = P_FNAME
            DATA_SHEET_NAME           = V_SHEET_NAME
       TABLES
            DATA_TAB                  = TLX
       EXCEPTIONS
            FILE_NOT_EXIST            = 1
            FILENAME_EXPECTED         = 2
            COMMUNICATION_ERROR       = 3
            OLE_OBJECT_METHOD_ERROR   = 4
            OLE_OBJECT_PROPERTY_ERROR = 5
            INVALID_FILENAME          = 6
            INVALID_PIVOT_FIELDS      = 7
            DOWNLOAD_PROBLEM          = 8
            OTHERS                    = 9.

  IF SY-SUBRC NE 0.
    WRITE:/ 'ERROR OPENING EXCEL'.
  ENDIF.
ELSE.
  WRITE:/ 'ERROR OR NO DATA'.
ENDIF.
```

See Also

ALSM_EXCEL_TO_INTERNAL_TABLE, KCD_EXCEL_OLE_TO_INT_CONVERT,
SAP_ CONVERT_TO_XLS_FORMAT

EXECUTE_WINWORD

Summary

Opens MS Word on the PC.

Description

Opens MS Word as an external application, if installed on the PC. It can also be opened with
a specific file.

Parameters

```
EXPORTING
      I_FILE  File to display after opening MS Word
```

Example

```
REPORT ZEXAMPLE.

CALL FUNCTION 'EXECUTE_WINWORD'
     EXPORTING
          I_FILE = 'C:\TEMP\DAILYDATA.RTF'
     EXCEPTIONS
          OTHERS = 1.
IF SY-SUBRC NE 0.
    WRITE:/ 'ERROR IN FUNCTION'.
ENDIF.
```

See Also

WS_EXCEL, GUI_EXEC, GUI_RUN

KCD_EXCEL_OLE_TO_INT_CONVERT

Summary

Uploads data directly from the Excel sheet.

Parameters

```
EXPORTING
      FILENAME           Filename and path to excel file
      I_BEGIN_COL        Excel column number to begin reading
      I_BEGIN_ROW        Excel row number to begin reading
      I_END_COL          Excel column number to end reading
      I_END_ROW          Excel row number to end reading
TABLES
      INTERN             Data from Excel file
```

Example

```
REPORT ZEXAMPLE.

FIELD-SYMBOLS: <FS1>.

DATA: BEGIN OF IEXCEL OCCURS 0.
        INCLUDE STRUCTURE KCDE_CELLS.
DATA: END OF IEXCEL.
DATA: BEGIN OF EXCEL_DATA OCCURS 0,
        VALUE_0001(50),
        VALUE_0002(50),
        VALUE_0003(50),
        VALUE_0004(50),
END OF EXCEL_DATA.
```

```
DATA:   VINDX(4) TYPE N,
        XLDATA(21).      "EXCEL_DATA-VALUE_....

PARAMETERS: P_FNAME LIKE RLGRAP-FILENAME DEFAULT 'C:\TEMP\TEST.XLS',
            NOHEADER AS CHECKBOX.

CALL FUNCTION 'KCD_EXCEL_OLE_TO_INT_CONVERT'
     EXPORTING
            FILENAME                  = P_FNAME
            I_BEGIN_COL               = 1
            I_BEGIN_ROW               = 1
            I_END_COL                 = 10
            I_END_ROW                 = 100
     TABLES
            INTERN                    = IEXCEL
     EXCEPTIONS
            INCONSISTENT_PARAMETERS   = 1
            UPLOAD_OLE                = 2
            OTHERS                    = 3.

SORT IEXCEL BY ROW COL.
LOOP AT IEXCEL.
  IF NOHEADER = 'X' AND IEXCEL-ROW = 1.
    CONTINUE.
  ENDIF.

  VINDX = IEXCEL-COL.
  CONCATENATE 'EXCEL_DATA-VALUE_' VINDX INTO XLDATA.
  ASSIGN (XLDATA) TO <FS1>.
  <FS1> = IEXCEL-VALUE.

  AT END OF ROW.
    APPEND EXCEL_DATA.
  ENDAT.
ENDLOOP.
WRITE:/ 'COLUMN A', 20 'COLUMN B', 40 'COLUMN C', 60 'COLUMN D'.
ULINE.
LOOP AT EXCEL_DATA.
  WRITE:/ EXCEL_DATA-VALUE_0001, 20 EXCEL_DATA-VALUE_0002,
        40 EXCEL_DATA-VALUE_0003, 60 EXCEL_DATA-VALUE_0004.
ENDLOOP.
```

See Also

ALSM_EXCEL_TO_INTERNAL_TABLE, EXCEL_OLE_STANDARD_DAT,
SAP_CONVERT_ TO_XLS_FORMAT

MS_EXCEL_OLE_STANDARD_DAT

Summary

Creates an MS Excel compatible file and automatically starts MS Excel.

Description

Input filename should end in ".DAT". The function resaves the file with an ".XLS" ending. If there is data in DATA_TAB, the function displays this in Excel instead of opening FILE_NAME. Beware: if you enter in an existing file FILE_NAME and data into DATA_TAB, the file FILE_NAME is deleted!

Parameters

```
EXPORTING
        FILE_NAME               Name of the Excel file to open
        CREATE_PIVOT            Create a pivot table sheet
        DATA_SHEET_NAME         Name on Excel sheet
        PIVOT_SHEET_NAME        Name of pivot table sheet
        PASSWORD                Password to protect file
        PASSWORD_OPTION         Password protect the file:
                                Value      Meaning
                                0          No password
                                1          Save with password from PASSWORD parameter
                                2          Create a new password
TABLES
        PIVOT_FIELD_TAB         Pivot data for Excel file
        DATA_TAB                Data for the Excel file
        FIELDNAMES              Table with column headers
```

Example

```
REPORT ZEXAMPLE.

PARAMETERS P_FNAME LIKE RLGRAP-FILENAME DEFAULT 'C:\TEMP\TEST.DAT'.

CALL FUNCTION 'MS_EXCEL_OLE_STANDARD_DAT'
     EXPORTING
         FILE_NAME                  = P_FNAME
     EXCEPTIONS
         FILE_NOT_EXIST             = 1
         FILENAME_EXPECTED          = 2
         COMMUNICATION_ERROR        = 3
         OLE_OBJECT_METHOD_ERROR    = 4
         OLE_OBJECT_PROPERTY_ERROR  = 5
         INVALID_FILENAME           = 6
         INVALID_PIVOT_FIELDS       = 7
         DOWNLOAD_PROBLEM           = 8
         OTHERS                     = 9.
IF SY-SUBRC NE 0.
  WRITE:/ 'ERROR OPENING', P_FNAME.
ENDIF.
```

RH_START_EXCEL_WITH_DATA

Summary

Starts Excel with the contents of an internal table.

Description

For all Excel versions earlier than 5.0, the module takes Version 4, since the others cannot be recognised from R/3. This module has good documentation.

Parameters

```
EXPORTING
        CHECK_VERSION           Check version of Excel
        DATA_NAME               Name of Excel file
        DATA_TYPE               Data transfer format:
                                Value   Meaning
                                ASC     ASCII
                                BIN     Binary
                                DBF     DBASE
                                IBM     ASCII with IBM code page conversion
                                WK1     Spreadsheet
                                DAT     ASCII data table with column tab (default)
        MACRO_NAME              Start a macro when Excel loads
        FORCE_START             Disable frontend installation check of Excel
        WAIT                    Start Excel modal or modeless
TABLES
        DATA_TAB                Data to put into Excel file
```

Example

```
REPORT ZEXAMPLE.

DATA:   T_LST LIKE ABAPLIST OCCURS 0 WITH HEADER LINE.
DATA:   BEGIN OF T_L,
        LINE(120),
        END OF T_L.
DATA:   TLX LIKE T_L OCCURS 0 WITH HEADER LINE.

PARAMETERS:  P_FNAME LIKE RLGRAP-FILENAME,
             P_DATUM LIKE SY-DATUM,
             P_WERKS LIKE T001W-WERKS.

SUBMIT RM07MLBD                         "REPORT OF STOCK LEVELS
        WITH DATUM EQ P_DATUM
        WITH WERKS EQ P_WERKS
        EXPORTING LIST TO MEMORY AND RETURN.

CALL FUNCTION 'LIST_FROM_MEMORY'
        TABLES
                LISTOBJECT = T_LST.
```

```
CALL FUNCTION 'LIST_TO_ASCI'
     TABLES
          LISTASCI              = TLX
          LISTOBJECT            = T_LST
     EXCEPTIONS
          EMPTY_LIST            = 1
          LIST_INDEX_INVALID    = 2
          OTHERS                = 3.


IF SY-SUBRC EQ 0 AND NOT T_LST IS INITIAL.

  CALL FUNCTION 'RH_START_EXCEL_WITH_DATA'
      EXPORTING
           DATA_NAME              = P_FNAME
      TABLES
           DATA_TAB               = TLX
      EXCEPTIONS
           NO_BATCH               = 1
           EXCEL_NOT_INSTALLED    = 2
           WRONG_VERSION          = 3
           INTERNAL_ERROR         = 4
           INVALID_TYPE           = 5
           CANCELLED              = 6
           DOWNLOAD_ERROR         = 7
           OTHERS                 = 8.


  IF SY-SUBRC NE 0.
    WRITE:/ 'ERROR DOWNLOADING EXCEL FILE'.
  ENDIF.
ELSE.
  WRITE:/ 'ERROR OR NO DATA'.
ENDIF.
```

See Also

ALSM_EXCEL_TO_INTERNAL_TABLE, SAP_CONVERT_TO_XLS_FORMAT

RS_SEND_MAIL_FOR_SPOOLLIST

Summary

Sends message from the program to SAP office.

Description

Attachments cannot be added to the e-mail with this function.

Parameters

```
EXPORTING
      SPOOLNUMBER      Number of spool to send (optional)
      MAILNAME         Name of the recipient of a document (logon name)
      MAILTITEL        Subject of e-mail
      USER             User responsible for the transmission (optional)
TABLES
      TEXT             Message of e-mail
```

Example

See TXW_TEXTNOTE_EDIT

SAP_CONVERT_TO_XLS_FORMAT

Summary

Downloads internal table to Excel.

Description

Each field in the internal table is another column in the Excel sheet, and each new line in the internal table is a new row in the excel sheet. It will overwrite a file of the same name without warning.

Parameters

```
EXPORTING
      I_FILENAME       Excel filename
      I_APPL_KEEP      Display Excel inline (when not in batch mode)
TABLES
      I_TAB_SAP_DATA   Data for Excel sheet
```

Example

```
REPORT ZEXAMPLE.

TABLES USR03.

DATA:   BEGIN OF ISAPDAT OCCURS 0,
          BNAME LIKE USR03-BNAME,
          NAME1 LIKE USR03-NAME1,
          NAME2 LIKE USR03-NAME2,
        END OF ISAPDAT.

PARAMETERS P_FNAME LIKE RLGRAP-FILENAME
                              DEFAULT 'd:\sapdata.xls' OBLIGATORY.
```

```
SELECT * FROM USRO3 INTO CORRESPONDING FIELDS OF TABLE ISAPDAT.
SORT ISAPDAT.

CALL FUNCTION 'SAP_CONVERT_TO_XLS_FORMAT'
      EXPORTING
            I_FILENAME          = P_FNAME
      TABLES
            I_TAB_SAP_DATA      = ISAPDAT
      EXCEPTIONS
            CONVERSION_FAILED  = 1
            OTHERS             = 2.

IF SY-SUBRC EQ 0.
  WRITE:/ 'Download to Excel complete'.
ELSE.
  WRITE:/ 'Error with download'.
ENDIF.
```

See Also

ALSM_EXCEL_TO_INTERNAL_TABLE, EXCEL_OLE_STANDARD_DAT,
KCD_EXCEL_ OLE_TO_INT_CONVERT

SO_NEW_DOCUMENT_ATT_SEND_API1

Summary

Attaches a document to an e-mail.

Description

An e-mail can have numerous attachments and can be sent to multiple recipients. This function
is well documented.

Parameters

```
EXPORTING
      DOCUMENT_DATA        Attributes of new document
      PUT_IN_OUTBOX        Flag: move document to outbox after send
TABLES
      PACKING_LIST         Information about structure of data tables
      OBJECT_HEADER        Header data for document
      RECEIVERS            Document recipients with send attributes
```

Example

```
REPORT ZEXAMPLE.

DATA:     OBJPACK       LIKE SOPCKLSTI1 OCCURS 0 WITH HEADER LINE,
          OBJHEAD       LIKE SOLISTI1 OCCURS 0 WITH HEADER LINE,
```

```
            OBJBIN      LIKE SOLISTI1 OCCURS 0 WITH HEADER LINE,
            OBJTXT      LIKE SOLISTI1 OCCURS 0 WITH HEADER LINE,
            RECLIST     LIKE SOMLRECI1 OCCURS 0 WITH HEADER LINE,
            DOC_CHNG    LIKE SODOCCHGI1,
            TAB_LINES   LIKE SY-TABIX.


PARAMETER P_EADDR LIKE RECLIST-RECEIVER.  "EXTERNAL E-MAIL ADDRESS


DOC_CHNG-OBJ_NAME  = 'SENDFILE'.
DOC_CHNG-OBJ_DESCR = 'SEND EXTERNAL MAIL'.


OBJTXT = 'LINE 1 OF MESSAGE'.
APPEND OBJTXT.
OBJTXT = 'LINE 2 OF MESSAGE'.
APPEND OBJTXT.


DESCRIBE TABLE OBJTXT LINES TAB_LINES.
READ TABLE OBJTXT INDEX TAB_LINES.
DOC_CHNG-DOC_SIZE = ( TAB_LINES - 1 ) * 255 + STRLEN( OBJTXT ).


CLEAR OBJPACK-TRANSF_BIN.
OBJPACK-HEAD_START  = 1.
OBJPACK-HEAD_NUM    = 0.
OBJPACK-BODY_START  = 1.
OBJPACK-BODY_NUM    = TAB_LINES.
OBJPACK-DOC_TYPE    = 'RAW'.
APPEND OBJPACK.


RECLIST-RECEIVER = P_EADDR.
RECLIST-REC_TYPE = 'U'.
APPEND RECLIST.

CALL FUNCTION 'SO_NEW_DOCUMENT_ATT_SEND_API1'
     EXPORTING
                DOCUMENT_DATA                 = DOC_CHNG
                PUT_IN_OUTBOX                 = 'X'
     TABLES
                PACKING_LIST                  = OBJPACK
                OBJECT_HEADER                 = OBJHEAD
                CONTENTS_BIN                  = OBJBIN
                CONTENTS_TXT                  = OBJTXT
                RECEIVERS                     = RECLIST
     EXCEPTIONS
                TOO_MANY_RECEIVERS            = 1
                DOCUMENT_NOT_SENT             = 2
                OPERATION_NO_AUTHORIZATION    = 3
                OTHERS                        = 4.
IF SY-SUBRC EQ 0.
  WRITE:/ 'E-MAIL MESSAGE SENT TO', P_EADDR.
ELSE.
  WRITE:/ 'COULD NOT SEND E-MAIL TO', P_EADDR.
ENDIF.
```

See Also

SO_NEW_DOCUMENT_SEND_API1

SO_NEW_DOCUMENT_SEND_API1

Summary

Sending express mail (SAP office).

Description

The user ID is case-sensitive.

Parameters

```
EXPORTING
        DCUMENT_DATA       Attributes of new document
        DOCUMENT_TYPE      Sending format of document
        PUT_IN_OUTBOX      Move document to outbox after sending
IMPORTING
        SENT_TO_ALL        Indicator: document sent to all recipients
TABLES
        OBJECT_HEADER      Document header
        OBJECT_CONTENT     Document contents
        RECEIVERS          Document recipients with send attributes
```

Example

```
REPORT ZEXAMPLE.

TABLES: KNA1,
        MAKT.

DATA:  V_DOCDATA       LIKE SODOCCHGI1,
       I_MSG           LIKE SOLI OCCURS 0 WITH HEADER LINE,
       I_TO            LIKE SOMLRECI1 OCCURS 0 WITH HEADER LINE.

PARAMETERS P_RECE LIKE SOMLRECI1-RECEIVER.

SELECT * FROM MAKT UP TO 100 ROWS.
  CONCATENATE MAKT-MATNR MAKT-MAKTX INTO I_MSG-LINE SEPARATED BY SPACE.
  APPEND I_MSG.
ENDSELECT.

MOVE: P_RECE     TO I_TO-RECEIVER,
      'X'        TO I_TO-EXPRESS,
      'B'        TO I_TO-REC_TYPE.
APPEND I_TO.
```

```
WRITE 'THESE MATERIALS WERE UPDATED:'     TO V_DOCDATA-OBJ_DESCR.

CALL FUNCTION 'SO_NEW_DOCUMENT_SEND_API1'
     EXPORTING
               DOCUMENT_DATA                = V_DOCDATA
     TABLES
               OBJECT_CONTENT               = I_MSG
               RECEIVERS                    = I_TO
     EXCEPTIONS
               TOO_MANY_RECEIVERS           = 1
               DOCUMENT_NOT_SENT            = 2
               DOCUMENT_TYPE_NOT_EXIST      = 3
               OPERATION_NO_AUTHORIZATION   = 4
               PARAMETER_ERROR              = 5
               X_ERROR                      = 6
               ENQUEUE_ERROR                = 7
               OTHERS                       = 8.

IF SY-SUBRC EQ 0.
  WRITE:/ 'DOCUMENT SENT'.
ELSE.
  WRITE:/ 'DOCUMENT NOT SENT'.
ENDIF.
```

See Also

SO_NEW_DOCUMENT_ATT_SEND_API1

WS_EXCEL

Summary

Starts EXCEL on the PC.

Parameters

```
EXPORTING
       FILENAME    Excel filename
TABLES
       DATA        Excel data
```

Example

```
REPORT ZEXAMPLE.

DATA:  T_LST LIKE ABAPLIST OCCURS 0 WITH HEADER LINE.
DATA:  BEGIN OF T_L,
       LINE(120),
       END OF T_L.
DATA:  TLX LIKE T_L OCCURS 0 WITH HEADER LINE.
```

```
PARAMETERS:  P_FNAME LIKE RLGRAP-FILENAME,
             P_DATUM LIKE SY-DATUM,
             P_WERKS LIKE T001W-WERKS.
SUBMIT RM07MLBD                             "REPORT OF STOCK LEVELS
        WITH DATUM EQ P_DATUM
        WITH WERKS EQ P_WERKS
        EXPORTING LIST TO MEMORY AND RETURN.

CALL FUNCTION 'LIST_FROM_MEMORY'
    TABLES
        LISTOBJECT     = T_LST.

CALL FUNCTION 'LIST_TO_ASCI'
    TABLES
        LISTASCI           = TLX
        LISTOBJECT         = T_LST
    EXCEPTIONS
        EMPTY_LIST         = 1
        LIST_INDEX_INVALID = 2
        OTHERS             = 3.

IF SY-SUBRC EQ 0 AND NOT T_LST IS INITIAL.

  CALL FUNCTION 'WS_EXCEL'
      EXPORTING
          FILENAME = P_FNAME
      TABLES
          DATA     = TLX.

  IF SY-SUBRC NE 0.
    WRITE:/ 'ERROR OPENING EXCEL FILE'.
  ENDIF.
ELSE.
  WRITE:/ 'ERROR OR NO DATA'.
ENDIF.
```

See Also

EXECUTE_WINWORD, GUI_EXEC

Popup Dialogues 9

SAP has many built-in functions that display popup dialogue screens. Many, especially the confirmation prompt dialogues, are very similar in function. The screen-shots below should help you in choosing the right dialogue for your program.

Confirmation Prompt Dialogues

These function modules create dialogue boxes in which you question whether the user wishes to perform a processing step with loss of data.

C14A_POPUP_ASK_FILE_OVERWRITE

Summary

Asks if file can be overwritten.

Description

If the file already exists, it asks if it can be overwritten.

Parameters

```
IMPORTING
    E_FLG_CONTINUE        Flag indicating whether to overwrite or not
```

Example

See C13Z_FILE_DOWNLOAD_ASCII

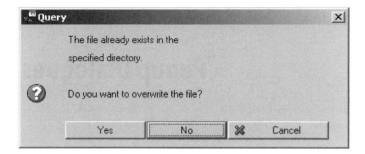

CJDB_POPUP_TO_HANDLE_TIME_OUT

Summary

Asks for next step after timeout.

Description

Displays this pop if a process takes longer than a pre-determined runtime.

Parameters

```
IMPORTING
     ANSWER              Return code of button clicked:
                         Value       Meaning
                         W           Process in online mode
                         B           Process in background mode
                         C           Cancel selection screen
                         ' '         Default; all other buttons
```

Example

```
REPORT ZEXAMPLE.
TABLES BSEG.
DATA: START_TIME          LIKE SY-UZEIT,
      ACTUAL_TIME         LIKE SY-UZEIT,
      RUN_TIME            TYPE I,
      TIME_OUT_STRING(5)  TYPE C,
      ACTION(1),
      REC_COUNT           TYPE I.

PARAMETERS TIME_OUT TYPE I DEFAULT 10.    "max runtime in seconds

IF TIME_OUT LE 0.
  PERFORM GET_TIME_OUT_SETTINGS CHANGING TIME_OUT.
ENDIF.

WRITE:/ 'Max run-time allowed:', TIME_OUT.
ULINE.
```

```
GET TIME FIELD START_TIME.

SELECT * FROM BSEG.
  GET TIME FIELD ACTUAL_TIME.

  RUN_TIME = ACTUAL_TIME - START_TIME.
  IF RUN_TIME < 0.
    ADD 86400 TO RUN_TIME.
  ENDIF.

  IF RUN_TIME > TIME_OUT.
    CALL FUNCTION 'CJDB_POPUP_TO_HANDLE_TIME_OUT'
        IMPORTING
             E_ACTION = ACTION.
    CASE ACTION.
      WHEN 'W'.        "online
        GET TIME FIELD START_TIME.
        REC_COUNT = REC_COUNT + 1.
      WHEN OTHERS.
        EXIT.
    ENDCASE.
    CLEAR ACTION.
  ELSE.
    REC_COUNT = REC_COUNT + 1.
  ENDIF.
ENDSELECT.

WRITE:/ 'Number of records counted in table BSEG:', REC_COUNT.

*&---------------------------------------------------------------------*
*&                      Form GET_TIME_OUT_SETTINGS
*&---------------------------------------------------------------------*
*&                      Get SAP's default
*&---------------------------------------------------------------------*
FORM GET_TIME_OUT_SETTINGS CHANGING P_P_TIME_OUT.
  CALL 'C_SAPGPARAM'     ID   'NAME' FIELD 'rdisp/max_wprun_time'
                         ID   'VALUE' FIELD TIME_OUT_STRING.
  P_P_TIME_OUT = TIME_OUT_STRING.
  IF P_P_TIME_OUT <= 0.
    P_P_TIME_OUT = 2147483647.    "Max value possible for TYPE I
  ENDIF.
ENDFORM.        "GET_TIME_OUT_SETTINGS
```

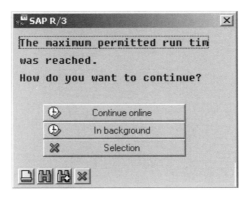

POPUP_TO_CONFIRM

Summary

Confirms an action before it is carried out.

Description

Clicking "Yes" returns "J", an abbreviation of the German word "Ja" meaning "Yes"; clicking "No" returns "N" meaning "Nein"; and clicking "Cancel" returns "A", an abbreviation of the German word "Abbrechen" meaning "Break off". This function is well documented.

Parameters

```
EXPORTING
    TITLEBAR          Text in popup title
    TEXT_QUESTION     Question displayed to user
    TEXT_BUTTON_1     Text on the first pushbutton
    ICON_BUTTON_1     Icon on first pushbutton
    TEXT_BUTTON_2     Text on the second pushbutton
    ICON_BUTTON_2     Icon on second pushbutton
IMPORTING
    ANSWER            Return code of button clicked
```

Example

```
REPORT ZEXAMPLE.
TABLES MARA.
DATA: V_ANS, V_MSG(255), C_ROWS(4).

PARAMETER P_ROWS TYPE I.

C_ROWS = P_ROWS.
CONCATENATE 'SELECT' C_ROWS 'ROWS FROM MARA?' INTO V_MSG
                                    SEPARATED BY SPACE.

CALL FUNCTION 'POPUP_TO_CONFIRM'
    EXPORTING
        TITLEBAR          = 'SELECT ROWS FROM MARA'
        TEXT_QUESTION     = V_MSG
        TEXT_BUTTON_1     = 'YES'
        ICON_BUTTON_1     = 'ICON_OKAY'
        TEXT_BUTTON_2     = 'NO'
        ICON_BUTTON_2     = 'ICON_CANCEL'
    IMPORTING
        ANSWER            = V_ANS.

IF V_ANS EQ '1'.
  SELECT * FROM MARA UP TO P_ROWS ROWS.
    WRITE:/ MARA-MATNR.
```

```
  ENDSELECT.
  ULINE.
  WRITE:/ C_ROWS, 'SELECTED'.
ELSE.
  WRITE:/ 'NO RECORDS SELECTED'.
ENDIF.
```

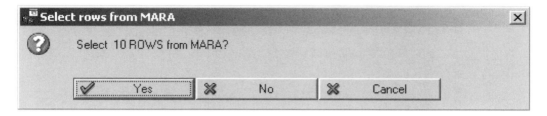

See Also

POPUP_TO_DECIDE

POPUP_TO_CONFIRM_DATA_LOSS

Summary

Confirms an action before carrying out.

Description

Simpler version of POPUP_TO_CONFIRM_LOSS_OF_DATA. The popup automatically displays the text "Changed data will be lost".

Parameters

```
EXPORTING
    TITEL           Text in popup title
IMPORTING
    ANSWER          Return code of button clicked
```

Example

```
REPORT ZEXAMPLE.
DATA V_ANS.

CALL FUNCTION 'POPUP_TO_CONFIRM_DATA_LOSS'
    EXPORTING
        TITEL     = 'DELETE ROWS FROM MARA'
    IMPORTING
        ANSWER    = V_ANS.
```

```
IF V_ANS EQ 'J'.
* CODE TO DELETE RECORDS HERE....
  WRITE:/ 'RECORDS IN MARA DELETED'.
ELSE.
  WRITE:/ 'NO RECORDS DELETED'.
ENDIF.
```

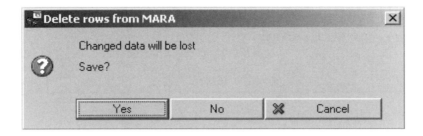

POPUP_TO_CONFIRM_LOSS_OF_DATA

Summary

Confirms an action before it is carried out.

Description

The popup automatically displays the text "Data will be lost".

Parameters

```
EXPORTING
    TEXTLINE1    Information message to the user
    TEXTLINE2    Optional second line of information to the user
    TITEL        Text in title of dialogue box
IMPORTING
    ANSWER       Return code of button clicked
```

Example

```
REPORT ZEXAMPLE.
DATA V_ANS.

CALL FUNCTION 'POPUP_TO_CONFIRM_LOSS_OF_DATA'
    EXPORTING
        TEXTLINE1 = 'CLICKING YES WILL DELETE ALL RECORDS IN MARA'
        TEXTLINE2 = 'DO YOU WANT TO DELETE THE RECORDS?'
        TITEL     = 'DELETE RECORDS FROM MARA'
    IMPORTING
        ANSWER    = V_ANS.
```

```
IF V_ANS EQ 'J'.
* CODE TO DELETE HERE....
  WRITE:/ 'RECORDS IN MARA DELETED'.
ELSE.
  WRITE:/ 'NO RECORDS DELETED'.
ENDIF.
```

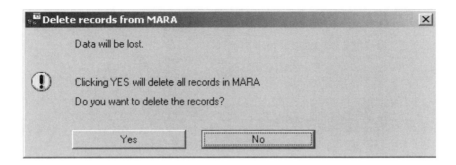

POPUP_TO_CONFIRM_STEP

Summary

Questions whether to perform the next processing step.

Parameters

```
EXPORTING
     TEXTLINE1     Information message to the user
     TEXTLINE2     Optional second line of information to the user
     TITEL         Text in title of dialogue box
IMPORTING
     ANSWER        Return code of button clicked
```

Example

```
REPORT ZEXAMPLE.
DATA V_ANS.

CALL FUNCTION 'POPUP_TO_CONFIRM_STEP'
     EXPORTING
          TEXTLINE1 = 'CLICKING YES WILL DELETE ALL RECORDS IN MARA'
          TEXTLINE2 = 'DO YOU WANT TO DELETE THE RECORDS?'
          TITEL     = 'DELETE RECORDS FROM MARA'
     IMPORTING
          ANSWER    = V_ANS.
```

```
IF V_ANS EQ 'J'.
* CODE TO DELETE HERE....
  WRITE:/ 'RECORDS IN MARA DELETED'.
ELSE.
  WRITE:/ 'NO RECORDS DELETED'.
ENDIF.
```

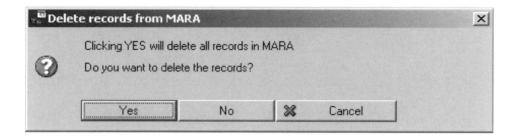

POPUP_TO_CONFIRM_WITH_MESSAGE

Summary

Simpler version of POPUP_TO_CONFIRM_LOSS_OF_DATA.

Description

Can display up to five lines of text to the user.

Parameters

```
EXPORTING
    DIAGNOSETEXT1    First line of information to the user
    DIAGNOSETEXT2    Second line of information to the user
    DIAGNOSETEXT3    Third line of information to the user
    TEXTLINE1        Fourth line of information to the user
    TEXTLINE2        Fifth line of information to the user
    TITEL            Text in title of dialogue box
IMPORTING
    ANSWER           Return code of button clicked
```

Example

```
REPORT ZEXAMPLE.
DATA: V_ANS,
      V_ERRORS(2)   TYPE C VALUE '98',
      V_WARNINGS(2) TYPE C VALUE '3',
```

```
        V_DIAG1(255)  VALUE 'ERROR MESSAGES OCCURRED',
        V_DIAG2(255)  VALUE 'WARNING MESSAGES OCCURRED'.

CONCATENATE V_ERRORS V_DIAG1 INTO V_DIAG1 SEPARATED BY SPACE.
CONCATENATE V_WARNINGS V_DIAG2 INTO V_DIAG2 SEPARATED BY SPACE.

CALL FUNCTION 'POPUP_TO_CONFIRM_WITH_MESSAGE'
EXPORTING
        DIAGNOSETEXT1 = 'ANALYSIS OF INPUT FILE COMPLETED WITH ERRORS:'
        DIAGNOSETEXT2 = V_DIAG1
        DIAGNOSETEXT3 = V_DIAG2
        TEXTLINE1     = 'ANALYSIS CANNOT CONTINUE WITH THESE INPUT ERRORS.'
        TEXTLINE2     = 'DELETE THE RECORDS?'
        TITEL         = 'FILE INPUT ANALYSIS'
IMPORTING
        ANSWER        = V_ANS.

IF V_ANS EQ 'J'.
* CODE TO DELETE HERE....
   WRITE:/ 'RECORDS IN MARA DELETED'.
ELSE.
   WRITE:/ 'NO RECORDS DELETED'.
ENDIF.
```

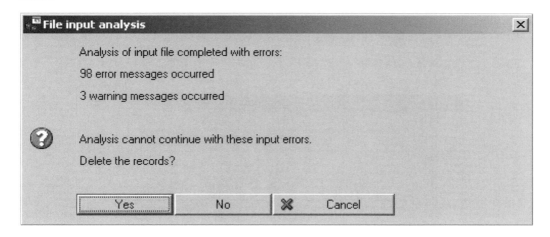

POPUP_TO_CONFIRM_WITH_VALUE

Summary

Displays a numeric value with a message.

Description

This is an obsolete function as of Version 4.6B.

Parameters

```
EXPORTING
     OBJECTVALUE
     TEXT_AFTER      Text displayed after OBJECTVALUE
     TEXT_BEFORE     Text displayed before OBJECTVALUE
     TITEL           Text in title of popup
IMPORTING
     ANSWER          Return code of button clicked
```

Example

```
REPORT ZEXAMPLE.
DATA V_ANS.

CALL FUNCTION 'POPUP_TO_CONFIRM_WITH_VALUE'
     EXPORTING
          OBJECTVALUE   = '1024'
          TEXT_AFTER    = 'RECORDS SELECTED'
          TEXT_BEFORE   = 'A TOTAL OF'
          TITEL         = 'RECORDS SELECTED'
     IMPORTING
          ANSWER        = V_ANS.

IF V_ANS EQ 'J'.
  WRITE:/ 'CONFIRMED NUMBER OF RECORDS SELECTED'.
ELSE.
  WRITE:/ 'RECORDS NOT CONFIRMED'.
ENDIF.
```

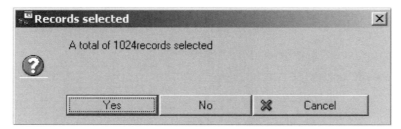

Display Input Check Dialogues

These function modules display dialogue boxes in which the user may select data.

POPUP_GET_VALUES

Summary

Dialogue box for data display and input.

Parameters

```
EXPORTING
    POPUP_TITLE     Text title on dialogue box
IMPORTING
    RETURNCODE      Return code of button selected
TABLES
    FIELDS          Fields to display
```

Example

```
REPORT ZEXAMPLE.
TABLES USR02.
DATA: RC TYPE C,
      V_BNAME   LIKE USR02-BNAME,
      V_TRDAT   LIKE USR02-TRDAT,
      ITAB      LIKE SVAL OCCURS 0 WITH HEADER LINE.

ITAB-TABNAME    = 'USR02'.
ITAB-FIELDNAME  = 'BNAME'.
ITAB-VALUE      = USR02-BNAME.
ITAB-FIELDTEXT  = 'LOGON ID'.
ITAB-NOVALUEHLP = 'X'.
APPEND ITAB.

ITAB-TABNAME    = 'USR02'.
ITAB-FIELDNAME  = 'TRDAT'.
ITAB-VALUE      = USR02-TRDAT.
ITAB-FIELDTEXT  = 'LAST LOGON'.
ITAB-NOVALUEHLP = 'X'.
APPEND ITAB.

CALL FUNCTION 'POPUP_GET_VALUES'
    EXPORTING
        POPUP_TITLE = 'USERS LOGGED IN ON A DATE'
    IMPORTING
        RETURNCODE  = RC
    TABLES
        FIELDS      = ITAB.

IF RC NE 'A'.          "USER CLICKED OK BUTTON
  READ TABLE ITAB INDEX 1.  "BNAME
  V_BNAME = ITAB-VALUE.
  READ TABLE ITAB INDEX 2.  "TRDAT
  V_TRDAT = ITAB-VALUE.

  SELECT SINGLE * FROM USR02 WHERE BNAME EQ V_BNAME AND
                                   TRDAT EQ V_TRDAT.
  IF SY-SUBRC NE 0.
    WRITE:/ V_BNAME, 'DID NOT LOG IN ON THE', V_TRDAT.
  ELSE.
    WRITE:/ V_BNAME, 'DID LOG IN ON THE', V_TRDAT.
  ENDIF.
ENDIF.
```

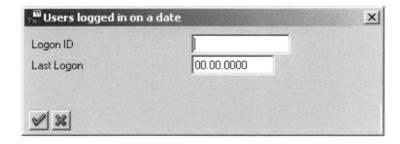

POPUP_GET_VALUES_DB_CHECKED

Summary

Dialogue box for data to be input and checked against the database.

Description

An error message will popup if the value entered by the user does not exist in the system.

Parameters

```
EXPORTING
    CHECK_EXISTENCE    Compare entered value against database
    POPUP_TITLE        Text title of dialogue box
IMPORTING
    RETURNCODE         Return code of button selected by user
TABLES
    FIELDS             Table containing table, field, and data
```

Example

```
REPORT ZEXAMPLE.
TABLES: MARA, MAKT.
DATA: RC        TYPE C,
      IFIELDS   LIKE SVAL OCCURS 0 WITH HEADER LINE.

SELECT SINGLE MATNR FROM MARA INTO MARA-MATNR.
IFIELDS-TABNAME     = 'MARA'.
IFIELDS-FIELDNAME   = 'MATNR'.
IFIELDS-VALUE       = MARA-MATNR.
APPEND IFIELDS.

CALL FUNCTION 'POPUP_GET_VALUES_DB_CHECKED'
    EXPORTING
        CHECK_EXISTENCE = 'X'
        POPUP_TITLE     = 'MATERIALS CHECK'
```

```
    IMPORTING
          RETURNCODE        = RC
    TABLES
          FIELDS            = IFIELDS.

IF RC NE 'A'.
  READ TABLE IFIELDS INDEX 1.
  SELECT SINGLE MAKTX FROM MAKT INTO MAKT-MAKTX WHERE MATNR = IFIELDS-VALUE.

  WRITE:/ IFIELDS-VALUE, ':', MAKT-MAKTX.
ENDIF.
```

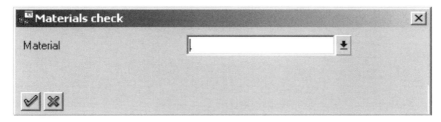

POPUP_GET_VALUES_SET_MAX_FIELD

Summary

Specifies number of fields to display in dialogue.

Description

If more than the maximum numbers of fields are specified, the dialogue box is displayed in scroll mode and with a scrollbar. The change is made in the local memory of the function group, and remains valid as long as the calling program is active. This function is well documented.

Parameters

```
EXPORTING
    NUMBER_OF_FIELDS     Maximum number of fields on a dialogue before scrolling
```

Example

```
REPORT ZEXAMPLE.
TABLES USR02.
DATA: RC        TYPE C,
      V_BNAME   LIKE USR02-BNAME,
      V_TRDAT   LIKE USR02-TRDAT,
      ITAB      LIKE SVAL OCCURS 0 WITH HEADER LINE.

ITAB-TABNAME     = 'USR02'.
ITAB-FIELDNAME   = 'BNAME'.
```

```
ITAB-VALUE        = USR02-BNAME.
ITAB-FIELDTEXT    = 'LOGON ID'.
ITAB-NOVALUEHLP   = 'X'.
APPEND ITAB.

ITAB-TABNAME      = 'USR02'.
ITAB-FIELDNAME    = 'TRDAT'.
ITAB-VALUE        = USR02-TRDAT.
ITAB-FIELDTEXT    = 'LAST LOGON DATE'.
ITAB-NOVALUEHLP   = 'X'.
APPEND ITAB.

ITAB-TABNAME      = 'USR02'.
ITAB-FIELDNAME    = 'LTIME'.
ITAB-VALUE        = USR02-LTIME.
ITAB-FIELDTEXT    = 'LAST LOGON TIME'.
ITAB-NOVALUEHLP   = 'X'.
APPEND ITAB.

CALL FUNCTION 'POPUP_GET_VALUES_SET_MAX_FIELD'
    EXPORTING
        NUMBER_OF_FIELDS   = '2'.

CALL FUNCTION 'POPUP_GET_VALUES'
    EXPORTING
        POPUP_TITLE        = 'USERS LOGGED IN ON A DATE'
    IMPORTING
        RETURNCODE         = RC
    TABLES
        FIELDS             = ITAB.

IF RC NE 'A'.        "USER CLICKED OK BUTTON
  READ TABLE ITAB INDEX 1.  "BNAME
  V_BNAME = ITAB-VALUE.
  READ TABLE ITAB INDEX 2.  "TRDAT
  V_TRDAT = ITAB-VALUE.

SELECT SINGLE * FROM USR02 WHERE BNAME EQ V_BNAME AND TRDAT EQ V_TRDAT.
  IF SY-SUBRC NE 0.
    WRITE:/ V_BNAME, 'DID NOT LOG IN ON THE', V_TRDAT.
  ELSE.
    WRITE:/ V_BNAME, 'DID LOG IN ON THE', V_TRDAT.
  ENDIF.
ENDIF.
```

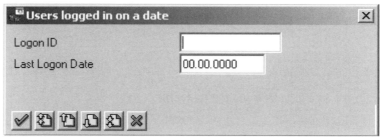

POPUP_GET_VALUES_USER_BUTTONS

Summary

Dialogue box for requesting values and offering user pushbuttons.

Description

This function is well documented.

Parameters

```
EXPORTING
     POPUP_TITLE          Title of popup
     FORMNAME             Name of the external subroutine for processing
     PROGRAMNAME          Name of the module pool from FORMNAME
     F4_FORMNAME          Name of the external subroutine for F4 help
     F4_PROGRAMNAME       Name of the module pool from F4_FORMNAME
     OK_PUSHBUTTONTEXT    Standard pushbutton text
     ICON_OK_PUSH         Icon for standard pushbutton
     FIRST_PUSHBUTTON     Text of the first additional pushbutton
     ICON_BUTTON_1        Icon for the first additional pushbutton
IMPORTING
     RETURNCODE           Return code of button selected by user
TABLES
     FIELDS               Table containing table, field, and data
```

Example

```
REPORT ZEXAMPLE.
TABLES: MARA, MAKT.
DATA: ITAB          LIKE SVAL OCCURS 0 WITH HEADER LINE,
      RC            TYPE C,
      V_CONTRACT    LIKE SVAL-VALUE,
      V_DESCR       LIKE SVAL-VALUE.

ITAB-TABNAME    = 'BDLSERVICE'.
ITAB-FIELDNAME  = 'CONTRACT'.
ITAB-VALUE      = ' '.
ITAB-FIELDTEXT  = 'CONTRACT'.
ITAB-NOVALUEHLP = ' '.
APPEND ITAB.

ITAB-TABNAME    = 'BDLSERVICE'.
ITAB-FIELDNAME  = 'DESCR'.
ITAB-VALUE      = ' '.
ITAB-FIELDTEXT  = 'DESCRIPTION'.
ITAB-NOVALUEHLP = ' '.
APPEND ITAB.
```

```
CALL FUNCTION 'POPUP_GET_VALUES_USER_BUTTONS'
     EXPORTING
          POPUP_TITLE        = 'ENTER SERVICE'
          PROGRAMNAME        = 'BDLTREDF'
          FORMNAME           = 'HANDLE_OK_CODE'
          F4_PROGRAMNAME     = 'BDLTREDF'
          F4_FORMNAME        = 'HANDLE_F4'
          OK_PUSHBUTTONTEXT  = 'DISPLAY'
          ICON_OK_PUSH       = 'ICON_DETAIL'
          FIRST_PUSHBUTTON   = 'MAINTENANCE'
          ICON_BUTTON_1      = 'ICON_MAINTENANCE_OBJECT_LIST'
     IMPORTING
          RETURNCODE         = RC
     TABLES
          FIELDS             = ITAB.

IF RC NE 'A'.
  READ TABLE ITAB INDEX 1.   "CONTRACT
  V_CONTRACT = ITAB-VALUE.
  READ TABLE ITAB INDEX 2.   "DESCR
  V_DESCR = ITAB-VALUE.

  WRITE:/ V_CONTRACT, V_DESCR.
ENDIF.
```

POPUP_GET_VALUES_USER_CHECKED

Summary

Input data to be checked in a user exit.

Description

This function is well documented.

Parameters

```
EXPORTING
     FORMNAME           Name of subroutine
     POPUP_TITLE        Text of title line
     PROGRAMNAME        Program containing the subroutine
```

```
IMPORTING
    RETURNCODE        User response
TABLES
    FIELDS            Table containing table, field, and data
```

Example

```
REPORT ZEXAMPLE.
TABLES USR02.

DATA: BEGIN OF IFIELDS OCCURS 1.
        INCLUDE STRUCTURE SVAL.
DATA: END OF IFIELDS.

DATA: BEGIN OF IERRORS OCCURS 1.
        INCLUDE STRUCTURE SVALE.
DATA: END OF IERRORS.

DATA: RC, G_REPID LIKE SY-REPID.

G_REPID = SY-REPID.
IFIELDS-TABNAME     = 'USR02'.
IFIELDS-FIELDNAME   = 'BNAME'.
IFIELDS-FIELD_OBL   = 'X'.
APPEND IFIELDS.

CALL FUNCTION 'POPUP_GET_VALUES_USER_CHECKED'
    EXPORTING
        FORMNAME      = 'CHECK_USER'
        POPUP_TITLE   = 'CHECK USERNAME'
        PROGRAMNAME   = G_REPID
    IMPORTING
        RETURNCODE    = RC
    TABLES
        FIELDS        = IFIELDS.

IF RC  <> 'A'.
  WRITE:/ IFIELDS-VALUE, 'EXISTS'.
ENDIF.

*--------------------------------------------------------------------------*
*                            FORM CHECK_USER                               *
*--------------------------------------------------------------------------*
*              CHECK IF USERNAME ENTERED BY USER EXISTS IN SAP             *
*--------------------------------------------------------------------------*
FORM CHECK_USER TABLES IFIELDS STRUCTURE SVAL
                 CHANGING IERRORS STRUCTURE SVALE.

  CLEAR IERRORS.
  READ TABLE IFIELDS INDEX 1.
  SELECT SINGLE BNAME FROM USR02 INTO USR02-BNAME
                            WHERE BNAME EQ IFIELDS-VALUE.

  IF SY-SUBRC NE 0.
    IERRORS-ERRORTAB    = 'USR02'.
    IERRORS-ERRORFIELD = 'BNAME'.
```

```
    IERRORS-MSGTY  = 'I'.
    IERRORS-MSGID  = 'TR'.
    IERRORS-MSGNO  = '809'.
  ENDIF.
ENDFORM.
```

See Also

POPUP_GET_VALUES_USER_HELP

POPUP_GET_VALUES_USER_HELP

Summary

Branching in a user F1 or F4 help.

Description

This function is well documented.

Parameters

```
EXPORTING
    F4_FORMNAME       Name of the subroutine for F4 help
    F4_PROGRAMNAME    Name of the program containing the F4_FORMNAME subroutine
    FORMNAME          Name of subroutine
    POPUP_TITLE       Text of title line
    PROGRAMNAME       Program containing the subroutine
IMPORTING
    RETURNCODE        User response
TABLES
    FIELDS            Table containing table, field, and data
```

Example

```
REPORT ZEXAMPLE.
TABLES USR02.

DATA: BEGIN OF IFIELDS OCCURS 1.
        INCLUDE STRUCTURE SVAL.
DATA: END OF IFIELDS.
```

```
DATA: BEGIN OF IERRORS OCCURS 1.
        INCLUDE STRUCTURE SVALE.
DATA: END OF IERRORS.

DATA: RC, G_REPID LIKE SY-REPID.

G_REPID = SY-REPID.
IFIELDS-TABNAME     = 'USR02'.
IFIELDS-FIELDNAME   = 'BNAME'.
IFIELDS-FIELD_OBL   = 'X'.
APPEND IFIELDS.

CALL FUNCTION 'POPUP_GET_VALUES_USER_HELP'
    EXPORTING
        F4_FORMNAME       = 'PROFIL_IN_POPUP_PF4_HILFE'
        F4_PROGRAMNAME    = 'SAPLOC15'
        FORMNAME          = 'CHECK_USER'
        POPUP_TITLE       = 'SELECT USERNAME'
        PROGRAMNAME       = G_REPID
    IMPORTING
        RETURNCODE        = RC
    TABLES
        FIELDS            = IFIELDS.

IF RC  <> 'A'.
  WRITE:/ IFIELDS-VALUE, 'EXISTS'.
ENDIF.

*--------------------------------------------------------------------*
*                          FORM CHECK_USER                           *
*--------------------------------------------------------------------*
*              CHECK IF USERNAME ENTERED BY USER EXISTS IN SAP        *
*--------------------------------------------------------------------*
FORM CHECK_USER TABLES IFIELDS STRUCTURE SVAL
                  CHANGING IERRORS STRUCTURE SVALE.
  CLEAR IERRORS.
  READ TABLE IFIELDS INDEX 1.
  SELECT SINGLE BNAME FROM USR02 INTO USR02-BNAME
                              WHERE BNAME EQ IFIELDS-VALUE.

  IF SY-SUBRC NE 0.
    IERRORS-ERRORTAB    = 'USR02'.
    IERRORS-ERRORFIELD  = 'BNAME'.
    IERRORS-MSGTY       = 'I'.
    IERRORS-MSGID       = 'TR'.
    IERRORS-MSGNO       = '809'.
  ENDIF.
ENDFORM.
```

See Also

POPUP_GET_VALUES_USER_CHECKED

Popup Screens

These dialogue screens are designed mostly for specific situations.

COPO_POPUP_TO_DISPLAY_TEXTLIST

Summary

Dialogue box displays help when F1 is pressed.

Parameters

```
EXPORTING
     TASK              Processing type
                       Value          Meaning
                       DISPLAY        Display text as read-only
                       DECIDE         Let user decide whether to keep or change text

     TITEL             Text title on dialogue box
TABLES
     TEXT_TABLE        Help information to display
```

Example

```
REPORT ZEXAMPLE.
PARAMETERS P_TEST AS CHECKBOX.
DATA I_TXT LIKE TLINE OCCURS 0 WITH HEADER LINE.

AT SELECTION-SCREEN ON HELP-REQUEST FOR P_TEST.
  MOVE 'PARAMETER: P_TEST' TO I_TXT-TDLINE.
  APPEND I_TXT.
  MOVE 'CHECK THIS BOX TO RUN THE PROGRAM IN TEST MODE' TO I_TXT-TDLINE.
  APPEND I_TXT.
  MOVE 'UNCHECK THE BOX TO RUN THE PROGRAM IN OPERATIONAL MODE' TO I_TXT-TDLINE.
  APPEND I_TXT.

  CALL FUNCTION 'COPO_POPUP_TO_DISPLAY_TEXTLIST'
      EXPORTING
           TASK         = 'DISPLAY'
           TITEL        = 'HELP FOR CHECKBOX'
      TABLES
           TEXT_TABLE   = I_TXT
      EXCEPTIONS
           OTHERS       = 1.
```

```
IF SY-SUBRC NE 0.
  WRITE:/ 'ERROR DISPLAYING HELP DIALOG BOX'.
ENDIF.
```

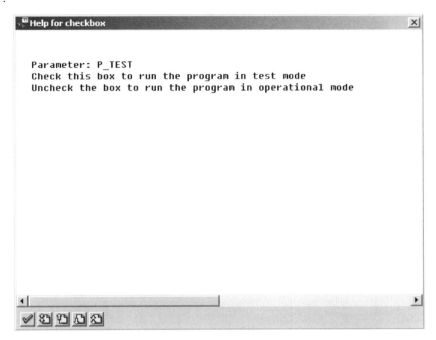

See Also

HELP_START

CORRESPONDENCE_POPUP_EMAIL

Summary

Dialogue box for requesting e-mail address.

Description

Does not actually e-mail the address – just asks for the e-mail address.

Parameters

```
EXPORTING
    I_INTAD        Default e-mail address
IMPORTING
    E_ANSWER       'J' for Yes, 'N' for No
    E_INTAD        E-mail address entered
```

Example

```
REPORT ZEXAMPLE.

DATA: V_ANS,
      V_EMAILADDR(130).

CALL FUNCTION 'CORRESPONDENCE_POPUP_EMAIL'
     EXPORTING
          I_INTAD      = 'DEFAULT@NOSUCHPLACE.COM'
     IMPORTING
          E_ANSWER     = V_ANS
          E_INTAD      = V_EMAILADDR.

IF V_ANS EQ 'J'.
  WRITE:/ 'E-MAIL ADDRESS CONFIRMED AS:', V_EMAILADDR.
ENDIF.
```

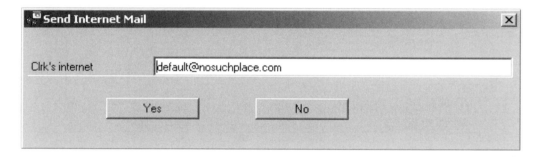

EPS_PROGRESS_POPUP

Summary

Creates a number of graphical popups with different levels of progress.

Description

This can leave quite a number of dialogue screens open on the users PC if the progress interval is too small. You should always remember to code the automatic closing of all the dialogues when finished. SAPGUI_PROGRESS_INDICATOR is probably a better solution.

Parameters

```
EXPORTING
     BTN_TXT             Text for button in third line
     CURVAL_G2           Current value\progress of metre
     MAXVAL_G2           Maximum value\progress
```

```
POPUP_STAT        Dialogue parameter
POPUP_TITLE       Title of the progress display
TEXT_1            Text, right justified in first line
TEXT_2            Text, right justified in second line
TEXT_3            Text, right justified in third line
TEXT_4            Text, right justified in fourth line
TEXT_G1           Main message text in first line
TEXT_G2           Main message text in third line
TITLE_G2          Title under progress metre
WINID             Window unique ID (handle)
```

Example

```
REPORT ZEXAMPLE.
DATA: PER TYPE I VALUE 0,
      EVENT(6) TYPE C.


DO 4 TIMES.
  PER = PER + 25.
  CALL FUNCTION 'EPS_PROGRESS_POPUP'
       EXPORTING
              BTN_TXT            = 'CANCEL'
              CURVAL_G2          = PER
              MAXVAL_G2          = '100'
              POPUP_STAT         = '1'
              POPUP_TITLE        = 'CLIENT COPY'
              TEXT_1             = 'SYSTEMS BEING COPIED:'
              TEXT_2             = 'DEVELOPMENT'
              TEXT_3             = 'TESTING'
              TEXT_4             = 'QUALITY'
              TEXT_G1            = 'COPYING DATA FROM PRODUCTION SYSTEMS'
              TEXT_G2            = 'PROGRESS:'
              TITLE_G2           = 'CLIENT COPY PROGRESS METER'
              WINID              = 100
       EXCEPTIONS
              GRAPH_RECEIVE      = 1
              INVALID_LAYOUT     = 2
              OTHERS             = 3.


  IF SY-SUBRC NE 0.
    WRITE:/ 'THERE WAS AN ERROR GENERATING THE GRAPH'.
  ENDIF.
ENDDO.


*  CLOSE THE GRAPHS
CALL FUNCTION 'PROGRESS_POPUP'
     EXPORTING
          STAT          = '2'
          WINID         = 100.
CALL FUNCTION 'GRAPH_DIALOG'
     EXPORTING
          CLOSE         = 'X'.
```

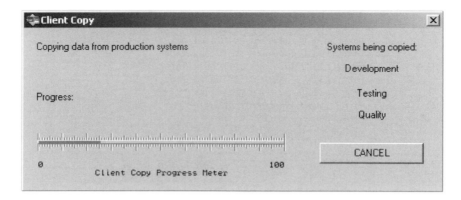

See Also

See SAPGUI_PROGRESS_INDICATOR

ERGO_TEXT_SHOW

Summary

Displays text in a documentation window.

Parameters

```
EXPORTING
      TEXTNAME              Name of the general text is displayed
      ID                    Documentation class ID (TX for general text)
      LANGU                 Language in which the text is displayed
```

Example

```
REPORT ZEXAMPLE.

PARAMETERS:   P_TNAME LIKE DOKHL-OBJECT DEFAULT 'ERGP2880',
              P_ID LIKE DOKHL-ID DEFAULT 'RE'.

CALL FUNCTION 'ERGO_TEXT_SHOW'
      EXPORTING
            TEXTNAME          = P_TNAME
            ID                = P_ID
            LANGU             = SY-LANGU
      EXCEPTIONS
            TEXT_NOT_FOUND    = 01.
IF SY-SUBRC NE 0.
  WRITE:/ 'COULD NOT LOCATE TEXT OBJECT FOR', P_TNAME, P_ID.
ENDIF.
```

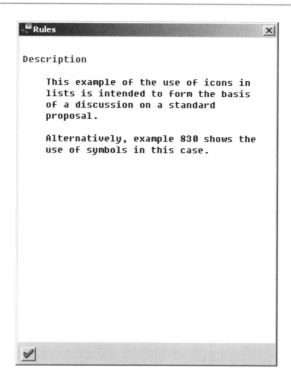

See Also

COPO_POPUP_TO_DISPLAY_TEXTLIST

F4_CLOCK

Summary

Displays a clock in a popup window.

Parameters

```
EXPORTING
    START_TIME      Initial time displayed on clock
    DISPLAY         Allow user to change time
IMPORTING
    SELECTED_TIME   Time entered by user
```

Example

```
REPORT ZEXAMPLE.
DATA V_CTIME LIKE SY-UZEIT.
```

```
CALL FUNCTION 'F4_CLOCK'
     EXPORTING
          START_TIME     = SY-UZEIT
     IMPORTING
          SELECTED_TIME  = V_CTIME.

WRITE:/ 'THE TIME ENTERED WAS:', V_CTIME.
```

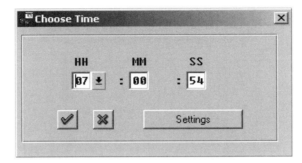

F4_DATE

Summary

Displays a calendar in a popup window.

Parameters

```
EXPORTING
     DATE_FOR_FIRST_MONTH     Initial date displayed in dialogue
IMPORTING
     SELECT_DATE              Date selected from dialogue
```

Example

```
REPORT ZEXAMPLE.
DATA:  V_AMTH   LIKE ISELLIST-MONTH,
       V_DATE   LIKE SY-DATUM,
       V_SDATE  LIKE SY-DATUM.

V_AMTH = SY-DATUM(6).
CALL FUNCTION 'POPUP_TO_SELECT_MONTH'
     EXPORTING
          ACTUAL_MONTH         = V_AMTH
     IMPORTING
          SELECTED_MONTH       = V_AMTH.

CONCATENATE V_AMTH '01' INTO V_DATE.
CALL FUNCTION 'F4_DATE'
     EXPORTING
          DATE_FOR_FIRST_MONTH  = V_DATE
```

```
     IMPORTING
          SELECT_DATE                 = V_SDATE
     EXCEPTIONS
          CALENDAR_BUFFER_NOT_LOADABLE  = 1
          DATE_AFTER_RANGE            = 2
          DATE_BEFORE_RANGE           = 3
          DATE_INVALID                = 4
          FACTORY_CALENDAR_NOT_FOUND  = 5
          HOLIDAY_CALENDAR_NOT_FOUND  = 6
          PARAMETER_CONFLICT          = 7
          OTHERS                      = 8.

IF SY-SUBRC EQ 0.
  WRITE:/ 'DATE SELECTED:', V_SDATE.
ELSE.
  WRITE:/ 'DATE SELECTION ERROR'.
ENDIF.
```

See Also

POPUP_TO_SELECT_MONTH

F4_FILENAME

Summary

Selects files on local PC.

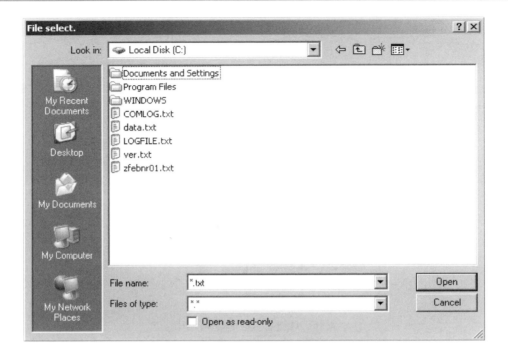

Parameters

```
IMPORTING
    FILE_NAME    File selected on local PC
```

Example

```
REPORT ZEXAMPLE.
DATA: SERVER   LIKE  MSXXLIST-NAME,
      V_SPATH  LIKE  IBIPPARMS-PATH.
      V_LPATH  LIKE  IBIPPARMS-PATH.

PARAMETERS P_FNAME TYPE IBIPPARMS-PATH.   "SERVER PATH

CALL FUNCTION 'TH_SELECT_SERVER'
    IMPORTING
        SERVER = SERVER.

CALL FUNCTION 'F4_FILENAME_SERVER' DESTINATION SERVER
    EXPORTING
        PFAD              = P_FNAME
    IMPORTING
        FILE_NAME         = V_SPATH
    EXCEPTIONS
        NO_FILE_ON_SERVER = 1
        OTHERS            = 2.
```

```
IF SY-SUBRC NE 0.
  WRITE:/ 'ERROR SELECTING FILE FROM', SERVER.
ENDIF.

CALL FUNCTION 'F4_FILENAME'
     IMPORTING
         FILE_NAME = V_LPATH.

WRITE:/ 'SERVER FILE AND PATH:', V_SPATH,
        'LOCAL FILE AND PATH:', V_LPATH.
```

See Also

F4_FILENAME_SERVER, KD_GET_FILENAME_ON_F4, WS_FILENAME

F4_FILENAME_SERVER

Summary

Selects files on server.

Parameters

```
EXPORTING
    PFAD          Directory on server
IMPORTING
    FILE_NAME     File selected on server
```

Example

See F4_FILENAME

See Also

F4_FILENAME

F4_USER

Summary

Popup of logon IDs.

Description

Displays only the first 200.

Parameters

```
EXPORTING
    OBJECT        User ID
IMPORTING
    RESULT        User ID selected from dialogue box
```

Example

```
REPORT ZEXAMPLE.
DATA: V_USRID LIKE SY-UNAME,
      V_LOCK.

CALL FUNCTION 'F4_USER'
    IMPORTING
        RESULT          = V_USRID.

CALL FUNCTION 'USER_EXISTS'
    EXPORTING
        BNAME           = V_USRID
    IMPORTING
        LOCKED          = V_LOCK
```

```
      EXCEPTIONS
           USER_DONT_EXIST        = 1
           USER_EXISTS            = 2
           OTHERS                 = 3.

IF SY-SUBRC EQ 2.
  IF V_LOCK EQ 'X'.
    WRITE:/ V_USRID, 'EXISTS AND IS LOCKED'.
  ELSE.
    WRITE:/ V_USRID, 'EXISTS AND IS UNLOCKED'.
  ENDIF.
ELSEIF SY-SUBRC EQ 1.
  WRITE:/ V_USRID, 'DOES NOT EXIST'.
ELSE.
  WRITE:/ 'ERROR FINDING USER'.
ENDIF.
```

FITRV_CALCULATOR

Summary

Pops up a working calculator.

Parameters

```
EXPORTING
     INPUT_VALUE    Initial value
     CURRENCY       Output formatted to this currency
IMPORTING
     OUTPUT_VALUE   Result
```

Example

```
REPORT ZEXAMPLE.

DATA AMOUNT_OUT(35) TYPE C.

PARAMETERS:  P_AMT_IN (35)     TYPE C,
             P_WAERS           TYPE TCURC-WAERS.

SHIFT P_AMT_IN LEFT DELETING LEADING SPACE.
CALL FUNCTION 'FITRV_CALCULATOR'
     EXPORTING
          INPUT_VALUE          = P_AMT_IN
          CURRENCY             = P_WAERS
     IMPORTING
          OUTPUT_VALUE         = AMOUNT_OUT
     EXCEPTIONS
          INVALID_INPUT        = 1
          CALCULATION_CANCELED = 2
          OTHERS               = 3.
```

```
IF SY-SUBRC EQ 0.
  SHIFT AMOUNT_OUT LEFT DELETING LEADING SPACE.
  WRITE:/ 'THE FINAL ANSWER IS:', AMOUNT_OUT.
ELSE.
  WRITE:/ 'CALCULATOR CANCELLED'.
ENDIF.
```

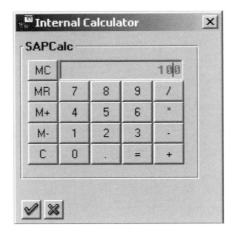

HELP_START

Summary

Help values on database fields.

Description

Useful at the Process on Value-Request stage for those fields that do not provide F4 help at the DDIC level.

Parameters

```
EXPORTING
    HELP_INFOS          Structure with values passed to help processor
TABLES
    DYNPSELECT          Screen selection in flow logic
    DYNPVALUETAB        Screen values in flow logic
```

Example

```
REPORT ZEXAMPLE.
DATA: BEGIN OF HELP_INFOS.
        INCLUDE STRUCTURE HELP_INFO.
DATA: END OF HELP_INFOS.
```

```
DATA:  BEGIN OF DYNPSELECT OCCURS 0.
         INCLUDE STRUCTURE DSELC.
DATA:  END OF DYNPSELECT.
DATA:  BEGIN OF DYNPVALUETAB OCCURS 0.
         INCLUDE STRUCTURE DVAL.
DATA:  END OF DYNPVALUETAB.

PARAMETERS:  P_TABLE(30),
             P_FIELD(30).

IF NOT P_TABLE IS INITIAL AND
   NOT P_FIELD IS INITIAL.
  CLEAR HELP_INFOS.
  HELP_INFOS-CALL        = 'D'.
  HELP_INFOS-SPRAS       = SY-LANGU.
  HELP_INFOS-DOCUID      = 'FE'.
  HELP_INFOS-TITLE       = SY-TITLE.
  HELP_INFOS-TABNAME     = P_TABLE.
  HELP_INFOS-FIELDNAME   = P_FIELD.
  HELP_INFOS-PROGRAM     = SY-REPID.
  HELP_INFOS-DYNPRO      = SY-DYNNR.
  HELP_INFOS-REPORT      = SY-REPID.
  HELP_INFOS-DYNPPROG    = SY-REPID.

  CALL FUNCTION 'HELP_START'
       EXPORTING
            HELP_INFOS    = HELP_INFOS
       TABLES
            DYNPSELECT    = DYNPSELECT
            DYNPVALUETAB  = DYNPVALUETAB.
ELSE.
  WRITE:/ 'ENTER IN A TABLE NAME AND A FIELD NAME'.
ENDIF.
```

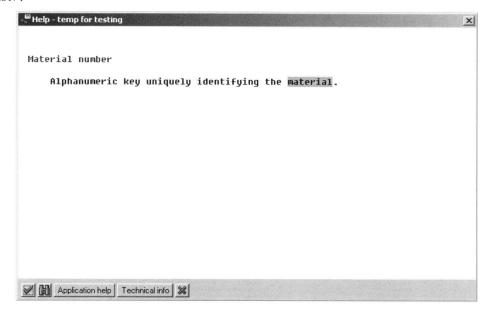

See Also

COPO_POPUP_TO_DISPLAY_TEXTLIST, HELP_VALUES_GET_WITH_DD_TABLE, HELP_VALUES_GET_WITH_TABLE

HELP_VALUES_GET_NO_DD_NAME

Summary

Displays help values for fields.

Description

This is obsolete. Use F4IF_INT_TABLE_VALUE_REQUEST instead.

Parameters

```
EXPORTING
     SELECTFIELD   Chosen table field
     TITLE         Title of the F4 popup
IMPORTING
     IND           Index of the selected field
TABLES
     FIELDS        Internal table structure
     FULL_TABLE    Internal table of data
```

Example

```
REPORT ZEXAMPLE.

TABLES RTXTH.

DATA: BEGIN OF TEXT_TAB OCCURS 0,
        TEXT_NAME LIKE RTXTH-TEXT_NAME,
        UPD_USER LIKE RTXTH-UPD_USER,
        UPD_DATE LIKE RTXTH-UPD_DATE,
        UPD_TIME LIKE RTXTH-UPD_TIME,
      END OF TEXT_TAB.

DATA: IRTXTH LIKE RTXTH OCCURS 0 WITH HEADER LINE,
      FIELD_TAB LIKE HELP_VALUE OCCURS 0 WITH HEADER LINE,
      TABINDEX LIKE SY-TABIX.

PARAMETERS: P_ACLASS LIKE RTXTH-APPLCLASS,
            P_TTYPE LIKE RTXTH-TEXT_TYPE.
SELECT * FROM RTXTH INTO TABLE IRTXTH WHERE APPLCLASS = P_ACLASS
                                        AND TEXT_TYPE = P_TTYPE.

IF NOT IRTXTH[] IS INITIAL.
  LOOP AT IRTXTH.
    MOVE-CORRESPONDING IRTXTH TO TEXT_TAB.
```

```
      APPEND TEXT_TAB.
   ENDLOOP.

   FIELD_TAB-SELECTFLAG   = 'X'.
   FIELD_TAB-TABNAME      = 'RTXTH'.
   FIELD_TAB-FIELDNAME    = 'TEXT_NAME'.
   APPEND FIELD_TAB.
   CLEAR FIELD_TAB-SELECTFLAG.
   FIELD_TAB-FIELDNAME    = 'UPD_USER'.
   APPEND FIELD_TAB.
   FIELD_TAB-FIELDNAME    = 'UPD_DATE'.
   APPEND FIELD_TAB.
   FIELD_TAB-FIELDNAME    = 'UPD_TIME'.
   APPEND FIELD_TAB.

   CALL FUNCTION 'HELP_VALUES_GET_NO_DD_NAME'
        EXPORTING
             SELECTFIELD            = 'TEXT_NAME'
             TITEL                  = 'REPORT TEXTS'
        IMPORTING
             IND                    = TABINDEX
        TABLES
             FIELDS                 = FIELD_TAB
             FULL_TABLE             = TEXT_TAB
        EXCEPTIONS
             FULL_TABLE_EMPTY       = 1
             NO_TABLESTRUCTURE_GIVEN = 2.

   IF SY-SUBRC EQ 0.
     IF NOT TABINDEX IS INITIAL.
       READ TABLE TEXT_TAB INDEX TABINDEX.
       WRITE:/ TEXT_TAB-TEXT_NAME.
     ENDIF.
   ENDIF.
 ELSE.
   WRITE:/ 'NO DATA FOUND FOR', P_ACLASS, P_TTYPE, 'NOT FOUND IN RTXTH'.
 ENDIF.
```

Text name		UPD_USER	UPD_DATE	UPD_TIME
01RICASP	112PLANMR	SAP	04.05.1998	16:15:24
01RICASP	113PLANPMR	SAP	04.05.1998	16:58:22
01RICASP	114PLANIR	SAP	04.05.1998	17:00:48
01RICASP	121PLANBUDRM	SAP	04.05.1998	17:10:08
01RICASP	123BUDGM	SAP	04.05.1998	17:06:54
01RICASP	128PLABUDCON	SAP	04.05.1998	17:12:04
01RICASP	131BUDGAUPR	SAP	04.05.1998	17:15:32
01RICASP	132BUDGAUM	SAP	04.05.1998	17:17:51
01RICASP	133PLANAVR	SAP	04.05.1998	17:19:45
01RICASP	134BUDGAVOE	SAP	04.05.1998	17:20:55
01RICASP	138BUDGAUMU	SAP	04.05.1998	17:31:23

Report Texts

See Also

F4IF_INT_TABLE_VALUE_REQUEST

HELP_VALUES_GET_WITH_DD_NAME

Summary

Displays the F4 values for any database field.

Description

This is obsolete. Use F4IF_INT_TABLE_VALUE_REQUEST instead. This function module serves to display an internal table with dictionary reference.

Parameters

```
EXPORTING
    SELECTFIELD            Chosen table field
    TITLE                  Title of the F4 popup
    TABLENAME              Database table
    USE_USER_SELECTIONS    Use specified selection conditions:
                           Value      Meaning
                           ' '        Generic selection
                           D          Multi-selections from screen
                           S          Selections from user-defined table
IMPORTING
    IND                    Index of the selected field
TABLES
    FIELDS                 Internal table structure
    USER_SEL_FIELDS        Specified selection conditions on dialogue
```

Example

```
REPORT ZEXAMPLE.
TABLES TSTCT.

DATA:   TABLE LIKE HELP_INFO-TABNAME VALUE 'TSTCT',
        FIELD LIKE HELP_INFO-FIELDNAME VALUE 'TCODE',
        IND LIKE SY-INDEX.

DATA:   ITSTC LIKE TSTC OCCURS 0 WITH HEADER LINE,
        USRSEL LIKE DYNPREAD OCCURS 0 WITH HEADER LINE.

CONCATENATE TABLE FIELD INTO USRSEL-FIELDNAME SEPARATED BY '-'.
MOVE 'SE*' TO USRSEL-FIELDVALUE.
APPEND USRSEL.
```

```
SELECT * FROM TSTCT INTO TABLE ITSTC WHERE SPRSL EQ SY-LANGU.

CALL FUNCTION 'HELP_VALUES_GET_WITH_DD_NAME'
     EXPORTING
          SELECTFIELD                   = FIELD
          TABLENAME                     = TABLE
          TITEL                         = 'TCODE HELP VALUES'
          USE_USER_SELECTIONS           = 'S'
     IMPORTING
          IND                           = IND
     TABLES
          FULL_TABLE                    = ITSTC
          USER_SEL_FIELDS               = USRSEL
     EXCEPTIONS
          NO_TABLEFIELDS_IN_DICTIONARY  = 01
          NO_TABLESTRUCTURE_GIVEN       = 02
          MORE_THAN_ONE_SELECTFIELD     = 03
          NO_SELECTFIELDS               = 04.
IF SY-SUBRC EQ 0.
  READ TABLE ITSTC INDEX IND.
  WRITE:/ 'TRANSACTION SELECTED:', ITSTC-TCODE+1.
ELSE.
  WRITE:/ 'ERROR WITH POPUP HELP'.
ENDIF.
```

Language	TCode	Transaction text
EN	SE01	Transport Organizer
EN	SE03	Workbench Organizer: Tools
EN	SE06	Set Up Workbench Organizer
EN	SE07	CTS Status Display
EN	SE09	Workbench Organizer
EN	SE10	Customizing Organizer
EN	SE11	ABAP/4 Dictionary Maintenance
EN	SE12	ABAP/4 Dictionary Display
EN	SE13	Maintain Technical Settings (Tables)
EN	SE14	Utilities for Dictionary Tables
EN	SE15	ABAP/4 Repository Information System
EN	SE16	Data Browser
EN	SE17	General Table Display
EN	SE18	Business Add-Ins: Definitions
EN	SE19	Business Add-Ins: Implementations
EN	SE24	Class Builder
EN	SE25	*** reserved ***
EN	SE26	*** reserved ***
EN	SE29	Application Packets
EN	SE30	ABAP Objects Runtime Analysis
EN	SE32	ABAP Text Element Maintenance
EN	SE32_OLD	ABAP Text Element Maintenance
EN	SE32_WB99	ABAP Text Element Maintenance
EN	SE33	Context Builder
EN	SE35	ABAP/4 Dialog Modules
EN	SE36	Logical databases
EN	SE37	ABAP Function Modules
EN	SE38	ABAP Editor
EN	SE39	Splitscreen Editor: Program Compare
EN	SE40	MP: Standards Maint. and Translation
EN	SE41	Menu Painter

See Also

F4IF_INT_TABLE_VALUE_REQUEST

HELP_VALUES_GET_WITH_DD_TABLE

Summary

Help values on database tables.

Description

Pops up your own set of values when you do a drop down on a field on a selection screen for database tables.

Parameters

```
EXPORTING
    FIELDNAME           Table field name
    FIELDTABNAME        Dictionary table name
    SELECTFIELD         Position of field to be selected
    SHFIELDS            Display field positions
    TABKEY              Generic dictionary table key
    TABNAME             Database selection table
IMPORTING
    SELECTVALUE         Selected value from dialogue box
```

Example

```
REPORT ZEXAMPLE.
DATA E_FRGAB LIKE RM06B-FRGAB.

PARAMETERS:  P_TABLE(30) DEFAULT 'T161E',
             P_FIELD(30) DEFAULT 'FRGAB'.

IF NOT P_TABLE IS INITIAL AND
   NOT P_FIELD IS INITIAL.

  CALL FUNCTION 'HELP_VALUES_GET_WITH_DD_TABLE'
      EXPORTING
          FIELDNAME               = P_FIELD
          FIELDTABNAME            = P_TABLE
          SELECTFIELD             = 2
          SHFIELDS                = '23'
          TABKEY                  = '*'
          TABNAME                 = P_TABLE
      IMPORTING
          SELECTVALUE             = E_FRGAB
```

```
      EXCEPTIONS
            FIELD_NOT_IN_DDIC              = 01
            MORE_THEN_ONE_SELECTFIELD     = 02
            NO_SELECTFIELD                = 03
            TABLE_NOT_IN_DDIC             = 04
            DATABASE_ERROR                = 05.

  IF SY-SUBRC EQ 0.
    WRITE:/ 'DATA FROM TABLE:', E_FRGAB.
  ENDIF.
ELSE.
  WRITE:/ 'ENTER A TABLE NAME AND A FIELD NAME'.
ENDIF.
```

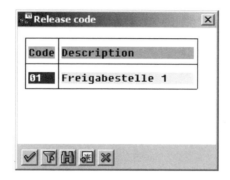

See Also

HELP_START, HELP_VALUES_GET_WITH_TABLE

HELP_VALUES_GET_WITH_TABLE

Summary

Lists help values on selection screen.

Description

Marked as obsolete.

Parameters

```
EXPORTING
    FIELDNAME               Name of field from table
    TABNAME                 Name of database table
    TITLE_IN_VALUES_LIST    Title of dialogue box
IMPORTING
    SELECT_VALUE            Value selected from list
```

```
TABLES
    FIELDS                        Internal table containing fields to display
    VALUETAB                      Internal table containing field data to display
```

Example

```
REPORT ZEXAMPLE.
TABLES T000.

DATA: BEGIN OF ICLIENTS OCCURS 0.
        INCLUDE STRUCTURE T000.
DATA: END OF ICLIENTS.

DATA: BEGIN OF IFIELDS OCCURS 0.
        INCLUDE STRUCTURE HELP_VALUE.
DATA: END OF IFIELDS.

DATA: BEGIN OF IVALUES OCCURS 0,
      MANDT LIKE T000-MANDT,
      SEP1,
      MTEXT LIKE T000-MTEXT,
      SEP2,
      ORT01 LIKE T000-ORT01,
      END OF IVALUES.

DATA SELECTED_CLIENT LIKE TEMSG-CLIENT.

SELECT * FROM T000 INTO TABLE ICLIENTS.
SORT ICLIENTS BY MANDT ASCENDING.

LOOP AT ICLIENTS.
  IVALUES-MANDT   = ICLIENTS-MANDT.
  IVALUES-MTEXT   = ICLIENTS-MTEXT.
  IVALUES-ORT01   = ICLIENTS-ORT01.
  APPEND IVALUES.
ENDLOOP.

IFIELDS-TABNAME    = 'T000'.
IFIELDS-FIELDNAME  = 'MANDT'.
IFIELDS-SELECTFLAG = 'X'.
APPEND IFIELDS.

CALL FUNCTION 'HELP_VALUES_GET_WITH_TABLE'
    EXPORTING
        FIELDNAME             = 'MANDT'
        TABNAME               = 'T000'
        TITLE_IN_VALUES_LIST  = 'CLIENTS'
        TITEL                 = 'CLIENT LIST'
    IMPORTING
        SELECT_VALUE          = SELECTED_CLIENT
    TABLES
        FIELDS                = IFIELDS
        VALUETAB              = IVALUES
```

```
      EXCEPTIONS
            FIELD_NOT_IN_DDIC            = 1
            MORE_THEN_ONE_SELECTFIELD   = 2
            NO_SELECTFIELD              = 3
            OTHERS                      = 4.

IF SY-SUBRC EQ 0.
  WRITE:/ SELECTED_CLIENT.
ELSE.
  WRITE:/ 'ERROR SELECTING CLIENT'.
ENDIF.
```

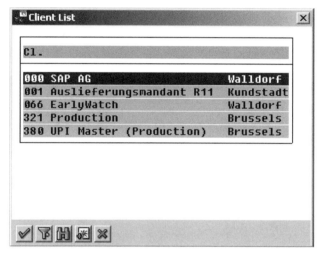

See Also

HELP_START, HELP_VALUES_GET_WITH_TABLE,
HELP_VALUES_GET_WITH_DD_TABLE

KD_GET_FILENAME_ON_F4

Summary

Selects files on the local PC.

Parameters

```
EXPORTING
    MASK                    Display files of type
    STATIC                  Keep last path selected
CHANGING
    FILE_NAME               Filename and path selected
```

Example

```
REPORT ZEXAMPLE.

PARAMETERS P_FNAME LIKE RLGRAP-FILENAME.

AT SELECTION-SCREEN ON VALUE-REQUEST FOR P_FNAME.
  CALL FUNCTION 'KD_GET_FILENAME_ON_F4'
       EXPORTING
             MASK        = ',TEXTFILES,*.TXT'
             STATIC      = 'X'
       CHANGING
             FILE_NAME   = P_FNAME.

START-OF-SELECTION.
  WRITE:/ 'FILE CHOSEN:', P_FNAME.
```

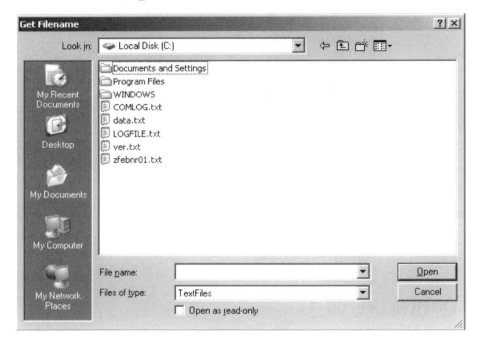

See Also

F4_FILENAME

MD_POPUP_SHOW_INTERNAL_TABLE

Summary

Pops up contents of internal table.

Description

There must be at least two entries in the internal table before the popup displays any data.

Parameters

```
EXPORTING
    TITLE          Title of popup title
IMPORTING
    INDEX          Table index of internal table
TABLES
    VALUES         Data from internal table
    COLUMNS        Columns of table data
```

Example

```
REPORT ZEXAMPLE.
TABLES T001W.

DATA: BEGIN OF ITAB OCCURS 0,
        WERKS LIKE T001W-WERKS,
        NAME1 LIKE T001W-NAME1,
      END OF ITAB.

DATA: BEGIN OF ICOLS OCCURS 0.
        INCLUDE STRUCTURE HELP_VALUE.
DATA: END OF ICOLS.
DATA V_INDX LIKE SY-INDEX.

ICOLS-TABNAME      = 'T001W'.
ICOLS-FIELDNAME    = 'WERKS'.
ICOLS-SELECTFLAG   = 'X'.
APPEND ICOLS.
ICOLS-TABNAME      = 'T001W'.
ICOLS-FIELDNAME    = 'NAME1'.
APPEND ICOLS.

SELECT-OPTIONS: S_WERKS FOR T001W-WERKS.

SELECT * FROM T001W WHERE WERKS IN S_WERKS.
  ITAB-WERKS  = T001W-WERKS.
  ITAB-NAME1  = T001W-NAME1.
  APPEND ITAB.
ENDSELECT.

SORT ITAB BY WERKS.
CALL FUNCTION 'MD_POPUP_SHOW_INTERNAL_TABLE'
     EXPORTING
          TITLE     = 'SELECT A VALUE'
     IMPORTING
          INDEX     = V_INDX
```

```
      TABLES
           VALUES    = ITAB
           COLUMNS   = ICOLS
      EXCEPTIONS
           LEAVE     = 1
           OTHERS    = 2.

IF SY-SUBRC EQ 0.
  READ TABLE ITAB INDEX V_INDX.
  WRITE:/ ITAB-WERKS, ITAB-NAME1.
ENDIF.
```

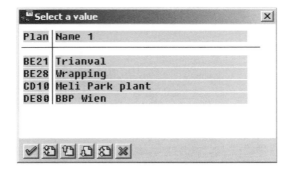

See Also

POPUP_WITH_TABLE_DISPLAY

POPUP_CONTINUE_YES_NO

Summary

Pops up with the response alternatives "Yes" and "No".

Description

Clicking "Yes" returns "J", an abbreviation of the German word "Ja" meaning "Yes"; clicking "No" returns "N" meaning "Nein". This function is well documented.

Parameters

```
EXPORTING
    TEXTLINE1      Line 1 of message
    TEXTLINE2      Line 2 of message
    TITEL          Text title of dialogue
IMPORTING
    ANSWER         Button code clicked by user
```

Example

```
REPORT ZEXAMPLE.
DATA V_ANS.

CALL FUNCTION 'POPUP_CONTINUE_YES_NO'
     EXPORTING
          TEXTLINE1   = 'DO YOU WANT TO SIGNOFF?'
          TEXTLINE2   = 'UNSAVED DATA WILL BE LOST'
          TITEL       = 'SIGNOFF SYSTEM'
     IMPORTING
          ANSWER      = V_ANS.

WRITE:/ V_ANS.
```

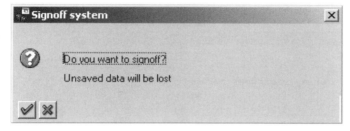

POPUP_DISPLAY_TEXT

Summary

Displays help documentation.

Description

Displays the documentation (document class DT) associated with an object (program, function, etc). These are held in Table DOKHL. They can be created with the object or in Transaction SE61.

Parameters

```
EXPORTING
     LANGUAGE          Language of documentation
     POPUP_TITLE       Title of popup
     TEXT_OBJECT       Object name
IMPORTING
     CANCELLED         Indicator if user clicks cancel on dialogue
```

Example

```
REPORT ZEXAMPLE.
TABLES DOKHL.
DATA V_CAN.
```

```
PARAMETERS P_TXTOBJ LIKE DOKHL-OBJECT DEFAULT 'SPO_EXAMPLE_1'.

CALL FUNCTION 'POPUP_DISPLAY_TEXT'
     EXPORTING
          POPUP_TITLE       = 'DOCUMENTATION TEXT'
          TEXT_OBJECT       = P_TXTOBJ
     IMPORTING
          CANCELLED         = V_CAN
     EXCEPTIONS
          TEXT_NOT_FOUND    = 1
          OTHERS            = 2.

IF SY-SUBRC NE 0.
  WRITE:/ 'CANNOT DISPLAY DOCUMENTATION FOR', P_TXTOBJ.
ENDIF.
```

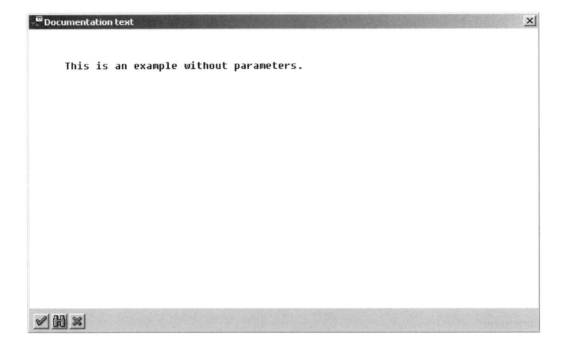

See Also

POPUP_DISPLAY_TEXT_WITH_PARAMS

POPUP_DISPLAY_TEXT_WITH_PARAMS

Summary

Displays help documentation with parameters.

Description

Displays the documentation (document class DT) associated with an object (program, function, etc). These are held in Table DOKHL. They can be created with the object or in Transaction SE61.

Parameters

```
EXPORTING
     LANGUAGE        Language of documentation
     POPUP_TITLE     Title of popup
     TEXT_OBJECT     Object name
IMPORTING
     CANCELLED       Indicator if user clicks cancel on dialogue
TABLES
     PARAMETERS      Replacements to parameters in object
```

Example

```
REPORT ZEXAMPLE.
TABLES DOKHL.
DATA V_CAN.

DATA: BEGIN OF PARAMS OCCURS 0.
         INCLUDE STRUCTURE SPAR.
DATA: END OF PARAMS.

PARAMETERS P_TXTOBJ LIKE DOKHL-OBJECT DEFAULT 'SPO_EXAMPLE_2'.

PARAMS-PARAM  = 'V1'.
PARAMS-VALUE  = 'WITH'.
APPEND PARAMS.
PARAMS-PARAM  = 'V2'.
PARAMS-VALUE  = 'NUMBERED TEXTS'.
APPEND PARAMS.

CALL FUNCTION 'POPUP_DISPLAY_TEXT_WITH_PARAMS'
     EXPORTING
         POPUP_TITLE       = 'DOCUMENTATION'
         TEXT_OBJECT       = P_TXTOBJ
     IMPORTING
         CANCELLED         = V_CAN
     TABLES
         PARAMETERS        = PARAMS
     EXCEPTIONS
         ERROR_IN_TEXT     = 1
         TEXT_NOT_FOUND    = 2
         OTHERS            = 3.

IF SY-SUBRC NE 0.
  WRITE:/ 'CANNOT DISPLAY DOCUMENTATION FOR', P_TXTOBJ.
ENDIF.
```

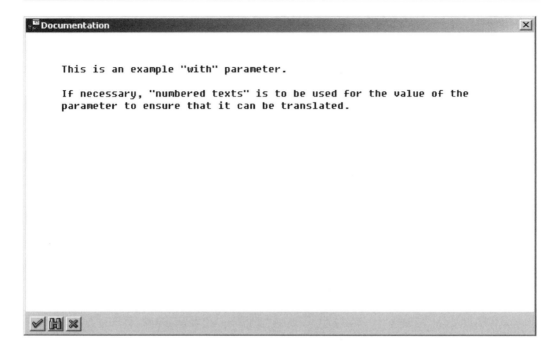

See Also

POPUP_DISPLAY_TEXT

POPUP_FOR_INTERACTION

Summary

General purpose popup box.

Parameters

```
EXPORTING
    HEADLINE            Text title of dialogue box
    TEXT1               Line 1 of message
    TEXT2               Line 2 of message
    TEXT3               Line 3 of message
    TEXT4               Line 4 of message
    TEXT5               Line 5 of message
    TEXT6               Line 6 of message
    TICON               Type of icon displayed:
                        Value       Meaning
                        I           Information
                        W           Warning
```

```
                        E                Error
                        Q                Question
                        C                Critical
                        ' '              No icon
        BUTTON_1         Text on first button
        BUTTON_2         Text on second button
        BUTTON_3         Text on third button
IMPORTING
        BUTTON_PRESSED   Code of button clicked by user (1, 2, or 3)
```

Example

```
REPORT ZEXAMPLE.
TABLES: USR02.

DATA: V_ANS,
      V_TIME(20),
      V_TEXT1(35) VALUE 'DATA FOR',
      V_TEXT3(35) VALUE 'LOGON ID:',
      V_TEXT4(35) VALUE 'CREATED ON:',
      V_TEXT5(35) VALUE 'LAST LOGON:'.


PARAMETERS: P_BNAME LIKE USR02-BNAME OBLIGATORY.

SELECT SINGLE * FROM USR02 WHERE BNAME EQ P_BNAME.

IF SY-SUBRC NE 0.
  CONCATENATE V_TEXT1 P_BNAME INTO V_TEXT1 SEPARATED BY SPACE.
  V_TEXT3 = 'NO DATA FOUND'.
  CLEAR: V_TEXT4, V_TEXT5.
ELSE.
  CONCATENATE:  V_TEXT1 P_BNAME INTO V_TEXT1 SEPARATED BY SPACE,
                V_TEXT3 P_BNAME INTO V_TEXT3 SEPARATED BY SPACE,
                V_TEXT4 USR02-ERDAT INTO V_TEXT4 SEPARATED BY SPACE,
                USR02-TRDAT USR02-LTIME INTO V_TIME,
                V_TEXT5 V_TIME INTO V_TEXT5 SEPARATED BY SPACE.
ENDIF.

CALL FUNCTION 'POPUP_FOR_INTERACTION'
     EXPORTING
         HEADLINE          = 'USER INFORMATION'
         TEXT1             = V_TEXT1
         TEXT2             = ' '
         TEXT3             = V_TEXT3
         TEXT4             = V_TEXT4
         TEXT5             = V_TEXT5
         TEXT6             = ' '
         TICON             = 'I'
         BUTTON_1          = 'OK'
     IMPORTING
         BUTTON_PRESSED    = V_ANS.

WRITE:/ 'ANSWER:', V_ANS.
```

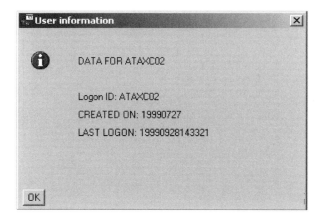

POPUP_NO_LIST

Summary

Displays standard dialogue box if no data.

Parameters

None

Example

```
REPORT ZEXAMPLE.
TABLES USR02.

SELECT SINGLE * FROM USR02 WHERE BNAME EQ 'NOSUCHUSER'.

IF SY-SUBRC NE 0.
  CALL FUNCTION 'POPUP_NO_LIST'.
ELSE.
  WRITE:/ 'NOSUCHUSER FOUND IN SYSTEM!'.
ENDIF.
```

POPUP_TO_DECIDE

Summary

Provides user with several choices as push buttons.

Parameters

```
EXPORTING
     TEXTLINE1          Line 1 of message
     TEXTLINE2          Line 2 of message
     TEXTLINE3          Line 3 of message
     TEXT_OPTION1       Text of first button
     TEXT_OPTION2       Text of second button
     TITEL              Text title of dialogue
IMPORTING
     ANSWER             Code of button clicked by user (1, 2, or 3)
```

Example

```
REPORT ZEXAMPLE.
DATA V_ANS.

CALL FUNCTION 'POPUP_TO_DECIDE'
     EXPORTING
          TEXTLINE1    = '6000 RECORDS WILL BE DELETED'
          TEXTLINE2    = 'THIS ACTION CANNOT BE UNDONE!'
          TEXTLINE3    = 'DO YOU REALLY WANT TO DELETE?'
          TEXT_OPTION1 = 'YES'
          TEXT_OPTION2 = 'NO'
          TITEL        = 'CHOOSE'
     IMPORTING
          ANSWER       = V_ANS.

IF V_ANS EQ '1'.
  WRITE:/ 'RECORDS DELETED'.
ELSEIF V_ANS EQ '2'.
  WRITE:/ 'RECORDS NOT DELETED'.
ELSE.
  WRITE:/ 'CANCELLED - RECORDS NOT DELETED'.
ENDIF.
```

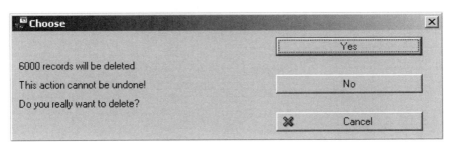

See Also

POPUP_TO_CONFIRM, POPUP_TO_DECIDE_WITH_MESSAGE

POPUP_TO_DECIDE_LIST

Summary

Provide user with several choices as radio buttons.

Parameters

```
EXPORTING
    TEXTLINE1           First information text line
    TEXTLINE2           Second information text line
    TEXTLINE3           Third information text line
    TITEL               Header of popup box
IMPORTING
    ANSWER              Cancel or table index to options
TABLES
    T_SPOPLI            Options for display
```

Example

```
REPORT ZEXAMPLE.

DATA BEGIN OF ISPOPLI OCCURS 1.
       INCLUDE STRUCTURE SPOPLI.
DATA END OF ISPOPLI.

DATA V_ANS.

START-OF-SELECTION.
  PERFORM FILL_SPOPLI.

  CALL FUNCTION 'POPUP_TO_DECIDE_LIST'
       EXPORTING
           TEXTLINE1           = 'CHOOSE A REPORTING LANGUAGE'
           TITEL               = 'CHOOSE A LANGUAGE'
       IMPORTING
           ANSWER              = V_ANS
       TABLES
           T_SPOPLI            = ISPOPLI
       EXCEPTIONS
           NOT_ENOUGH_ANSWERS  = 1
           TOO_MUCH_ANSWERS    = 2
           TOO_MUCH_MARKS      = 3
         OTHERS                = 4.
```

```
  IF SY-SUBRC EQ 0.
    IF V_ANS NE 'A'.
      READ TABLE ISPOPLI INDEX V_ANS.
      WRITE:/ 'YOU HAVE CHOSEN THE', ISPOPLI-VAROPTION, 'LANGUAGE.'.
    ELSE.
      WRITE:/ 'YOU HAVE NOT CHOSEN ANY LANGUAGE'.
    ENDIF.
  ELSE.
    WRITE:/ 'ERROR WITH POPUP'.
  ENDIF.

*&---------------------------------------*
*&                 FORM FILL_SPOPLI
*&---------------------------------------*
FORM FILL_SPOPLI.
  MOVE 'ENGLISH (EN)' TO ISPOPLI-VAROPTION.
  APPEND ISPOPLI.
  MOVE 'GERMAN (DE)' TO ISPOPLI-VAROPTION.
  APPEND ISPOPLI.
  MOVE 'SPANISH (ES)' TO ISPOPLI-VAROPTION.
  APPEND ISPOPLI.
  MOVE 'ITALIAN (IT)' TO ISPOPLI-VAROPTION.
  APPEND ISPOPLI.
  MOVE 'JAPANESE (JA)' TO ISPOPLI-VAROPTION.
  APPEND ISPOPLI.
  MOVE 'GREEK (EL)' TO ISPOPLI-VAROPTION.
  APPEND ISPOPLI.
ENDFORM.                    " FILL_SPOPLI
```

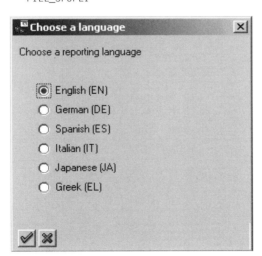

POPUP_TO_DECIDE_WITH_MESSAGE

Summary

Displays diagnosis text to user.

Description

Similar to POPUP_TO_DECIDE.

Parameters

```
EXPORTING
    DIAGNOSETEXT1        Line 1 of message
    DIAGNOSETEXT2        Line 2 of message
    DIAGNOSETEXT3        Line 3 of message
    TEXTLINE1            Line 4 of message
    TEXTLINE2            Line 5 of message
    TEXTLINE3            Line 6 of message
    TEXT_OPTION1         Text of first button
    TEXT_OPTION2         Text of second button
    TITEL               Text title of dialogue
IMPORTING
    ANSWER              Code of button clicked by user (1, 2, or 3)
```

Example

```
REPORT ZEXAMPLE.
DATA V_ANS.

CALL FUNCTION 'POPUP_TO_DECIDE_WITH_MESSAGE'
    EXPORTING
        DIAGNOSETEXT1    = '6000 RECORDS WILL BE DELETED'
        DIAGNOSETEXT2    = 'THIS ACTION CANNOT BE UNDONE!'
        DIAGNOSETEXT3    = 'DO YOU REALLY WANT TO DELETE?'
        TEXTLINE1        = 'YES WILL DELETE THE RECORDS'
        TEXTLINE2        = 'NO WILL NOT DELETE THE RECORDS'
        TEXTLINE3        = 'CANCEL WILL NOT DELETE THE RECORDS'
        TEXT_OPTION1     = 'YES'
        TEXT_OPTION2     = 'NO'
        TITEL            = 'CHOOSE NEXT STEP'
    IMPORTING
        ANSWER           = V_ANS.

IF V_ANS EQ '1'.
  WRITE:/ 'RECORDS DELETED'.
ELSEIF V_ANS EQ '2'.
  WRITE:/ 'RECORDS NOT DELETED'.
ELSE.
  WRITE:/ 'CANCELLED - RECORDS NOT DELETED'.
ENDIF.
```

See Also

POPUP_TO_DECIDE

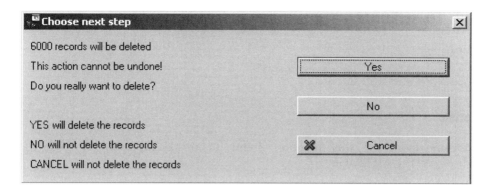

POPUP_TO_DISPLAY_TEXT

Summary

A dialogue box with a two-line message.

Parameters

```
EXPORTING
    TITEL               Text title of dialogue box
    TEXTLINE1           Line 1 of message
    TEXTLINE2           Line 2 of message
```

Example

```
REPORT ZEXAMPLE.
DATA: V_MSG1(20), V_MSG2(20).

CONCATENATE: 'TODAY IS THE' SY-DATUM INTO V_MSG1 SEPARATED BY SPACE,
             'THE TIME IS' SY-UZEIT INTO V_MSG2 SEPARATED BY SPACE.

CALL FUNCTION 'POPUP_TO_DISPLAY_TEXT'
    EXPORTING
        TITEL       = 'INFORMATION REQUEST'
        TEXTLINE1   = V_MSG1
        TEXTLINE2   = V_MSG2.
```

POPUP_TO_INFORM

Summary

Displays several lines of text.

Description

The documentation of this function seems to mistakenly point to POPUP_TO_CONFIRM_WITH_MESSAGE.

Parameters

```
EXPORTING
    TITEL               Title of dialogue box
    TXT1                Line 1 of message
    TXT2                Line 2 of message
    TXT3                Line 3 of message
    TXT4                Line 4 of message
```

Example

```
REPORT ZEXAMPLE.

CALL FUNCTION 'POPUP_TO_INFORM'
    EXPORTING
        TITEL = 'CONFIGURATION SETTINGS'
        TXT1  = 'THE CONFIGURATION CHANGES'
        TXT2  = 'MADE TO THE SYSTEM HAVE'
        TXT3  = 'BEEN SUCCESSFULLY SAVED.'.
```

POPUP_TO_SELECT_MONTH

Summary

Popup to choose a month and year.

Parameters

```
EXPORTING
      ACTUAL_MONTH        Initial year and month to display (format: YYYYMM)
IMPORTING
      SELECTED_MONTH      Year and month selected (format: YYYYMM)
```

Example

See F4_DATE

See Also

F4_DATE

POPUP_WITH_TABLE_DISPLAY

Summary

Displays internal table data in a popup table.

Parameters

```
EXPORTING
      ENDPOS_COL          Last column position
      ENDPOS_ROW          Last row position
      STARTPOS_COL        First column position
      STARTPOS_ROW        First row position
      TITLETEXT           Text title of dialogue
IMPORTING
      CHOISE              Index to row displayed on screen
TABLES
      VALUETAB            Internal table containing data
```

Example

```
REPORT ZEXAMPLE.
TABLES USRO2.
DATA: BEGIN OF IUSR OCCURS 0,
        BNAME LIKE USRO2-BNAME,
        TAB1(2),
```

```
        TRDAT LIKE USR02-TRDAT,
        TAB2(2),
  END OF IUSR.
DATA: IUSRDAT LIKE IUSR OCCURS 20 WITH HEADER LINE.

DATA: V_USRLINES TYPE I,
      V_BEGROW TYPE SY-CUROW VALUE 1,
      V_ANS LIKE SY-TABIX.

PARAMETERS: V_LINES TYPE I DEFAULT 5.

IF V_LINES LE 0.
  V_LINES = 5.
ENDIF.

SELECT * FROM USR02 UP TO V_LINES ROWS.
  IUSRDAT-BNAME  = USR02-BNAME.
  IUSRDAT-TRDAT  = USR02-TRDAT.
  APPEND IUSRDAT.
ENDSELECT.

DESCRIBE TABLE IUSRDAT LINES V_USRLINES.
V_USRLINES = V_BEGROW + V_USRLINES.

CALL FUNCTION 'POPUP_WITH_TABLE_DISPLAY'
    EXPORTING
        ENDPOS_COL    = 30
        ENDPOS_ROW    = V_USRLINES
        STARTPOS_COL  = 2
        STARTPOS_ROW  = V_BEGROW
        TITLETEXT     = 'USER DISPLAY'
    IMPORTING
        CHOISE        = V_ANS
    TABLES
        VALUETAB      = IUSRDAT
    EXCEPTIONS
        BREAK_OFF     = 1
        OTHERS        = 2.
IF SY-SUBRC EQ 0.
  READ TABLE IUSRDAT INDEX V_ANS.
  WRITE:/ IUSRDAT-BNAME, IUSRDAT-TRDAT.
ENDIF.
```

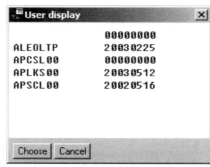

See Also

MD_POPUP_SHOW_INTERNAL_TABLE

SO_EXPRESS_FLAG_SET

Summary

Popup after user performs an action.

Description

This function can be used to send a message in background mode.

Parameters

```
EXPORTING
     TEXT_INFO          Text of message
     INBOX              Flag to display inbox button
     POPUP_TITLE        Text of title to dialogue box
TABLES
     REC_TAB            Recipients
```

Example

```
REPORT ZEXAMPLE.

DATA: IMSG LIKE SOTXTINFO OCCURS 0 WITH HEADER LINE,
      IREC LIKE SOOS7 OCCURS 0 WITH HEADER LINE,
      V_FROM (30).

PARAMETERS: P_REC LIKE SY-UNAME OBLIGATORY.

CONCATENATE 'MESSAGE FROM' SY-UNAME '.' INTO V_FROM SEPARATED BY SPACE.
IMSG-MSGID    = 'F0'.
IMSG-MSGNO    = '257'.
IMSG-MSGV1    = V_FROM.
IMSG-MSGV2    = 'THE RECORDS HAVE BEEN VERIFIED.'.
IMSG-MSGV3    = 'THERE WERE 0 ERRORS.'.

IREC-RECNAM = P_REC.
IREC-RECESC = 'B'.
APPEND IREC.

CALL FUNCTION 'SO_EXPRESS_FLAG_SET'
     EXPORTING
          TEXT_INFO         = IMSG
          INBOX             = ' '
          POPUP_TITLE       = 'VERIFICATION INFORMATION'
```

```
     TABLES
          REC_TAB             = IREC
     EXCEPTIONS
          NO_RECEIVER_EXIST  = 1
          OFFICE_NAME_ERROR  = 2
          OTHERS             = 3.

IF SY-SUBRC EQ 0.
  WRITE:/ 'MESSAGE SENT TO', P_REC.
ELSE.
  WRITE:/ 'MESSAGE NOT SENT TO', P_REC.
ENDIF.
```

See Also

TH_POPUP

TERM_CONTROL_EDIT

Summary

Pops up mini-text editor.

Description

More powerful than TXW_TEXTNOTE_EDIT, as it allows language and a customised text on the titlebar.

Parameters

```
EXPORTING
    TITEL              Title on dialogue box
TABLES
    TEXTLINES          Internal table containing data from text editor
```

Example

```
REPORT ZEXAMPLE.
CONSTANTS C_BASIS_SUPPORT LIKE USR02-BNAME VALUE 'PCWIL00'.
```

```
DATA: BEGIN OF ITXT OCCURS 0.
        INCLUDE STRUCTURE TXW_NOTE.
DATA: END OF ITXT.

START-OF-SELECTION.
PERFORM FILL_HEADER.

ITXT-LINE = '*************************************************************'.
  APPEND ITXT.
  ITXT-LINE = 'PLEASE ENTER TO SEND THIS INFORMATION TO BASIS SUPPORT'.
  APPEND ITXT.
  ITXT-LINE = 'OR CLICK CANCEL'.
  APPEND ITXT.

  CALL FUNCTION 'TERM_CONTROL_EDIT'
      EXPORTING
          TITEL           = 'BASIS SUPPORT REQUEST'
      TABLES
          TEXTLINES       = ITXT
      EXCEPTIONS
          USER_CANCELLED  = 1
          OTHERS          = 2.

  IF SY-SUBRC EQ 0.
    PERFORM SEND_MSG.
  ENDIF.
  WRITE:/ 'FINISHED'.

*-------------------------------------------------------------------
* FORM FILL_HEADER
*-------------------------------------------------------------------
FORM FILL_HEADER.
  ITXT-LINE = 'SAP BASIS SUPPORT TEAM - USER REQUEST FORM'.
  APPEND ITXT.
  ITXT-LINE = '= = = = = = = = = = = = = = = = = = = = = = = = = = = '.
  APPEND ITXT.
  ITXT-LINE = 'PLEASE FILL OUT DETAILS OF YOUR REQUEST BELOW AND RETURN.'.
  APPEND ITXT.
  ITXT-LINE = '----------------------------------------------------------'.
  APPEND ITXT.
  ITXT-LINE = 'NAME:'.
  APPEND ITXT.
  ITXT-LINE = 'SAP LOGON ID:'.
  APPEND ITXT.
  ITXT-LINE = 'PRIORITY OF REQUEST:'.
  APPEND ITXT.
  ITXT-LINE = 'DETAILS OF REQUEST:'.
  APPEND ITXT.

ENDFORM.

*&------------------------------------------------------------------*
*& FORM SEND_MSG
*&------------------------------------------------------------------*
FORM SEND_MSG.
  DATA: V_MSG LIKE SOLI OCCURS 0 WITH HEADER LINE,
        V_LNS TYPE I.
```

```
DESCRIBE TABLE ITXT LINES V_LNS.
V_LNS = V_LNS - 3.


LOOP AT ITXT FROM 1 TO V_LNS.
  V_MSG-LINE  = ITXT-LINE.
  APPEND V_MSG.
ENDLOOP.


CALL FUNCTION 'RS_SEND_MAIL_FOR_SPOOLLIST'
     EXPORTING
          MAILNAME    = C_BASIS_SUPPORT
          MAILTITEL   = 'BASIS SUPPORT REQUEST'
     TABLES
          TEXT        = V_MSG
     EXCEPTIONS
          ERROR       = 1
          OTHERS      = 2.


ENDFORM.                          " SEND_MSG
```

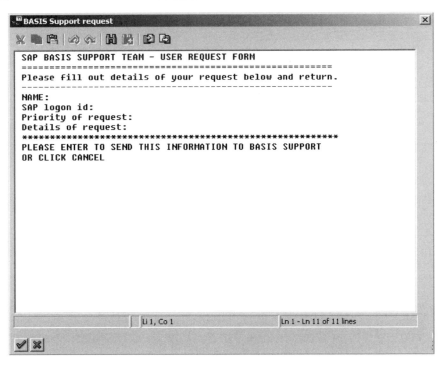

See Also

TXW_TEXTNOTE_EDIT

TH_POPUP

Summary

Displays a popup dialogue on a specific users screen.

Parameters

```
EXPORTING
     CLIENT            Send message to user on this client (default = all clients)
     USER              Logon ID of user to receive message
     MESSAGE           One-line message
     CUT_BLANKS        Remove trailing blanks from message
```

Example

```
REPORT ZEXAMPLE.
TABLES USR02.

DATA: BEGIN OF IUSRS OCCURS 0,
        BNAME LIKE USR02-BNAME,
      END OF IUSRS.
DATA: BEGIN OF IERRS OCCURS 0,
        BNAME LIKE USR02-BNAME,
      END OF IERRS.

SELECT-OPTIONS S_BNAME FOR USR02-BNAME.
PARAMETER P_MSG(128).

SELECT BNAME FROM USR02 INTO TABLE IUSRS WHERE BNAME IN S_BNAME.
IF NOT IUSRS[] IS INITIAL.
  LOOP AT IUSRS.
    CALL FUNCTION 'TH_POPUP'
         EXPORTING
               CLIENT            = SY-MANDT
               USER              = IUSRS-BNAME
               MESSAGE           = P_MSG
               CUT_BLANKS        = 'X'
         EXCEPTIONS
               USER_NOT_FOUND    = 1
               OTHERS            = 2.
    IF SY-SUBRC NE 0.
      IERRS-BNAME = IUSRS-BNAME.
      APPEND IERRS.
    ENDIF.
  ENDLOOP.
ELSE.
  WRITE:/ 'NO USER FOUND'.
ENDIF.

IF NOT IERRS[] IS INITIAL.
  WRITE:/ 'THE MESSAGE WAS NOT SENT TO THE FOLLOWING:'.
```

```
    LOOP AT IERRS.
      WRITE:/ IERRS-BNAME.
    ENDLOOP.
ENDIF.
```

See Also

SO_EXPRESS_FLAG_SET

TXW_TEXTNOTE_EDIT

Summary

Pops up mini-text editor.

Description

TERM_CONTROL_EDIT is more powerful.

Parameters

```
EXPORTING
     EDIT_MODE       Flag whether information data is passed into internal table
TABLES
     T_TXWNOTE       Internal table containing data from text editor
```

Example

```
REPORT ZEXAMPLE.
CONSTANTS C_BASIS_SUPPORT LIKE USR02-BNAME VALUE 'PCWIL00'.

DATA: BEGIN OF ITXT OCCURS 0.
         INCLUDE STRUCTURE TXW_NOTE.
DATA: END OF ITXT.
```

```
START-OF-SELECTION.
  PERFORM FILL_HEADER.

  IF SY-UCOMM NE 'CANC'.
ITXT-LINE = '**************************************************************'.
    APPEND ITXT.
    ITXT-LINE = 'PLEASE ENTER TO SEND THIS INFORMATION TO BASIS SUPPORT'.
    APPEND ITXT.
    ITXT-LINE = 'OR CLICK CANCEL'.
    APPEND ITXT.


    CALL FUNCTION 'TXW_TEXTNOTE_EDIT'
         EXPORTING
             EDIT_MODE   = 'X'
         TABLES
             T_TXWNOTE   = ITXT.
  ENDIF.

  IF SY-UCOMM NE 'CANC'.
    PERFORM SEND_MSG.
  ENDIF.
    WRITE:/ 'FINISHED'.

*----------------------------------------------------------------------
* FORM FILL_HEADER
*----------------------------------------------------------------------
FORM FILL_HEADER.
  ITXT-LINE  = 'SAP BASIS SUPPORT TEAM - USER REQUEST FORM'.
  APPEND ITXT.
  ITXT-LINE  = ' = = = = = = = = = = = = = = = = = = = = = = = = ='.
  APPEND ITXT.
  ITXT-LINE  = 'PLEASE FILL OUT DETAILS OF YOUR REQUEST BELOW AND RETURN.'.
  APPEND ITXT.
  ITXT-LINE  = '---------------------------------------------------------'.
  APPEND ITXT.
  ITXT-LINE  = 'NAME:'.
  APPEND ITXT.
  ITXT-LINE  = 'SAP LOGON ID:'.
  APPEND ITXT.
  ITXT-LINE  = 'PRIORITY OF REQUEST:'.
  APPEND ITXT.
  ITXT-LINE  = 'DETAILS OF REQUEST:'.
  APPEND ITXT.


  CALL FUNCTION 'TXW_TEXTNOTE_EDIT'
       TABLES
             T_TXWNOTE = ITXT.
ENDFORM.

*&---------------------------------------------------*
*& FORM SEND_MSG
*&---------------------------------------------------*
FORM SEND_MSG.
  DATA: V_MSG LIKE SOLI OCCURS 0 WITH HEADER LINE,
        V_LNS TYPE I.
```

```
DESCRIBE TABLE ITXT LINES V_LNS.
V_LNS = V_LNS - 3.

LOOP AT ITXT FROM 1 TO V_LNS.
  V_MSG-LINE = ITXT-LINE.
  APPEND V_MSG.
ENDLOOP.
CALL FUNCTION 'RS_SEND_MAIL_FOR_SPOOLLIST'
     EXPORTING
          MAILNAME        = C_BASIS_SUPPORT
          MAILTITEL       = 'BASIS SUPPORT REQUEST'
     TABLES
          TEXT            = V_MSG
     EXCEPTIONS
          ERROR           = 1
          OTHERS          = 2.
ENDFORM.                              " SEND_MSG
```

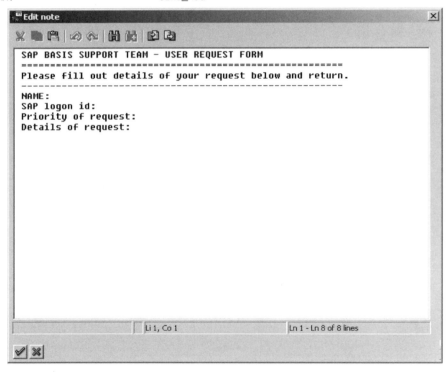

See Also

TERM_CONTROL_EDIT

WS_MSG

Summary

Displays a one-line message.

Description

Does not affect the flow logic of the program.

Parameters

```
EXPORTING
  MSG_TYPE                    Type of icon to display:
                              Value     Meaning
                              I         Information
                              W         Warning
                              E         Error
                              Q         Question
                              C         Critical
                              ' '       No icon
  TEXT                        Message to display on dialogue
  TITL                        Text of dialogue title
```

Example

```
REPORT ZEXAMPLE.
TABLES USR02.

PARAMETERS P_BNAME LIKE USR02-BNAME.

SELECT SINGLE BNAME FROM USR02 INTO USR02-BNAME WHERE BNAME EQ P_BNAME.
IF SY-SUBRC NE 0.
  CALL FUNCTION 'WS_MSG'
      EXPORTING
          MSG_TYPE  = 'E'
          TEXT      = 'USER DOES NOT EXIST'
          TITL      = 'USER LOGON ID CHECK'.
ELSE.
  CALL FUNCTION 'WS_MSG'
      EXPORTING
          MSG_TYPE  = 'I'
          TEXT      = 'USER ID EXISTS'
          TITL      = 'USER LOGON ID CHECK'.
ENDIF.
```

Miscellaneous

10

Individually, these functions cover-specific topics, and as a whole, they span a huge range of available functionality in the SAP system.

Jobs

BP_JOB_DELETE

Summary

Deletes background job(s).

Description

Deletion is unconditional, except that active jobs cannot be deleted and a job cannot delete itself. Aborted jobs, however, are deleted. Logs are deleted, if they exist with the job.

Parameters

```
EXPORTING
        JOBCOUNT                        Job identification number
        JOBNAME                         Job name
```

Example

See BP_JOB_SELECT

BP_JOB_SELECT

Summary

Returns a table with job(s) details.

Parameters

```
EXPORTING
      JOBSELECT_DIALOG              Display popup to select job (Transaction SP01)
TABLES
      JOBSELECT_JOBLIST             Criteria for job listing
```

Example

```
REPORT ZEXAMPLE.

DATA: JOBLIST LIKE TBTCJOB OCCURS 0 WITH HEADER LINE,
      JOBDETS LIKE BTCSELECT,
      JOBLOG  LIKE TBTC5 OCCURS 0 WITH HEADER LINE,
      V_ANS.

PARAMETERS P_UNAME LIKE SY-UNAME DEFAULT SY-UNAME OBLIGATORY.

IF NOT P_UNAME IS INITIAL.
  JOBDETS-JOBNAME     = '*'.
  JOBDETS-USERNAME    = P_UNAME.
  JOBDETS-FROM_DATE   = SY-DATUM.
  JOBDETS-TO_DATE     = SY-DATUM.
  JOBDETS-NO_DATE     = 'X'.
  JOBDETS-WITH_PRED   = 'X'.
  JOBDETS-PRELIM      = 'X'.
  JOBDETS-SCHEDUL     = 'X'.
  JOBDETS-READY       = 'X'.
  JOBDETS-RUNNING     = 'X'.
  JOBDETS-FINISHED    = 'X'.
  JOBDETS-ABORTED     = 'X'.
ENDIF.

CALL FUNCTION 'BP_JOB_SELECT'
    EXPORTING
        JOBSELECT_DIALOG    = 'Y'
        JOBSEL_PARAM_IN     = JOBDETS
    TABLES
        JOBSELECT_JOBLIST   = JOBLIST
    EXCEPTIONS
        INVALID_DIALOG_TYPE = 1
        JOBNAME_MISSING     = 2
        NO_JOBS_FOUND       = 3
        SELECTION_CANCELED  = 4
        USERNAME_MISSING    = 5
        OTHERS              = 6.

IF SY-SUBRC EQ 0.
  IF NOT JOBLIST[] IS INITIAL.
    READ TABLE JOBLIST INDEX 1.

    CALL FUNCTION 'BP_JOBLOG_READ'
        EXPORTING
            JOBCOUNT            = JOBLIST-JOBCOUNT
            JOBNAME             = JOBLIST-JOBNAME
```

```
        TABLES
            JOBLOGTBL                = JOBLOG
        EXCEPTIONS
            CANT_READ_JOBLOG         = 1
            JOBCOUNT_MISSING         = 2
            JOBLOG_DOES_NOT_EXIST    = 3
            JOBLOG_IS_EMPTY          = 4
            JOBLOG_NAME_MISSING      = 5
            JOBNAME_MISSING          = 6
            JOB_DOES_NOT_EXIST       = 7
            OTHERS                   = 8.


IF JOBLOG[] IS INITIAL.
  WRITE:/ 'NO JOB LOG FOUND'.
ELSE.
  CALL FUNCTION 'POPUP_TO_CONFIRM'
        EXPORTING
            TITLEBAR                 = 'DELETE JOB LOGS'
            TEXT_QUESTION            = 'JOB LOGS FOUND. DELETE?'
            POPUP_TYPE               = 'W'
        IMPORTING
            ANSWER                   = V_ANS.
ENDIF.


IF V_ANS EQ '1'.
  CALL FUNCTION 'BP_JOB_DELETE'
        EXPORTING
            JOBCOUNT                     = JOBLIST-JOBCOUNT
            JOBNAME                      = JOBLIST-JOBNAME
        EXCEPTIONS
            CANT_DELETE_EVENT_ENTRY    = 1
            CANT_DELETE_JOB            = 2
            CANT_DELETE_JOBLOG         = 3
            CANT_DELETE_STEPS          = 4
            CANT_DELETE_TIME_ENTRY     = 5
            CANT_DERELEASE_SUCCESSOR   = 6
            CANT_ENQ_PREDECESSOR       = 7
            CANT_ENQ_SUCCESSOR         = 8
            CANT_ENQ_TBTCO_ENTRY       = 9
            CANT_UPDATE_PREDECESSOR    = 10
            CANT_UPDATE_SUCCESSOR      = 11
            COMMIT_FAILED              = 12
            JOBCOUNT_MISSING           = 13
            JOBNAME_MISSING            = 14
            JOB_DOES_NOT_EXIST         = 15
            JOB_IS_ALREADY_RUNNING     = 16
            NO_DELETE_AUTHORITY        = 17
            OTHERS                     = 18.
    IF SY-SUBRC EQ 0.
      WRITE:/ JOBLIST-JOBCOUNT, JOBLIST-JOBNAME, 'LOG DELETED'.
      EXIT.
    ELSE.
      WRITE:/ JOBLIST-JOBCOUNT, JOBLIST-JOBNAME, 'LOG NOT DELETED'.
    ENDIF.
```

```
    ELSE.
      CALL FUNCTION 'BP_JOBLOG_SHOW'
            EXPORTING
                  JOBCOUNT                      = JOBLIST-JOBCOUNT
                  JOBNAME                       = JOBLIST-JOBNAME
            EXCEPTIONS
                  ERROR_READING_JOBDATA     = 1
                  ERROR_READING_JOBLOG_DATA = 2
                  JOBCOUNT_MISSING          = 3
                  JOBLOG_DOES_NOT_EXIST     = 4
                  JOBLOG_IS_EMPTY           = 5
                  JOBLOG_SHOW_CANCELED      = 6
                  JOBNAME_MISSING           = 7
                  JOB_DOES_NOT_EXIST        = 8
                  NO_JOBLOG_THERE_YET       = 9
                  NO_SHOW_PRIVILEGE_GIVEN   = 10
                  OTHERS                    = 11.
    ENDIF.
  ELSE.
    WRITE:/ 'NO JOBS FOR', P_UNAME.
    EXIT.
  ENDIF.
ENDIF.
```

BP_JOBLOG_READ

Summary

Fetches job log executions.

Description

Reads the contents of a job-processing log into an internal table for further processing.

Parameters

```
EXPORTING
      JOBCOUNT                  Job identification number
      JOBNAME                   Job name
TABLES
      JOBLOGTBL                 Job log entries in list format
```

Example

See BP_JOB_SELECT

See Also

BP_JOBLOG_SHOW

BP_JOBLOG_SHOW

Summary

Displays job log in window.

Parameters

```
EXPORTING
      JOBCOUNT            Job identification number
      JOBNAME             Job name
```

Example

See BP_JOB_SELECT

See Also

BP_JOBLOG_READ

JOB_CLOSE

Summary

Schedules a background job.

Description

Used to schedule the job, including how it should be started (time, date, etc.).

Parameters

```
EXPORTING
      JOBCOUNT            Job identification number
      JOBNAME             Job name
IMPORTING
      JOB_WAS_RELEASED    Flag if job is released (X if true)
```

Example

See JOB_OPEN

See Also

JOB_OPEN

JOB_OPEN

Summary

Creates a background job.

Parameters

```
EXPORTING
      JOBGROUP      Group to which the job is to be assigned
      JOBNAME       Job name
IMPORTING
      JOBCOUNT      ID number of background job
```

Example

```
REPORT ZEXAMPLE.

DATA: JOBCOUNT  LIKE TBTCJOB-JOBCOUNT,
      IMMEDIATE LIKE SY-BATCH VALUE 'X',
      REL,
      JOBNAME   LIKE TBTCJOB-JOBNAME,
      STEPNUM   LIKE TBTCJOB-STEPCOUNT.

PARAMETERS: P_RPT LIKE SY-REPID,
            P_VAR LIKE RALDB-VARIANT.

JOBNAME = P_RPT.

CALL FUNCTION 'JOB_OPEN'
      EXPORTING
            JOBGROUP          = 'QUEUE'
            JOBNAME           = JOBNAME
      IMPORTING
            JOBCOUNT          = JOBCOUNT
      EXCEPTIONS
            CANT_CREATE_JOB   = 1
            INVALID_JOB_DATA  = 2
            JOBNAME_MISSING   = 3
            OTHERS            = 4.
IF SY-SUBRC EQ 0.
  CALL FUNCTION 'JOB_SUBMIT'
      EXPORTING
            AUTHCKNAM               = SY-UNAME
            JOBCOUNT                = JOBCOUNT
            JOBNAME                 = JOBNAME
            REPORT                  = P_RPT
            VARIANT                 = P_VAR
      IMPORTING
            STEP_NUMBER             = STEPNUM
      EXCEPTIONS
            BAD_PRIPARAMS           = 1
            BAD_XPGFLAGS            = 2
```

```
                    INVALID_JOBDATA        = 3
                    JOBNAME_MISSING        = 4
                    JOB_NOTEX              = 5
                    JOB_SUBMIT_FAILED      = 6
                    LOCK_FAILED            = 7
                    PROGRAM_MISSING        = 8
                    PROG_ABAP_AND_EXTPG_SET = 9
                    OTHERS                 = 10.
    IF SY-SUBRC EQ 0.
      CALL FUNCTION 'JOB_CLOSE'
            EXPORTING
                  JOBCOUNT               = JOBCOUNT
                  JOBNAME                = JOBNAME
                  STRTIMMED              = IMMEDIATE
            IMPORTING
                  JOB_WAS_RELEASED       = REL
            EXCEPTIONS
                  CANT_START_IMMEDIATE = 1
                  INVALID_STARTDATE    = 2
                  JOBNAME_MISSING      = 3
                  JOB_CLOSE_FAILED     = 4
                  JOB_NOSTEPS          = 5
                  JOB_NOTEX            = 6
                  LOCK_FAILED          = 7
                  OTHERS               = 8.
      IF SY-SUBRC EQ 0.
        IF REL EQ 'X'.
          WRITE:/ JOBNAME, 'WAS RELEASED. CHECK SM37.'.
        ELSE.
          WRITE:/ JOBNAME, 'WAS NOT RELEASED'.
        ENDIF.
      ELSE.
        WRITE:/ JOBNAME, 'NOT CLOSED'.
      ENDIF.
    ELSE.
      WRITE:/ JOBNAME, 'NOT SUBMITTED'.
    ENDIF.
  ELSE.
    WRITE:/ JOBNAME, 'NOT CREATED'.
  ENDIF.
```

See Also

JOB_CLOSE

JOB_SUBMIT

Summary

Adds a step (program) to a background job.

Description

This is not allowed in update task mode as the function uses COMMIT.

Parameters

```
EXPORTING
        AUTHCKNAM       Background user name for authorisation check
        JOBCOUNT        ID number of background job
        JOBNAME         Job name
        REPORT          Report to run in the background job
        VARIANT         Variant for the specified report
IMPORTING
        STEP_NUMBER     Step number in job
```

Example

See JOB_OPEN

See Also

JOB_CLOSE, JOB_OPEN

Numbers

CLOI_PUT_SIGN_IN_FRONT

Summary

Moves the negative sign from the left-hand side of a number to the right-hand side of the number.

Description

The result will be left justified like a character field.

Parameters

```
CHANGING
      VALUE             Value to change
```

Example

```
REPORT ZEXAMPLE.
PARAMETERS P_VAL(10) TYPE C OBLIGATORY DEFAULT '100.15-'.
```

```
WRITE:/ 'BEFORE:', P_VAL.
CALL FUNCTION 'CLOI_PUT_SIGN_IN_FRONT'
    CHANGING
        VALUE    = P_VAL.
WRITE:/ 'AFTER:', P_VAL.
```

G_DECIMAL_PLACES_GET

Summary

Number of decimal places set for currency.

Parameters

```
EXPORTING
      CURRENCY          Currency key
IMPORTING
      DECIMAL_PLACES    Number of decimal places in currency key
```

Example

```
REPORT ZEXAMPLE.

DATA V_DEC LIKE TCURX-CURRDEC.

PARAMETERS P_WAERS LIKE TCURC-WAERS.

CALL FUNCTION 'G_DECIMAL_PLACES_GET'
    EXPORTING
        CURRENCY       = P_WAERS
    IMPORTING
        DECIMAL_PLACES = V_DEC.

WRITE:/ 'NUMBER OF DECIMAL PLACES:', V_DEC.
```

NUMERIC_CHECK

Summary

Returns the format of a number.

Parameters

```
EXPORTING
      STRING_IN       Number in
```

```
IMPORTING
        STRING_OUT        Formatted number out
        HTYPE             Data type:
                          Value     Views
                          CHAR      String
                          NUMC      Numeric (default)
```

Example

```
REPORT ZEXAMPLE.
DATA: VALUEOUT(70), DTYPE LIKE DD01V-DATATYPE.

PARAMETERS VALUEIN(70).

CALL FUNCTION 'NUMERIC_CHECK'
    EXPORTING
        STRING_IN  = VALUEIN
    IMPORTING
        STRING_OUT = VALUEOUT
        HTYPE      = DTYPE.

WRITE:/ VALUEIN, VALUEOUT, DTYPE.
```

QF05_RANDOM

Summary

Returns a random number between 0 and 1.

Description

This function is documented.

Parameters

```
EXPORTING
        RAN_SEED          Initial 'seed' value
IMPORTING
        RAN_NUMBER        Random number
        RAN_SEED          Generated new 'seed' value
```

Example

```
REPORT ZEXAMPLE.

DATA: V_SEED LIKE QF00-RAN_SEED VALUE 1,
      V_RAN  LIKE QF00-RAN_NUMBER.
```

```
DO 20 TIMES.
  CALL FUNCTION 'QF05_RANDOM'
      EXPORTING
            RAN_SEED    = V_SEED
      IMPORTING
            RAN_NUMBER  = V_RAN
            RAN_SEED    = V_SEED.
  WRITE:/ V_RAN.
ENDDO.
```

See Also

QF05_RANDOM_INTEGER

QF05_RANDOM_INTEGER

Summary

Returns a random number.

Description

There is some documentation for this function. The number lies between a maximum and minimum parameter range.

Parameters

```
EXPORTING
      RAN_INT_MAX    Maximum random number
      RAN_INT_MIN    Minimum random number
IMPORTING
      RAN_INT        Random number generated
```

Example

```
REPORT ZEXAMPLE.

DATA RANINT LIKE QF00-RAN_INT.

PARAMETERS: P_MAX   LIKE QF00-RAN_INT DEFAULT 100,
            P_MIN   LIKE QF00-RAN_INT DEFAULT 1,
            P_TIMES TYPE I DEFAULT 10.

WRITE:/ 'RANDOM NUMBER'.
ULINE.
DO P_TIMES TIMES.
```

```
CALL FUNCTION 'QF05_RANDOM_INTEGER'
     EXPORTING
          RAN_INT_MAX   = P_MAX
          RAN_INT_MIN   = P_MIN
     IMPORTING
          RAN_INT       = RANINT
     EXCEPTIONS
          INVALID_INPUT = 1
          OTHERS        = 2.
IF SY-SUBRC EQ 0.
  WRITE:/ RANINT.
ELSE.
  WRITE:/ 'COULD NOT GENERATE RANDOM NUMBER'.
ENDIF.
ENDDO.
```

See Also

QF05_RANDOM

Printing

ADDRESS_INTO_PRINTFORM

Summary

Formats an address for printing according to the postal regulations of recipient countries.

Description

The country-specific formatting of the address is decided by the three-character country code in field LAND1 in the input address. The function module is well documented in the online help.

Parameters

```
EXPORTING
     ADDRESS_1                 Transfer table containing unformatted address
     ADDRESS_TYPE              Flag type of destination address (person/company):
                               Value   Meaning
                               " "     Company addresses
                               1       Normal addresses
                               2       Personal address
                               3       Person at company addresses
     SENDER_COUNTRY            Country key of sender
IMPORTING
     ADDRESS_PRINTFORM_TABLE   The formatted address
```

Example

```
REPORT ZEXAMPLE.

TYPE-POOLS: SZADR.
DATA: V_ADDRESS                        LIKE  ADRS1,
      I_ADDRESS_PRINTFORM_TABLE        TYPE  SZADR_PRINTFORM_TABLE,
      I_ADDRESS_PRINTFORM_TABLE_LINE   TYPE  SZADR_PRINTFORM_TABLE_LINE.

PARAMETERS:  P_NAME     LIKE V_ADDRESS-NAME1,
             P_STREET   LIKE V_ADDRESS-STREET,
             P_HNUM     LIKE V_ADDRESS-HOUSE_NUM1,
             P_CITY     LIKE V_ADDRESS-CITY1,
             P_PCODE    LIKE V_ADDRESS-POST_CODE1,
             P_DCTRY    LIKE T005-LAND1, "DESTINATION COUNTRY
             P_SCTRY    LIKE T005-LAND1. "SENDING COUNTRY

V_ADDRESS-NAME1        = P_NAME.
V_ADDRESS-STREET       = P_STREET.
V_ADDRESS-HOUSE_NUM1   = P_HNUM.
V_ADDRESS-CITY1        = P_CITY.
V_ADDRESS-POST_CODE1   = P_PCODE.
V_ADDRESS-COUNTRY      = P_DCTRY.

CALL FUNCTION 'ADDRESS_INTO_PRINTFORM'
     EXPORTING
          ADDRESS_1               = V_ADDRESS
          ADDRESS_TYPE            = '1'
          SENDER_COUNTRY          = P_SCTRY
     IMPORTING
          ADDRESS_PRINTFORM_TABLE = I_ADDRESS_PRINTFORM_TABLE.

LOOP AT I_ADDRESS_PRINTFORM_TABLE INTO I_ADDRESS_PRINTFORM_TABLE_LINE.
  WRITE:/ I_ADDRESS_PRINTFORM_TABLE_LINE-ADDRESS_LINE.
ENDLOOP.
```

FM_SELECTION_CRITERIA_PRINT

Summary

Displays criteria used in selection screen.

Parameters

None.

Example

```
REPORT ZEXAMPLE.
TABLES USR01.
```

```
DATA: BEGIN OF SELECTIONS OCCURS 0,
        FLAG,
        OLENGHT TYPE X,
        LINE LIKE RALDB-INFOLINE,
      END OF SELECTIONS.

SELECT-OPTIONS: S_USRID FOR USR01-BNAME.
PARAMETER: P_COMMNT(30).

WRITE:/ 'Output with PRINT_SELECTIONS:' COLOR COL_HEADING.
NEW-LINE.

CALL FUNCTION 'PRINT_SELECTIONS'
        EXPORTING
                RNAME      = SY-CPROG
                RVARIANTE  = SY-SLSET
                MODE       = 0
        TABLES
                INFOTAB    = SELECTIONS.

LOOP AT SELECTIONS.
        WRITE SELECTIONS-LINE.
        NEW-LINE.
ENDLOOP.
NEW-PAGE.

WRITE:/ 'Output with FM_SELECTION_CRITERIA_PRINT:' COLOR COL_HEADING.
NEW-LINE.

CALL FUNCTION 'FM_SELECTION_CRITERIA_PRINT'
        EXPORTING
                I_REPORT_NAME  = SY-CPROG
        EXCEPTIONS
                OTHERS         = 1.
```

See Also

PRINT_SELECTIONS

GET_PRINT_PARAMETERS

Summary

Reads and changes spool print parameters.

Description

This function is well documented in the online help.

Parameters

```
EXPORTING
        COPIES                  Number of copies to print
        COVER_PAGE              Flag to print a cover page
        DESTINATION             Name of printer
        IMMEDIATELY             Print immediatly
        LAYOUT                  Paper layout to use
        LINE_COUNT              Number of lines (rows)
        LINE_SIZE               Number of columns
        LIST_NAME               Spool request name
        LIST_TEXT               Spool request text
        NO_DIALOG               Flag to hide/show dialogue
        RECEIVER                Name of recipient
        PRIORITY                Printer priority
        USER
IMPORTING
        OUT_PARAMETERS          Settings of printer
        OUT_ARCHIVE_PARAMETERS  Archive settings of printer
```

Example

```
REPORT ZEXAMPLE.

DATA: INPARAMS LIKE PRI_PARAMS OCCURS O WITH HEADER LINE,
      OUTPARAMS LIKE PRI_PARAMS OCCURS O WITH HEADER LINE,
      ARCHIVE_PARAMETERS LIKE ARC_PARAMS,
      PLIST        LIKE PRI_PARAMS-PLIST,
      PRTXT        LIKE PRI_PARAMS-PRTXT,
      NO_DIALOG(1) TYPE X VALUE '01'.

DATA PKEY TYPE SYPRKEY.

CALL FUNCTION 'STORE_PRINT_PARAMETERS' "GENERATE KEY
    EXPORTING
        IN_PARAMETERS = INPARAMS
        APPLIKATION   = 'B'
        USER          = SY-UNAME
    IMPORTING
        KEY           = PKEY
    EXCEPTIONS
        ERROR_OCCURED = 1
        OTHERS        = 2.
IF SY-SUBRC NE O.
  WRITE:/ 'COULD NOT GET KEY'.
  EXIT.
ENDIF.

CALL FUNCTION 'LOAD_PRINT_PARAMETERS'
    EXPORTING
        KEY           = PKEY
    IMPORTING
        OUT_PARAMETERS = OUTPARAMS
```

```
      EXCEPTIONS
            ERROR_OCCURED  = 1
            OTHERS         = 2.
IF SY-SUBRC NE 0.
  WRITE:/ 'COULD NOT LOAD PRINT PARAMETERS'.
  EXIT.
ELSE.
  APPEND OUTPARAMS.
ENDIF.

LOOP AT OUTPARAMS.
  WRITE:/ 'SETTING PARAMETERS FOR', OUTPARAMS-PRREC.
  PLIST = OUTPARAMS-PRREC.
  PRTXT = 'ZEXAMPLE TEST'.
  CALL FUNCTION 'SET_PRINT_PARAMETERS'
       EXPORTING
            LIST_NAME            = PLIST
            LIST_TEXT            = PRTXT
            IN_PARAMETERS        = OUTPARAMS
            IN_ARCHIVE_PARAMETERS = ARCHIVE_PARAMETERS.
ENDLOOP.

CALL FUNCTION 'GET_PRINT_PARAMETERS'
     EXPORTING
          NO_DIALOG             = 'X'
     IMPORTING
          OUT_PARAMETERS        = OUTPARAMS
          OUT_ARCHIVE_PARAMETERS = ARCHIVE_PARAMETERS
     EXCEPTIONS
          ARCHIVE_INFO_NOT_FOUND = 1
          INVALID_PRINT_PARAMS   = 2
          INVALID_ARCHIVE_PARAMS = 3
          OTHERS                 = 4.
IF SY-SUBRC EQ 0.
  LOOP AT OUTPARAMS.
    WRITE:/ OUTPARAMS-PRREC, OUTPARAMS-PRTXT.
  ENDLOOP.
ELSE.
  WRITE:/ 'ERROR GETTING PRINT PARAMETERS'.
ENDIF.
```

See Also

SET_PRINT_PARAMETERS, LOAD_PRINT_PARAMETERS,
RSPO_RPRINT_SPOOLREQ, RSPO_OUTPUT_SPOOL_REQUEST

LOAD_PRINT_PARAMETERS

Summary

User default printer settings.

Parameters

```
EXPORTING
      KEY             Key for print parameter set
IMPORTING
      OUT_PARAMETERS  Settings of printer
```

Example

See GET_PRINT_PARAMETERS

See Also

STORE_PRINT_PARAMETERS, GET_PRINT_PARAMETERS

PRINT_SELECTIONS

Summary

Builds table of criteria used in selection screen.

Parameters

```
EXPORTING
      MODE         .        Not used
      RNAME                 Report name
      RVARIANTE             Variant name
TABLES
      INFOTAB               Table containing report criteria
```

Example

See FM_SELECTION_CRITERIA_PRINT

See Also

FM_SELECTION_CRITERIA_PRINT

SET_PRINT_PARAMETERS

Summary

Changes users print settings.

Parameters

```
EXPORTING
        COPIES                Number of copies to print
        COVER_PAGE            Flag to print a cover page
        DESTINATION           Name of printer
        LAYOUT                Paper layout to use
        LINE_COUNT            Number of lines (rows)
        LINE_SIZE             Number of columns
        LIST_NAME             Spool request name
        LIST_TEXT             Spool request text
        NO_DIALOG             Flag to hide/show dialogue
        RECEIVER              Name of recipient
        PRIORITY              Printer priority
        USER
IMPORTING
        OUT_PARAMETERS        Settings of printer
        OUT_ARCHIVE_PARAMETERS Archive settings of printer
```

Example

See GET_PRINT_PARAMETERS

See Also

GET_PRINT_PARAMETERS, STORE_PRINT_PARAMETERS

STORE_PRINT_PARAMETERS

Summary

Saves users current print settings.

Description

This function is well documented.

Parameters

```
EXPORTING
        IN_PARAMETERS    Parameters of printer
        APPLIKATION      Printing application
        USER             User
IMPORTING
        KEY              Unique key for print parameters
```

Example

See GET_PRINT_PARAMETERS

See Also

GET_PRINT_PARAMETERS, LOAD_PRINT_PARAMETERS

Programs and Transactions

BAPI_TRANSACTION_COMMIT

Summary

Explicitly commits a BAPI.

Description

When you call BAPIs in programs that change data in SAP, you should call this method after-wards to permanently write the changes to the database. There is good documentation with this function.

Parameters

```
EXPORTING
      WAIT       Use the command 'COMMIT AND WAIT' until completion of update
IMPORTING
      RETURN     Message return codes and descriptions
```

Example

```
REPORT ZEXAMPLE.

DATA: USRADDR      LIKE BAPIADDR3 OCCURS 0 WITH HEADER LINE,
      RET_GETDETAIL LIKE BAPIRET2 OCCURS 0 WITH HEADER LINE,
      RET_CHANGE   LIKE BAPIRET2 OCCURS 0 WITH HEADER LINE,
      RET_COMMIT   LIKE BAPIRET2 OCCURS 0 WITH HEADER LINE,
      RET_ROLLBACK LIKE BAPIRET2 OCCURS 0 WITH HEADER LINE.

PARAMETERS: P_USR LIKE SY-UNAME OBLIGATORY,
            P_NICKNM LIKE USRADDR-NICKNAME.

CALL FUNCTION 'BAPI_USER_GET_DETAIL'
    EXPORTING
        USERNAME   = P_USR
    IMPORTING
        ADDRESS    = USRADDR
    TABLES
        RETURN     = RET_GETDETAIL.
```

```
IF RET_GETDETAIL[] IS INITIAL.
  WRITE:/ P_USR, 'NICKNAME BEFORE CHANGE:', USRADDR-NICKNAME.
  USRADDR-NICKNAME = P_NICKNM.
  MODIFY USRADDR.

  CALL FUNCTION 'BAPI_USER_CHANGE'
      EXPORTING
          USERNAME      = P_USR
          ADDRESS       = USRADDR
      TABLES
          RETURN        = RET_CHANGE.

  IF RET_CHANGE[] IS INITIAL.
    CALL FUNCTION 'BAPI_TRANSACTION_COMMIT'
        EXPORTING
            WAIT          = 'X'
        IMPORTING
            RETURN        = RET_COMMIT.

    IF RET_COMMIT[] IS INITIAL.
      WRITE:/ P_USR, 'NICKNAME AFTER CHANGE:', USRADDR-NICKNAME.
    ELSE.
      CALL FUNCTION 'BAPI_TRANSACTION_ROLLBACK'
          IMPORTING
              RETURN        = RET_ROLLBACK.
      WRITE:/ P_USR, 'NOT UPDATED.'.
    ENDIF.
  ELSE.
    WRITE:/ 'COULD NOT MAKE', USRADDR-NICKNAME, 'CHANGE'.
  ENDIF.
ELSE.
  WRITE:/ 'ERROR RETRIEVING INFORMATION FOR', P_USR.
ENDIF.
```

See Also

BAPI_TRANSACTION_ROLLBACK

BAPI_TRANSACTION_ROLLBACK

Summary

Prevents permanent changes by BAPIs.

Description

If you call BAPIs in programs that change data in SAP, this method can prevent those changes being written to the database. The prerequisite is that these changes have not already been passed to the database with a COMMIT WORK command. This function is well documented.

Parameters

```
IMPORTING
      RETURN                    Message return codes and descriptions
```

Example

See BAPI_TRANSACTION_COMMIT

See Also

BAPI_TRANSACTION_COMMIT

DEQUEUE_ESFUNCTION

Summary

Unlocks an ABAP program so that it can be executed.

Description

Note that you should not use SY-REPID to pass your report name to the function. The value of SY-REPID will change as it is being passed to the function module and will no longer hold the value of the calling report.

Parameters

```
EXPORTING
      FUNCNAME                  Name of object to unlock
```

Example

See ENQUEUE_ESFUNCTION

See Also

DEQUEUE_ES_PROG, ENQUEUE_ESFUNCTION

ENQUE_SLEEP

Summary

Waits a specified period of time before continuing processing.

Parameters

```
EXPORTING
       SECONDS                    Number of seconds to delay
```

Example

```
REPORT ZEXAMPLE.

PARAMETERS: P_TIME TYPE I.

WRITE: / 'SECONDS OF DELAY CHOSEN:', P_TIME.

GET TIME.
WRITE: / 'START TIME:', SY-UZEIT.

CALL FUNCTION 'ENQUE_SLEEP'
    EXPORTING
        SECONDS          = P_TIME
    EXCEPTIONS
        SYSTEM_FAILURE   = 1
        OTHERS           = 2.

IF SY-SUBRC <> 0.
  WRITE:/ 'ERROR WITH SLEEP FUNCTION'.
ENDIF.

GET TIME.
WRITE: / 'END TIME:', SY-UZEIT.
```

See Also

RZL_SLEEP

ENQUEUE_ESFUNCTION

Summary

Locks an ABAP program so that it cannot be executed.

Description

The value of SY-REPID will change to the name of the function and cannot, therefore, be used to pass the report name to the function.

Parameters

```
EXPORTING
        FUNCNAME          Name of object to lock
        MODE_TFDIR        Type of lock:
                          Value        Meaning
                          E            Exclusive, cumulative (default)
                          S            Shared
                          X            Exclusive, non-cumulative
```

Example

```
REPORT ZEXAMPLE.

PARAMETERS P_PGM LIKE TFDIR-FUNCNAME OBLIGATORY.

CALL FUNCTION 'ENQUEUE_ESFUNCTION'
    EXPORTING
        FUNCNAME          = P_PGM
    EXCEPTIONS
        FOREIGN_LOCK      = 1
        SYSTEM_FAILURE    = 2
        OTHERS            = 3.
IF SY-SUBRC NE 0.
  WRITE:/ 'COULD NOT LOCK', P_PGM.
ELSE.
  WRITE:/ 'LOCKED', P_PGM.

  CALL FUNCTION 'DEQUEUE_ESFUNCTION'
      EXPORTING
          FUNCNAME = P_PGM.
  WRITE:/ 'UNLOCKED', P_PGM.
ENDIF.
```

See Also

DEQUEUE_ESFUNCTION, ENQUEUE_ES_PROG

GET_COMPONENT_LIST

Summary

Detailed description of fields from programs.

Parameters

```
EXPORTING
        PROGRAM           Program in which field is defined
        FIELDNAME         Name of field in program
TABLES
        COMPONENTS        Components of the field
```

Example

See GET_GLOBAL_SYMBOLS

See Also

See GET_GLOBAL_SYMBOLS, GET_INCLUDETAB, RS_GET_ALL_INCLUDES

GET_FIELDTAB

Summary

Retrieves table fields with field metadata.

Description

Obsolete. See DDIF_FIELDINFO_GET.

Parameters

```
EXPORTING
        LANGU           Language of field texts
        WITHTEXT        Indicator to retrieve field texts
        TABNAME         Table name
TABLES
        FIELDTAB        Table fields with field metadata
```

Example

```
REPORT ZEXAMPLE.

DATA: BEGIN OF FIELDINFO OCCURS 0.
        INCLUDE STRUCTURE DFIES.
DATA: END OF FIELDINFO.

PARAMETERS TABNAME LIKE SUBDFIES-TABNAME.

CALL FUNCTION 'GET_FIELDTAB'
     EXPORTING
        TABNAME           = TABNAME
     TABLES
        FIELDTAB          = FIELDINFO
     EXCEPTIONS
        INTERNAL_ERROR    = 1
        NO_TEXTS_FOUND    = 2
        TABLE_HAS_NO_FIELDS = 3
        TABLE_NOT_ACTIV   = 4
        OTHERS            = 5.
```

```
IF SY-SUBRC EQ 0.
  WRITE:/ 'Structure of', TABNAME,
      / 'Field Name', 20 'Field Type', 40 'Field Size'.
  ULINE.
  LOOP AT FIELDINFO.
  WRITE:/ FIELDINFO-FIELDNAME, 20 FIELDINFO-INTTYPE, 40 FIELDINFO-LENG.
  ENDLOOP.
ELSE.
  WRITE:/ 'Error retrieving field data'.
ENDIF.
```

See Also

DDIF_FIELDINFO_GET

GET_GLOBAL_SYMBOLS

Summary

Returns all components of a program.

Description

Returns a list of all tables, select options, and the text definitions for selection screens.

Parameters

```
EXPORTING
      PROGRAM        Program name
TABLES
      FIELDLIST      List of objects in program
```

Example

```
REPORT ZEXAMPLE.

DATA: BEGIN OF FLIST OCCURS 0.
      INCLUDE STRUCTURE RFIELDLIST.
DATA: END OF FLIST.

DATA: BEGIN OF COMP OCCURS 0.
      INCLUDE STRUCTURE RSTRUCINFO.
DATA: END OF COMP.

DATA FNAM LIKE SCR_PFIELD-FNAM.

PARAMETERS PROG LIKE SY-REPID DEFAULT SY-REPID.
```

```
CALL FUNCTION 'GET_GLOBAL_SYMBOLS'
    EXPORTING
        PROG            = PROG
    TABLES
        FIELDLIST       = FLIST.

LOOP AT FLIST.
*   REMOVE AUTOMATICALLY-GENERATED ABAP SYMBOLS:
    CHECK FLIST-NAME(2)   NE '%_'.
    CHECK FLIST-NAME(2)   NE '<%'.
    CHECK FLIST-NAME(3)   NE '*%_'.
    CHECK FLIST-NAME(1)   NE '-'.
    CHECK FLIST-NAME(2)   NE '#-'.
    CHECK FLIST-NAME(2)   NE ')-'.
    CHECK FLIST-NAME      NE 'SCREEN'.
    CHECK FLIST-NAME(8)   NE '$$MAND$$'.
    CHECK FLIST-NAME      NE '?NOT_ASSIGNED?'.
    CHECK FLIST-NAME      NE 'DUMMY$$'.
    CHECK FLIST-NAME      NE 'SPACE'.
    CHECK FLIST-NAME      NE 'SY'.
    CHECK FLIST-NAME      NE 'SYST'.
    CHECK FLIST-NAME      NE 'VARI'.
    CHECK FLIST-NAME      NE 'RSJOBINFO'.
    CHECK FLIST-LENG      NE 0.
    CHECK FLIST-TYPE      NE 'H'.

    IF FLIST-TYPE CO 'UV'.  "FIELDS (U) AND STRUCTURES (V)
      CALL FUNCTION 'GET_COMPONENT_LIST'
          EXPORTING
              PROG        = PROG
              FIELDNAME   = FLIST-NAME
          TABLES
              COMPONENTS  = COMP.

    LOOP AT COMP.
      CLEAR FNAM.
      CONCATENATE FLIST-NAME '-' COMP-COMPNAME INTO FNAM.
      WRITE:/1 FNAM, 30 COMP-OLEN, 40 COMP-TYPE.
    ENDLOOP.
  ENDIF.
ENDLOOP.
```

See Also

See GET_COMPONENT_LIST, GET_INCLUDETAB, RS_GET_ALL_INCLUDES

GET_INCLUDETAB

Summary

Returns a list of all INCLUDES in a program.

Parameters

```
EXPORTING
      PROGNAME    Program name
TABLES
      INCLTAB    List of includes in program
```

Example

```
REPORT ZEXAMPLE.

DATA: BEGIN OF INCTAB OCCURS 0,
      LINE(8),
    END OF INCTAB.

PARAMETERS P_PNAME LIKE TRDIR-NAME.

CALL FUNCTION 'GET_INCLUDETAB'
    EXPORTING
        PROGNAME    = P_PNAME
    TABLES
        INCLTAB    = INCTAB.
WRITE:/ 'INCLUDES DEFINED IN', P_PNAME.
ULINE.
LOOP AT INCTAB.
  WRITE:/ INCTAB-LINE.
ENDLOOP.
```

See Also

GET_COMPONENT_LIST, GET_GLOBAL_SYMBOLS, RS_GET_ALL_INCLUDES

RFC_ABAP_INSTALL_AND_RUN

Summary

Runs an ABAP program that is stored in table PROGRAM.

Description

The function crashes if runtime exceeds the RDISP/MAX_WPRUN_TIME value setting.

Parameters

```
IMPORTING
      ERRORMESSAGE    Error message from function
TABLES
      PROGRAM          Program source code
      WRITES           Output from program
```

Example

```
REPORT ZEXAMPLE.

DATA: PROGRAM LIKE PROGTAB OCCURS 0 WITH HEADER LINE,
      WRITES  LIKE LISTZEILE OCCURS 0 WITH HEADER LINE,
      ERRMSG  LIKE SY-MSGV1.

PARAMETERS P_PROG LIKE PROGTAB-LINE.

READ REPORT P_PROG INTO PROGRAM.
LOOP AT PROGRAM.
  IF PROGRAM-LINE+1(1) = 'R'.
    IF PROGRAM-LINE+1(6) = 'RSCHED'.
      SHIFT PROGRAM LEFT BY 8 PLACES.
      MODIFY PROGRAM.
    ENDIF.
  ELSE.
    DELETE PROGRAM.
  ENDIF.
ENDLOOP.

* CALL P_PROG IN THE REMOTE SYSTEM
CALL FUNCTION 'RFC_ABAP_INSTALL_AND_RUN' DESTINATION 'RFC_LINK'
    IMPORTING
        ERRORMESSAGE = ERRMSG
    TABLES
        PROGRAM      = PROGRAM
        WRITES       = WRITES.
```

RPY_TRANSACTION_READ

Summary

This is used for transactions, programs, and screens.

Description

Given a transaction, this returns the initial program and screen. Or inputting a program and screen, it returns the transactions which use that program and screen.

Parameters

```
EXPORTING
      TRANSACTION         Name of transaction to read
      PROGRAM             Program name
      DYNPRO              Screen number
```

```
        TRANSACTION_TYPE   Type of transaction:
                           Value     Meaning
                           T         Transaction
                           D         Transaction
                           R         Report
                           A         Inspection
TABLES
        TCODES             Transaction and program data
```

Example

```
REPORT ZEXAMPLE.

DATA ITCODES LIKE TSTC OCCURS O WITH HEADER LINE.

PARAMETERS P_TCODE LIKE TSTC-TCODE.

CALL FUNCTION 'RPY_TRANSACTION_READ'
     EXPORTING
          TRANSACTION       = P_TCODE
     TABLES
          TCODES            = ITCODES
     EXCEPTIONS
          PERMISSION_ERROR = 1
          CANCELLED        = 2
          NOT_FOUND        = 3
          OBJECT_NOT_FOUND = 4
          OTHERS           = 5.
IF SY-SUBRC EQ O.
  WRITE:/ 'PROGRAM', 20 'SCREEN'.
  LOOP AT ITCODES.
    WRITE:/ ITCODES-PGMNA, 20 ITCODES-DYPNO.
  ENDLOOP.
ELSE.
  WRITE:/ 'COULD NOT READ', P_TCODE.
ENDIF.
```

RS_GET_ALL_INCLUDES

Summary

Returns a list of all INCLUDES in a program.

Parameters

```
EXPORTING
        PROGNAME             Program name
        WITH_INACTIVE_INCLS  Return inactive INCLUDES
TABLES
        INCLUDETAB           List of includes in program
```

Example

```
REPORT ZEXAMPLE.
DATA: BEGIN OF INCL_TAB OCCURS 0.
        INCLUDE STRUCTURE D010INC.
DATA: END OF INCL_TAB.

PARAMETERS P_PROG LIKE SY-REPID.

CALL FUNCTION 'RS_GET_ALL_INCLUDES'
    EXPORTING
        PROGRAM            = P_PROG
    TABLES
        INCLUDETAB         = INCL_TAB
    EXCEPTIONS
        NOT_EXISTENT       = 1
        NO_PROGRAM         = 2
        OTHERS             = 3.

SORT INCL_TAB.
LOOP AT INCL_TAB.
  WRITE:/ INCL_TAB.
ENDLOOP.
```

See Also

GET_COMPONENT_LIST, GET_GLOBAL_SYMBOLS, GET_INCLUDETAB

RZL_SLEEP

Summary

Pauses the program a defined number of seconds.

Description

Default is 5 seconds.

Parameters

```
EXPORTING
    SECONDS             Number of seconds to delay
```

Example

```
REPORT ZEXAMPLE.

PARAMETERS: P_TIME TYPE I.

WRITE: / 'SECONDS OF DELAY CHOSEN:', P_TIME.

GET TIME.
WRITE: / 'START TIME:', SY-UZEIT.
```

```
CALL FUNCTION 'RZL_SLEEP'
     EXPORTING
          SECONDS        = P_TIME
     EXCEPTIONS
          ARGUMENT_ERROR = 1
          OTHERS         = 2.

IF SY-SUBRC <> 0.
  WRITE:/ 'ERROR WITH SLEEP FUNCTION'.
ENDIF.
GET TIME.
WRITE: / 'END TIME:', SY-UZEIT.
```

See Also

ENQUE_SLEEP

SAPGUI_SET_FUNCTIONCODE

Summary

Simulates a keystroke in an ABAP report.

Description

EnjoySAP controls ignore this functionality, and it is only possible to use in dialogue mode. There is good documentation with this function.

Parameters

```
EXPORTING
       FUNCTIONCODE       Function code to simulate
```

Example

```
REPORT ZEXAMPLE.

CALL FUNCTION 'SAPGUI_SET_FUNCTIONCODE'
     EXPORTING
          FUNCTIONCODE          = '=BACK'
     EXCEPTIONS
          FUNCTION_NOT_SUPPORTED = 1
          OTHERS                = 2.

IF SY-SUBRC EQ 0.
  WRITE:/ 'WAIT A SECOND - TAKING YOU BACK TO PREVIOUS SCREEN...'.
ELSE.
  WRITE:/ 'ERROR CALLING BACK FUNCTION CODE'.
ENDIF.
```

Text and Strings

CLPB_EXPORT

Summary

Sends text table to clipboard of the presentation server.

Description

After the function module has been called, you can paste this text with CTRL-V, e.g. into the Windows editor. This function is well documented.

Parameters

```
TABLES
    DATA_TAB                Data from clipboard
```

Example

```
REPORT ZEXAMPLE.

*   BEFORE RUNNING THIS EXAMPLE, PASTE SOME TEXT INTO THE PCs CLIPBOARD

DATA: BEGIN OF TAB OCCURS 1,
        TEXT(80),
      END OF TAB.
DATA: EMPTY(1).

CALL FUNCTION 'CLPB_IMPORT'
    IMPORTING
        EMPTY       = EMPTY
    TABLES
        DATA_TAB    = TAB
    EXCEPTIONS
        CLPB_ERROR = 01.
IF SY-SUBRC EQ 0.
  IF EMPTY EQ SPACE.
    WRITE:/ 'CURRENT DATA IN CLIPBOARD:', TAB-TEXT.
  ELSE.
    WRITE:/ 'NO DATA IN CLIPBOARD'.
  ENDIF.
ELSE.
  WRITE:/ 'ERROR READING CLIPBOARD DATA'.
ENDIF.

LOOP AT TAB.
  TAB-TEXT = 'CLIPBOARD UPDATED BY SAP'.
  MODIFY TAB.
ENDLOOP.
```

```
CALL FUNCTION 'CLPB_EXPORT'
    TABLES
         DATA_TAB   = TAB
    EXCEPTIONS
         CLPB_ERROR = 01.
IF SY-SUBRC EQ 0.
  WRITE:/ 'CLIPBOARD CONTENTS CHANGED - PLEASE CHECK'.
ELSE.
  WRITE:/ 'ERROR CHANGING CLIPBOARD DATA'.
ENDIF.
```

See Also

CLPB_IMPORT

CLPB_IMPORT

Summary

Loads text table from clipboard of the presentation server.

Description

When the function module is called, an internal table is returned with the selected text. Only ASCII objects are copied from the clipboard.

Parameters

```
IMPORTING
       EMPTY        Flag indicating whether any data is on clipboard (X = empty)
TABLES
       DATA_TAB     Table into which clipboard contents are placed
```

Example

See CLPB_EXPORT

See Also

CLPB_EXPORT

RKD_WORD_WRAP

Summary

Converts a long string or phrase into several lines.

Parameters

```
EXPORTING
        TEXTLINE        Long text phrase
        DELIMITER       Separator symbol
        OUTPUTLEN       Maximum output before break
IMPORTING
        OUT_LINE1       Output line 1
        OUT_LINE2       Output line 2
        OUT_LINE3       Output line 3
```

Example

```
REPORT ZEXAMPLE.

DATA: TEXT_LINE1(15),
      TEXT_LINE2(5).


PARAMETERS P_TEXT(20).


CALL FUNCTION 'RKD_WORD_WRAP'
     EXPORTING
            TEXTLINE            = P_TEXT
            OUTPUTLEN           = 15
     IMPORTING
            OUT_LINE1           = TEXT_LINE1
            OUT_LINE2           = TEXT_LINE2
     EXCEPTIONS
            OUTPUTLEN_TOO_LARGE = 1.


WRITE:/ 'BEFORE ->', P_TEXT.
ULINE.
WRITE:/ 'AFTER ->',
      / 'LINE 1:', TEXT_LINE1,
      / 'LINE 2:', TEXT_LINE2.
```

See Also

SWA_STRING_SPLIT, STRING_SPLIT, TEXT_SPLIT

SCP_REPLACE_STRANGE_CHARS

Summary

Replaces special letters with normal text.

Description

Special and national characters are replaced in such a way that the text remains reasonably legible. The character set 1146 is used by default. Some of the replacements made in this set are

- Æ ==> AE   (AE)
- Â ==> A   (A circumflex)
- Ä ==> Ae   (A dieresis)
- £ ==> L   (sterling)

Run program RSCP0007 for more examples. Note that the new text can be longer than the old.

Parameters

```
EXPORTING
        INTEXT            Input text with special characters
        INTEXT_LG         Number of bytes in input text
        INTER_CP          Character set to convert input (default: 1146)
        INTER_BASE_CP     For AS400/unicode character sets
        IN_CP             Character set of input text (default: system set)
        REPLACEMENT       Use this character if alternative character not found
IMPORTING
        OUTTEXT           Output text with special characters replaced
        OUTUSED           Length of output text
        OUTOVERFLOW       Flag set if output text does not fit into OUTTEXT
```

Example

```
REPORT ZEXAMPLE.

DATA: V_OUTTEXT(20),
      V_OFLOW.

PARAMETER P_GWORD(20) DEFAULT 'SPAß'.

CALL FUNCTION 'SCP_REPLACE_STRANGE_CHARS'
     EXPORTING
         INTEXT            = P_GWORD
     IMPORTING
         OUTTEXT           = V_OUTTEXT
         OUTOVERFLOW       = V_OFLOW
     EXCEPTIONS
         INVALID_CODEPAGE  = 1
         CODEPAGE_MISMATCH = 2
         INTERNAL_ERROR    = 3
         CANNOT_CONVERT    = 4
         FIELDS_NOT_TYPE_C = 5
         OTHERS            = 6.
```

```
IF SY-SUBRC EQ 0.
  IF V_OFLOW EQ 'X'.
    WRITE:/ 'OVERFLOW: INCREASE OUTPUT TEXT LENGTH'.
  ENDIF.
  WRITE:/ 'INPUT', 30 'OUTPUT'.
  ULINE.
  WRITE:/ P_GWORD, 30 V_OUTTEXT.
ELSE.
  WRITE:/ 'ERROR CONVERTING TEXT'.
ENDIF.
```

SPELL_AMOUNT

Summary

Converts numbers and figures into words.

Description

This function is used mostly with cheques to get the textual amount of the cheque figure.

Parameters

```
EXPORTING
      AMOUNT        Amount/number that is to be converted
      CURRENCY      Currency of amount
      FILLER        Filler for output field (default = SPACE)
      LANGUAGE      Language indicator for conversion in words
IMPORTING
      IN_WORDS      Field string with amount/number and figure in words of LANGUAGE
```

Example

```
REPORT ZEXAMPLE.
TABLES SPELL.

PARAMETERS AMT LIKE REGUD-SWNES.

CALL FUNCTION 'SPELL_AMOUNT'
    EXPORTING
        LANGUAGE  = SY-LANGU
        CURRENCY  = 'EUR'
        AMOUNT    = AMT
    IMPORTING
        IN_WORDS  = SPELL
    EXCEPTIONS
        NOT_FOUND = 1
        TOO_LARGE = 2.
```

```
IF SY-SUBRC EQ 0.
  WRITE:/ SPELL-WORD.
ELSE.
  WRITE:/ 'ERROR WITH CONVERTING NUMBER'.
ENDIF.
```

See Also

HRCM_AMOUNT_TO_STRING_CONVERT, HRCM_STRING_TO_AMOUNT_CONVERT

STRING_CENTER

Summary

Centres a string within another.

Description

This function is obsolete, but well documented. Use the WRITE … CENTERED TO statement instead.

Parameters

```
EXPORTING
        STRING          Source string
IMPORTING
        CSTRING         Centred destination string
```

Example

```
REPORT ZEXAMPLE.

PARAMETERS P_STR(40).

CALL FUNCTION 'STRING_CENTER'
     EXPORTING
          STRING   = P_STR
     IMPORTING
          CSTRING  = P_STR
     EXCEPTIONS
          TOO_SMALL = 1
          OTHERS    = 2.

IF SY-SUBRC EQ 0.
  WRITE:/ 'STRING CENTERED:', P_STR.
ELSE.
  WRITE:/ 'ERROR CENTERING STRING'.
ENDIF.
```

STRING_CONCATENATE

Summary

Joins two strings together.

Description

This function is obsolete, but well documented. Use the CONCATENATE statement instead.

Parameters

```
EXPORTING
        STRING1         First input string
        STRING2         Second input string
IMPORTING
        STRING          Concatenated string
```

Example

```
REPORT ZEXAMPLE.

DATA V_OUT(40).

PARAMETERS:  P_STR1(20),
             P_STR2(20).

CALL FUNCTION 'STRING_CONCATENATE'
    EXPORTING
         STRING1    = P_STR1
         STRING2    = P_STR2
    IMPORTING
         STRING     = V_OUT
    EXCEPTIONS
         TOO_SMALL = 1
         OTHERS    = 2.

IF SY-SUBRC EQ 0.
  WRITE:/ 'CONCATENATED STRING:', V_OUT.
ELSE.
  WRITE:/ 'ERROR IN CONCATENATING STRING'.
ENDIF.
```

See Also

See STRING_CONCATENATE_3

STRING_CONCATENATE_3

Summary

Joins three strings together.

Description

This function is obsolete, but well documented. Use the CONCATENATE statement instead.

Parameters

```
EXPORTING
       STRING1         First input string
       STRING2         Second input string
       STRING3         Third input string
IMPORTING
       STRING          Concatenated string
```

Example

```
REPORT ZEXAMPLE.

DATA V_OUT(60).

PARAMETERS:  P_STR1(20),
             P_STR2(20),
             P_STR3(20).

CALL FUNCTION 'STRING_CONCATENATE_3'
     EXPORTING
          STRING1    = P_STR1
          STRING2    = P_STR2
          STRING3    = P_STR3
     IMPORTING
          STRING     = V_OUT
     EXCEPTIONS
          TOO_SMALL = 1
          OTHERS    = 2.

IF SY-SUBRC EQ 0.
  WRITE:/ 'CONCATENATED STRING:', V_OUT.
ELSE.
  WRITE:/ 'ERROR IN CONCATENATING STRING'.
ENDIF.
```

See Also

See STRING_CONCATENATE

STRING_LENGTH

Summary

Returns the length of a string.

Description

This function is obsolete, but well documented. Use the STRLEN statement instead.

Parameters

```
EXPORTING
       STRING          Source string
IMPORTING
       LENGTH          Numeric length of string
```

Example

```
REPORT ZEXAMPLE.

DATA V_OUT TYPE I.

PARAMETERS P_STR(20).

CALL FUNCTION 'STRING_LENGTH'
    EXPORTING
        STRING = P_STR
    IMPORTING
        LENGTH = V_OUT.

WRITE:/ P_STR, 'HAS', V_OUT, 'CHARACTERS'.
```

STRING_MOVE_RIGHT

Summary

Shifts string to the right.

Description

This function is obsolete, but well documented. Use the SHIFT statement instead.

Parameters

```
EXPORTING
       STRING          Input string
IMPORTING
       RSTRING         Right-aligned string
```

Example

```
REPORT ZEXAMPLE.

DATA V_OUT TYPE I.

PARAMETERS P_STR(20).

WRITE:/ P_STR.

CALL FUNCTION 'STRING_MOVE_RIGHT'
     EXPORTING
          STRING    = P_STR
     IMPORTING
          RSTRING   = P_STR
     EXCEPTIONS
          TOO_SMALL = 1
          OTHERS    = 2.

IF SY-SUBRC EQ 0.
  WRITE:/ P_STR.
ELSE.
  WRITE:/ 'ERROR MOVING STRING RIGHT'.
ENDIF.
```

STRING_REVERSE

Summary

Returns a string in reverse order.

Description

This function is well documented.

Parameters

```
EXPORTING
     STRING        Character string to be reversed
     LANG          Language of string
IMPORTING
     RSTRING       Reversed character string
```

Example

```
REPORT ZEXAMPLE.

PARAMETERS P_STR(20).

WRITE:/ P_STR.
```

```
CALL FUNCTION 'STRING_REVERSE'
    EXPORTING
          STRING     = P_STR
          LANG       = SY-LANGU
    IMPORTING
          RSTRING    = P_STR
    EXCEPTIONS
          TOO_SMALL  = 1
          OTHERS     = 2.


IF SY-SUBRC EQ 0.
  WRITE:/ P_STR.
ELSE.
  WRITE:/ 'ERROR REVERSING STRING'.
ENDIF.
```

STRING_SPLIT

Summary

Splits a string into smaller string.

Description

This function is obsolete, but well documented. Use the SPLIT string AT delimiter INTO head tail statement instead.

Parameters

```
EXPORTING
      DELIMITER      Character at which to split string
      STRING         String to split
IMPORTING
      HEAD           Head of STRING in front of DELIMITER
      TAIL           Tail of STRING after DELIMITER
```

Example

```
REPORT ZEXAMPLE.

DATA: V_HEAD(10), V_TAIL(10).

PARAMETERS: P_STR(20),
            P_DEM.
```

```
CALL FUNCTION 'STRING_SPLIT'
     EXPORTING
          DELIMITER = P_DEM
          STRING    = P_STR
     IMPORTING
          HEAD      = V_HEAD
          TAIL      = V_TAIL
     EXCEPTIONS
          NOT_FOUND = 1
          NOT_VALID = 2
          TOO_LONG  = 3
          TOO_SMALL = 4
          OTHERS    = 5.

IF SY-SUBRC EQ 0.
  WRITE:/ 'HEAD:', V_HEAD,
        / 'TAIL:', V_TAIL.
ELSE.
  WRITE:/ 'ERROR SPLITTING STRING'.
ENDIF.
```

See Also

SWA_STRING_SPLIT, TEXT_SPLIT

STRING_UPPER_LOWER_CASE

Summary

Converts string to proper case.

Description

Delimiter can be a maximum of 40 characters.

Parameters

```
EXPORTING
      DELIMITER     Indicator to capitalise next character
      STRING1       Input string
IMPORTING
      STRING        Proper case string
```

Example

```
REPORT ZEXAMPLE.

DATA: V_HEAD(10), V_TAIL(10).
```

```
PARAMETERS:  P_STR(20),
             P_DEM.

CALL FUNCTION 'STRING_UPPER_LOWER_CASE'
     EXPORTING
          DELIMITER = P_DEM
          STRING1   = P_STR
     IMPORTING
          STRING    = P_STR
     EXCEPTIONS
          NOT_VALID = 1
          TOO_LONG  = 2
          TOO_SMALL = 3
          OTHERS    = 4.

IF SY-SUBRC EQ 0.
  WRITE:/ P_STR.
ELSE.
  WRITE:/ 'ERROR CONVERTING STRING'.
ENDIF.
```

SWA_STRING_SPLIT

Summary

Splits a string into smaller strings.

Description

Apply OSS note 571426 if it has not been applied already, as this prevents ABAP short dumps, caused by coding errors in this module. Maximum string split is 255 characters.

Parameters

```
EXPORTING
      INPUT_STRING            String to be split
      MAX_COMPONENT_LENGTH    Maximum length of the sections
      TERMINATING_SEPARATORS  Separators, remain unchanged, default: '>=)],.'
      OPENING_SEPARATORS      Characters, on continuation line, default '<([ '
TABLES
      STRING_COMPONENTS       Table of divided strings
```

Example

```
REPORT ZEXAMPLE.

DATA: BEGIN OF I_INSTR OCCURS 0,
      LINE TYPE STRING,
      END OF I_INSTR.
```

```
DATA: I_STRCOMP LIKE SWASTRTAB OCCURS 0 WITH HEADER LINE.

*   SOME SAMPLE DATA:
I_INSTR-LINE = 'THIS IS A VERY LONG LINE, THAT HAS TO'.
APPEND I_INSTR.
I_INSTR-LINE = 'BE SPLIT INTO LINES OF 20 CHARACTERS.'.
APPEND I_INSTR.

LOOP AT I_INSTR.
  CLEAR: I_STRCOMP, I_STRCOMP[].

  CALL FUNCTION 'SWA_STRING_SPLIT'
      EXPORTING
            INPUT_STRING                = I_INSTR-LINE
            MAX_COMPONENT_LENGTH        = 20
      TABLES
            STRING_COMPONENTS           = I_STRCOMP
      EXCEPTIONS
            MAX_COMPONENT_LENGTH_INVALID = 1
            OTHERS                      = 2.

  IF SY-SUBRC EQ 0.
    LOOP AT I_STRCOMP.
      WRITE:/ I_STRCOMP-STR.
    ENDLOOP.
  ELSE.
    WRITE:/ 'ERROR SPLITTING STRING', I_INSTR-LINE.
  ENDIF.
ENDLOOP.
```

See Also

```
STRING_SPLIT, TEXT_SPLIT, RKD_WORD_WRAP
```

TEXT_SPLIT

Summary

Splits text into smaller strings.

Parameters

```
EXPORTING
      LENGTH       Position at which to split string
      TEXT         Input string
IMPORTING
      LINE         Text before position split
      REST         Text after position split
```

Example

```
REPORT ZEXAMPLE.
DATA: SLINE(30),
      SREST(30).

PARAMETERS:  P_TEXT(30) TYPE C,
             P_SPLIT TYPE I.

CALL FUNCTION 'TEXT_SPLIT'
    EXPORTING
        LENGTH = P_SPLIT
        TEXT   = P_TEXT
    IMPORTING
        LINE   = SLINE
        REST   = SREST.

WRITE:/ 'ORIGINAL STRING:', P_TEXT.
WRITE:/ 'TEXT BEFORE POSITION SPLIT:', SLINE,
        'TEXT AFTER POSITION SPLIT:', SREST.
```

See Also

SWA_STRING_SPLIT, STRING_SPLIT, RKD_WORD_WRAP

Various

CALL_BROWSER

Summary

Calls default web browser or file manager.

Description

If no parameter values are filled in, the PC's file manager (e.g. Explorer) is called.

Parameters

```
EXPORTING
     URL                  URL path for browser
     BROWSER_TYPE         Browser software (Internet Explorer, Netscape, etc.)
     CONTEXTSTRING        String to identify browser (if more than one opened)
     WINDOW_NAME          Name of browser in ITS system
```

Example

```
REPORT ZEXAMPLE.

DATA: BROWSER_TYPE    LIKE TOLE-APP VALUE 'INTERNETEXPLORER.APPLICATION',
      LV_HELP_MODE    TYPE CHAR1,
      LV_WINDOW_NAME  TYPE SYDATAR.


PARAMETER P_URL(132) DEFAULT 'http://service.sap.com'.


*  if WebGUI, open new browser window
CALL FUNCTION 'GET_WEBGUI_HELP_MODE'
     IMPORTING
          HELP_MODE = LV_HELP_MODE.


IF LV_HELP_MODE  = 'X'.
  LV_WINDOW_NAME  = 'SAPNet'.
ELSE.
  LV_WINDOW_NAME  = SPACE.
ENDIF.


CALL FUNCTION 'CALL_BROWSER'
     EXPORTING
          URL                    = P_URL
          BROWSER_TYPE           = BROWSER_TYPE
          WINDOW_NAME            = LV_WINDOW_NAME
     EXCEPTIONS
          FRONTEND_NOT_SUPPORTED = 1
          FRONTEND_ERROR         = 2
          PROG_NOT_FOUND         = 3
          NO_BATCH               = 4
          UNSPECIFIED_ERROR      = 5
          OTHERS                 = 6.

IF SY-SUBRC NE 0.
  WRITE:/ 'Browser not called.'.
ENDIF.
```

CHANGEDOCUMENT_READ_HEADERS

Summary

Gets the change document header.

Description

Gets the change document header and puts the results in an internal table. There is some documentation with this function.

Parameters

```
EXPORTING
        OBJECTCLASS             Object class for determining change document number
        OBJECTID                Object ID
        USERNAME                Changed by
TABLES
        I_CDHDR                 Table with document header information
```

Example

```
REPORT ZEXAMPLE LINE-SIZE 255.
TABLES TCDOBT.

DATA:  ICDHDR LIKE CDHDR OCCURS 0 WITH HEADER LINE,
       IEDITPOS LIKE CDSHW OCCURS 0 WITH HEADER LINE,
       VDATE(20).

PARAMETERS: P_OBJCLA LIKE TCDOBT-OBJECT OBLIGATORY,
            P_OBJID  LIKE CDHDR-OBJECTID,
            P_UNAME  LIKE SY-UNAME DEFAULT SY-UNAME,
            P_DATUM  LIKE SY-DATUM DEFAULT SY-DATUM.

PERFORM RPT_HEADERS.

CALL FUNCTION 'CHANGEDOCUMENT_READ_HEADERS'
     EXPORTING
            OBJECTCLASS             = P_OBJCLA
            OBJECTID                = P_OBJID
            USERNAME                = P_UNAME
            DATE_OF_CHANGE          = P_DATUM
     TABLES
            I_CDHDR                 = ICDHDR
     EXCEPTIONS
            NO_POSITION_FOUND       = 1
            WRONG_ACCESS_TO_ARCHIVE = 2
            TIME_ZONE_CONVERSION_ERROR = 3
            OTHERS                  = 4.

IF SY-SUBRC EQ 0.
  IF NOT ICDHDR[] IS INITIAL.
    LOOP AT ICDHDR.
      CLEAR VDATE.
      CONCATENATE ICDHDR-UDATE ICDHDR-UTIME INTO VDATE SEPARATED BY SPACE.
      WRITE:/ ICDHDR-OBJECTID, 15 ICDHDR-USERNAME, 30 VDATE, 45 ICDHDR-TCODE.
      CALL FUNCTION 'CHANGEDOCUMENT_READ_POSITIONS'
           EXPORTING
                 CHANGENUMBER = ICDHDR-CHANGENR
           TABLES
                 EDITPOS      = IEDITPOS.
      LOOP AT IEDITPOS.
        WRITE:/60 IEDITPOS-FNAME, 75 IEDITPOS-F_OLD, 90 IEDITPOS-F_NEW.
      ENDLOOP.
    ENDLOOP.
```

```
    ELSE.
      WRITE:/ 'NO DOCUMENTS FOUND FOR', P_OBJCLA, P_OBJID.
    ENDIF.
    WRITE:/ 'ERROR ACCESSING DOCUMENT HEADER'.
ENDIF.


*&-------------------------------------------------------------------*
*& FORM RPT_HEADERS
*&-------------------------------------------------------------------*
FORM RPT_HEADERS.
  SELECT SINGLE OBTEXT FROM TCDOBT INTO TCDOBT-OBTEXT
                               WHERE OBJECT EQ P_OBJCLA AND
                                     SPRAS = SY-LANGU.
  WRITE:/ 'OBJECTCLASS:', TCDOBT-OBTEXT.
  WRITE:/ 'OBJECT ID', 15 'CHANGED BY', 30 'CHANGED ON', 45 'CHANGED WITH',
            60 'FIELD CHANGED', 75 'OLD VALUE', 90 'NEW VALUE'.
  ULINE.
ENDFORM.                        " RPT_HEADERS
```

See Also

CHANGEDOCUMENT_READ_POSITIONS

CHANGEDOCUMENT_READ_POSITIONS

Summary

Gets the details of a change document.

Description

Gets the details of a change document and stores them in an internal table. This will tell you whether a field was changed, deleted, or updated. There is some documentation with this function.

Parameters

```
EXPORTING
      CHANGENUMBER              Change document number
TABLES
      EDITPOS                   Table with detailed information
```

Example

See CHANGEDOCUMENT_READ_HEADERS

See Also

CHANGEDOCUMENT_READ_HEADERS

CL_TABLE_EDITOR

Summary

Displays and edits internal table data.

Description

Click the SAVE button on the toolbar after each operation.

Parameters

```
EXPORTING
        FIELDLENGTH           Length of the field of the internal table (maximum 70)
        HEADLINE              Heading in the title bar of the editor screen
TABLES
        INTTAB                Internal table containing the data that is being edited
```

Example

```
REPORT ZEXAMPLE.

DATA: BEGIN OF ITAB OCCURS 0,
        ROWA(5),
        ROWB(30),
      END OF ITAB.

DATA: CMT(30),
      LINENUM(5).

DO 10 TIMES.
  CLEAR CMT.
  LINENUM = SY-INDEX.
  CONCATENATE 'Comment line number' LINENUM INTO CMT.
  ITAB-ROWA = SY-INDEX.
  ITAB-ROWB = CMT.
  APPEND ITAB.
ENDDO.

CALL FUNCTION 'CL_TABLE_EDITOR'
    EXPORTING
        FIELDLENGTH = '35'
        HEADLINE    = 'Internal Table Editor'
    TABLES
        INTTAB      = ITAB.
```

```
SORT ITAB.
LOOP AT ITAB.
  WRITE:/ ITAB-ROWA,
          ITAB-ROWB.
ENDLOOP.
```

CSAP_MAT_BOM_READ

Summary

Displays simple material BOMs.

Description

You cannot display long texts, sub-items, classification data of BOM items for batches, and it can only display one alternative or variant (default: 01). See the good online documentation for more information.

Parameters

```
EXPORTING
        MATERIAL        Material number
        PLANT           Plant of material
        BOM_USAGE       BOM usage (default: 01)
IMPORTING
        FL_WARNING      Flag of errors in log
TABLES
        T_STKO          BOM items
        T_STPO          BOM headers
```

Example

```
REPORT ZEXAMPLE.
TABLES: MARA.

DATA: ISTKO LIKE STKO_API02 OCCURS 0,
      ISTPO LIKE STPO_API02 OCCURS 0,
      WA_ISTKO LIKE ISTKO WITH HEADER LINE,
      WA_ISTPO LIKE ISTPO WITH HEADER LINE.

DATA V_FLGWARN LIKE CAPIFLAG-FLWARNING.

PARAMETERS P_MATNR LIKE MARA-MATNR.

PERFORM HEADERS.
```

```
SELECT SINGLE * FROM MARA INTO MARA WHERE MATNR EQ P_MATNR.
IF SY-SUBRC EQ 0.
  CALL FUNCTION 'CSAP_MAT_BOM_READ'
      EXPORTING
            MATERIAL   = P_MATNR
            BOM_USAGE  = '1'
      IMPORTING
            FL_WARNING = V_FLGWARN
      TABLES
            T_STKO     = ISTKO
            T_STPO     = ISTPO
      EXCEPTIONS
            ERROR      = 1.
  IF SY-SUBRC NE 0.
    WRITE:/ 'ERROR RETRIEVING CHARACTERISTICS'.
  ELSE.
    LOOP AT ISTKO INTO WA_ISTKO.
      WRITE:/ P_MATNR, 20 WA_ISTKO-BASE_UNIT.
      LOOP AT ISTPO INTO WA_ISTPO.
        WRITE:/40 WA_ISTPO-COMPONENT, 60 WA_ISTPO-COMP_UNIT.
      ENDLOOP.
    ENDLOOP.
  ENDIF.
ELSE.
  WRITE:/ P_MATNR, 'NOT FOUND'.
ENDIF.

*&-------------------------------------------------------------------*
*& FORM HEADERS
*&-------------------------------------------------------------------*
FORM HEADERS.
  WRITE:/ 'MATERIAL', 20 'BASE UNIT', 40 'COMPONENT', 60 'COMPONENT UNIT'.
  ULINE.
ENDFORM.                        " HEADERS
```

DDIF_FIELDINFO_GET

Summary

Dynamically accesses field metadata.

Description

This function is well documented.

Parameters

```
EXPORTING
      TABNAME        Name of the table for which information is required
      LANGU          Language of the texts
TABLES
      DFIES_TAB      Field List
```

Example

```
REPORT ZEXAMPLE.

DATA ITAB LIKE DFIES OCCURS 0 WITH HEADER LINE.

PARAMETERS P_TAB LIKE DCOBJDEF-NAME.

CALL FUNCTION 'DDIF_FIELDINFO_GET'
     EXPORTING
          TABNAME        = P_TAB
          LANGU          = SY-LANGU
     TABLES
          DFIES_TAB      = ITAB
     EXCEPTIONS
          NOT_FOUND      = 1
          INTERNAL_ERROR = 2
          OTHERS         = 3.
IF SY-SUBRC EQ 0.
  WRITE:/ P_TAB.
  ULINE.
  LOOP AT ITAB.
    WRITE:/ ITAB-FIELDNAME.
  ENDLOOP.
ELSE.
  WRITE:/ 'ERROR RETRIEVING DATA FOR', P_TAB.
ENDIF.
```

See Also

GET_FIELDTAB

FORMAT_MESSAGE

Summary

Formats error message for display.

Description

WRITE_MESSAGE can only replace ampersands (&) in a message and not the dollar ($) character that some messages use as a place holder. FORMAT_MESSAGE can do both.

Parameters

```
EXPORTING
     ID                      ID of message class
     LANG                    Language of message
     NO                      Message number in class
     V1                      Message text for first parameter
```

	V2	Message text for second parameter
	V3	Message text for third parameter
	V4	Message text for fourth parameter
IMPORTING		
	MSG	Full message for display

Example

```
REPORT ZEXAMPLE.
TABLES T100.

DATA: MSG_LST LIKE SWAEXERROR OCCURS 0 WITH HEADER LINE,
      MSG_TEXT(60).

PARAMETERS: P_ARBGB LIKE T100-ARBGB DEFAULT 'F0'.

SELECT * FROM T100 UP TO 50 ROWS   WHERE ARBGB EQ P_ARBGB
                                     AND SPRSL = SY-LANGU.
  MSG_LST-MSGID  = T100-ARBGB.
  MSG_LST-MSGNO  = T100-MSGNR.
  APPEND MSG_LST.
ENDSELECT.

WRITE / 'ERROR MESSAGES' COLOR COL_HEADING.
LOOP AT MSG_LST.
  CONCATENATE MSG_LST-MSGTY MSG_LST-MSGNO '(' MSG_LST-MSGID ')' INTO MSG_TEXT.
  WRITE: / MSG_TEXT COLOR COL_NORMAL NO-GAP.

  CALL FUNCTION 'FORMAT_MESSAGE'
       EXPORTING
             ID        = MSG_LST-MSGID
             LANG      = SY-LANGU
             NO        = MSG_LST-MSGNO
             V1        = MSG_LST-MSGV1
             V2        = MSG_LST-MSGV2
             V3        = MSG_LST-MSGV3
             V4        = MSG_LST-MSGV4
       IMPORTING
             MSG       = MSG_TEXT
       EXCEPTIONS
             NOT_FOUND = 01.
  WRITE: AT 12(68) MSG_TEXT COLOR COL_NORMAL.
ENDLOOP.
```

See Also

WRITE_MESSAGE

K_WERKS_OF_BUKRS_FIND

Summary

Returns a list of all plants for a given company code.

Parameters

```
EXPORTING
      BUKRS            Company code
TABLES
      ITAB_001W        Internal table of all plants associated with BUKRS
```

Example

```
REPORT ZEXAMPLE.

DATA IPLANTS LIKE T001W OCCURS 0 WITH HEADER LINE.

PARAMETERS P_BUKRS LIKE T001-BUKRS.

CALL FUNCTION 'K_WERKS_OF_BUKRS_FIND'
     EXPORTING
          BUKRS            = P_BUKRS
     TABLES
          ITAB_001W        = IPLANTS
     EXCEPTIONS
          NO_ENTRY_IN_T001K = 1
          NO_ENTRY_IN_T001W = 2
          OTHERS            = 3.
IF SY-SUBRC NE 0.
  WRITE:/ 'NO PLANTS FOUND FOR', P_BUKRS.
ELSE.
  WRITE:/ 'PLANTS ASSOCIATED WITH', P_BUKRS.
  ULINE.
  SORT IPLANTS BY WERKS.
  LOOP AT IPLANTS.
    WRITE:/ IPLANTS-WERKS, IPLANTS-NAME1.
  ENDLOOP.
ENDIF.
```

MATERIAL_BTCI_SELECTION_NEW

Summary

Selects the correct views on the material master.

Description

The content in the select views screen is dependent on which material has been chosen. Therefore, when using call transaction/batch input (MM02), you cannot use a fixed index to refer to selections on the select views screen. Use this function module to find the correct index of a view.

Parameters

```
EXPORTING
        MATERIAL            Material number
        SELECTION           Maintenance code:
                            Value       Views
                            A           Work scheduling
                            B           Accounting 1
                                        Accounting 2
                            C           Classification
                            D           MRP1
                                        MRP2
                                        MRP3
                                        MRP4
                            E           Purchasing
                                        Foreign trade: import data
                                        Purchase order text
                            G           Costing 1
                                        Costing 2
                            K           Basic data 1
                                        Basic data 2
                            L           General plant data / storage 1
                                        General plant data / storage 2
                            Q           Quality management
                            V           Sales: sales organisation data 1
                                        Sales: sales organisation data 2
                                        Sales: general/plant data
                                        Foreign trade: export data
                                        Sales text
                            X           Plant stock
        TCODE               Transaction code
TABLES
        BTCI_D0070          Table containing views from maintenance code
```

Example

```
REPORT ZEXAMPLE.
TABLES MARA.


DATA: LETTERS(26) VALUE 'ABCDEFGHIJKLMNOPQRSTUVWXYZ',
      REF LIKE T130M-PSTAT,
      IBTC LIKE BDCDATA OCCURS 0 WITH HEADER LINE.
DATA: BEGIN OF ITAB OCCURS 0,
        REF,
        MAT LIKE MARA-MATNR,
        FNAM LIKE IBTC-FNAM,
        FVAL LIKE IBTC-FVAL,
      END OF ITAB.


REF = LETTERS(1).
DO 25 TIMES.
```

```
SELECT * FROM MARA UP TO 20 ROWS.
  CALL FUNCTION 'MATERIAL_BTCI_SELECTION_NEW'
       EXPORTING
             MATERIAL    = MARA-MATNR
             SELECTION   = REF
             TCODE       = 'MM02'
       TABLES
             BTCI_D0070  = IBTC
       EXCEPTIONS
             OTHERS      = 1.

  IF SY-SUBRC EQ 0.
    LOOP AT IBTC WHERE FVAL EQ 'X'.
      ITAB-MAT = MARA-MATNR.
      ITAB-REF = REF.
      ITAB-FNAM = IBTC-FNAM.
      APPEND ITAB.
    ENDLOOP.
  ENDIF.
  CLEAR: IBTC, IBTC[].
 ENDSELECT.
 REF = LETTERS+SY-INDEX(1).
ENDDO.

SORT ITAB BY REF MAT FNAM.
LOOP AT ITAB.
  WRITE:/ ITAB-MAT, 20 ITAB-REF, 40 ITAB-FNAM.
ENDLOOP.
```

MATERIAL_BTCI_TEXT

Summary

BDC fields and OK codes for materials.

Parameters

```
EXPORTING
      BILD              Screen number
      FCODE             Function code
      INLINE_COUNT      Size of online area in lines
      NODATA_SIGN       Character for no data
TABLES
      TEXTTAB           Table with texts for the screen
      BTCI_TEXT         Batch data
```

Example

```
REPORT ZEXAMPLE.

DATA: XBEST LIKE BMMH7 OCCURS 0 WITH HEADER LINE,
      BTCI_TEXT LIKE BDCDATA OCCURS 0 WITH HEADER LINE.
```

```
PARAMETERS: P_SCRN    LIKE T138B-DYPNO DEFAULT '0232',
            P_FCODE   LIKE T138B-FCODE DEFAULT 'E2',
            P_ROWS    LIKE SY-STEPL DEFAULT 4,
            P_NODATA LIKE BGR00-NODATA.

CALL FUNCTION 'MATERIAL_BTCI_TEXT'
     EXPORTING
            BILD        = P_SCRN
            FCODE       = P_FCODE
            INLINE_COUNT = P_ROWS
            NODATA_SIGN  = P_NODATA
     TABLES
            TEXTTAB     = XBEST
            BTCI_TEXT   = BTCI_TEXT.

WRITE:/ 'PROGRAM', 15 'SCREEN NUMBER', 35 'FIELD', 45 'VALUE'.
ULINE.
LOOP AT BTCI_TEXT.
  WRITE:/ BTCI_TEXT-PROGRAM, 15 BTCI_TEXT-DYNPRO, 35 BTCI_TEXT-FNAM, 45 BTCI_TEXT-FVAL.
ENDLOOP.
```

REGISTRY_GET

Summary

Reads an entry from the registry.

Description

For use only in the Windows OS. Run the Windows program REGEDT32 to display the registry.

Parameters

```
EXPORTING
      SECTION    Section in registry
      KEY        Key in registry
IMPORTING
      VALUE      Retrieve registry value
```

Example

```
REPORT ZEXAMPLE.

DATA GET_VAL(40).

PARAMETERS: SET AS CHECKBOX, GET AS CHECKBOX DEFAULT 'X',
            PRO_SECT LIKE RLGRAP-FILENAME DEFAULT 'EXCEL.APPLICATION',
            PRO_KEY LIKE RLGRAP-FILENAME DEFAULT 'CURVER',
            SET_VAL LIKE RLGRAP-FILENAME.
```

```
IF SET <> SPACE.
  CALL FUNCTION 'REGISTRY_SET'
       EXPORTING
             KEY     = PRO_KEY
             SECTION = PRO_SECT
             VALUE   = SET_VAL.
  WRITE: / 'SET_VAL = ', SET_VAL.
ENDIF.

IF GET <> SPACE.
  CALL FUNCTION 'REGISTRY_GET'
       EXPORTING
             SECTION = PRO_SECT
             KEY     = PRO_KEY
       IMPORTING
             VALUE   = GET_VAL.
  WRITE: / 'GET_VAL = ', GET_VAL.
ENDIF.
```

See Also

REGISTRY_SET

REGISTRY_SET

Summary

Sets an entry in the registry.

Description

For use only in the Windows OS. Indiscriminate changes with this function can cause major problems on your computer, so exercise extreme care.

Parameters

```
EXPORTING
       KEY        Key in registry
       SECTION    Section in registry
       VALUE      Value to save in registry
```

Example

See REGISTRY_GET

See Also

REGISTRY_GET

RV_ORDER_FLOW_INFORMATION

Summary

Reads sales document flow.

Parameters

```
EXPORTING
        COMWA         Document number
TABLES
        VBFA_TAB      Document flow
```

Example

```
REPORT ZEXAMPLE.
TABLES VBCO6.

DATA:   VBFA_TAB LIKE VBFA OCCURS 0 WITH HEADER LINE.
DATA:   BEGIN OF ITAB OCCURS 0,
            VBTYP_N LIKE VBFA_TAB-VBTYP_N,
            VBELN LIKE VBFA_TAB-VBELN,
        END OF ITAB.

PARAMETERS P_VBELN LIKE VBCO6-VBELN.

VBCO6-VBELN = P_VBELN.

CALL FUNCTION 'RV_ORDER_FLOW_INFORMATION'
     EXPORTING
         COMWA           = VBCO6
     TABLES
         VBFA_TAB        = VBFA_TAB
     EXCEPTIONS
         NO_VBFA       = 1
         NO_VBUK_FOUND = 2
         OTHERS        = 3.

IF SY-SUBRC <> 0.
  WRITE:/ 'ERROR GETTING INFORMATION FOR', P_VBELN.
ELSE.
  DELETE VBFA_TAB WHERE ( MANDT IS INITIAL AND VBTYP_N <> '+' ).
  DELETE VBFA_TAB WHERE VBELV IS INITIAL.
  SORT VBFA_TAB BY VBELV.
  DELETE ADJACENT DUPLICATES FROM VBFA_TAB COMPARING VBELV.

  LOOP AT VBFA_TAB.
    CASE VBFA_TAB-VBTYP_N.
      WHEN '+'.                   "ACC DOC
        ITAB-VBTYP_N = VBFA_TAB-VBTYP_N.
        ITAB-VBELN = VBFA_TAB-VBELN.
        APPEND ITAB.
```

```
          WHEN '6'.                "CREDIT MEMO
            ITAB-VBTYP_N = VBFA_TAB-VBTYP_N.
            ITAB-VBELN = VBFA_TAB-VBELN.
            APPEND ITAB.
          WHEN '5' OR 'M'.         "DELIVERY DOC
            ITAB-VBTYP_N = VBFA_TAB-VBTYP_N.
            ITAB-VBELN = VBFA_TAB-VBELV.
            APPEND ITAB.
          WHEN 'J'.               "SCHEDULING AGREE
            ITAB-VBTYP_N = VBFA_TAB-VBTYP_N.
            ITAB-VBELN = VBFA_TAB-VBELN.
            APPEND ITAB.
     ENDCASE.
   ENDLOOP.                       "VBFA_TAB

   WRITE:/ 'FLOW FOR:', P_VBELN.
   ULINE.
   WRITE:/ 'ACCOUNTING', 15 'CREDIT', 25 'DELIVERY', 35 'SCHEDULING'.
   ULINE.
   LOOP AT ITAB.
     CASE ITAB-VBTYP_N.
       WHEN '+'.                "ACC DOC
         WRITE:/ ITAB-VBELN.
       WHEN '6'.                "CREDIT MEMO
         WRITE:/15 ITAB-VBELN.
       WHEN '5'.                "DELIVERY DOC
       WHEN 'M'.
         WRITE:/25 ITAB-VBELN.
       WHEN 'J'.                "SCHEDULING
         WRITE:/35 ITAB-VBELN.
     ENDCASE.
   ENDLOOP.
 ENDIF.
```

WRITE_MESSAGE

Summary

Formats error message for display.

Description

This function only replaces ampersands (&) in a message and not the dollar ($) character that some messages use as a place holder. FORMAT_MESSAGE can do both.

Parameters

```
EXPORTING
     MSGID      ID of message class
     MSGNO      Message number in class
     MSGV1      Message text for first parameter
```

```
            MSGV2        Message text for second parameter
            MSGV3        Message text for third parameter
            MSGV4        Message text for fourth parameter
            MSGV5        Message text for fifth parameter
IMPORTING
            ERROR        Error in building message
            MESSG        Message text
            MSGLN        Length of message
```

Example

```
REPORT ZEXAMPLE.
TABLES T100.

DATA:  IMESS LIKE MESSAGE OCCURS 0 WITH HEADER LINE,
       MSG_LST LIKE SWAEXERROR OCCURS 0 WITH HEADER LINE.

DATA:  MSGLN LIKE SY-FDPOS,
       ERROR_FLAG TYPE C.

PARAMETERS P_ARBGB LIKE T100-ARBGB DEFAULT 'F0'.

SELECT * FROM T100 UP TO 100 ROWS WHERE ARBGB EQ P_ARBGB AND SPRSL = SY-LANGU.
  MSG_LST-MSGID  = T100-ARBGB.
  MSG_LST-MSGNO  = T100-MSGNR.
  APPEND MSG_LST.
ENDSELECT.

WRITE / 'ERROR MESSAGES' COLOR COL_HEADING.

LOOP AT MSG_LST.
  CALL FUNCTION 'WRITE_MESSAGE'
       EXPORTING
             MSGID = MSG_LST-MSGID
             MSGNO = MSG_LST-MSGNO
             MSGTY = MSG_LST-MSGTY
             MSGV1 = MSG_LST-MSGV1
             MSGV2 = MSG_LST-MSGV2
             MSGV3 = MSG_LST-MSGV3
             MSGV4 = MSG_LST-MSGV4
       IMPORTING
             ERROR = ERROR_FLAG
             MESSG = IMESS
             MSGLN = MSGLN.

  IF ERROR_FLAG IS INITIAL.
    WRITE:/ IMESS-MSGTX.
  ELSE.
    WRITE:/ '@09@ ERROR BUILING MESSAGE TEXT'.
  ENDIF.
ENDLOOP.
```

See Also

FORMAT_MESSAGE

Appendix

This appendix lists the tables used in the examples throughout the book:

BKPF   Accounting document header
BSEG   Accounting document line items
DD02L   SAP data dictionary tables
DOKHL   Documentation header
ITCPO   SAPscript output interface
KNA1   Customer master general data
LIPS   SD document line items
MAKT   Material textual descriptions
MARA   Master master
MARM   Units of measure for materials
MDCAL   Date fields for accessing calendar
MDKP   Header data for MRP document
MSXXLIST   System list structure
RTXTH   Header table for report texts
SPELL   Transfer structure for amounts rendered in words
T000   Client master
T001R   Rounding rules of companies
T001W   Plants
T006   Units of measurement
T006A   Units of measurement by language
T006D   Dimensions
T006T   Dimension texts
T009   Fiscal year variants
T100   Messages
T559R   Rounding rules
TBIER   Direct input (DI): results table
TBIST   Direct input (DI) control: restart capability
TCDOBT   Texts for objects for change document creation
TCURC   Currency codes
TFACD   Factory calendar definition
TSP01   Spool requests
TSTCT   Transaction code texts
TTXID   Valid text IDs

TVAKT	Sales document types: texts
USR01	User master record (runtime data)
USR02	User logon data
USR03	User address data
VARIT	Variant texts
VBCO6	Sales document access methods: key fields

Index

A

ABAP4_CALL_TRANSACTION 1
  see HLP_MODE_CREATE
  see TH_REMOTE_TRANSACTION
  see TRANSACTION_CALL
ADD_TIME_TO_DATE 93
  see C14B_ADD_TIME
  see DATE_IN_FUTURE
  see MONTH_PLUS_DETERMINE
  see RE_ADD_MONTH_TO_DATE
  see RP_CALC_DATE_IN_INTERVAL
  see SUBTRACT_TIME_FROM_DATE
ADDRESS_INTO_PRINTFORM 332
ALSM_EXCEL_TO_INTERNAL_TABLE 237
  see EXCEL_OLE_STANDARD_DAT
  see KCD_EXCEL_OLE_TO_INT_CONVERT
  see MS_EXCEL_OLE_STANDARD_DAT
  see RH_START_EXCEL_WITH_DATA
  see SAP_CONVERT_TO_XLS_FORMAT
  see WS_EXCEL
ARFC_GET_TID 2
  see TERMINAL_ID_GET
  see TH_USER_INFO
AUTHORITY_CHECK_DATASET 3

B

BAPIs
  see BAPI_CURRENCY_CONV_TO_
    EXTERNAL
  see BAPI_CURRENCY_CONV_TO_
    INTERNAL
  see BAPI_TRANSACTION_COMMIT
  see BAPI_TRANSACTION_ROLLBACK
BAPI_CURRENCY_CONV_TO_EXTERNAL 47
  see BAPI_CURRENCY_CONV_TO_INTERNAL
BAPI_CURRENCY_CONV_TO_INTERNAL 48
  see BAPI_CURRENCY_CONV_TO_EXTERNAL

BAPI_TRANSACTION_COMMIT 339
  see BAPI_TRANSACTION_ROLLBACK
BAPI_TRANSACTION_ROLLBACK 340
  see BAPI_TRANSACTION_COMMIT
BP_EVENT_RAISE 5
  see GET_JOB_RUNTIME_INFO
BP_JOB_DELETE 321
  see BP_JOB_SELECT
BP_JOB_SELECT 321
  see BP_JOB_DELETE
BP_JOBLOG_READ 324
  see BP_JOBLOG_SHOW
BP_JOBLOG_SHOW 325
  see BP_JOBLOG_READ
browser
  see CALL_BROWSER

C

calculator
  see FITRV_CALCULATOR
C13Z_FILE_DOWNLOAD_ASCII 151
  see C13Z_FILE_DOWNLOAD_BINARY
C13Z_FILE_DOWNLOAD_BINARY 155
  see C13Z_FILE_DOWNLOAD_ASCII
C13Z_FILE_UPLOAD_ASCII 156
  see C13Z_FILE_UPLOAD_BINARY
C13Z_FILE_UPLOAD_BINARY 157
  see C13Z_FILE_UPLOAD_ASCII
C14A_POPUP_ASK_FILE_OVERWRITE 253
C14B_ADD_TIME 95
  see ADD_TIME_TO_DATE
CALL_BROWSER 366
CAT_CHECK_RFC_DESTINATION 6
  see CAT_PING
  see TH_SERVER_LIST

CAT_PING 7
  see CAT_CHECK_RFC_DESTINATION
CF_UT_UNIT_CONVERSION 49
  see CONVERSION_FACTOR_GET
  see MD_CONVERT_MATERIAL_UNIT
  see MATERIAL_UNIT_CONVERSION
CHANGEDOCUMENT_READ_HEADERS 367
  see CHANGEDOCUMENT_READ_
    POSITIONS
CHANGEDOCUMENT_READ_POSITIONS 369
  see CHANGEDOCUMENT_READ_HEADERS
CJDB_POPUP_TO_HANDLE_TIME_OUT 254
CL_TABLE_EDITOR 370
clipboard
  see CLPB_EXPORT
  see CLPB_IMPORT
clock
  see F4_CLOCK
CLOI_PUT_SIGN_IN_FRONT 328
CLPB_EXPORT 352
  see CLPB_IMPORT
CLPB_IMPORT 353
  see CLPB_EXPORT
COMMIT_TEXT 217
  see SAVE_TEXT
COMPUTE_YEARS_BETWEEN_DATES 95
  see FIMA_DAYS_AND_MONTH_AND_
    YEARS
CONVERSION_EXIT_ALPHA_INPUT 50
  see CONVERSION_EXIT_ALPHA_OUTPUT
CONVERSION_EXIT_ALPHA_OUTPUT 51
  see CONVERSION_EXIT_ALPHA_INPUT
CONVERSION_EXIT_AUART_INPUT 51
  see CONVERSION_EXIT_AUART_OUTPUT
CONVERSION_EXIT_AUART_OUTPUT 52
  see CONVERSION_EXIT_AUART_INPUT
CONVERSION_EXIT_CUNIT_INPUT 53
  see CONVERSION_EXIT_CUNIT_
    OUTPUT
CONVERSION_EXIT_CUNIT_OUTPUT 54
  see CONVERSION_EXIT_CUNIT_INPUT
CONVERSION_EXIT_LDATE_OUTPUT 96
CONVERSION_EXIT_LUNIT_INPUT 55
  see CONVERSION_EXIT_LUNIT_OUTPUT
CONVERSION_EXIT_LUNIT_OUTPUT 56
  see CONVERSION_EXIT_LUNIT_INPUT
CONVERSION_FACTOR_GET 57
  see CF_UT_UNIT_CONVERSION
  see MATERIAL_UNIT_CONVERSION
  see MD_CONVERT_MATERIAL_UNIT

CONVERT_ABAPSPOOLJOB_2_PDF 59
  see CONVERT_OTFSPOOLJOB_2_PDF
  see SX_OBJECT_CONVERT_OTF_PDF
CONVERT_DATE_INPUT 97
  see CONVERT_DATE_TO_INTERNAL
CONVERT_DATE_TO_EXTERNAL 98
  see CONVERT_DATE_INPUT
  see CONVERT_DATE_TO_EXTERNAL
CONVERT_DATE_TO_INTERNAL 99
  see CONVERT_DATE_INPUT
  see CONVERT_DATE_TO_EXTERNAL
CONVERT_OTFSPOOLJOB_2_PDF 61
  see CONVERT_ABAPSPOOLJOB_2_PDF
  see SX_OBJECT_CONVERT_OTF_PDF
CONVERT_TO_FOREIGN_CURRENCY 63
  see CONVERT_TO_LOCAL_CURRENCY
CONVERT_TO_LOCAL_CURRENCY 64
  see CONVERT_TO_FOREIGN_CURRENCY
COPF_DETERMINE_DURATION 100
  see COMPUTE_YEARS_BETWEEN_DATES
  see DAYS_BETWEEN_TWO_DATES
  see HR_HK_DIFF_BT_2_DATES
COPO_POPUP_TO_DISPLAY_TEXTLIST 272
  see ERGO_TEXT_SHOW
  see HELP_START
CORRESPONDENCE_POPUP_EMAIL 273
CREATE_TEXT 218
  see DELETE_TEXT
CSAP_MAT_BOM_READ 371
currency
  see CONVERT_TO_FOREIGN_CURRENCY
  see CONVERT_TO_LOCAL_CURRENCY
  see CURRENCY_AMOUNT_SAP_TO_IDOC
  see CURRENCY_CODE_ISO_TO_SAP
  see CURRENCY_CODE_SAP_TO_ISO
CURRENCY_AMOUNT_SAP_TO_IDOC 66
CURRENCY_CODE_ISO_TO_SAP 67
  see CURRENCY_CODE_SAP_TO_ISO
CURRENCY_CODE_SAP_TO_ISO 68
  see CURRENCY_CODE_ISO_TO_SAP

D

DATE_CHECK_PLAUSIBILITY 101
  see RP_CHECK_DATE
DATE_CHECK_WORKINGDAY 102
  see DATE_CHECK_WORKINGDAY_
    MULIPLE
  see DATE_CONVERT_TO_FACTORYDATE
  see DATE_CONVERT_TO_WORKINGDAY

DATE_CHECK_WORKINGDAY_MULIPLE 103
  see DATE_CHECK_WORKINGDAY
  see DATE_CONVERT_TO_FACTORYDATE
  see DATE_CONVERT_TO_WORKINGDAY
DATE_COMPUTE_DAY 105
  see DAY_IN_WEEK
  see WEEKDAY_GET
DATE_CONV_EXT_TO_INT 106
  see CONVERT_DATE_INPUT
  see CONVERT_DATE_TO_INTERNAL
DATE_CONVERT_TO_FACTORYDATE 107
  see DATE_CHECK_WORKINGDAY
  see DATE_CHECK_WORKINGDAY_
    MULIPLE
  see DATE_CONVERT_TO_WORKINGDAY
DATE_CONVERT_TO_WORKINGDAY 109
  see DATE_CHECK_WORKINGDAY
  see DATE_CHECK_WORKINGDAY_
    MULIPLE
  see DATE_CONVERT_TO_FACTORYDATE
DATE_CREATE 110
  see DATE_IN_FUTURE
  see MONTH_PLUS_DETERMINE
  see RE_ADD_MONTH_TO_DATE
  see RP_CALC_DATE_IN_INTERVAL
  see SUBTRACT_TIME_FROM_DATE
DATE_GET_WEEK 110
  see DAY_IN_WEEK
DATE_IN_FUTURE 112
  see ADD_TIME_TO_DATE
  see C14B_ADD_TIME
  see DATE_IN_FUTURE
  see MONTH_PLUS_DETERMINE
  see RE_ADD_MONTH_TO_DATE
  see RP_CALC_DATE_IN_INTERVAL
  see SUBTRACT_TIME_FROM_DATE
DATE_STRING_CONVERT 68
DATE_TO_PERIOD_CONVERT 113
  see HR_PAYROLL_PERIOD_GET
DATUMSAUFBEREITUNG 115
DAY_ATTRIBUTES_GET 116
DAY_IN_WEEK 117
  see DATE_COMPUTE_DAY
  see DATE_GET_WEEK
  see WEEKDAY_GET
DAYS_BETWEEN_TWO_DATES 118
  see COMPUTE_YEARS_BETWEEN_DATES
  see FIMA_DAYS_AND_MONTH_AND_YEARS
DDIF_FIELDINFO_GET 372
  see GET_FIELDTAB

DELETE_TEXT 220
  see CREATE_TEXT
DEQUEUE_ES_PROG 8
  see DEQUEUE_ESFUNCTION
  see ENQUEUE_ES_PROG
DEQUEUE_ESFUNCTION 341
  see DEQUEUE_ES_PROG
  see ENQUEUE_ES_PROG
  see ENQUEUE_ESFUNCTION
DIMENSION_CHECK 69
  see DIMENSION_GET
DIMENSION_GET 71
  see DIMENSION_CHECK
  see DIMENSION_GET_FOR_UNIT
DIMENSION_GET_FOR_UNIT 71
  see DIMENSION_GET
directory
  see EPS_GET_DIRECTORY_LISTING
  see GUI_CREATE_DIRECTORY
  see GUI_REMOVE_DIRECTORY
  see RZL_READ_DIR
  see TMP_GUI_DIRECTORY
  see TMP_GUI_DIRECTORY_LIST_FILES
documentation
  see COPO_POPUP_TO_DISPLAY_TEXTLIST
  see ERGO_TEXT_SHOW
  see HELP_START
DOWNLOAD 157
  see C13Z_FILE_DOWNLOAD_ASCII
  see C13Z_FILE_DOWNLOAD_BINARY
  see GUI_DOWNLOAD
  see WRITE_FILE_LOCAL
  see WS_DOWNLOAD
DYNP_VALUES_READ 189
  see DYNP_VALUES_UPDATE
  see RPY_DYNPRO_READ
  see RS_COVERPAGE_SELECTIONS
DYNP_VALUES_UPDATE 193
  see DYNP_VALUES_READ
  see RPY_DYNPRO_READ
  see RS_COVERPAGE_SELECTIONS

E

EASTER_GET_DATE 118
EDIT_TEXT 221
  see CREATE_TEXT
email
  see CORRESPONDENCE_POPUP_EMAIL
  see RFC_MAIL

see RS_SEND_MAIL_FOR_SPOOLLIST
see SO_EXPRESS_FLAG_SET
see SO_NEW_DOCUMENT_ATT_SEND_API1
see SO_NEW_DOCUMENT_SEND_API1
see TH_POPUP
ENQUE_SLEEP 341
   see RZL_SLEEP
ENQUEUE_ES_PROG 8
   see DEQUEUE_ES_PROG
   see ENQUEUE_ESFUNCTION
ENQUEUE_ESFUNCTION 342
   see DEQUEUE_ES_PROG
   see DEQUEUE_ESFUNCTION
   see ENQUEUE_ES_PROG
EPS_GET_DIRECTORY_LISTING 160
   see RZL_READ_DIR
   see TMP_GUI_DIRECTORY
   see TMP_GUI_DIRECTORY_LIST_FILES
EPS_GET_FILE_ATTRIBUTES 161
   see EPS_GET_DIRECTORY_LISTING
EPS_PROGRESS_POPUP 274
   see SAPGUI_PROGRESS_INDICATOR
ERGO_TEXT_SHOW 276
   see COPO_POPUP_TO_DISPLAY_TEXTLIST
   see HELP_START
errors
   see FORMAT_MESSAGE
   see WRITE_MESSAGE
excel
   see ALSM_EXCEL_TO_INTERNAL_TABLE
   see EXCEL_OLE_STANDARD_DAT
   see KCD_EXCEL_OLE_TO_INT_CONVERT
   see MS_EXCEL_OLE_STANDARD_DAT
   see RH_START_EXCEL_WITH_DATA
   see SAP_CONVERT_TO_XLS_FORMAT
   see WS_EXCEL
EXCEL_OLE_STANDARD_DAT 238
   see ALSM_EXCEL_TO_INTERNAL_TABLE
   see KCD_EXCEL_OLE_TO_INT_CONVERT
   see MS_EXCEL_OLE_STANDARD_DAT
   see RH_START_EXCEL_WITH_DATA
   see SAP_CONVERT_TO_XLS_FORMAT
   see WS_EXCEL
EXECUTE_WINWORD 240
   see GUI_EXEC
   see GUI_RUN
external programs
   see EXECUTE_WINWORD
   see GUI_EXEC
   see GUI_RUN

see SXPG_COMMAND_EXECUTE
see WS_EXCEL
see WS_EXECUTE

F

F4_CLOCK 277
F4_DATE 278
   see POPUP_TO_SELECT_MONTH
F4_FILENAME 279
   see F4_FILENAME_SERVER
   see KD_GET_FILENAME_ON_F4
   see WS_FILENAME
F4_FILENAME_SERVER 281
   see F4_FILENAME
   see KD_GET_FILENAME_ON_F4
   see WS_FILENAME
F4_USER 282
F4IF_INT_TABLE_VALUE_REQUEST 193
   see HELP_VALUES_GET_NO_DD_NAME
factory date
   see DATE_CHECK_WORKINGDAY_MULIPLE
   see DATE_CONVERT_TO_FACTORYDATE
   see FACTORYDATE_CONVERT_TO_DATE
FACTORYDATE_CONVERT_TO_DATE 119
   see DATE_CONVERT_TO_FACTORYDATE
   see DATE_CONVERT_TO_WORKINGDAY
files
   see AUTHORITY_CHECK_DATASET
   see C13Z_FILE_DOWNLOAD_ASCII
   see C13Z_FILE_DOWNLOAD_BINARY
   see C13Z_FILE_UPLOAD_ASCII
   see C13Z_FILE_UPLOAD_BINARY
   see C14A_POPUP_ASK_FILE_
      OVERWRITE
   see EPS_GET_FILE_ATTRIBUTES
   see F4_FILENAME
   see F4_FILENAME_SERVER
   see GUI_DELETE_FILE
   see GUI_UPLOAD
   see KD_GET_FILENAME_ON_F4
   see SPLIT_FILE_AND_PATH
   see WS_FILE_DELETE
   see WS_FILENAME
FIMA_DAYS_AND_MONTHS_AND_YEARS 120
   see COMPUTE_YEARS_BETWEEN_DATES
   see DAYS_BETWEEN_TWO_DATES
   see HR_HK_DIFF_BT_2_DATES
   see SD_DATETIME_DIFFERENCE
   see SWI_DURATION_DETERMINE

FIRST_AND_LAST_DAY_IN_YEAR_GET 121
  see DATE_TO_PERIOD_CONVERT
  see LAST_DAY_IN_PERIOD_GET
  see PERIOD_DAY_DETERMINE
FIRST_DAY_IN_PERIOD_GET 122
  see DATE_TO_PERIOD_CONVERT
  see LAST_DAY_IN_PERIOD_GET
  see PERIOD_DAY_DETERMINE
FITRV_CALCULATOR 283
FM_SELECTION_CRITERIA_PRINT 333
  see PRINT_SELECTIONS
FORMAT_MESSAGE 373
  see WRITE_MESSAGE
FTP_COMMAND 9
  see FTP_CONNECT
FTP_CONNECT 10
  see CAT_CHECK_RFC_DESTINATION
  see FTP_COMMAND
  see FTP_DISCONNECT
FTP_DISCONNECT 12
  see CAT_CHECK_RFC_DESTINATION
  see FTP_COMMAND
  see FTP_CONNECT

G

G_DECIMAL_PLACES_GET 329
GET_COMPONENT_LIST 343
  see GET_GLOBAL_SYMBOLS
  see GET_INCLUDETAB
GET_CURRENT_YEAR 122
GET_FIELDTAB 344
  see DDIF_FIELDINFO_GET
GET_GLOBAL_SYMBOLS 345
  see GET_COMPONENT_LIST
  see GET_INCLUDETAB
  see RS_GET_ALL_INCLUDES
GET_INCLUDETAB 346
  see GET_COMPONENT_LIST
  see GET_GLOBAL_SYMBOLS
  see RS_GET_ALL_INCLUDES
GET_JOB_RUNTIME_INFO 13
  see BP_EVENT_RAISE
GET_PRINT_PARAMETERS 334
  see LOAD_PRINT_PARAMETERS
  see RSPO_FIND_SPOOL_REQUESTS
  see RSPO_RPRINT_SPOOLREQ
  see SET_PRINT_PARAMETERS
GUI_CREATE_DIRECTORY 162
GUI_DELETE_FILE 164
  see WS_FILE_DELETE

GUI_DOWNLOAD 165
  see C13Z_FILE_DOWNLOAD_ASCII
  see C13Z_FILE_DOWNLOAD_BINARY
  see DOWNLOAD
  see WRITE_FILE_LOCAL
  see WS_DOWNLOAD
GUI_EXEC 13
  see EXECUTE_WINWORD
  see GUI_RUN
  see WS_EXECUTE
  see WS_EXCEL
GUI_GET_DESKTOP_INFO 14
  see IW_C_GET_FRONTEND_VERSION
  see WS_QUERY
GUI_REMOVE_DIRECTORY 166
GUI_RUN 16
  see EXECUTE_WINWORD
  see GUI_EXEC
  see WS_EXECUTE
  see WS_EXCEL
GUI_UPLOAD 166
  see C13Z_FILE_UPLOAD_ASCII
  see C13Z_FILE_UPLOAD_BINARY
  see RZL_READ_FILE
  see UPLOAD
  see WS_UPLOAD
GWY_READ_CONNECTIONS 17

H

HELP_START 284
  see COPO_POPUP_TO_DISPLAY_TEXTLIST
  see ERGO_TEXT_SHOW
  see HELP_VALUES_GET_WITH_DD_TABLE
HELP_VALUES_GET_NO_DD_NAME 286
  see F4IF_INT_TABLE_VALUE_REQUEST
HELP_VALUES_GET_WITH_DD_NAME 288
  see F4IF_INT_TABLE_VALUE_REQUEST
HELP_VALUES_GET_WITH_DD_TABLE 290
  see HELP_START
  see HELP_VALUES_GET_WITH_TABLE
HELP_VALUES_GET_WITH_TABLE 291
  see HELP_START
  see HELP_VALUES_GET_WITH_DD_TABLE
HLP_MODE_CREATE 18
  see ABAP4_CALL_TRANSACTION
  see TH_REMOTE_TRANSACTION
  see TRANSACTION_CALL
HOLIDAY_CHECK_AND_GET_INFO 123
  see HOLIDAY_GET

HOLIDAY_GET 124
   see HOLIDAY_CHECK_AND_GET_INFO
H_BEN_GET_DATE_INTERSECTION 126
H_DISPLAY_BASIC_LIST 194
H_GET_LEAVE_DATA 128
H_HK_DIFF_BT_2_DATES 30
   see COMPUTE_YEARS_BETWEEN_DATES
   see DYS_BETWEEN_TWO_DATES
   see FMA_DAYS_AND_MONTHS_AND_
     YEARS
   see SD_DATETIME_DIFFERENCE
   see SI_DURATION_DETERMINE
HR_IE_NUM_PRSI_WEEKS 131
   see DATE_GET_WEEK
HR_PAYROLL_PERIODS_GET 132
   see DATE_TO_PERIOD_CONVERT
   see HR_TIME_RESULTS_GET_DATE
HR_ROUND_NUMBER 72
   see ROUND
   see ROUND_AMOUNT
HR_TIME_RESULTS_GET
   see HR_PAYROLL_PERIODS_GET
HRCM_AMOUNT_TO_STRING_CONVERT
   73
   see HRCM_STRING_TO_AMOUNT_
     CONVERT
HRCM_STRING_TO_AMOUNT_CONVERT 74
   see HRCM_AMOUNT_TO_STRING_
     CONVERT

I

INIT_TEXT 222
   see CREATE_TEXT
IP
   see ARFC_GET_TID
   see TERMINAL_ID_GET
   see TH_USER_INFO
internet
   see CALL_BROWSER
   see WWW_ITAB_TO_HTML
   see WWW_LIST_TO_HTML
IW_C_GET_FRONTEND_VERSION 19
   see GUI_GET_DESKTOP_INFO

J

jobs
   see BP_EVENT_RAISE
   see BP_JOB_DELETE

   see BP_JOB_SELECT
   see BP_JOBLOG_READ
   see BP_JOBLOG_SHOW
   see GET_JOB_RUNTIME_INFO
   see JOB_CLOSE
   see JOB_OPEN
   see JOB_SUBMIT
JOB_CLOSE 325
   see JOB_OPEN
JOB_OPEN 326
   see JOB_CLOSE
JOB_SUBMIT 327
   see JOB_CLOSE
   see JOB_OPEN

K

K_ABC_DOKU_SHOW 195
   see RS_TOOL_ACCESS
K_WERKS_OF_BUKRS_FIND 374
KCD_EXCEL_OLE_TO_INT_CONVERT
   241
   see ALSM_EXCEL_TO_INTERNAL_
     TABLE
   see EXCEL_OLE_STANDARD_DAT
   see MS_EXCEL_OLE_STANDARD_DAT
   see RH_START_EXCEL_WITH_DATA
   see SAP_CONVERT_TO_XLS_
     FORMAT
   see WS_EXCEL
KD_GET_FILENAME_ON_F4 293
   see F4_FILENAME

L

LAST_DAY_IN_PERIOD_GET 135
   see DATE_TO_PERIOD_CONVERT
   see FIRST_DAY_IN_PERIOD_GET
LIST_DOWNLOAD 167
   see STRR_GET_REPORT
LIST_FROM_MEMORY 196
   see WRITE_LIST
LIST_TO_ASCI 197
   see LIST_FROM_MEMORY
LOAD_PRINT_PARAMETERS 336
   see GET_PRINT_PARAMETERS
   see STORE_PRINT_PARAMETERS
locking
   see ENQUEUE_ES_PROG
   see ENQUEUE_ESFUNCTION

M

MATERIAL_BTCI_SELECTION_NEW 375
MATERIAL_BTCI_TEXT 377
MATERIAL_UNIT_CONVERSION 75
   see CF_UT_UNIT_CONVERSION
   see CONVERSION_FACTOR_GET
   see MD_CONVERT_MATERIAL_UNIT
MD_CONVERT_MATERIAL_UNIT 76
   see CF_UT_UNIT_CONVERSION
   see CONVERSION_FACTOR_GET
   see MATERIAL_UNIT_CONVERSION
MD_POPUP_SHOW_INTERNAL_TABLE
   294
   see POPUP_WITH_TABLE_DISPLAY
microsoft access
   see STRUCTURE_EXPORT_TO_
      MSACCESS
   see TABLE_EXPORT_TO_MSACCESS
microsoft excel
   see ALSM_EXCEL_TO_INTERNAL_TABLE
   see EXCEL_OLE_STANDARD_DAT
   see KCD_EXCEL_OLE_TO_INT_CONVERT
   see MS_EXCEL_OLE_STANDARD_DAT
   see RH_START_EXCEL_WITH_DATA
   see SAP_CONVERT_TO_XLS_FORMAT
   see WS_EXCEL
microsoft word
   see EXECUTE_WINWORD
months
   see DATE_IN_FUTURE
   see MONTH_NAMES_GET
   see MONTH_PLUS_DETERMINE
   see RE_ADD_MONTH_TO_DATE
   see RP_CALC_DATE_IN_INTERVAL
   see RP_LAST_DAY_OF_MONTHS
MONTH_NAMES_GET 135
MONTH_PLUS_DETERMINE 137
   see DATE_IN_FUTURE
   see F4_DATE
   see POPUP_TO_SELECT_MONTH
   see RE_ADD_MONTH_TO_DATE
   see RP_CALC_DATE_IN_INTERVAL
MS_EXCEL_OLE_STANDARD_DAT 242
   see ALSM_EXCEL_TO_INTERNAL_TABLE
   see EXCEL_OLE_STANDARD_DAT
   see KCD_EXCEL_OLE_TO_INT_CONVERT
   see RH_START_EXCEL_WITH_DATA
   see SAP_CONVERT_TO_XLS_FORMAT
   see WS_EXCEL

N

NUMBER_GET_NEXT 227
   see NUMBER_RANGE_OBJECT_LIST
NUMBER_RANGE_DEQUEUE 227
   see NUMBER_RANGE_ENQUEUE
NUMBER_RANGE_ENQUEUE 228
   see NUMBER_RANGE_DEQUEUE
NUMBER_RANGE_INTERVAL_LIST 228
   see NUMBER_RANGE_OBJECT_LIST
NUMBER_RANGE_OBJECT_CLOSE 229
   see NUMBER_RANGE_OBJECT_MAINTAIN
NUMBER_RANGE_OBJECT_DELETE 229
   see NUMBER_RANGE_OBJECT_MAINTAIN
NUMBER_RANGE_OBJECT_GET_INFO 230
   see NUMBER_RANGE_OBJECT_READ
NUMBER_RANGE_OBJECT_INIT 230
   see NUMBER_RANGE_OBJECT_MAINTAIN
NUMBER_RANGE_OBJECT_LIST 231
   see NUMBER_RANGE_INTERVAL_LIST
NUMBER_RANGE_OBJECT_MAINTAIN 233
NUMBER_RANGE_OBJECT_READ 235
   see NUMBER_RANGE_OBJECT_GET_INFO
NUMBER_RANGE_OBJECT_UPDATE 236
   see NUMBER_RANGE_OBJECT_MAINTAIN
NUMERIC_CHECK 329

O

OTF
   see SAPSCRIPT

P

pause
   see sleep
PDF
   see CONVERT_ABAPSPOOLJOB_2_PDF
   see CONVERT_OTFSPOOLJOB_2_PDF
   see SX_OBJECT_CONVERT_OTF_PDF
period
   see DATE_TO_PERIOD_CONVERT
   see FIRST_AND_LAST_DAY_IN_YEAR_GET
   see HR_PAYROLL_PERIOD_GET
   see PERIOD_DAY_DETERMINE
   see RKE_ADD_TO_PERIOD
PERIOD_DAY_DETERMINE 137
   see FIRST_AND_LAST_DAY_IN_YEAR_
      GET
plant
   see K_WERKS_OF_BUKRS_FIND

POPUP_CONTINUE_YES_NO 296
POPUP_DISPLAY_TEXT 297
   see POPUP_DISPLAY_TEXT_WITH_PARAMS
POPUP_DISPLAY_TEXT_WITH_PARAMS 298
   see POPUP_DISPLAY_TEXT
POPUP_FOR_INTERACTION 300
POPUP_GET_VALUES 262
POPUP_GET_VALUES_DB_CHECKED 264
   see POPUP_GET_VALUES_USER_CHECKED
   see POPUP_GET_VALUES_USER_HELP
POPUP_GET_VALUES_SET_MAX_FIELD 265
POPUP_GET_VALUES_USER_BUTTONS 267
POPUP_GET_VALUES_USER_CHECKED 268
   see POPUP_GET_VALUES_DB_CHECKED
   see POPUP_GET_VALUES_USER_HELP
POPUP_GET_VALUES_USER_HELP 270
   see POPUP_GET_VALUES_DB_CHECKED
   see POPUP_GET_VALUES_USER_CHECKED
POPUP_NO_LIST 302
POPUP_TO_CONFIRM 256
   see POPUP_TO_CONFIRM_DATA_LOSS
   see POPUP_TO_CONFIRM_STEP
   see POPUP_TO_CONFIRM_WITH_VALUE
POPUP_TO_CONFIRM_DATA_LOSS 257
   see POPUP_TO_CONFIRM
   see POPUP_TO_CONFIRM_STEP
   see POPUP_TO_CONFIRM_WITH_VALUE
POPUP_TO_CONFIRM_LOSS_OF_DATA 258
POPUP_TO_CONFIRM_STEP 259
   see POPUP_TO_CONFIRM
   see POPUP_TO_CONFIRM_DATA_LOSS
   see POPUP_TO_CONFIRM_WITH_VALUE
POPUP_TO_CONFIRM_WITH_MESSAGE 260
POPUP_TO_CONFIRM_WITH_VALUE 261
   see POPUP_TO_CONFIRM
   see POPUP_TO_CONFIRM_DATA_LOSS
   see POPUP_TO_CONFIRM_STEP
POPUP_TO_DECIDE 303
POPUP_TO_DECIDE_LIST 304
POPUP_TO_DECIDE_WITH_MESSAGE 305
   see POPUP_TO_DECIDE
POPUP_TO_DISPLAY_TEXT 307
POPUP_TO_INFORM 308
POPUP_TO_SELECT_MONTH 308
   see F4_DATE
POPUP_WITH_TABLE_DISPLAY 309
   see MD_POPUP_SHOW_INTERNAL_TABLE
printing
   see ADDRESS_INTO_PRINTFORM
   see FM_SELECTION_CRITERIA_PRINT

   see GET_PRINT_PARAMETERS
   see LOAD_PRINT_PARAMETERS
   see PRINT_SELECTIONS
   see PRINT_TEXT
   see PRINT_TEXT_ITF
   see RSPO_FIND_SPOOL_REQUESTS
   see RSPO_RPRINT_SPOOLREQ
   see SET_PRINT_PARAMETERS
PRINT_SELECTIONS 337
   see FM_SELECTION_CRITERIA_PRINT
PRINT_TEXT 222
   see PRINT_TEXT_ITF
PRINT_TEXT_ITF 223
   see PRINT_TEXT
PROFILE_GET 168
   see PROFILE_SET
PROFILE_SET 169
   see PROFILE_GET

Q

QF05_RANDOM 330
   see QF05_RANDOM_INTEGER
QF05_RANDOM_INTEGER 331
   see QF05_RANDOM

R

random
   see QF05_RANDOM
   see QF05_RANDOM_INTEGER
RE_ADD_MONTH_TO_DATE 138
   see DATE_IN_FUTURE
   see MONTH_PLUS_DETERMINE
   see RP_CALC_DATE_IN_INTERVAL
READ_TEXT 224
   see CREATE_TEXT
REGISTRY_GET 378
   see REGISTRY_SET
REGISTRY_SET 379
   see REGISTRY_GET
RFC
   see CAT_CHECK_RFC_DESTINATION
   see CAT_PING
   see RFC_ABAP_INSTALL_AND_RUN
   see RFC_MAIL
   see TH_SERVER_LIST
RFC_ABAP_INSTALL_AND_RUN 347
RFC_MAIL 20
   see CAT_CHECK_RFC_DESTINATION
   see SO_NEW_DOCUMENT_ATT_SEND_API1
   see SO_NEW_DOCUMENT_SEND_API1

RH_GET_DATE_DAYNAME 139
  see WEEKDAY_GET
RH_START_EXCEL_WITH_DATA 244
  see ALSM_EXCEL_TO_INTERNAL_TABLE
  see EXCEL_OLE_STANDARD_DAT
  see KCD_EXCEL_OLE_TO_INT_CONVERT
  see MS_EXCEL_OLE_STANDARD_DAT
  see SAP_CONVERT_TO_XLS_FORMAT
  see WS_EXCEL
RKD_WORD_WRAP 353
RKE_ADD_TO_PERIOD 139
  see DATE_TO_PERIOD_CONVERT
RKE_TIMESTAMP_CONVERT_INPUT 140
  see RKE_TIMESTAMP_CONVERT_OUTPUT
RKE_TIMESTAMP_CONVERT_OUTPUT 141
  see RKE_TIMESTAMP_CONVERT_INPUT
ROUND 77
  see HR_ROUND_NUMBER
  see ROUND_AMOUNT
ROUND_AMOUNT 79
  see ROUND
  see HR_ROUND_NUMBER
RP_CALC_DATE_IN_INTERVAL 142
  see DATE_IN_FUTURE
  see MONTH_PLUS_DETERMINE
  see RE_ADD_MONTH_TO_DATE
RP_CHECK_DATE 142
  see DATE_CHECK_PLAUSIBILITY
RP_LAST_DAY_OF_MONTHS 143
  see MONTH_NAMES_GET
RPY_DYNPRO_READ 198
  see DYNP_VALUES_READ
  see RS_COVERPAGE_SELECTIONS
RPY_TRANSACTION_READ 348
  see GET_COMPONENT_LIST
  see GET_GLOBAL_SYMBOLS
RS_COVERPAGE_SELECTIONS 199
  see DYNP_VALUES_READ
  see RPY_DYNPRO_READ
  see RS_REFRESH_FROM_SELECTOPTIONS
RS_CREATE_VARIANT 200
  see RS_VARIANT_DELETE
RS_DELETE_PROGRAM 170
RS_GET_ALL_INCLUDES 349
  see GET_COMPONENT_LIST
  see GET_GLOBAL_SYMBOLS
  see GET_INCLUDETAB
  see RPY_TRANSACTION_READ
RS_REFRESH_FROM_SELECTOPTIONS 202
  see RS_COVERPAGE_SELECTIONS
RS_SEND_MAIL_FOR_SPOOLLIST 245

RS_SET_SELSCREEN_STATUS 203
RS_TOOL_ACCESS 204
  see K_ABC_DOKU_SHOW
RS_VARIANT_CONTENTS 206
RS_VARIANT_DELETE 206
  see RS_CREATE_VARIANT
RS_VARIANT_EXISTS 207
RS_VARIANT_TEXT 207
RS_VARIANT_VALUES_TECH_DATA 208
RSPO_DOWNLOAD_SPOOLJOB 171
RSPO_FIND_SPOOL_REQUESTS 20
RSPO_OUTPUT_SPOOL_REQUEST 22
  see GET_PRINT_PARAMETERS
  see RSPO_FIND_SPOOL_REQUESTS
  see RSPO_RPRINT_SPOOLREQ
RSPO_RPRINT_SPOOLREQ 23
  see GET_PRINT_PARAMETERS
  see RSPO_FIND_SPOOL_REQUESTS
RV_ORDER_FLOW_INFORMATION 380
RZL_READ_DIR 172
  see EPS_GET_DIRECTORY_LISTING
RZL_READ_FILE 173
  see GUI_UPLOAD
  see UPLOAD
  see WS_UPLOAD
RZL_SLEEP 350
  see ENQUE_SLEEP
RZL_SUBMIT 209
RZL_WRITE_FILE_LOCAL 174
  see DOWNLOAD
  see GUI_DOWNLOAD
  see WS_DOWNLOAD

S

SAP_CONVERT_TO_XLS_FORMAT 246
  see ALSM_EXCEL_TO_INTERNAL_TABLE
  see EXCEL_OLE_STANDARD_DAT
  see KCD_EXCEL_OLE_TO_INT_CONVERT
  see MS_EXCEL_OLE_STANDARD_DAT
  see RH_START_EXCEL_WITH_DATA
  see WS_EXCEL
SAPGUI_PROGRESS_INDICATOR 209
  see EPS_PROGRESS_POPUP
SAPGUI_SET_FUNCTIONCODE 351
SAPSCRIPT
  see CONVERT_OTFSPOOLJOB_2_PDF
  see SX_OBJECT_CONVERT_OTF_PDF
  see SX_OBJECT_CONVERT_OTF_PRT
  see SX_OBJECT_CONVERT_OTF_RAW

SAPWL_GET_SUMMARY_STATISTIC 23
  see SAPWL_WORKLOAD_GET_DIRECTORY
  see SAPWL_WORKLOAD_GET_STATISTIC
SAPWL_WORKLOAD_GET_DIRECTORY 25
  see SAPWL_GET_SUMMARY_STATISTIC
  see SAPWL_WORKLOAD_GET_STATISTIC
SAPWL_WORKLOAD_GET_STATISTIC 26
  see SAPWL_GET_SUMMARY_STATISTIC
  see SAPWL_WORKLOAD_GET_DIRECTORY
SAVE_LIST 210
SAVE_TEXT 224
  see CREATE_TEXT
SCP_REPLACE_STRANGE_CHARS 354
SD_DATETIME_DIFFERENCE 144
selections
  see DYNP_VALUES_READ
  see DYNP_VALUES_UPDATE
  see RPY_DYNPRO_READ
  see RS_COVERPAGE_SELECTIONS
SET_PRINT_PARAMETERS 337
  see GET_PRINT_PARAMETERS
SHOW_JOBSTATE 27
SI_UNIT_GET 80
sleep
  see ENQUE_SLEEP
  see RZL_SLEEP
SO_EXPRESS_FLAG_SET 311
  see TH_POPUP
SO_NEW_DOCUMENT_ATT_SEND_API1 247
  see SO_NEW_DOCUMENT_SEND_API1
SO_NEW_DOCUMENT_SEND_API1 249
  see SO_NEW_DOCUMENT_ATT_SEND_API1
SO_SPLIT_FILE_AND_PATH 175
  see GUI_CREATE_DIRECTORY
SO_SPOOL_READ 29
  see RSPO_RETURN_ABAP_SPOOLJOB
  see SO_WIND_SPOOL_LIST
SO_WIND_SPOOL_LIST 30
  see SO_SPOOL_READ
SPELL_AMOUNT 356
  see HRCM_AMOUNT_TO_STRING_
    CONVERT
  see HRCM_STRING_TO_AMOUNT_
    CONVERT
spool
  see CONVERT_ABAPSPOOLJOB_2_PDF
  see CONVERT_OTFSPOOLJOB_2_PDF
  see RS_SEND_MAIL_FOR_SPOOLLIST
  see RSPO_DOWNLOAD_SPOOLJOB
  see RSPO_FIND_SPOOL_REQUESTS

  see RSPO_OUTPUT_SPOOL_REQUEST
  see RSPO_RETURN_ABAP_SPOOLJOB
  see RSPO_RPRINT_SPOOLREQ
  see SO_SPOOL_READ
  see SO_WIND_SPOOL_LIST
STORE_PRINT_PARAMETERS 338
  see GET_PRINT_PARAMETERS
  see LOAD_PRINT_PARAMETERS
  see SET_PRINT_PARAMETERS
STRING_CENTER 357
STRING_CONCATENATE 358
  see STRING_CONCATENATE_3
STRING_CONCATENATE_3 359
  see STRING_CONCATENATE
STRING_LENGTH 360
STRING_MOVE_RIGHT 360
STRING_REVERSE 361
STRING_SPLIT 362
  see SWA_STRING_SPLIT
  see TEXT_SPLIT
STRING_UPPER_LOWER_CASE 363
STRR_GET_REPORT 175
  see LIST_DOWNLOAD
STRUCTURE_EXPORT_TO_MSACCESS 176
  see TABLE_EXPORT_TO_MSACCESS
SUBTRACT_TIME_FROM_DATE 145
  see ADD_TIME_TO_DATE
  see C14B_ADD_TIME
  see COMPUTE_YEARS_BETWEEN_DATES
  see DATE_IN_FUTURE
  see MONTH_PLUS_DETERMINE
  see RE_ADD_MONTH_TO_DATE
  see RP_CALC_DATE_IN_INTERVAL
SWA_STRING_SPLIT 364
  see STRING_SPLIT
  see TEXT_SPLIT
SWI_DURATION_DETERMINE 146
SUBTRACT_TIME_FROM_DATE 145
  see ADD_TIME_TO_DATE
  see C14B_ADD_TIME
  see RP_CALC_DATE_IN_INTERVAL
SX_OBJECT_CONVERT_OTF_PDF 81
  see CONVERT_OTFSPOOLJOB_2_PDF
  see SX_OBJECT_CONVERT_OTF_PRT
  see SX_OBJECT_CONVERT_OTF_RAW
SX_OBJECT_CONVERT_OTF_PRT 84
  see CONVERT_OTFSPOOLJOB_2_PDF
  see SX_OBJECT_CONVERT_OTF_PDF
  see SX_OBJECT_CONVERT_OTF_RAW
SX_OBJECT_CONVERT_OTF_RAW 84

see CONVERT_OTFSPOOLJOB_2_PDF
see SX_OBJECT_CONVERT_OTF_PDF
see SX_OBJECT_CONVERT_OTF_PRT
SXPG_CALL_SYSTEM 31
  see SXPG_COMMAND_CHECK
  see SXPG_COMMAND_EXECUTE
  see SXPG_COMMAND_LIST_GET
SXPG_COMMAND_CHECK 33
  see SXPG_CALL_SYSTEM
SXPG_COMMAND_EXECUTE 34
  see SXPG_CALL_SYSTEM
SXPG_COMMAND_LIST_GET 35
  see SXPG_CALL_SYSTEM

T

TABLE_EXPORT_TO_MSACCESS 178
  see STRUCTURE_EXPORT_TO_MSACCESS
TERM_CONTROL_EDIT 312
  see TXW_TEXTNOTE_EDIT
TERMINAL_ID_GET 35
  see ARFC_GET_TID
  see TH_USER_INFO
TEXT_SPLIT 365
  see SWA_STRING_SPLIT
  see STRING_SPLIT
TH_DELETE_USER 36
TH_ENVIRONMENT 37
TH_POPUP 315
  see SO_EXPRESS_FLAG_SET
TH_REMOTE_TRANSACTION 38
  see ABAP4_CALL_TRANSACTION
  see HLP_MODE_CREATE
  see TRANSACTION_CALL
TH_SERVER_LIST 39
  see CAT_CHECK_RFC_DESTINATION
TH_USER_INFO 39
  see ARFC_GET_TID
  see TERMINAL_ID_GET
  see TH_USER_LIST
TH_USER_LIST 41
  see TH_USER_INFO
time
  see ADD_TIME_TO_DATE
  see C14B_ADD_TIME
  see DATE_IN_FUTURE
  see MONTH_PLUS_DETERMINE
  see RE_ADD_MONTH_TO_DATE
  see RP_CALC_DATE_IN_INTERVAL
  see SUBTRACT_TIME_FROM_DATE

timeout
  see CJDB_POPUP_TO_HANDLE_TIME_
  OUT
TMP_GUI_DIRECTORY_LIST_FILES 179
  see EPS_GET_DIRECTORY_LISTING
  see TMP_GUI_READ_DIRECTORY
  see RZL_READ_DIR
TMP_GUI_READ_DIRECTORY 180
  see TMP_GUI_DIRECTORY_LIST_FILES
transaction
  see ABAP4_CALL_TRANSACTION
  see HLP_MODE_CREATE
  see RPY_TRANSACTION_READ
  see TH_REMOTE_TRANSACTION
  see TRANSACTION_CALL
TRANSACTION_CALL 42
  see ABAP4_CALL_TRANSACTION
  see HLP_MODE_CREATE
  see TH_REMOTE_TRANSACTION
TXW_TEXTNOTE_EDIT 316
  see TERM_CONTROL_EDIT

U

UNIT_CONVERSION_SIMPLE 85
  see HR_ROUND_NUMBER
  see ROUND
UNIT_CONVERSION_WITH_FACTOR 86
UNIT_CORRESPONDENCE_CHECK 87
UNIT_GET 88
  see DIMENSION_GET
UNIT_OF_MEASURE_ISO_TO_SAP 90
  see UNIT_OF_MEASURE_SAP_TO_ISO
UNIT_OF_MEASURE_SAP_TO_ISO 91
  see UNIT_OF_MEASURE_ISO_TO_SAP
UNIT_OF_MEASUREMENT_HELP 92
units
  see CF_UT_UNIT_CONVERSION
  see CONVERSION_FACTOR_GET
  see DIMENSION_GET
  see MATERIAL_UNIT_CONVERSION
  see MD_CONVERT_MATERIAL_UNIT
  see SI_UNIT_GET
  see UNIT_CONVERSION_SIMPLE
  see UNIT_CONVERSION_WITH_FACTOR
  see UNIT_CORRESPONDENCE_CHECK
  see UNIT_GET
  see UNIT_OF_MEASUREMENT_HELP
  see UNIT_OF_MEASURE_ISO_TO_SAP
  see UNIT_OF_MEASURE_SAP_TO_ISO

unlocking
   see DEQUEUE_ES_PROG
   see DEQUEUE_ESFUNCTION
UPLOAD 181
   see C13Z_FILE_UPLOAD_ASCII
   see C13Z_FILE_UPLOAD_BINARY
   see GUI_UPLOAD
   see RZL_READ_FILE
   see UPLOAD_FILES
   see WS_UPLOAD
UPLOAD_FILES 182
   see C13Z_FILE_UPLOAD_ASCII
   see C13Z_FILE_UPLOAD_BINARY
   see GUI_UPLOAD
   see RZL_READ_FILE
   see UPLOAD
   see WS_UPLOAD
USER_EXISTS 42
   see F4_USER

V

variants
   see RS_CREATE_VARIANT
   see RS_VARIANT_CONTENTS
   see RS_VARIANT_DELETE
   see RS_VARIANT_EXISTS
   see RS_VARIANT_TEXT
   see RS_VARIANT_VALUES_TECH_DATA
VRM_SET_VALUES 211

W

WDKAL_DATE_ADD_FKDAYS 147
   see WEEK_GET_NR_OF_WORKDAYS
week
   see DATE_COMPUTE_DAY
   see DATE_GET_WEEK
   see DAY_IN_WEEK
   see HR_IE_NUM_PRSI_WEEKS
   see WDKAL_DATE_ADD_FKDAYS
   see WEEK_GET_FIRST_DAY
   see WEEK_GET_NR_OF_WORKDAYS
   see WEEKDAY_GET
WEEK_GET_FIRST_DAY 148
   see DATE_GET_WEEK
WEEK_GET_NR_OF_WORKDAYS 149
   see WDKAL_DATE_ADD_FKDAYS
WEEKDAY_GET 150
   see DAY_IN_WEEK
   see RH_GET_DATE_DAYNAME

working date
   see DATE_CHECK_WORKINGDAY
   see DATE_CHECK_WORKINGDAY_
      MULIPLE
   see DATE_CONVERT_TO_WORKINGDAY
WRITE_LIST 212
   see LIST_FROM_MEMORY
WRITE_MESSAGE 381
   see FORMAT_MESSAGE
WS_DOWNLOAD 183
   see C13Z_FILE_DOWNLOAD_ASCII
   see C13Z_FILE_DOWNLOAD_BINARY
   see DOWNLOAD
   see GUI_DOWNLOAD
   see RZL_WRITE_FILE_LOCAL
WS_EXCEL 250
   see ALSM_EXCEL_TO_INTERNAL_TABLE
   see EXCEL_OLE_STANDARD_DAT
   see KCD_EXCEL_OLE_TO_INT_CONVERT
   see MS_EXCEL_OLE_STANDARD_DAT
   see RH_START_EXCEL_WITH_DATA
   see SAP_CONVERT_TO_XLS_FORMAT
WS_EXECUTE 43
   see GUI_EXEC
   see GUI_RUN
   see SXPG_COMMAND_EXECUTE
WS_FILE_DELETE 184
   see GUI_DELETE_FILE
WS_FILENAME_GET 184
WS_MSG 318
WS_QUERY 44
   see GUI_GET_DESKTOP_INFO
WS_UPLOAD 185
   see C13Z_FILE_UPLOAD_ASCII
   see C13Z_FILE_UPLOAD_BINARY
   see GUI_UPLOAD
   see RZL_READ_FILE
   see UPLOAD
WWW_ITAB_TO_HTML 213
   see WWW_LIST_TO_HTML
WWW_LIST_TO_HTML 214
   see WWW_ITAB_TO_HTML

Y

years
   see COMPUTE_YEARS_BETWEEN_DATES
   see FIMA_DAYS_AND_MONTH_AND_
      YEARS
   see HR_HK_DIFF_BT_2_DATES